P9-CEG-791

Marvin K. Mayers

CHRISTIANITY CONFRONTS CULTURE

A Strategy for Cross-Cultural Evangelism

Academie Books Grand Rapids, Michigan
Zondervan Publishing House

to Marilyn

ACADEMIE BOOKS are published by Zondervan Publishing House, 1415 Lake Drive, S.E., Grand Rapids, Michigan 49506

CHRISTIANITY CONFRONTS CULTURE

Copyright © 1974 by The Zondervan Corporation
Library of Congress Catalog Card Number 73-13068

Appreciation is expressed to the following for the use of copyrighted material:

Evangelical Missions Quarterly for excerpts from the article "Why Pentecostal Churches Are Growing Faster in Italy."

International Review of Missions for a case study from "The Educational Value of Initiatory Rites."

Moody Monthly for "My Hippie Brother." Reprinted by permission from the October, 1969, issue of *Moody Monthly*. © 1969 Moody Bible Institute of Chicago.

Practical Anthropology for a conflict situation from the article "The Social Context of Guilt and Forgiveness."

The Chicago Tribune for quotations from the article "The Decision-Making Process in Japan."

Word Books, Waco, Texas, for the story "If I Forbid Ken to Drink," from *Are You Fun to Live With?* by Lionel Whiston. Copyright © 1969.

Grateful acknowledgment is also made for the use of occasional Scripture verses from the following versions of the Bible:

The Living Bible. Copyright © 1971 by Tyndale House Publishers, Wheaton, Illinois.

The New Testament in Modern English. Copyright © 1958, 1959, 1960 by J. B. Phillips, published by The Macmillan Company.

The Revised Standard Version of the Bible. Copyright © 1952 by The Division of Christian Education, National Council of the Churches of Christ in the United States of America.

ISBN 0-310-28891-6

Printed in the United States of America

86 87 88 — 20 19 18 17 16 15 14 13

contents

54300

acknowledgments

The principles of crosscultural communication included in this volume grew out of my professional studies in social anthropology. They were first tested out in the mission field while I was serving with Wycliffe Bible Translators. Later, in my teaching at Wheaton College, a perceptually popular course began to develop around these principles. In developing the course, this volume grew, as did other supplementary materials such as the Philippine case study referred to in the text, a Latin American case study, a book of brief cases and, in fact, a total life way. I have sought to apply the principles in my home, with my friends, in my teaching experience, with my colleagues — in fact, in every aspect of my life. Though the results have not always been as I might have wanted them to be, it has been exciting to see the development of sound interpersonal relationships within the crosscultural challenges of my life.

It is for this reason that I must acknowledge the contribution made to this volume by my family, my friends, my students, and my colleagues. Without their help and inspiration I would have given up the task long ago. Further, my appreciation extends to my beloved friends among the Pocomchi (Guatemala) and those in the Philippines who have given me the opportunity of knowing them and working with them in sharpening up these tools among them. Special recognition must go to my wife, Marilyn, who has suffered through my field blunders, the agonies of graduate work, and the hammering out of this material. She has been my adviser and typist in many aspects of the program. Special contributions were made by John Snarey, who wrote the role-playing situations at the end of chapter 5 and the message for translation at the end of chapter 15; and by Gene Carol Olsen, who is co-author of the case studies found on pages 277-363. Also, I acknowledge the assistance of David App, Rich Butman, and John Snarey in the bibliographic work; Carol Dockstader Evans, Marjorie Garrison, Marti Hausch, Douglas Kell, and Philip Yancey in editorial work; and Mary Arnell, Judy Fulops, and Pauline Roelofs in typing assistance.

As this approach to crosscultural communications has become a life way, an unexpected bonus has been mine. I have found that the principles applied in the human arena of life have opened up new experiences and insights in my spiritual life, thus developing a whole new relationship with my God.

preface

As Christians, we believe in an unchanging Christ — "Jesus Christ, the same yesterday, today and forever" (Hebrews 13:8). The concept "eternal" expresses for us His enduring, unchanged nature, and provides a deep sense of security to attend our thoughts of Christ and God. The fact that He is our firm foundation allows us to view Him as *forever the same.*

As human beings, we live in an ever-changing world.[1] The seasons provide change in the world of nature. The cycle of family development from formation to final disintegration pushes us into a life of physical, emotional, and spiritual change. The changes taking place in our own bodies give us aggressive feelings when we realize growth and maturing, and they give us pause for thought when we sense physical, emotional, and intellectual disorders. Each day we awaken to a world new in many respects — a world recreated out of the experience of the past and shaped by the potential of the future.

We cannot step twice into the same river, not merely because the water has flowed by, but because we have become different persons in the meantime.[2]

Each generation faces a new combination of forces poised to shape and mold it. Although technological developments are the most obvious indicators of change, we miss some of the most significant changes if we focus only upon the products our society develops. Many important factors lie in the areas of social, religious, political, and economic concerns.

As North Americans, we travel far more than ever before and exceedingly more than we might have imagined a few short years ago. Airplanes carrying five hundred passengers fly daily to great cities of the world. Smaller planes brave the same routes, carrying millions of passengers yearly on shorter runs. Automobiles, buses and trains fill in where planes do not go or are not selected by the traveler. In itself travel has no special significance

---

1. Alvin Toffler, *Future Shock* (New York: Random House, 1970). One of the most recent of the books alerting us to the tremendous changes in our world today.

2. T. S. Eliot, *The Cocktail Party* (New York: Harcourt, Brace, 1950). A comedy.

from the point of view of the Christian, but what results from the travel takes on tremendous meaning. The American Christian comes into face-to-face contact with hundreds and thousands of people different from himself. The differences range from subtle changes of dress and technology to radical changes of conceptualizing morality and ethics.

The Swiss, living in the midst of linguistic and ethnic diversity, have adapted to social and cultural changes deriving from linguistic divergence and cultural nuance. They learn at an early age to speak numerous languages fluently, to deal with people of diverse ethnic backgrounds and to be aware of difference. They can then more readily apply these principles of sound interpersonal relations within their own nation and cope with the lesser diversity of subcultural and dialectal variations. Such subtle, natural applications might totally escape the casual observer.

Contrarily, the American has grown up in a "one-culture" world.[3] Frequently he enters high school or even college before becoming aware of dialectal differences in the English language. Instead of accepting and working with the differences he does encounter, all too often he has learned the monocultural ethnocentric approach of ridicule and mockery which tells the speaker with the "accent" that he is an oddball, an outsider, and thus rejected. A series of defense mechanisms protects the average American from being hurt by the difference of language or culture. The *superior-inferior* categories quickly label the other person as inferior when he differs in language or culture. Further, the *right-wrong* categories convince him that his way is right and make him satisfied with his own way of life, and thus dissatisfied with the other person's way of life. As a result, "difference" becomes "oddness." The American may react to speech and dress as strange. Divergence of thought and belief is classified as pagan, heathen, or uncivilized. Ethnic and class lines dissect sharply and serve to establish one's security rather than draw together compatible people and separate incompatibles, the normal function of stratification within society.

In light of the unchanging nature of Christ and the continual change within the sphere of the human being, the question is naturally forced upon us: "How can the American Christian work with change in a change setting?" The average American Christian, unprepared to cope with change, responds primarily

3. Harold Ordway Rugg, *American Culture: An Introduction to Problems of* (New York: Ginn and Company, 1931).

in one of two ways. He may cling tenaciously to every form or expression to which he has become accustomed. Every rite and ritual thus has significance in itself. Every institution must remain constant over time. Every word must have fixed meaning. He follows the path of the traditionalist who firms and finalizes every cultural and linguistic form and expression, and responds defensively to every change and innovation introduced into his sociocultural setting.

Another choice the Christian may make is to give up all form. So a continual movement persists in Christian circles to do away with rite and ritual, form and expression. And with every destructuring, new forms take hold and entrap. These forms, however, are not built upon a base of principle such as is characteristic of the traditional society, but on a relativistic or antinomian base: "We do it because we like to do it this way," or in more sacred terms, "God has led us to do it this way." The firm foundation of sound principle comes only after years of rebuilding confidence in oneself, one's associates, and one's God.

The witness of the Gospel of Jesus Christ has suffered from both approaches and responses too long. It is time to instruct another way: *the way of the Gospel of Jesus Christ, and not the Gospel encased in one's ethnocentrism.* When ethnocentrism captures the Gospel, a pattern of enslavement ensues, evidenced by reactions of nationalism, low motivation in growth, and overall spiritual death. This is not to castigate the Christian alone, for his peers outside the church have their problems with change. The difference is that the Christian "should know better."

At a time when studies in history, literature, theology, and other disciplines deriving from the humanities and the humanities-oriented social sciences were considered adequate for missionary preparation, I was enlisted in a mission enterprise with my wife, and entered Central America. During my first term of service in Guatemala, numerous problems arose that were impossible of solution with the tools I had available to me. From time to time consultants would shed light on a problem or two but by the end of that tour, I was convinced that most of these problems simply had to be left in the "hands of the Lord" to resolve. I did have an uneasy feeling about that since I had the distinct impression, at times, that my wife and I had been adding to the problems rather than providing answers to them.

During our furlough, we were privileged to attend the University of Chicago to pursue advanced studies in linguistics. My wife chose to study in the humanities division, and I chose the social sciences division and entered the department of anthropology. It was there that I came into contact, for the first time, with social anthropologists and the teachings of the British school of social anthropology. Resolutions to the various problems I had left behind in the field began to fill my mind. I experienced what I now call my "behavioral sciences conversion." I had gone to Central America as a change agent under the direction of the Spirit of God, but I had not been trained as a change agent, nor had I been given the tools that should have been given to one who was committed to changing another. Therefore the changes introduced into the total setting by my introduction of the Gospel were partial, inconsistent, resisted, or modified in ways over which I had no control.

I do not suggest that my training in social anthropology was a cure-all for every problem, but I realized that many problems we had faced in our mission program were problems amenable to solution with the proper tools. Our second term on the field proved this in a large percentage of cases. It was therefore with a great deal of anticipation that I accepted the offer of Wheaton College to teach during our second furlough year. It was my desire to prepare materials within a total teaching program that would adequately prepare a Christian for crosscultural encounter so that there could be maximum impact on the lives of the members of the host culture. Apparently the Lord knew that a year was not sufficient for such a task and has given us an extended period in which to complete this task.

THE LEARNING MOSAIC

The material of the volume is presented chapter by chapter and appears simply to be linear progression of various parts of the whole. This perception is simply an artifact of the reading-writing process. In order to present all the parts as a complete whole, the sequence proceeds from the contributions of social psychology (model one), to that of sociology (model two), to that of anthropology (model three), and finally to that of education (model four). All the parts make up a whole, not in the sense that nothing more can be added or changed, for additions and corrections can be made by anyone grasping the whole and working within it. But the point is to be made that none of the parts has any significance apart from the whole.

The material need not be taught or learned sequentially, even though the average reader/learner will likely attempt to learn it in this way. It is suggested that effective principles of crosscultural communication will be most effectively learned as a mosaic in which a person studying the models applies them to life. He may not need all the models during any one lived experience. Thus he applies those models that appear to be useful in understanding that one lived experience. As he lives more and gains more insight, he learns to apply all the models and finally relaxes within the change process much like one learning to drive an automobile: after weeks of concentrating on the parts of the driving process, brakes, steering, safety belt, etc., he finally sits back and "drives the car."

When the material is being learned by one individual, then any life experience is adequate for contemplation and analysis. However, when more than one person is involved in the learning experience, it is convenient to use "case studies." A case study is life experience to which all the members of the learning group can relate. It must communicate "reality" to all the members of the group. Basic details of the case are recorded and the group proceeds to reach consensus on these and any other details needed for an adequate discussion of the case. Once this consensus is reached, the models of biculturalism or any comparable model can be applied, not to resolve the case finally, but rather to have the experience of application of the models so that through this practice any actual lived experience can be approached with confidence. Everyone in the group thus lives the same experience together and has common information with which to interact.

For the student of crosscultural communication, the greatest gain can come as he selects some group of which he is a part now and will be throughout the period of his study of the materials. Then he can apply the various models as he encounters needs or challenges within the group process.

glossary of terms

Acculturation is the process by which culture is transmitted through continuous firsthand contact of groups with different cultures.

Archiving, as referring to research, is that research undertaken in any body of available records, either *official,* as in the written records of some group or organization, or a depository of records as the collection of original writings of an author; or *unofficial,* as in any library.

Conceptual translation is that for which language and culture equivalence is based on the larger concept being communicated, rather than on a word-for-word equivalence, therefore resulting in a less literal and more understandable translation.

Culture ideal is a verbalized formulation of normative patterns for behavior as stated by the members of a given society.

Culture pattern is a form of behavior that has become normative by the concensus of the members of a society.

Drift, in linguistic terminology, describes the process by which a language, or linguistic prototype, slowly changes. The concept was originally developed by Edward Sapir and was taken into the domain of culture by Melville Herskovits to refer to the same phenomenon occurring in the larger cultural matrix.

Experimentation refers to research involving the use of a carefully defined population being tested for change and compared to a control population in which that change is not introduced. Referring to the life processes, it involves the trying of some aspect of a life-style or culture not characteristic of one's own to see if it is compatible within one's own.

Form/meaning composite, or f/m, is the correlation of meaning with its expression, the form of expression communicating the specific meaning intended. In the process of change the form may remain constant while the meaning changes or is lost completely as in the case of "survivals." In certain cases, the meaning will remain constant and the form will change and become more varied, producing a number of expressions communicating the same meaning.

Functional equivalent is the form of one social and linguistic system that completely expresses the meaning intended by a different form in a distinct social and linguistic system. It is to be differentiated from the direct equivalent which seeks to maintain the same form across cultural boundaries.

Grammatical translation is one that is "correct" grammatically, though attention may not be paid fully to the semantic organization of the language and culture.

Hypothesis is a tentative theory or supposition provisionally adopted to explain certain facts and to guide in the investigation of others.

Innovation is the introduction of something new or novel.

Interviewing, referring to research, involves the questioning of a person either *informally* as in conversation or in either unstructured interviews (allowing the person to say what he pleases on a given subject) or structured interviews; or *formally* as with questionnaires.

Life-way, used interchangeably with culture, sociocultural setting, norm, *nomos,* or system, refers to that totality of being and experience expressed by a given person within the total context of his life.

Life-way translation, or impact translation, is that which forms out of the life-way or total sociocultural setting of an individual through effective functional equivalence and thus speaks directly to the "heart" of the person with impact. It is to be distinguished both from a word-for-word, or literal, translation and from a concept translation, each of which falls short of this totality of communication.

Literal translation is a word-for-word translation relying on direct equivalence of words to carry the thought intended and thus falling short of both correctness of meaning and impact on the life of the hearer. It is responded to by the reader as "written for those over there."

Participant observation, referring to research, is the process of observing while participating in the life-way of the people being studied. The observation is not random; it develops through careful training in awareness of what to look for and how to allow the natural culture patterns to be discovered.

Process of abstraction is that operation of the mind by which thought is separated from that which is being considered. Conceptual models such as the ones used in this book or in a text on theology or philosophy are not the real themselves, but rather abstractions from the real so that the person thinking will be able to control the real more readily than would otherwise be possible.

Society is the interaction of people sharing a given culture, resulting in a sociocultural setting.

Structural units are those forms settled upon by the concensual process within society that regulate and control behavior. They can be referred to as "organization," "network of social relations," "social controls," etc.

Validating the society is the act of accepting a society *as it is* without explanation or apology. The society is adjudged worthy of being heard and thus worthy of respect equally with any other society.

Walking pattern is the pattern of movement resulting from the day schedule calling for someone to be at a given place at a given time or in a given sequence of events.

1

exploring the subject of change

To change means to alter, to make different, to cause to pass from one state to another.[1]

Change is that alteration brought about by interplay among the following forces and movements: tradition, drift, process, tension, adaptation, innovation.

Change is involved in *tradition* in the sense that the firming of a form with the dynamics of the change process effects a very subtle variety of change.[2] For example, members of the youth subculture in American society respond to "rebellion" immediately and automatically as good. Adult subculture responds to it immediately and automatically as evil. The expression has remained the same but the meaning has changed across cultural boundaries. The two groups will have difficulty communicating simply because a form, utilized by two groups within the whole, refers to two different experiences of life: one pleasurable and the other unpleasurable. Thus the tradition has been maintained; yet it has also been eroded at one point.

1. "Change." *Webster's Unabridged Dictionary* (Springfield, Mass.: G. & C. Merriam Co.)

2. George M. Foster, *A Cross-Cultural Anthropological Analysis of a Technical Aid Program* (Washington, D.C.: Smithsonian Institute of Social Anthropology, 1951), *Traditional Cultures: and the Impact of Technological Change* (New York: Harper and Row, 1962), and *Applied Anthropology* (Boston: Little Brown and Co., 1969).

The process by which tradition effects change inconsistently and erratically for the desired effect, or for the undesired one, is termed *drift*.[3] This process takes place when a number of people adopt certain deviations from established norms and continue the tendency until it becomes a trend. The use of pews in churches illustrate this point. Benches were provided at first for use only by the wealthy and prestigious while attending the divine service, but eventually they were provided for everyone attending, and we now have a difficult time imagining what Christianity would be like without pews. Pews have nothing to do with true worship, and in fact may even hinder effective worship for some.

Process includes a series of interlinked events commencing under certain defined conditions and concluding under certain other defined conditions.[4] Life and the continued association it brings are forever linking and interlinking parts of the whole of social interaction and thus forming new patterns and mosaics.

Tension results when two life-ways refuse to yield to each other.[5] Tension can be constructive and creative or it can be destructive. In any case, tension introduces change, since it causes selection from alternatives in the decision-making process. For example, a household in tension selects from a wider range of alternatives than does a household without it.

Adaptation to a second society, or *acculturation*[6] as the process is termed technically, occurs when two or more previously separated cultures come into contact with each other to a degree sufficient to produce significant changes in either or both. The demand for acculturation may also be faced when one encounters another subculture within his own society. In one sense, every interpersonal encounter is one where two subcultures are involved and so ultimately every encounter becomes an opportunity to practice adaptation.

Innovation follows the introduction of anything new within the source society.[7] Whereas acculturation introduces a flow of new items, practices, and ideas across cultural boundaries, inno-

3. Melville Herskovits, *Cultural Dynamics* (New York: Alfred A. Knopf, 1964).

4. E. E. Evans-Pritchard, *The Values of Primitive Society* (Oxford: Blackwell, 1954).

5. Raymond Firth, *Elements of Social Organization* (London: Watts, 1952).

Bronislaw Malinowski, *The Dynamics of Culture Change* (New Haven: Yale University Press, 1945).

6. Herskovits, *Cultural Dynamics*.

7. Homer Garner Barnett, *Innovation: The Basis of Culture Change* (New York: McGraw-Hill, 1953).

vation develops from within the society when any parts of the society are rearranged.

CHANGE AND THE MISSION OF THE CHURCH

Change seriously affects the mission of the church in either Christian growth or in evangelism. A traditional program within the church may force a continual flow of membership out of the church in search of meaning. Or some members may conform so completely to the traditional program of the church or mission that it loses vitality or self-motivation. The church thus drifts from truth to falsehood without ever realizing what is happening, "having a form of godliness, but denying the power thereof" (2 Tim. 3:5). The process of change goes on so subtly and so thoroughly in every aspect of life that a program without built-in mechanisms to cope with change may drift toward falsehood in every part of its program and ministry. Those within the program who want to stand on principle and search for meaningful belief and practice may very quickly find themselves at odds with the institution and thus in tension. If the institution responds by developing new programs, it can tap this tension constructively, but generally, within the church, belief is so closely tied into the life-way that the tension introduces undesired disorganization and destruction. There is so little understanding of cultural differences that the church and its mission extension refuse to prepare for multicultural confrontation and thus any adjustment or adaptation to more than one life-way is banned on the grounds of compromise of belief. Even innovation within the church arouses suspicion, since it resembles that which exists outside the culture or the subculture of the church. If it has not been done before, its soundness is questioned. The end result is a static world view that places high value on changelessness and on the continual reinforcing of "form" or the way something is expressed, instead of on meaning. This approach to life constructs a body of culture-based rituals that one is supposed to follow to have the life of Christ.

Since biblical Christianity is a dynamic process born in a change setting and since it introduces change in the life of individuals and society, it resists being bound by the narrow ethnocentrism and restricting legalisms that often characterize the established church. Thus there arises in each generation a reformation. Christ led the great reformation of the New Testament times, for He was the One through whom the new covenant came into being. Luther instigated a far-reaching reformation now termed "the Protestant Reformation." Inter-Varsity was the forerunner of a new reformation for our contemporary period which opened the way for revisions within the denominational program of protestantism at a time when the Protestant Reformation was ossifying into firmly established lines with specific expressions which may or may not have been related to truth. A similar reformation is developing with the introduction of the small-group ministry of the Keith Miller variety;[8] and still another with the burgeoning development of the "Jesus Movement."[9]

THE NATURE OF MISSION

Because the beliefs of Christianity are so different from those of other religions, some change will be necessary if the missionary is doing his work. Note the following contrast:

HINDU: Let us understand, and we will believe.
MISSIONARY: Believe, and you will understand.

The mission of the true Church of Jesus Christ is to introduce Christ into the lives of people everywhere: "As ye go into all the world, share your faith" (from the Greek). The missionary thus becomes an *agent of change* whether he likes it or not. The Gospel of Jesus Christ is tied to no one culture and allows the individual to transcend his own culture.[10] This does not in any way imply that we must attempt to establish a "Christian culture." Rather, it leads to a specific culture being regenerated by the work of grace within the hearts and lives of the Christians living within the culture. Christianity can permeate any part of the sociocultural setting or make the whole over anew. An American can become a Christian as an American, without being made over into a Nigerian. A Nigerian can become a Christian as a Nigerian without becoming an American. The

---

8. The small-group movement has been suggested and developed through the efforts of the following, among many others:
Keith Miller, *A Taste of New Wine* (Waco, Texas: Word Books, 1965).
Eugene Nida, *Religion Across Cultures* (New York: Harper and Row, 1968).
Bruce Larson and Ralph Osborne, *The Emerging Church* (Waco, Texas: Word Books, 1970).
9. Earle Cairns, "Marks of a Jesus Revolution," *HIS* (December, 1971), 8-10.
Billy Graham, *The Jesus Generation* (Grand Rapids: Zondervan Publishing House, 1971).
Ronald M. Enroth, Edward E. Erickson, Jr., and C. Breckinridge Peters, *The Jesus People* (Grand Rapids: Wm. B. Eerdmans Publishing Co., 1972).
10. For another point of view, read Richard H. Niebuhr, *Christ and Culture* (New York: Harper and Row, 1956).

excitement of Christianity springs from Christ living "in me," to make me pleasing to Him through the working of His Holy Spirit.

Not only will I remain an American, but I will also become the very finest American possible. My sense of responsibility to my nation and to my way of life will be continually refined and developed. This does not mean I will agree with whatever is labeled "American," but I will responsibly share in every aspect of American life open to me. The same potential applies to everyone who comes to Christ in the conversion-regeneration process. Ideally, he will become a full and completely responsible member of his family, his interest groups, his governmental groups. Gaining fulfillment in these various ways, he will become fully responsible to God. Perfection will not come in any realm, but the progress toward perfection will show in this life and be completed in the life to come.

PREPARATION FOR MISSION

Every existing Christian mission sincerely endeavors to introduce Christ to the peoples of the world. Just what this implies in the specific ministries of each group depends on the training and insight of each member of that mission — qualities developed in large measure by a specific training process.[11] The average Christian missionary of the evangelical protestant faith is recruited through some church or Christian contact on a university, college, or Bible college campus. The mission is likely to employ language or words as the primary means of recruitment, though at times audio-visual aids are used in the way of recordings, slides, or films. The recruit maintains contact with the mission by being placed on a mailing list. When the recruit is ready to proceed with his missionary enterprises, the mission recruitment personnel process his application and proceed to investigate his credentials. These credentials consist primarily of a college degree and a seminary degree or equivalent. He is expected to have received a general education, during the college program, with special stress on biblical studies. During his seminary training he should have studied "sound" theology, which the mission has likely assumed to be doctrinal in nature.

When the recruit is received into the mission, he becomes

11. This process is reflected in every issue of any mission periodical or house organ. At times it comes out specifically in a total article as in the July to August 1971 issue of the Sudan Interior Mission publication, *Africa Now*.

part of a very formal sending organization. Responsibility for fund raising for his travel and support may fall on the individual or be shared in part by the mission. The mission, however, takes upon itself the actual collecting and sending of the funds. Further, the new member is under the jurisdiction and supervision of the mission in matters relating to orientation, outfitting, and placement. The mission may tacitly recognize the leading of the Holy Spirit in the life of the individual, but it usually assumes that the Holy Spirit is working through the mission itself for all final decisions regarding the member.

The member is now part of a formal sequencing of activities that starts with his deputation, followed by placement in the field which divides into two-to-six-year periods broken by further deputation in the home country. The sequence ends with retirement either on the field or in the home country.

Throughout this entire sequence of training and events, the missionary is seldom required to have coursework or to attend special seminars on crosscultural communication, working with peoples of other societies, culture change, or related programs. This is significant in light of the fact that when he enters the mission he faces a crosscultural challenge. Further challenges come when he enters the field of his choice, becomes part of the missionary group working there, returns home on furlough, enters one kind of church after another during his furlough period, returns to the field of his choice, and leaves on furlough again — repeating the process until he finally retires.[12] Each challenge leaves him with just a little less motivation for facing up to change and the challenge of change. Unless the missionary is quite flexible and adapts to new and different situations readily, by the time he retires, he will have been depleted of any toleration to adapt to any new situation.

The exciting aspect of today's learning explosion is that any person can be trained to face the challenges of change quite naturally and without anxiety. This training derives from the behavioral sciences which, when teamed up with sound theology, can help the missionary introduce the Gospel of Jesus Christ

---

12. No "orientation" program for missionaries is complete unless the missionary is prepared to encounter each of these experiences from a crosscultural encounter. Otherwise, "culture shock" will set in to a greater or lesser degree, leaving the missionary less effective than he could be or might otherwise hope to be whether at "home" or "abroad." Whereas the more traditional mission spends most of its energies orienting the new recruit to its program, the Peace Corps attempts to orient the new recruit to the people among whom he is to work.

without its being encumbered with the cultural baggage of the sending society. The missionary at ease within the change setting can be sure that the message he is communicating is truly the message of salvation in Jesus Christ.

THE ROLE OF THE BEHAVIORAL SCIENCES

The behavioral sciences stand midpoint along a continuum from the humanities and the physical sciences. Whereas the humanities tend to start with fact or idea and relate this to behavior, the behavioral sciences begin with human behavior and attempt to determine how idea grows from behavior or how fact is significant in relation to behavior. Whereas the physical sciences utilize the inductive, generalizing, or hypothesizing procedure to determine regularity of natural law or the out-working of a scientific principle, the behavioral sciences must apply this approach to human behavior, not to physical processes. Human behavior is far more difficult to work with since it is patterned but not fully predictable. At the moment a rule or law is established to explain human behavior, someone will deviate from the previous pattern. Thus, the behavioral scientist may prove a hypothesis to a large degree but never finally establish it. Behavioral sciences are nonetheless useful in working with behavior, but there must always be the possibility for exception, something the physical sciences less frequently have to concern themselves with.

Whereas the other social sciences, of which the behavioral sciences form an integral part, generally rely on archiving as a primary tool of research, e.g., a study of books,[13] the behavioral sciences, although utilizing archiving in ethnohistory, primarily use the research tools of participant observation, the interview (including questionnaires and statistical validation) and experimentation. (See chapter 14.)

For example, considering the problem of missionary furloughs, the humanities would focus on the history of the work-furlough program of missions; the relationship this had to the mission and its program in the field; and the social, political, and religious situation that gave rise to a five-year-work-and-one-year-furlough arrangement, as well as other related concerns. A physical scientist would likely concern himself more with the properties of speed and sound involved in the transportation of missionaries to and from the field, or some other

---

13. John Madge, *The Tools of the Social Sciences* (Garden City, New York: Doubleday, 1965).

related concern within the realm of the physical sciences. The behavioral scientist, without ignoring the contribution to his studies of the other disciplines, would be more interested in exploring the response of the missionary to the five-one program, the function of the furlough within the total concern of missions, how missions are modifying their furlough program in the light of new developments in the world, the nature of contemporary air transportation and what this means to missionaries living in a plane age rather than in a ship age, and the pressures on the missionary family in terms of American culture demands for extensive education of the children of established time limits (i.e., twelve years for precollege education and four for college education — no more and no less). The behavioral scientist would research these concerns in archives such as libraries and mission offices, observe the current practices within the missions to determine the effectiveness of present and traditional programs, set up interviews both of the informal variety similar to conversations and of the formal type of written questionnaire, and finally structure various experimental programs to determine if, for example, an airplane society might affect furloughs designed for a ship society. Finally, the behavioral scientist would begin preparing information-educational programs and materials for the missions as a service to their missionaries that would in effect prepare them for each major aspect of the furlough program. One key part of this would be a special orientation program for the missionaries, debriefing them concerning their work on the field and briefing them on the changes effected during the work period of four to six years on the society they left behind, as well as the subtle but significant changes effected on themselves during this period.

The behavioral sciences have had little to do with the traditional missionary program for a number of reasons:

1. There has been an unfortunate confusion of behavioral sciences with the psychology of John B. Watson called "behaviorism"[14] and referred to as behavioristic or behavioral. This is a psychological theory rooted in the physical sciences and has very little to do with true behavioral sciences within the social sciences.

2. The behavioral sciences study human behavior and then ask the questions of morality and ethics, of belief and practice. Many Christians have falsely assumed that since they have asked

---

14. John Broadus Watson, *Behaviorism* (Chicago: University of Chicago Press, 1957).

that question first, they were putting man first, as do the so-called "humanists." This assumption has produced a tragic misunderstanding and breakdown of confidence in the fields covered by the behavioral sciences, including psychology, sociology, anthropology, and other disciplines having a similar approach. The misunderstanding developed naturally, perhaps, since some behavioral scientists follow this line of reasoning: Since human behavior is so obvious and so all-encompassing, there must be nothing more than that. Emile Durkheim suggested that all society is the interaction of human beings.[15] This viewpoint allows no place for the supernatural. Durkheim's point of view does not receive universal acceptance. A Christian can hold other fully acceptable views and receive the support of scholars in the field. This is the same principle that has been applied to theological studies for many generations. Naturalistic or modernistic theologians are studied for what contribution they can make, but a Christian theologian has vast room to work and can make significant contribution to the Christian community. Cannot this same utilization by Christians be extended to the researched facts and ideas of the behavioral scientist?

3. Another taboo that falls on behavioral science is that "Christian" and behavioral science ideas at times run counter to each other. History contains many such conflicts. Copernicus, Darwin, Freud, and others have come under the ire of Christianity for their "heretical ideas," but time and careful research have upheld *some* of their key ideas, though perhaps not their entire viewpoint.

4. The language or dialect of the behavioral sciences also differs from that of the humanities (chart 1) which dominates history, theology, and philosophy. The latter dialect has become largely the dialect of Christianity. "Historical process" is much

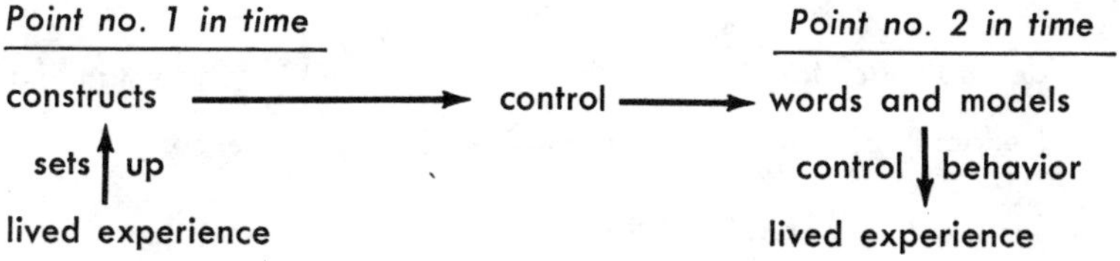

Point no. 1 in time		*Point no. 2 in time*
constructs ⟶	control ⟶	words and models
sets ↑ up		control ↓ behavior
lived experience		lived experience

Chart 1. The Humanities and Human Behavior

---

15. Emile Durkheim, *The Elementary Forms of the Religious Life* (Glencoe, Illinois: The Free Press, 1947). A study in the sociology of religion.

more acceptable than "sociocultural change" of the behavioral science dialect usage. "Rational" and "existential" terminology is much more commonplace than is the "linear" and "mosaic" terminology of behavioral scientists.

The humanities are both worthy and unworthy of such status within Christianity. They are worthy in the sense that any point of view gives us insight into the truth. They are also worthy in that very dedicated, careful men have worked within the various disciplines of the humanities to give us tremendously important insights into the nature of man and of the universe, as well as the relationship between God and man. They are unworthy in the sense that they too are human disciplines limited to language and human thought patterns. The language of the humanities is a dialect of the societies' language as is the language of any other field of knowledge. The elevation of one dialect above all others as a prestige dialect is the result of a social process, not of divine instruction. The thought forms of the humanities, which are a priori in nature, work with constructs and models[16] that are derived from human experience and then made to be controls of that human behavior.

The behavioral sciences (chart 2), on the other hand, continually ask questions concerning the lived experience: What is it? Who lived it? What does this imply concerning truth? In other words, behavioral scientists continually ask the question of the nature of the lived experience so that truth can relate directly to the person at a given time within a given culture and within the specific expression of that culture.

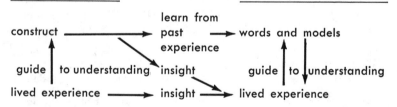

Chart 2. Behavioral Science and Human Behavior

16. All language is a representation of the real and so is a model or an abstraction from the real. At times it is useful to develop more specific models, both substantive and verbal, to supplement the insights gained from the more general and familiar models given us through language and culture. The model is not the real, but is useful in understanding the real. Once a model has served and passed its usefulness, it can be discarded or replaced.

Four questions are therefore necessary when dealing with the lived experience:

1. What is the norm? (See chapter 6.)
2. Is the person living in keeping with the norm?
3. Does the norm need changing?
4. Who is responsible for changing the norm?

The average, well-meaning person, untrained in crosscultural communication, asks only questions three and four. Thus, he will find that anything different from his own lived experience needs changing. When he gets to question four, therefore, he stands in the primary position of responsibility for changing the other norm. When one begins with the first question, however, a whole new experience awaits him. He becomes aware of difference. He knows that just because something is different, it does not automatically need changing. He becomes aware that the other person is as fully responsible as he is himself. Then when he gets to question three, he realizes that both norms may need changing, or that either his or the other norm may need changing, or that neither needs it. Then when he proceeds to the point of considering change, he does not go alone; he goes with the person of the other cultural viewpoint. And the Christian goes also with the Spirit of God guiding him.

Truth is of God and thus it is not something of human invention or construction. It is not something available only to the elite. It is available to all men,[17] of whatever culture or life-way, and it becomes meaningful to each one as he encounters it in relation to his lived experience. This does not mean that he will of necessity find truth, or recognize it when he finds it. For this reason the "good counselor" is always needed to ensure the effective communication of truth. The one who is a good counselor opens the way for each person, in whatever cultural setting, to know the truth. (See chapter 17.)

ANTHROPOLOGY AS ONE BEHAVIORAL SCIENCE

Anthropology is the study of man throughout all ages and in any sociocultural setting (chart 3) within which he is found. Social anthropology especially deals with the culture of people as it grows out of their social interaction. Thus we speak of the sociocultural setting and find man in groups carrying out activities within a value framework. This sociocultural setting provides the framework for meaning and significance within the life of the individual within the group, by organizing his life, giving an

17. This is what Calvin was intending when he spoke of "priesthood of believers," I feel.

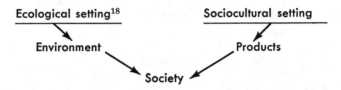

Chart 3. Ecological and Sociocultural Influences

arena of need fulfillment, and producing the automatic response to social controls.[19] With this new meaning the individual gains significance and identity. He is someone. He has a name, a language, a purpose. He is controlled by all of the forces within the sociocultural setting. The controls allow him to live without undue tension that would destroy him otherwise; they let him react to life with automatic responses so that he can devote the major part of his energies to creatively living within his environment. This sociocultural setting even *controls* the supernatural intrusion. It does not design it, nor create it, but it does bound it, limit it, amplify it and restrict it. Thus it was that Christ became a man, a son of a carpenter, living in Galilee, with the "stigma" of the Galileans, and was crucified and buried within the control of the culture. To the degree that Christ was man He was controlled by His culture, regardless of our judgment concerning its rightness or wrongness.

Since anthropology is the study of man,[20] one of the largest areas of concern to the anthropologist involves the comparison of man with man and the communication process that goes on among men. There have been some serious attempts to delineate this area of concern, but the material tends to be either theoretical with little practical application or practical with very little adequate theoretical framework.

18. Francis A. Schaeffer, *Pollution and the Death of Man* (Wheaton, Illinois: Tyndale House Publishers, 1970).

19. H. C. Bredemeier and R. M. Stevenson, *The Analysis of Social Systems* (New York: Holt, Rinehart, and Winston, 1962).

20. Texts for the introduction of anthropology as a discipline are:

Alan R. Beals with George and Louise Spindler, *Culture in Process* (New York: Holt, Rinehart and Winston, 1967).

Philip K. Bock, ed., *Culture Shock* (New York: Alfred A. Knopf, 1970). A reader in modern cultural anthropology.

E. Adamson Hoebel, *Anthropology: The Study of Man* (New York: McGraw-Hill, 1956).

Steve Grunlan; Marvin K. Mayers; John R. Snarey; *An Introduction to Anthropology for the Christian* (Wheaton, Illinois: Wheaton College, pre-publication manuscript).

This volume takes an eclectic approach to crosscultural communication and utilizes insights from the fields of social psychology, sociology, anthropology, and education — all from the perspective of crossing cultural and subcultural boundaries. There are four basic models: the acceptance of the person, the theory of natural groupings, the validity of distinct societies, and the support model. Although each of these is expanded in the following pages, no part can be separated from the whole. The acceptance of the person model is an integral part of the larger support concept. The theory of natural groupings must be worked out so that the crosscultural tools of relationships can be proven valid.

Radcliffe-Brown, Malinowski, and Evans-Pritchard, British social anthropologists, founded the primary theory of structure/function which suggests that every social structure serves some function within the whole structure.[21] Radcliffe-Brown specifically applied this theory to the network of social relations which gives society corporate identity, and man within that society, individual identity.

This view thus presents society as a system in balance. Whenever it is in disequilibrium or disorganization, it is working to return to the basic balance of the society. Man abuses the system, causing a dysfunction within the system of society that results in disorganization. Other forces may also serve to destroy the effective balance of the society.

An agent of change, seeking to change society or to introduce something new into it, must know the system currently operating and he can do this by examining the social control mechanisms that maintain the system. Once he grasps these through studying the behavior of participants in the system, he can define the system in its operation and also work to correct its abuses. As he aids the members of the society to live more meaningfully within their own society and within the subculture of that society, he will find many natural openings to share his own interests as well as many systematic reinforcements to the effective changes he is able to introduce.

In order to understand the various components and subsystems of the larger overall system, one needs conceptual

---

21. Refer to:
Evans-Pritchard, *Values of Primitive Society.*
Bronislaw Malinowski, *Coral Gardens and Their Magic* (London: G. Allen and Unwin, Ltd., 1935). A study in the Trobriand Islands.
A. R. Radcliffe-Brown, *Structure and Function in Primitive Society* (London: Cohen and West, 1952).

models that can be applied analytically to the system. These are provided in part in the works of Claude Levi-Strauss, Kenneth L. Pike, and others working in the area of ethnoscience;[22] in part by George Foster and the American applied anthropologists;[23] and by Melville Herskovits with his "dynamics" extension of principles of applied anthropology.[24]

Thus the approach of social anthropology is a systematic approach to the societies of the world, providing the investigator and analyst with a set of *principles* with which he can approach any society and discover the particular system operating in a given society. As the system is discovered for that society, the means of communicating effectively with its members will begin to reveal themselves. Once the guest within the new society begins to observe and operate within the system of the society, he needs to read all the material available on that society to hasten, when possible, his grasp of the entire system. In this way, the reading supports the effort rather than providing inadequate or incorrect information.

Thus, the approach of social anthropology is distinct from the more traditional approach to mission. For the sake of convenience, I will call the latter approach the *theological* approach to mission. It was sufficient, under this approach, for the new missionary to have the "truth," in which he was carefully instructed in Bible colleges and seminaries. Once he was in the field and dealing with the "heathen," the Holy Spirit would apply the truth to the other person's heart, and he would be converted. An unfortunate side effect of such an approach was the communication of much of the missionaries' culture with

22. Claude Levi-Straus, *Structural Anthropology* (New York: Basic Books, 1963, and *The Elementary Structure of Kinship* (Boston: Beacon Press, 1949; reprint ed. 1967).

23. There are some very fine materials available to the agent of change seeking to be effective in a society or subculture distinct from his own. In addition to the following, see section 3 of bibliography, pp. 369-372.

H. G. Barnett, *Innovation* (New York: McGraw-Hill, 1953).

Conrad M. Arensberg and Arthur H. Niehoff, *Introducing Social Change: A Manual for Community Development* (Chicago: Aldine, Atherton, 1971).

Warren G. Bennis; Kenneth D. Benne; and Robert Chin, *The Planning of Change* (New York: Holt, Rinehart and Winston, 1969).

James F. Downs, *The Two Worlds of Washo* (New York: Holt, Rinehart and Winston, 1966).

Eugene A. Nida, *Message and Mission* (New York: Harper and Row, 1960).

Kenneth L. Pike, *Stir — Change — Create* (Grand Rapids, Michigan: Wm. B. Eerdmans Publishing Co., 1967).

Foster (see footnote 2, p. 13).

24. Herskovits, *Cultural Dynamics*.

the "truth." The new convert not only accepted Christ but much of the missionaries' life-ways as well.

To counter the excesses of such an approach, an anthropological approach was developed by which the new missionary would learn as much as he could about the culture of the people he was going to serve. This will be called, here, the *ethnographic* approach. He would read all the books he could get his hands on and talk to everyone knowledgeable.

Unfortunately, two traps were lying in wait for the unwary missionary. There is no descriptive material on the culture and life-way of many peoples of the world, and much that is available is inadequate and inaccurate, primarily because of its lack of insight and its partial development. The missionary could enter the land of his choice and have false or scant information about the people and their culture. This would tend to hinder his work rather than aid it. When the material proved to be erroneous or inadequate, a bad attitude would develop on the part of the missionary toward all other similar types of material.

A second trap awaiting the unsuspecting and untrained missionary utilizing the ethnographic approach is that he would look for the things he had learned and overlook very important aspects of the life-way or culture that were far more significant to him in his work than that which was already learned.

THE ROLE OF THE HOLY SPIRIT

It is easy for someone to overlook the role of the Holy Spirit both in the development of an academic text and in the actual work in the field. There is no intention of replacing Him or according Him a lesser place in the role of mission by developing models of crosscultural communication. This approach is designed, rather, to restore the Holy Spirit to His rightful place in the mission enterprise. Traditional mission programs have all too frequently "set the stage" so to speak, so that the Holy Spirit has been forced to restage it or to "stumble over the props." This approach, on the other hand, provides for full cooperation with the Spirit of God thus allowing Him to complete His share of the responsibility for world mission in an effective way.

In the past, a tendency has prevailed of seeing God as an authoritarian leader, Jesus Christ as an incipient theologian, Paul as a theologian, and James as an inadequate theologian. This is unfortunate, since Paul and James and even Christ Himself were in essence behavioral scientists in the very best sense of the term. Jesus lived among men, and out of the experience of living among them, communicated the truth of God in a dynamic and forceful way. The Bible record thus becomes a guidebook by specifying various historical settings or situations in which man needed to approach the lived experience cautiously. James considered the behavior of man and very specifically shows him how he can best live with himself, with his fellowman, and with God. The behavioral science approach to life shared by Jesus, Paul, and James will be stressed repeatedly in this book, not to negate the important contribution of these men in various stages of theologizing, but to balance the picture somewhat and give us insights unavailable to us through other approaches.

Questions for discussion:

1. What is the true nature of Christian mission?

2. What serious questions or challenges are levelled at the North American missionary by citizens of other nations?

3. What tendencies do we show in our everyday lives that would be detrimental to our serving in another society?

4. Where do the behavioral sciences (anthropology, linguistics, psychology, sociology) stand as requirements for preparation for mission?

5. Seek out one way that the behavioral sciences could aid in your education or church ministry.

6. What has been the progress of change that Christianity has experienced through the ages?

7. How has Christianity come through this change process? Unscathed? Fairly well, though with some problems? Poorly? What makes you respond as you do?

8. How can we work with the change process to correct present lack, to adjust our progress to date, and to meet the challenge of change in the future?

Group activities and exercises:

1. Discovering differences: Let each group member circulate in the larger group and write down in list form all the cultural differences he discovers through visual or auditory stimuli, e.g., language differences, taste preferences, fashion distinctives, differential expectations of goals and aspirations, etc. Share these differences in the larger group audibly through a debriefing expe-

rience or by having two members of the group collate the lists and prepare a copy for everyone.

2. Role play, corporate: In groups of four or five have two- to three-minute skits prepared depicting some aspect of mission. Suggest that the skits have two parts, e.g., how others do it/how we would do it, before/after, as outsiders/as insiders. This is both to get acquainted and to tune into the differential perception of mission.

3. Name game — getting acquainted: In groups of twenty or fewer, sit in a circle and let the leader give his *first name*. The next person will then give the leader's first name and then his own. The third person will start again with the leader's first name, the second person's first name, and then his own. This will continue until everyone has had opportunity. The last person will be giving everyone's first name. Repeat the process, giving *full names* and letting the last person start this round. Following this second round, have a *specific interest* added to the full name, e.g., C. S. Lewis, sports, evangelism, etc. By the end of the round, everyone in the group should have a beginning acquaintance with everyone else.

An alternate experience uses three in a group and is presented as Experience #1, Pfeiffer and Jones.[25]

25. William J. Pfeiffer and John E. Jones, *A Handbook of Structured Experiences for Human Relations Training*, Vol. 1, Experience No. 1 (Iowa City, Iowa: University Associates Press, 1971).

MODEL 1

ACCEPTANCE OF THE PERSON

Acceptance of the Person is the beginning point of change.
This model includes four submodels briefly described below:

1. *The Prior Question of Trust* (PQT) is the question asked before all other questions: "Is what I am doing, thinking, or saying building or undermining trust?"
2. *The Acceptance of Self* permits the person to accept himself as he *is* at any given moment. He accepts himself as he is at that moment. Acceptance of self allows understanding of what is known and familiar to the person, thus preparing him to accept others (especially God whom he knows less).
3. *The Acceptance of the Other* is the extending of our self-acceptance to others so that we can interact and accept them as fully responsible members of their own life-way.
4. *Mutual Respect* involves balanced reciprocity in interpersonal relations leaving both persons intact and valid.

Acceptance of the Person
Trust
Acceptance of Self
Acceptance of the Other
Mutual Respect

2

trust

Ellen Cooper's family was one of the most respected in her part of the Ozarks. She and her three brothers had attended the State University and returned to the town where their family had lived for generations. She chose teaching and was happy in her work in the county high school.

Ellen's pastor encouraged her to go for several summers to a college in the East where she could get her M.A. in Christian Education. With this training she would be a great help to her church. There were so few local young people who were qualified to take a leading role in religious instruction. She seemed perfect for the job.

Ellen looked forward with real enthusiasm to her first trip north and her studies in a Christian college. She was warmly welcomed, and enjoyed the classes, shrugging off the teasing her classmates and teachers alike gave her about her mountain accent. She kept trying to remind herself that people tease only those they like.

One evening she entered the reception room with her Bible in her hand on her way to the evening service. "Hi, Ellen," one of the boys called, "What's that you're carrying? Not a Bible? I thought y'all's Bible was the Sears, Roebuck catalog."

Ellen laughed along with the others, but there was a hurt down inside that didn't quite go away, and seemed to grow as the unrelenting teasing continued.

31

Entering the dining room the last morning, she was greeted with, "Hey, Ellen, don't tell us you're wearing shoes! You can take them off now and keep them 'til next summer."

Next summer didn't come. Much to her pastor's disappointment, Ellen found that in succeeding summers she had to return to the university to take refresher courses for her high school teaching.

THE PRIOR QUESTION OF TRUST

When one approaches the task of mission, the questions naturally arise, "How can I win them to Christ? What board should I serve under? Where should I serve?"

In the marriage relationship or the relationship between boy and girl friends, the first questions that come to mind on Valentine's Day or at Christmas time is, "What should I give my true love? Should I give a card, a flower, a gift?" So, very naturally, the question of "gift" comes to mind.

In the home, the husband asks the question, "Should I do the dishes?" He therefore naturally considers the question of division of labor in the home; in American society his response will likely be, "No, there are other things that I have to do."

When children have done something wrong, the parents' response is to punish them immediately so they will be sure to know they have done wrong. The question of punishment is therefore the first one that comes to mind.

When Sunday morning comes, we ask the question, "Should we go to Sunday school or just to church?" Thus, we very naturally ask the question about Sunday activities.

When a question of ethnic difference arises, these questions also arise: "What are my rights as an American? as white? as black? What are my privileges in relation to these rights?" The answering of such questions of rights and privileges may readily lead to conflict.

In business or pleasure, selling or buying, lecturing or examining, the first questions that are considered are questions of action, participation, response; questions of who, what, when and why; questions of rights and privileges.

None of these is the first question that might best be thought of in settings involving crosscultural communication. The prior question to all of these is *the question of trust:* "Is what I am doing, thinking, or saying building trust or is it undermining trust? Is what I am doing, thinking, or saying *potential* for building trust or *potential* for undermining trust?"

When we ask the prior question of trust (PQT), we do not

know what the outcome will be, but we do know that a trust relationship[1] will develop that will open channels of communication rather than close them. When the question is not asked, there is the greater likelihood that these channels of communication will close, as was obvious in the case of the "mountain girl."

The point of mission leads to establishing a trust bond, first man-to-man and quite naturally then man-to-God. The mission to be approached will be that which permits a trust relationship. The place will be wherever one can be fulfilled as a Christian in his ministry with others. The lover will give only a card if a gift undermines trust for some reason. The husband will do the dishes if he senses that by doing them the trust bond between the husband and wife is strengthened. The father will withhold punishment if he feels that a direct, immediate punishment will result in the response, for example, "I can never do anything right." Later he might find opportunity to reveal to his child the wrong that he did, but he will do so in an atmosphere that will communicate to the child that he has done wrong and not one that will communicate to him that he never does anything right. The family will go to Sunday school if the trust relationship among them is developed by doing so, but they may need to avoid going, if only for a period, if the trust is undermined because of some condition within the experience. The white person will approach the black, and conversely, the black will approach the white in ways that respect the person and reveal this respect in action. In every aspect of life, from the least complex relationship to the most complex, the prior question of trust will open the way to effective communication within a growing trust relationship.

PQT AND INTERPERSONAL RELATIONSHIPS
Philippines

Whenever I enter a society that is not familiar to me, and of which I have not previously been a part, my practice is to visit with the local authorities and clue them in as to my reasons for being there. This was, therefore, the practice I followed when I entered the Philippines to live with a Filipino family in a rural city.[2] Upon reaching the city hall, however, I found that the mayor was out of town and the associate mayor was sitting in

---

1. It is this kind of relationship Carl Rogers is treating in *Freedom to Learn* (Columbus, Ohio: Charles E. Merrill Publishing Co., 1969).

2. Marvin K. Mayers, *Notes on Christian Outreach in a Philippine Community* (Pasadena, California: William Carey Library, 1970).

his place. After visiting awhile, I left. Later I approached my hosts regarding the possibility of holding a luncheon in one of the local restaurants in honor of the associate mayor.

At this point, I had already learned a number of things about the Philippines, for example, that the men like to belong to clubs such as Rotary or Lions Clubs. Either on the days set for their luncheons or on days when some of the members get together, they enjoy dining together at the most exclusive restaurants in town. I had also learned that the mayor was of the highest status in the community. Even though I was living with a very high status, prestigious family, it was my reaction that the mayor, as mayor, was above them.[3] Further, I had learned that it is common practice when beginning a relationship with Filipinos to give them favors or gifts.

What I had not learned was that though the mayor would be of higher status than my host, the associate mayor was not. Further, the men eat together only when there is a formal occasion — having a luncheon in honor of someone I did not know was not sufficient reason for doing so. Besides, a luncheon was too great a favor or gift at this stage of the relationship. A gift from the States would have been just right.

My hosts responded to the possibility of a luncheon in two ways. Verbally they said they would think about it. Nonverbally they communicated that I had really offended them. I had proceeded with a very fine principle — meet the authorities and be sure they know you and why you are there; but I had failed to continue asking the prior question of trust. In so doing, I offended my hosts, not only by giving them the impression that I did not care for the food they set before us, but also by suggesting that they were of lower status than the associate mayor. Had I continued asking the prior question of trust, I would likely have responded to the first visit with the associate mayor by sending a small gift. Then as the relationship developed, I could have had more encounters and reciprocated in more ways to establish the friendship. Had no relationship or friendship begun, I would have considered various alternatives and may

---

3. Stratification is needed in society to define one's relationship to others so the work of society can be done. The status-rank system of social stratification operating in the Philippines places everyone potentially on a status level either above or below everyone else. One's standing is thus established, not in relation to one's social role or job responsibility, but in relation to everyone above him and everyone below him. He tends to guard his position very carefully so that anyone moving up the status ladder becomes a threat to him and is thus resisted.

have finally rested in the realization that friendship was not necessary in light of the goal I was hoping to accomplish.

After sensing that I had offended my hosts, I began asking anew the prior question of trust. By being a little more careful to compliment the food without overdoing it, and by becoming more consciously aware of the status-rank stratification system operating in the society, I was able to make amends for my previous offense.

LEVELS OF TRUST (Chart 4)

Latin America

During my years of service in Latin America, I was constantly confronted with the question of whether to teach the Indian peoples to read in Spanish or in their own dialect. Upon asking the prior question of trust, it became very clear to me that they must be taught to read in Spanish if they are to become vital members of the larger community. Were they not taught to read Spanish and then later were they to enter into

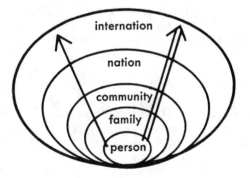

increasing complexity of involvement

increasing size

Chart 4. Levels of Trust

Reinforcing the trust bond on one level while at the same time understanding it on some other level ultimately undermines it on the starting level.

the Spanish-speaking society, they would not be well-prepared for that society. They could, moreover, very quickly associate their unfulfilled need with those who previously had the knowledge and the tools to teach them Spanish. I may have a very effective growing trust relationship with them at this moment, but if I were not preparing them for life in the larger community, I would actually be sowing seeds of distrust that would later result in a breakdown of trust within the community. They need to learn Spanish for their corporate identity as much as for their individual identity.

In answering the prior question of trust, there will not be an attempt on my part to inundate the Indians with Spanish. My responsibility is to work with them in developing a natural pride in their own language which they learned at their mother's knee and which is maximally meaningful to them. Without usage of their mother tongue there would be chaos, anomy, and unsettledness in their lived experience.[4] But my responsibility will not stop there. As they progress toward involvement in the national community, it should be my opportunity to move ahead of them and prepare the way, so to speak. I should know what they need before they sense their need. I should then proceed to teach them in the light of their actual identity and with their potential need in mind. A trust relationship will be building. At any point that trust is undermined, I should back off, take a new look at the whole, and move in again in the light of the new information I have been enabled to garner, as well as in the light of new associations I have been able to make.

In the development of an ongoing trust relationship in this way, my attempt is to *maneuver* them in their favor, not mine. To work with them solely with my own ends in view is to *manipulate* them. When people are manipulated, their natural response at the point of awareness is "You have taken advantage of me." Their response when maneuvered for their good in order to meet their sensed or stated goals is "We're glad you are here with us."

Aquacatec Indians

Some colleagues of mine in an Aquacatec Indian community in Central America were thinking of building a new home.

---

4. Many illustrations of this phenomenon could be cited. There is perhaps no more tragic experience for the members of a society than to be forced to learn a national or trade language and in the process lose their own before they are fully fluent in the new. They can speak of the superficial matters that concern them but have lost out on the deeper, more meaningful concerns of life.

They began asking the questions characteristic of this type of project: what size, what construction material, where to buy land, etc. The Indian Christians came to them and forced them to ask the prior question of trust. These believers were not only concerned with the trust relationship between the missionaries and the Indian believers, but also in the trust relationship building in their larger community. They wanted unbelieving Indian friends to respond automatically to them and their message in trust and confidence. Were the missionaries to have too large a home, trust would be undermined. It would also be undermined were they to have too small and simple a home. The believers, not with the motivation of keeping up with the Joneses, wanted their missionaries to have a home equivalent to that of the local Catholic priest. In this way they felt they would have the automatic trust of their friends and neighbors. The missionaries eventually built a home that was a bit more elaborate than they had originally intended, but the Indian believers liked to enter the home and were at ease there. Once the prior question of trust was asked, the other questions were readily resolved.

Pocomchi Indians

After we had been living in the highlands of Guatemala for some time, an Indian man came to the door and said, "I have no money; I have no food. Will you give me food?" As a Christian and a missionary I immediately thought of a number of questions. What should I give him? How much does he need? What does the Bible say about giving to a beggar? Is he saved? Can I help his family? Why doesn't he get a job? Does he really need help?

Answering these questions satisfactorily to myself led me to give him something to eat. The next week he was back again. I gave him more. He came weekly for a period and then started coming daily. I was still asking the same questions and still giving him the food I was able to supply. I had established a pattern of giving that had to continue until I began asking some other set of questions. But I had not been asking the prior question of trust.

Had I begun by asking this question in the light of levels of trust, I would have very quickly found out that in that community a beggar is welcome for a few months. After that the community slowly closes him out and communicates to him that he needs to move on; they have done their share. The beggar, in this case, didn't want to move on and was going now to those who would continue feeding him, namely, the outsiders, the missionaries. But at the moment that the community suggested he move on, the missionaries, by continuing to feed him, were undermining the trust base within the community, thus alienating themselves. The longer they would continue to feed the beggar, the more of a laughingstock they would become within the community, and the less they would be respected and trusted. The commands and teachings of the Scriptures are never designed to undermine trust. It is our lack of insight into the crosscultural challenge that causes us, however well-meaning we are, to undermine the trust relationship and in effect achieve the opposite to that which we intend.

Black-white tensions arise from cultural differences even as do tensions within the American-Filipino, American-Pocomchi encounters. Asking the prior question of trust lets one look for the differences that are significant between peoples and then look for ways to resolve or cope with these differences. The PQT thus gives one clearer vision to see through the seeming personal affront to the deeper meaning in the differences that do exist.

STAGES OF TRUST

Every trust relationship passes through what might be called *stages* in the development of trust within the relationship. These can be any kind of "milestone" that indicates to the participants the developing nature of their trust. They might be shared experiences, new relationships developed with others, or periods of trial and testing. The relationship builds when the stages of trust are passed effectively by all participants within the trust relationship. Trust is undermined when someone lags behind in the trust process as did Judas, one of the twelve disciples of Christ. He ultimately defected and had to be replaced.

American young people entering upon the path of courtship think in terms of dating, going steady, engagement, and finally the wedding. These are milestones of a sort, but they are more static than dynamic. In order to keep up with society's expectations, they will move from one stage to another even though trust and confidence in one stage of the relationship may not have been developed. They thus cover up, at times, the differential development of trust of the participants. Another, more dynamic set of stages of trust development might be: friendship, the building of confidence through the sharing of minor trials and challenges, the developing confidence of family, the building of confidence through more serious trials, and finally total trust and confidence. A way to chart such a developing love affair would then be as shown in chart 5.

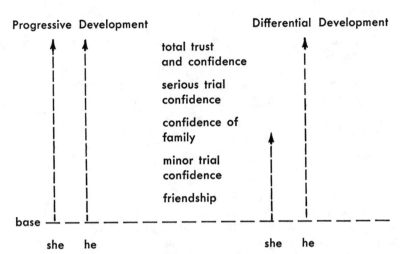

Chart 5. The Development of Trust in Courtship

When trust develops apace, with each one passing through the various stages together, the couple is fully ready for engagement and marriage. Their relationship has developed personally and in keeping with their societal norms and when marriage takes place, the two are ready physically, emotionally, and spiritually for each other. When there is a differential development of trust, one holds certain thoughts and concerns back from the other and is less than fully ready for marriage in the physical, emotional, and spiritual realms.

RECOGNITION OF A TRUST RELATIONSHIP

Although the relationship of the missionary to the target population in mission is not as intimate as that of husband and wife, the missionary must still be aware of developing stages of trust in the relationship and work to build trust, and not undermine it.

Within the crosscultural setting, verbal cues, such as words, pauses, and intonations, all are indicative of the nature of the trust relationship. Nonverbal cues, such as facial expressions, eye contact, positioning of hands and feet, yawns, drawl, and vibrato connected with speech, all signal the presence or absence

5. There are several excellent books that deal with kinesics (body motion) and proxemics (the use of space). Note especially the following, found in section 2 of the bibliography (pages 367-369): Birdwhistell, *Kinesics and Context;* Fast, *Body Language;* Hall, *The Hidden Dimension*

of trust.[5] Even as language differs from society to society, verbal and nonverbal cues also differ and must be learned.

When one becomes aware of the nature of the trust relationship that is building, a number of developments will become evident: there will be an increase of self-confidence; both parties will be themselves and develop uniquely — not apart from responsibility to the group of which they are a part; there will be an increasing awareness of the group, an inner and corporate relaxing which can be termed "peace," and a greater consistency of life. It is obvious that none of these characteristics were present in our opening case study.

SUMMARY

Before answering all other questions that arise within given situations, it is suggested that one face the prior question of trust. All other questions will be readily resolved as information is gathered and plans are executed that build the trust relationship rather than undermine it. Trust cannot be built within one level of a society that will adversely affect the trust relationship within the larger society. Those within the trust relationship pass through stages of trust development and need to be aware of the differential progress of trust development.

Verbal and nonverbal cues of behavior alert one to the true nature of the trust relationship, whether it is building or being undermined. These cues are different for each society and need to be learned as part of the language and culture.

Much of life is neutral to trust, therefore one needn't be "turned on" to trust in every experience of life. Someone who is always "working" the trust question may communicate another message — that he is in essence seeking to manipulate another to his ends. Someone who does not use it sufficiently may communicate an insensitivity, a lack of awareness of who the other person really is. An agent of change can rest in the natural bond of trust that is present between people and groups, but he should be aware of what he can do to correct a situation that proves to be one of undermining trust rather than building it.

> Love is very patient and kind, never jealous or envious, never boastful or proud, never haughty or selfish or rude. Love does not demand its own way. It is not irritable or touchy. It does not hold grudges and will hardly even notice

and *The Silent Language;* Hall and Whyte, "Intercultural Communication: A Guide to Men of Action"; Nierenberg and Calero, *How to Read a Person Like a Book;* Watson, *Proxemic Behavior: A Cross-Cultural Study.* Of these, the first is the most technical presentation and the second is the most popularized.

when others do it wrong. It is never glad about injustice, but rejoices whenever truth wins out. If you love someone you will be loyal to him no matter what the cost. You will always believe in him, always expect the best of him, and always stand your ground in defending him.

1 Cor. 13:4-7 *The Living Bible*

Such love builds trust relationships.

Questions for discussion:
1. What questions, other than the prior question of trust, do we generally ask in forming or developing a relationship? Specify.
2. What kinds of things do we tend to bring to a relationship?
3. What kinds of things do we tend to seek in, or take from, a relationship?
4. How do we tend to "let another person down"?
5. In what ways can we communicate our trust to another?
6. Begin to list the situations in which it would be necessary to have effective transfer of trust from one person to another.

Group activities — trust games:
1. "Pass the Bod" is a trust game that young people have liked so well they have made it a party game. With an effective debriefing session afterwards, it becomes a significant foundation block in the course. A group of seven or eight people stand or sit in a rather tight circle. One person stands in the center of the circle, closes his eyes, and proceeds to fall toward one side of the circle without moving his feet. The people in the circle extend their hands and gently pass the person in the center from one to the other, at times passing him across the circle.
2. "Lift the Bod." One person lies on the floor on his back with his eyes closed, his legs extended, his arms crossed. Seven or eight other people proceed to lift him over their heads proceeding very gradually until the person is as high as the group can lift him. They then lower him gradually and gently until he is again on the floor — but without the awareness that he has touched down.

The debriefing session following each of these experiences can involve the following questions:
   a. How did you feel during the experience? (Ask this of those falling or being lifted as well as of those in the circle.)
   b. When were your eyes "forced open"? This would be a sign of undermining of trust.
   c. Why do you think this is called a "trust" game?

    d. In what ways are you called upon to cooperate with your group members?

Group activities — exercises:

1. Individual response: Distribute slips of paper and ask each member of the group to describe briefly a situation that happened recently and that left "a bad taste in his mouth." When this is done, ask each one to focus on one participant in the situation drama — the one he tends to blame for the bad experience. *Then* ask him to record briefly how the situation might have turned out differently had he asked the prior question of trust.

2. Lived experience: Suggest that each group member practice using the prior question of trust for a few days. Have the members report orally or in writing the kinds of things that happened when they asked the trust question. Did they feel their relationships improved? What characteristic behavior attended the action built upon the prior question of trust?

Acceptance of the Person
Trust
Acceptance of Self
Acceptance of the Other
Mutual Respect

3

acceptance of the person: the self

Dear Ann Landers: Recently an irate mother wrote and asked why you never had any kind words for the unwed father. Your reply was very unsympathetic. You said you had no good-conduct medals lying around for unwed fathers and that it was always the girl who paid. You added, "The boy can go about his business . . . Nothing changes for him." I disagree. I am not an unwed father but my best buddy is. Believe me, he has paid plenty. He got the news when he was a junior in college. He actually wanted to marry the girl but her folks were against it, and she listened to them — not to him. His life changed that very day. He began to feel depressed and couldn't study. His grades went to the dogs. He flunked out and had to take a laborer's job. He is paying child support, and he will continue to pay until the child is twenty-one. The worst of it is the guy feels so guilty and worthless now that he refuses to take out a girl. He doesn't think he's good enough for anybody. Some unwed fathers may be bums, but some are good guys who made a mistake. In this case the girl made a better adjustment than the boy. She recently married a nice fellow and seems to be very happy. — For Justice[1]

ACCEPTANCE OF THE PERSON: THE SELF

Freedom to be what I am now, always . . . saying yes to all

---

1. From a column of Ann Landers.

43

that has been inside of me, to all that is, to all the potential of the will be. But how much easier it is to say yes to the possible with its hope, its perhaps, the tomorrowness, than to the now that is freedom, yes, maybe yes.[2]

Is there anything about you that you would change if you could? One young lady responds by saying, "I hated wearing glasses, and I resented the fact that my parents couldn't afford to give me contact lenses." Another asks the question, "Why did I ever have to work for money when other students had time to get to know each other and involve themselves in organizations?"

A young man writes, "I am absentminded when it comes to remembering errands to accomplish, so I began writing these things down rather than saying to myself, 'Oh, you'll remember to do that!'" "Another factor," states a young man, "is that I am a perfectionist. Not that everything has to be done exactly one hundred percent perfect before I will hand it in, but I will strive to do the best possible job I can in the amount of time available to me. This in itself represents a change from an earlier attitude of perfection or nothing at all. This change grew out of an acceptance of the impossibility of gaining perfection in school work."

The young man in the case study at the beginning of this chapter "doesn't think he's good enough for anybody." His failure to accept himself as a person who had done something, however wrong he might think it to be, adds additional barriers to his recovery and ultimate adjustment.

Acceptance of self is the beginning point of change: The person truly accepting himself as he is will not stay that way. He will change in keeping with what he truly is. The change process will not be erratic, nor hit-and-miss. It will cause the person to respond, "I'm glad it worked that way."

Rejection of self will continually leave the person wishing for effective change in his life and dissatisfied with the change process working in him.

THE DIFFICULTY OF ACCEPTING ONESELF

It is difficult for one to accept himself *as he is.* The easier path is one of rejection, of dissatisfaction with what one is, with what one has. Acceptance of self is a process, not to be achieved on the first try. Worked with until it becomes a way of life, it

---

2. Gwen Bailey, a student.

sets the scene for effective change in one's personal life and has beneficial results when one is dealing with others.

Others reject us, why shouldn't we reject ourselves? If we are the kinds of persons that others cut down, turn off, reject, what is there about us that is worthy of acceptance, or of self-respect? What does the young man of the case study have to reject — the pregnancy, payments, flunking out of college, his college, his job? Who rejects him — the girl, her parents, his perception that others do, he himself?

Our society sets such definite standards for us and we are unable to meet all of them. It becomes very easy to feel that we are inadequate in some way and succumb to an attitude of rejection of oneself. Many average students in school feel pressured to strive for grades that are in reality beyond their reach; and in striving they see the grade as an ultimate goal, obscuring for them the true goal of personal development. In the process of the grade struggle, they lose their self-respect through the rejection of their abilities.

The task of self-acceptance is further complicated by those who interpret the biblical injunction as implying "denial" of self. Certainly this interpretation points to a truth in that we dare not be proud of what we are or have, because it has been given to us from God. However — and this is important — the very moment of denial of self is the moment of acceptance of self. What we reject we are unable to turn over to someone else. When we accept ourselves at a given point, e.g., we say, "I'm a worrier," at that moment we are able to admit to God that we worry; then God can enter our lives and work with us as a worrier. That which we refuse to accept, we cling to, and the effect stays with us. It turns to selfishness, not selflessness.

Some segments of our evangelical tradition suggest to us that we are not good enough as we are. We have to be what "God tells us to be." We've got to follow a particular standard of Christian behavior. There is a "Christian" way that must be learned. This continually leaves the Christian with a basic discontent. He is always striving to be that which he is not. Such striving ends in a life of continual struggle and dissatisfaction, or one begins to put on a mask.[3] The mask effectively covers

---

3. For a discussion of the use of masks, read:

Erving Goffman, *The Presentation of Self in Everyday Life* (Garden City, New York: Doubleday, 1959).

Arthur J. Vidich and Joseph Bensman, *Small Town in Mass Society* (Garden City, New York: Doubleday, 1960). This book takes the reader behind the social mask/veneer of so many today.

what he really is, and communicates to others something that he is not now nor ever can be. The person wearing a mask comes through as a fake to others. The process of acceptance of self, and thus true denial of self, leads one on the path to Holy Spirit guidance of the Christian life through internal motivation. The change process starts from within the life and flows out into every contact and association beyond.

Another cause for Christians' rejecting themselves is that they feel they are not worthy of being Christians, of having God interested in them. A key reinforcement of this idea within the Christian community is Isaac Watts' song "At the Cross" in which the question is asked, would Christ die for "such a worm as I?" One of the pitfalls of reformed theology is that the individual is made to feel worthless before God. The reformers, I feel, never intended this thought development that has been reinforced through the centuries and now comes to us as "gospel truth." In our relationship to God, we are worth something to Him. Ephesians 1:18 speaks to this with impact: "God has been made rich because those who are Christ's have been given unto Him" *(The Living Bible)*. What the reformers were trying to convey was that the sinful self is unworthy. This is the tragic problem with Judaism. Its adherents do not recognize that Christ made freedom from sin and death possible for them by His death on the Cross. Through Christ we no longer have to live by a law, constantly trying to make ourselves right with God. When the Jew spends all of his time and energies trying to make himself right with God, he possesses no time, no standing, no insight by which to be of any service to God. Because of the sin in our lives and the fact that we are sinners, we are unworthy of meeting God *as we are* without someone or something to make us worthy. But He has taken our sin upon Himself through the blood of Christ and this leaves us as persons significant to God, something vital to God, something enriching God. *We are important to God, and God accepts us just as we are.*

Accepting yourself or being what you really are may be confused with what you think you ought to be. Someone who lives in keeping with what he thinks he ought to be can never accept himself as he is. Any basis for change rests on a shifting base. One can easily think of new ways in which he ought to be different, but until this change potential is built upon the solid

---

(The woman Jesus interviewed at Jacob's well was attempting to hide her true self when she said, "I have no husband." Christ smoothly unmasked her — and accepted the real person — John 4:16-18.)

foundation of what one is, it is spurious, shifting, uncertain, and inconsistent. Or, if acceptance is based on what we think we are, we may very readily perceive what we are correctly but we may also perceive what we are incorrectly.

JAMES AND A FORMULA

James, in the New Testament, has given us a guide to acceptance of ourselves.[4] In the opening four verses of the first chapter, he talks about accepting our *difficulties* which are potential for building us up and our *temptations* which are potential for tearing us down. The King James version uses only one word — "temptations." The Greek, however, shows the larger, broader impact of the two aspects of life — the difficulties and the temptations — and this is shown in the translation of *The Living Bible*.

James encourages us to accept our difficulties. They are ours, they are no one else's. They grow out of our uniqueness, both in dealing with others and in our own personality. "Work with your difficulties," he says; "Don't throw up your hands and retreat." We are to work with them, for they really develop uniqueness in us and have the potential for building up our lives in a positive sense. Each of us faces many difficulties during the course of our lives. I don't face any difficulty in working out a problem in construction, since I'm not engaged in construction. My difficulties involve students, working out difficult interpersonal relations among students and between students and teachers. My difficulties lie in preparing lectures, not in preparing architectural drawings. The difficulties I face are mine. They make me what I am. Facing up to my difficulties can help me become a mature person.

Almost in the same breath James tells us to accept our temptations. He doesn't say yield to them; he simply says accept them. The temptations we face are our own, not anyone else's. They have the potential for tearing us down if we yield to them. But they can strengthen us toward maturity. My temptations do not involve handling large sums of money as a bank teller does. I don't handle money. But, I do have the temptation to go to class partially prepared. I have the temptation to recommend

---

4. See James 1:1-19. James is reacted to by theologians as an "inadequate" or "immature" theologian. I do not see him as a theologian at all, but rather, as a behavioral scientist! He begins with human need, works with behavior patterns, suggests that anyone else can see what he sees and thus confirm his point of view. Thus his work is most important for the person studying human behavior, and especially for the person himself to understand better his own behavior.

someone more highly than he deserves for graduate school if I particularly like him. These are temptations. Mine make me uniquely me. Yours make you uniquely you.

Knowing yourself and understanding your own true identity includes accepting your difficulties and temptations as you become aware of them. James is not simply telling you to accept them, but he is saying further that it is tremendous that they are yours. It's great! "Then be happy," he says (James 1:2). With each step you take in life, you will face either a difficulty or a temptation, and James simply suggests that when you take the next step, you say, "Great, that's me!" Be "happy," know yourself, get up, start moving!

Many people think that if they want to know themselves, they have to look inward in an introversive way. Introversion and acceptance are two completely different things. Introversion comes from looking in, from minimum action. Acceptance comes from looking out, from maximum action. Introversiveness is a sickness. Acceptance of self leads to health. Introversion will make one dwell on what one is or thinks he is. Acceptance will cause one to move out and recognize a difficulty or temptation and in accepting it, be on the way to resolving the difficulty or standing firm to the temptation. What James is saying here is that "when the way is rough, your patience has a chance to grow" (1:3). Introversion leads to impatience. Acceptance leads to patience with oneself, and then with others. He goes on further: "Let [your patience] grow. Don't try to squirm out of your problems. For when your patience is finally in full bloom, then you will be ready for anything, strong in character, full and complete" (1:4).

Accepting Our Present

I was talking with a nurse recently. She said, "I just can't live with the incompetence of others. This affects what I do at the hospital; this affects what I do at home; this affects my relationships with other girls. The fellows think I'm a snob."

She probably is perceived as a snob by almost everyone, since she can't accept herself as she is, nor can she accept others as they are. She is trying to be something other than what she really is and in the process is trying to make others over, since she is unaccepting of them. We sat together and talked for a fifteen-minute period and with every indication from her of what she was, I said, "Great! That's you. Accept it." I suggested that over a twenty-four hour period, every time she had some little revelation of what she was through some action or thought, she would just say, "That's me! That's great! I accept myself just as I am. That's the way God accepts me." In a very remarkable and unique way, she began to pull out of her rejection pattern and became a person who was much more pleasant to live with.

Can we accept ourselves just as we are at any moment? Can I accept myself as a worrier? Yes! For in my acceptance of myself as a worrier, God has a solid base on which to build my life to what He wants for me. I'm not faking it with Him. Can I accept myself as rejected by someone? Yes, for from that moment on I'll be able to discover just why I'm being rejected and I can build toward a relationship that is meaningful with that person. Can I accept myself as having a dull spiritual life? Yes, for at that moment, I'll become motivated to do something about it. Can I accept myself as being licentious? Yes, for in that moment of acceptance, God can begin to make me a responsible person to His glory.

Thankfulness to God for all He does for us and "against" us is a direct route to acceptance. When rain spoils the plans for an outing and we are sitting in a worship service talking with God, it is difficult to thank God for the rain, but in the moment of thankfulness we share with Him in the acceptance of His perfect will.

I heard of a Summer Mission Project[5] recruit who was in Chicago. He was confronted by a couple of blacks, who looked menacingly at him. He could have stood up to them and fought, but as he said later, he realized he was "chicken" and just admitted to them that he was. You know, it was a funny thing, one of those blacks was also afraid but wouldn't admit it to his buddies. He wouldn't let himself admit to himself that he was afraid. Not long after, the black looked up the mission recruit and said, "I'm a chicken too. You're the first guy that ever played it straight to me. Let's talk."

Another Summer Mission Project worker was sent to work overseas. After some time she attempted to pray in the language of her host country but found it terribly difficult, since she had not mastered it well enough. There came a point during a prayer time with children when she just started praying in English. At that moment, the rapport between her and her friends rose sharply. She accepted herself as she was — an English-speaking American, trying to learn another language.

5. The Summer Mission Project is a student organization at Wheaton College that sends students into mission settings during the summer months for short-term mission service.

ACCEPTING OUR PAST AND FUTURE

Accepting ourselves as we are does not mean accepting ourselves only as we are at this moment. It means accepting also our past and future. A young woman from a Mennonite background asked me to supervise her work in an honors project that had to do with developing or understanding her faith. She said, "I'm not sure of what I believe." I said, "Then study your background. Know what it is in your Mennonite past that you accept, but also what you are right now rejecting. Above all, learn to accept your background. You'll find that this will bring a great deal of peace in accepting yourself as you are now." When she responded that she could never do that, I explained, "That's where you'll begin to find the basis for your own faith. This is the way of life through which you encountered God in the first place; the more you continue rejecting this past, the more difficult it will be for you to develop a personal faith."

Another illustration comes from my personal experience. As a boy, I memorized many passages of Scripture, short and long, meaningful and meaningless to me. When I grew older, I rejected this part of my background, feeling it was rote memory — useless and unworthy of a true Christian. Later I began to see its value and I accepted my "fundamentalist" past, including Bible memorization. Since that time, this memory work has proven useful repeatedly as I have prepared articles for publication, lectures for classes, discussions and special presentations. Because the Word of God lies behind my mind, so to speak, I can scan large passages without ever having to read them and I am able to draw out what is useful to confirm or negate the work I am doing.

When we reject our past, we often salvage the bad out of our background, that which is least useful to us. We don't intend to do this, but our rejection blinds us to what is most valuable. It focuses on what we didn't like, rather than on what is maximally useful to us for the present time; whereas acceptance allows us to consider all equally. Then in a sane, rational way, we select out of our past that which is useful to us. The young unwed father's rejection of his past affects his present and his future. It has delayed him in coming to terms with himself and with those about him.

What about the future? Some people are always looking ahead to tomorrow, and by this they run the risk of rejecting their past and their present. This is tragic. One day I saw a beautiful four-thousand-dollar organ. It was a marvelous instrument and I was tremendously excited. "Tomorrow I'll get that," I thought. "Not as a college professor," I realized. If I am to accept myself as I am today, and was yesterday, I must also accept myself as a person with a future in which there is not likely a place for a four-thousand-dollar organ. Things may change, but at this moment I accept myself as being unable to afford such an organ. And so I am at peace.

Acceptance of self gives us practice accepting that which is close to us. It allows us to practice on something that is real. Then, when we move out into the world among others, we can accept them more readily. The practice of self-acceptance has now become a way of life to us. We are ready to accept others as fully valid and unique. Practicing acceptance on that which we see and feel makes it easier to accept God whom we have not seen.

Those persons in the Scriptures who accepted themselves as they were had a vital role to play in the development of the Christian faith. Paul accepted his limitations and admitted them: "See with what large letters I am writing to you" (Gal. 6:11 RSV). And again, "I am in chains now . . ." (Eph. 6:20). Jesus said, "Take this cup away from me. Yet I want your will, not mine" (Mark 14:36). David sinned many times throughout his life, but there was an acceptance of what he was and did. The Psalms are full of the record of David's acceptance of himself, and the record is a moving testimony of a man growing before God.

Those who failed to accept themselves had a tragic role. I think especially of Saul, the king of Israel. Saul could never accept himself, therefore he continually drove himself and those about him mercilessly, creating all kinds of problems.[6]

SUMMARY

Acceptance of self is *the beginning point of change.* The person is not at that moment what he will eventually become, but it is acceptance that provides a solid base or foundation for change. At each step in the change process, one can accept himself as he is. In this way change will be in keeping with the person and what he truly is — not inconsistent with the person's life and development.

Interpersonal relations begin with the self. Some segments of evangelical Christianity have conveyed an unfortunate message to the individual: that one cannot accept himself as he is. One

---

6. Take note of Saul's experiences in 1 Samuel.

must always be seeing himself as he "ought to be." This has resulted in a wholesale rejection of self leading to various psychological conditions. God wants us to start with our lives where He starts, in full and complete acceptance of ourselves. Then, we can truly work with Him in the change process, becoming what He wants us to be through the leading of the Holy Spirit.

James is saying in Scripture, "Accept yourself as you are with your difficulties," i.e., that which is potential for building you up; "and with your temptations," i.e., that which is potential for tearing you down; then you will become mature and ready for anything. To reject yourself at this point will only produce immaturity and uncertainty.

The excitement of life lies with accepting one's past, present, and future. The degree to which one accepts his past determines the degree to which he will be able to realize the good of his background and select from it that which is useful to him at the lived moment. The degree to which one is able to accept his future determines the degree of peace within the ongoing development of his life.

The agent of change who approaches others while he is still unable to accept himself will communicate this self-rejection to other people. They will always doubt to some degree the value of that change that has not provided peace in the life of the agent of change.

Questions for discussion:
1. What do you find difficult to accept about yourself?
2. How do others limit your self-acceptance?
3. In what ways does self-rejection manifest itself in your life?
4. What biblical passages might help you accept yourself?
5. How does God accept you? As you are? As you ought to be? As others think you are or should be? As you would like to be?
6. Which do you think is most difficult — to accept one's past, one's present, or one's future?

Group activities and exercises:
1. Have the group members seek out from among their associations someone who does not accept himself as he is and someone who does. Have them compare orally or in writing the two kinds of experiences.
2. Plan, in writing, a program of change to reverse a pattern of self-rejection. Urge that the program be put into effect.

Acceptance of the Person
Trust
Acceptance of Self
Acceptance of the Other
Mutual Respect

4

acceptance of the person: the other

I have a roommate who is very insensitive to my thoughts and feelings, to my likes and dislikes. Just last night he came "bombing" into the room, dropped his books on my desk, threw his clothes on my bed, and then, to top it all off, he left a trail of cake crumbs all over the floor. The guy knows that I clean the room every night around six. I think I have a right to keep this place looking neat for my friends who drop in for the evening.

Another thing that bothers me is the way he just dumps his dirty clothes in the corner of the room. I have nothing against the guy being an athlete, but I do have something against peculiar odors. I wonder what he thinks the dirty clothes bag is for. (I asked him that question once and he just walked away as if he felt like saying, "Go hang it on your nose!") And another thing, why can't the guy put his things on his own desk and bed?!

He knows that all of these things bother me. I have tried to be patient with him and I've tried to understand his background. I have talked to him about the situation and, at one time, I even hung up his stuff for him. But now I am fed up with his deliberate insensitivity. I just shove his books under his bed and throw his clothes in the closet. This makes him mad, but that's tough! I've even come to the point of telling him to grow up, but he'll never change. I just avoid looking at him when he is in the room or elsewhere on campus. I think this guy is in for. . . .

53

How difficult it is for us to accept a person as he is, and work from there.

A number of years ago I walked out onto my porch in our small mountain village in Central America. I observed my neighbor, Fabian, starting down the trail. It was early in the morning for me, but he had probably been up an hour or more. I called to him and said, "Where are you going?" He indicated that he was going up the mountain to procure a cow for butchering the next day, the market day for that area. When I asked if I could accompany him, he readily agreed.

We started up the narrow, winding, steep trail and after a while he turned to me and said, "I'm tired; let's rest." I had become quite weary by that time, no doubt breathing heavily, so I responded happily, "I'm tired, too. Let's rest."

Now, I'm quite sure that he was not tired, but out of consideration for me he was willing to take a five-minute break.

We sat on the side of the mountain, looking eastward down the mountain valley. While we were sitting there chatting, Fabian was first to notice that the sun had begun to rise. He commented, "Here comes our father."

Since I was a missionary and was primed by my training, this was "just the ideal opportunity" to give a "Gospel witness." I turned to Fabian and exclaimed, "Fabian, that's not our father." He looked at me with a strange look on his face. I then proceeded to give him a half-hour eighth-grade science lecture on the topic of the sun. He didn't say much after that. In fact, in the following years of our friendship very little was said either about our conversation there on the mountainside, or about the Gospel I had begun to communicate to him.

Looking back, I realize that in rejecting his point of view, I failed to communicate that I was accepting him as a person. When I cut down his belief and his thought pattern, however wrong or right, or however superstitious or correct, he also read the message that I was cutting him down and rejecting him personally.

In my estimation, Fabian was one tremendous person; so I had no intention of rejecting him when I rejected his viewpoint. I didn't know that we were perceiving two different messages. Neither did I know that the possibility of two different messages even existed. Still further, I would not have known what to do if I had realized that there were two messages, or two parts to the same message. I had not been trained in effective communication, nor had I been warned that some people in the world see their entire experience as a "whole piece of cloth," where an attack in one aspect of life is an attack on the whole; where a criticism of a thought pattern is a criticism of the person himself. *In rejecting his point of view, I had unwittingly rejected him as a person.*

How many times in our interpersonal relations do we reject the other person's point of view, reject his action or statement, and wind up rejecting him as a person as well? We fail to recognize that there are two parts to a communication. We may want the other to know we accept him; however, he may see us as rejecting both his behavior *and* his person. How can we split these messages up and know what we are doing in the formation of a pattern of rejection?

It is our opportunity and responsibility in some way to get through to the other the message of our acceptance of him as a person even though we might disapprove of what he does. As a person he is loved and accepted by God, though his works are disapproved of God when they do not meet His standards.[1] Should we do less than accept the other person on this same basis?[2]

INSTANT REJECTION — A SIMULATION GAME

The game "Instant Rejection" is a game I developed to let each of us see to what degree we are acceptors or rejectors of others. The rules are quite simple. You select a person as the object of your rejection. Then, you proceed to work with all the tools at your disposal to reject that person and communicate the message of rejection to him. The following methods may be used:

You cut him off when he's talking to you.

You laugh after statements he addresses to you.

You question his facts.

You show him lack of trust and confidence.

You attempt to overprotect him.

You talk down to him.

---

1. Observe this process working in the encounter between Jesus and the woman taken in adultery in John 8:1-11.

2. The drive to be accepted is confirmed continually in the research and writings of psychologists, sociologists, and anthropologists. See the work of Peter Berger, Carl Rogers, Paul Tournier, and many others:

Peter L. Berger, *Invitation to Sociology: A Humanistic Perspective* (Garden City, New York: Doubleday, 1963).

Carl Rogers, *Freedom to Learn* (Columbus, Ohio: Charles E. Merrill Publishing Company, 1969).

Paul Tournier, *The Meaning of Persons* (New York: Harper and Row, 1957).

You overreact to something he says or does.
You avoid his eyes and forget his name.

I have guided many students in playing the game of "Instant Rejection." The amazing discovery they make is that this is the way they actually live. Rejecting other people is what they are doing continually. They have been trained to reject others. In the case study of this chapter, the one roommate had many things to reject about his roommate: his bombing into the room, his leaving a litter trail, his lack of a sense of "personal" property, the dropped clothes, the odor. It was quite easy to reject the other without thought.

ALIENATION

"Rejection produces alienation. Alienation is to cause to be estranged, to make inimical or indifferent where devotion or attachment formerly subsisted" (Webster). Alienation happens between two people, between a group and another person, or between two groups (see chapter 12). Alienation is cutting off; it is separating from. This may occur in actual alienation where someone is actually cut off from another person or group or in perceived alienation where it *appears* to the other person that he is being cut off. Either of these can be harmful, for alienation gives the feeling of being unwanted, of not having a place, of not being part of a group, whether this condition actually exists or not. As human beings, we have a drive, a desire to be accepted as part of some group, however large or small.

Today's world has produced many experiences of alienation. Youth in American society during the latter part of the decade of the sixties felt alienated. They responded to this feeling of alienation by withdrawing from society or by forming new groups, resulting in the resurgence of the "commune." The sense of alienation of communist China causes them to turn to the aid of "oppressed people." Alienation finds expression in war. Such alienation has caused underdeveloped nations to refuse to advance or to advance too rapidly for their own good. Some have sought to advance on their own or by seeking out questionable support from nations supplying this aid for ulterior motives. Alienation has undermined aid programs, mission programs, and educational efforts.

Rejection that results in alienation is likely to be reciprocated, producing further alienation. The rejected one, in fact, will do something to the other in such a way as to "get even" or "get back at him."

THE SNOB EFFECT

Rejection underlies the sense of alienation. There are many situations in life in which one can either sense rejection or can turn to reject someone. I will call the rejector "the snob." Rejection within a society has a "snob effect" on the one rejecting. He sees himself as the member of an elite group of some type and attempts both to remain within that group and to keep all others out. His victim, in turn, rejects this group and finds some satisfaction as a member of another group where he begins to react in the same way. He closes off the borders of that group to the outside and thus reinforces the identity of the group. The natural formation of groups within society is not a problem here except when exclusiveness is maintained by the group for selfish reasons. It is at this point that rejection of others becomes disastrous within the larger society.

The expression of nationalism in underdeveloped countries of the world is In part a response to rejection by outsiders. This expression may come as a formal rejection between governments or as an informal expression by outsiders in criticizing all the patterns of life they find in that country.

A non-American, responding to his experience of living in the United States, sensed the loss of self-respect involved in being forced to abandon what he was. "Neither can I be an American nor can I imitate them and pretend to be like them," he protested. "I want to be myself." He felt that to live among Americans he had to become something other than what he was. This does not mean just living a different way. To him this meant being made over into another person — abandoning what he was, his principles, and his responsibility to the whole of his former culture.

A young lady in the dormitory of a Christian college left after one year and explained, "I couldn't be myself. I couldn't dress right. I thought, upon coming, that I had some musical ability, but this was forever cut down. Nothing that I did was right, proper, or effective. I received no encouragement. I felt totally rejected."

REJECTION AND THE CHRISTIAN

Rejection infiltrates very subtly into our lives as Christians as well as into the ministry of the Gospel of Jesus Christ.

One evening I was speaking at a church that had planned a three-hour service. This was to include a period for spelling out the problem of concern, a time of small-group discussion, a sandwich supper, and a summary and challenge as the close. The subject was the general one of the church and the family, though the content focused on the generation gap.

The church members prided themselves on having effective communication with their teens, admitting only a small gap between the two subcultures. I was interested to observe just how correct this perception was. I noticed, first of all, that even though it was a rather large church, only a small number of young people attended this session designed especially to get teens together with their parents and other adults. I was told later that the young people figured there was very little in it for them.

The initial statement was made and then the larger group divided into smaller groups meeting separately. I had very little to do during the group discussion period, so I decided I would go from room to room and as much as possible refrain from intruding or interrupting. After sitting in on a few of the sessions, a pattern of response to the comments of young people began to form. The pattern followed this line: Whenever an adult spoke, he was supported or his thoughts were amplified. Whenever a young person spoke, I heard an audible chuckle from the audience, like a self-conscious giggle. The next statement would then come from an adult questioning the validity of the youth's statement. This pattern did not occur every time, but enough times to make me seek to further pursue some of the implications of such a response.

In the session following the group reports, I decided to introduce this observation. I then suggested that the church had a greater youth problem than they had anticipated, explaining that this was evidenced not only by the small youth turnout but also by the adult behavior toward youth.

Following the service, an attractive teenager approached me and said, "You're right! We have to live with that little laugh that degrades us so." A patterned response to youth and their ideas thus communicated rejection to them.

I was in another church, a Brethren Assembly, on the West Coast. After I had spoken, the young people gathered around me questioning me further concerning things I had commented on regarding contemporary music. Adult members also approached, some of them leaders of the church. Youth, adults, and I were all in conversation together. It seemed to me that a healthy discussion was going on. The adults appeared willing to let the young people play their kind of music in their youth groups as well as in the larger congregation. They were also allowed to develop this style into a Gospel witness. Since the discussion was going so well, I felt free to move to another group and began talking with them. However, as I looked around later, I noticed that the first group had dispersed. I learned afterward, much to my disappointment, that no further discussion was held and nothing further was done by the leaders on behalf of the youth. The subtle rejection of the youth, evident in the behavior of the adults, was effectively communicated to them. When an authority figure was no longer present, the adults felt no further obligation to pursue the subject.

The subtlety of such rejection is clearly evident when members of other ethnic groups join the conversation. It is this type of rejection that is termed "racism."

A young black spent a number of years in a white community and reported the questions asked of him during his stay there. "I bet your social life is real rough. I bet you have a real frustrating time. What sports do you play? Do negroes sunburn?" Such statements and questions very effectively alienate through the sense of rejection. The person feels invalid, unwanted.

Rejection, carried out by most of us, usually produces alienation. This rejection alienates all kinds of people, both of our society and of others. The way to avoid rejecting another person is to accept him completely and fully, *just as he is.* In interpersonal relations, start from a base of acceptance. Once you have an acceptance attitude in your mind, making it impossible for you to reject that other person, you will seek some way of communicating this acceptance. This again becomes an exciting "game" or exercise: how to communicate your acceptance to the other person.

Too often the Christian feels that he will be less than discerning, or that he will compromise his stand if he is to accept the other just as he is. This has produced divisions within the Church of Jesus Christ as well as alienation within the local fellowship of believers. The Christians in the early Church were known by their acceptance of one another. Non-Christians said, "See how they love one another," not, "See how they are continually producing alienation." *If our discernment or lack of compromise results in the rejection of persons, we need to re-examine the basis of our fellowship.* The love spoken of in the Bible does not result in alienation or rejection, but rather, it results in the full-orbed experience of fellowship and belonging.

ACCEPT-RESPECT VS. ACCEPT-BELIEVE

Acceptance of the person does not imply acceptance into

one's life of all that that person does, says, or believes. One does not have to believe the way another person does to accept him as a person. One does not even have to approve of what the other person believes to accept him as he is as the starting point for change. In fact, it is vitally important to be wise in distinguishing between what a person is and what he does, or between accepting a person and accepting what he does. Even though we do not need to accept-*believe* all that a person believes, we can still accept-*respect* what a person believes. Accept-respect suggests that we can accept a person, whatever he believes or does, and show him this acceptance or potential acceptance in the form of respect. We communicate to him in this way that he is a real and valid person in our eyes. *This may not be the way he ends up in our relationship — nor is this likely the way we will end up.* Accept-respect allows us to know the person as he is and begin working with him in the change process.

Accept-believe means that we accept by believing and taking into our lives and experiences that which we accept. Respect yields to embracing the belief as a belief.

Acceptance of the person does not call for accept-believe, although it may develop into this. Rather, it calls for accept-respect.[3] The other person does not expect us to do everything he does, believe as he believes, think as he thinks. Rather, he assumes that we will be what *we* are; only then will he accept us as we are, and respect both our person and what we do. When we abandon what we are, he will lose respect for us. Young people in American society lose respect for that adult who tries to be too much like youth — wearing the same clothes, talking the same dialect, participating in the very same activities. Youth do not want their elders to adopt all of their practices, all of their details of life. The same applies to peoples of other societies. They simply want the respect of others, not conformity to their pattern of life. They know that respect will lead the other to an effective adaptation to the culture and life-way. Conformity will undermine the trust relationship in time and disrupt interpersonal relationships rather than build them.

Peoples of other societies do not expect the missionary to dress just as they do, live in the same kind of house as they do, or follow their practices. They do not expect us to abandon our principles in becoming like them. They do not want us to be-

---

3. For further discussion of the accept-respect attitude, refer to Carl Rogers' discussion of accepting and "prizing" the other in *Freedom to Learn* (Columbus, Ohio: Charles E. Merrill Publishing Co., 1969).

come ethical relativists. *They want us to be persons of principle so they can trust us.* At the same time, they expect that we will work with them and let them be people of principle as well, people deserving of respect.

DISCERNMENT

Acceptance of the person implies discernment. It does not negate it. In other words, we do not accept a person irrespective of a quality of life. Rather, our acceptance grows and develops in keeping with that person as he grows in maturity. We accept the person at every moment of his experience. As we grow together, the intensity of our acceptance increases. As we grow apart, our acceptance is still there, but the intensity of our feelings lessens.

The same principle holds as far as the other's actions are concerned. We always accept him as a person, and as his actions show increasing maturity, our acceptance increases in intensity of feeling. Thus, acceptance is primary and prior to all feelings and emotions extended toward others and is rooted in trust.

Frequently the realization of one's worthiness for acceptance comes a long time after any initial attempt at acceptance, for it takes time to gain full knowledge of another's personal and social being. This is the underlying principle involved in Christ's urging to forgive "seventy times seven." A period of time is thus made available for each to know the other and sense the full realization of the worth of each other within the context of individual and sociological difference. Christ also illustrated the principle by continually trusting and accepting when we would have given up and failed to trust and accept.

THE BIBLE AND ACCEPTANCE

The Bible offers a number of clear illustrations of acceptance of the person of which only a few will be presented here.

One of the most dramatic of these occurred between Eli and Hannah in the Old Testament.[4] Eli communicated to Hannah, "You are a beautiful person, a wonderful woman, God give you what you ask." We would no doubt have questioned her life-style, since she was a second wife of a man and thus living in a polygamous household. We would have viewed her with sus-picion long after Eli, who at first had thought she was drunk because she moved her lips strangely, but then recognized his mistake and acted in accordance with his new perception with-

---

4. 1 Samuel 1:9-18.

out further question. Eli accepted her as a person, just as she was, and encouraged her in her request to God.

A woman, taken in the act of adultery one day, was brought to Jesus. Jesus, in talking with her after her accusers had gone, communicated two messages to her (or two parts of the same message). One was a nonverbal message that communicated to her that she was a fantastic person, a beautiful person. The second message, this time a verbal one, indicated disapproval of the practice of adultery: "Go and sin no more." The evidence for the two parts of the message is quite clear. She (or another whom Jesus had accepted and forgiven in much the same way) responded to the first by returning at a later date and anointing the Savior with precious ointment — a deed she would likely not have done had she thought that Jesus was rejecting her person. She responded to the second (apparently, since there is lack of indication to the contrary in the Scriptures) by making her behavior as beautiful as her person; i.e., she was no longer an adulteress.[5]

The "love" chapter of the Bible, 1 Corinthians 13, deals with this problem also. One of the most telling statements in that chapter is the simple statement "[Love] will hardly even notice when others do it wrong."

Carl Rogers spells out a number of ways that enable us to create a helping relationship, or, in the terminology of this chapter, to become an acceptor of persons rather than one who rejects.

Rogers sums up his thoughts in this way: "The degree to which I can create relationships which facilitate the growth of the other as a separate person, is the measure of the growth I have achieved in myself."[6]

We should ask ourselves these questions:

1. Can I in some way which will be perceived by the other person as trustworthy, be as dependable or consistent in some deep sense? Do I realize that being trustworthy does not demand that I be rigidly consistent but that I be dependably real?
2. Can I be expressive enough as a person so that what I am will be communicated unambiguously?
3. Can I let myself experience positive attitudes toward this

5. John 8:1-11.
6. Carl Rogers, *On Becoming A Person* (Boston: Houghton Mifflin, 1961), pp. 50-56.

other person — attitudes of warmth, caring, liking, interest, respect?

4. Can I be strong enough as a person to be separate from the other? Can I be a sturdy respector of my own feelings and my own needs, as well as his? Can I acknowledge my own feelings and, if need be, express them as something belonging to me and separate from his feelings?
5. Am I secure enough within myself to permit him his separateness? Can I permit him to be what he is — honest or deceitful, infantile or adult, despairing or overconfident?
6. Can I let myself enter fully into the world of his feelings and personal meanings and see these as he does? Can I step into his private world so completely that I lose all desire to evaluate or judge it? Can I enter it so sensitively that I can move about in it freely, without trampling on meanings which are precious to him?
7. Can I receive him as he is? Can I communicate this attitude? Or can I only receive him conditionally, acceptant of some aspects of his feelings and silently or openly disapproving of other aspects?
8. Can I act with sufficient sensitivity in the relationship so that my behavior will not be perceived as a threat?
9. Can I free him from the threat of external evaluation?
10. Can I meet this other individual as a person who is in process of *becoming,* or will I be bound by his past and by my past?

ACCEPTANCE AND MISSION

A first need for an attitude of acceptance in mission is in the matter of recruiting. The personnel of a mission board needs the attitude of acceptance toward *new recruits.* Youth always appears distinct from the adult in some way, either in dress, hair style, vocabulary, or learning/doing ideas. The adult has difficulty working his way through the differences of language and fashion to find the true nature of responsibility as expressed by youth.[7] Therefore, the adult vitally needs an attitude of acceptance so that petty concerns and misunderstandings do not mar the progress of the young person through the process of recruitment. Therefore, it is not only important that the missionary learn to accept others within another country or culture,

---

7. It is unfortunate in any age that "man looks on the outward appearance"; however, we may be grateful that the Lord looks on the heart (1 Samuel 16:7 RSV).

but it is also equally significant for all of us to exercise this same acceptance within our own culture and subculture.

There are two different kinds of Christian educational institutions: the Bible college and the Christian liberal arts college. The former has stricter controls over the expressions of language and dress, whereas the latter tends to follow the lead in language and fashion of the secular college or university. Mission executives become wary of the graduates of the Christian liberal arts college, since they do not appear to be dedicated or as dedicated to Christ as their Bible college counterparts. They naturally gravitate to the latter group that appears to understand them more completely, and with which they feel most comfortable. Such perceptions may mislead the mission board if it focuses only on the stereotyped groups. The mission representative needs crosscultural tools, for he may find, all too late, that the more normal-appearing youth, though he dresses and speaks correctly, is as radical and rebellious as those encountered in the secular university; and further, the extreme-appearing youth on the Christian liberal arts campus may be just as sincere in his dedication to Christ as his counterpart on the Bible college campus. In many ways, he may be more capable of doing the job the mission wishes to have accomplished.

Second, when the missionary enters the *missionary subculture overseas,* he needs an attitude of acceptance also. The other missionaries probably come from his own society, but they still have sociocultural distinctions derived both from their background and from their experience in the host country, that can produce irritations in the life of the new worker. Such distinctions are intensified in another society. Every encounter within the missionary subculture must be considered as a multicultural situation. Members within both his own and other missions are distinct in numerous ways. Not all share his approach, his belief, his principles, but he can be accepted for what he is and he can also accept the other as a valid person, with a right to his own belief and practice.

Third, in his dealings with the *citizens of his host country,* the missionary needs the attitude of acceptance. The national *can* and *must* be taken just as he is. This is *not* the way he will continue to be, nor is the missionary what he will eventually be, but it is absolutely vital that each be accepted just as he is and not be viewed in terms of the standards and beliefs of the other. Rogers talks about this right and privilege as being "free from the threat of external evaluation." The member of the host nation can become the finest Christian in keeping with what he is. He does not need to be made over into an American, a Canadian, or a Britisher. Belief in Jesus Christ can regenerate his own life and, through this change, his society. This change will still follow the cultural ways of his people and be in keeping with it. If a man belongs to a society where men and women eat separately, becoming a Christian will not cause them to eat together. In fact, eating together may not necessarily indicate growth in the Christian life, and eating separately will not indicate sin in the life. The people can become the finest Christians and grow in Christ and yet continue to have division of the sexes in the experience of eating. It is possible that a family of that culture, by following the western practice of eating together, might express a number of tragic non-Christian attitudes that could destroy their family and limit their testimony within the community. Though Christianity may not cause them to change their culture, it will cause their hearts to change; and whether their practice will be to eat separately or together, there will be a growing bond of Christian love and fellowship which over a period of time will unite the family in a true unity, reinforcing the vitality of the family within that society.

Thus, acceptance must become the foundation for all interpersonal relations so that the missionary can come to a sure and complete understanding of what each person is, and how he can best reach him for Christ and encourage his true growth in Christ.

When an attitude of rejection underlies the message of Christian love, the nationals immediately respond with further rejection. A missionary thus loses the whole purpose of his ministry.

A fourth and final aspect of missions in which a missionary needs the attitude of acceptance is *within his own family.* The missionary family is made up of a multicultural group. The parents belong to the adult subculture of their home society. They have children born either within that society or within the host society. Each child develops differently in keeping with the multiplicity of experiences both in his parents' home society and in the host society. The critical challenge to this attitude of acceptance is when the child returns home to enter the youth subculture of his parents' society. His preparation for this entry was made primarily in contact with the adult subculture of this society and the youth subculture of the host society. If the parents withdraw their acceptance support at this critical time, the missionary child will seek out replacement support, and may find himself in the company of cop-outs or drug users.

SUMMARY

The acceptance of the other person deals with the acceptance-rejection patterns underlying interpersonal relationships. Rejection produces alienation; acceptance reverses alienation and is the sound foundation for true Christian love. The average person is trained through the socialization process to reject someone different from himself. The expression of this rejection leads from self to one's neighbor, to the stranger, and ultimately to God Himself. Here centers the importance of the Christian message of love, for the Gospel would reverse the process of rejection and insure acceptance.

The acceptance of the person, *as he is* at any moment in time, is simply the starting point in change. What that person is, is not what he will become, nor will the person dealing with him remain unchanged. Both will change in a way that will improve them. They will emerge in a better condition, with a more healthy relationship. The acceptance of the person precedes any involvement with that person within a change relationship. The agent of change will get nowhere if he evokes a rejection response. Complete openness in acceptance will encourage the other also to be completely open; thus, openness provides fertile soil for change.

Questions for discussion:

1. What kinds of things do you find it difficult to accept in another person?
2. What kinds of things do you find it difficult to accept in a group or an organization?
3. In what ways does one manifest or show this rejection? Physiologically? Psychologically? Sociologically? By body movement? By spatial arrangement?
4. How did Jesus show His acceptance of the other person?
5. How would Christian mission be carried out were one to accept the other just as he is at every moment in time? What problems might one face?
6. How can one reject a point of view without rejecting the person?
7. How does one go about reversing the process of rejection?
8. What do you perceive is the nature of "everyman's" behavior, acceptance or rejection?

Group activities and exercises:

1. Conceptualize a class, church, or family situation in which the

group members approach the situation with a rejection attitude. Then conceptualize that same situation if acceptance were practiced.

2. Study the book of James in the Bible and see what James is saying about acceptance of the other person. What generalizations would you make from the teachings of James?

3. Send the group members out into their everyday experiences to observe behavior of others. Have them report back any observed behavior that has surprised them. Debrief this kind of exercise with the following questions:
   a. What surprised you?
   b. Would this same thing surprise anyone else?
   c. How did you react to such surprise behavior?

4. Role play, corporate: Have the group members divide into groups of four to six and prepare an acceptance/rejection skit. For example, take a situation out of the life of Christ and if it was an acceptance-of-the-other experience, role play it first as acceptance and then do it as if those who were acceptors of others in the first instance changed to rejectors in this one. Talk about the impact of rejection on the group, especially their reaction to Christ being depicted as a rejector. Then talk about the related roles and how each group member fit into his assigned role. An excellent situation to try is that of the mothers bringing their children to Christ and having the disciples turn them away.

5. Experiment: Send each group member out to accept or reject someone. Let the acceptance or rejection develop for a period of time until behavior is modified. Have the person report on the behavioral response of the other person. (Caution: Be quite careful in selecting the object of rejection and carrying out the rejection part of this exercise, since relationships can be permanently affected.)

Acceptance of the Person
Trust
Acceptance of Self
Acceptance of the Other
Mutual Respect

5

---

mutual respect

A prominent, well-to-do family in California had a son who was expected to follow in the steps of the father and maintain the social position of the family in the community. After finishing high school, the boy joined a so-called hippie group.

Later on, he decided to go to college in England and arranged with his father to spend a year there. The father promised to pay the transportation and the college costs for the first year. Without the parents being aware of it, the boy met his girl friend in New York and the two of them left for England where they lived together and spent the money the father had provided for college, doing the things they were interested in, but without attending school.

When the year expired, the fellow and his girl returned to the states as husband and wife. They asked permission to live with his parents until they could get established, and part of their request included money. They needed ready cash to carry them over until they could support themselves.

Three current points of view regarding interpersonal relations leave the relationship partial and potential by loss of trust as well as loss of self-respect. These points of view are that of the traditionalist, that of the relativist or antinomian, and that of the adherents of situation ethics. (See chart 6.) These views develop partial relationships, since someone in the relationship

68

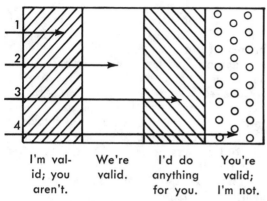

1. traditionalist

2. mutual respect

3. situationist

4. antinomian

| I'm val-id; you aren't. | We're valid. | I'd do anything for you. | You're valid; I'm not. |

Chart 6. Ways Interpersonal Relationships May Develop

is bound to come out on the short end. He will be the one that will abandon his principles, if only in part, and thus be less than a truly "whole person."

The *traditionalist* sees his world as one that never changes and should never change. In other words, the other person must at least partially abandon what he is — his principles, his beliefs, and his life-way — to conform to the traditionalist, in order to get along with him. The traditionalist focuses primarily on form or expression, rather than on meaning. The form is to remain the same whatever the cost. If the form or expression remains constant through time, then it most certainly follows, as far as he is concerned, that the meaning will also remain constant through time.

Were the father, in the opening case study, a traditionalist, he would insist on the couple's apology, an immediate wedding, a change of dress, and he would proceed to urge a "return" to logical "middle-class" thinking.

"A traditionalist" is not synonymous with "a member of a *traditional society*."[1] A traditional society is one that has changed little through time, though it may very well have effective

1. See:
George Dalton, *Tribal and Peasant Economics* (Garden City, New York: Doubleday, 1967).
George M. Foster, *A Cross-Cultural Anthropological Analysis of a Technical Aid Program* (Washington, D.C.: Smithsonian Institute of Social Anthropology, 1951), *Traditional Cultures and the Impact of Technological Change* (New York: Harper and Row, 1962), and *Applied Anthropology* (Boston: Little Brown and Co., 1969).

mechanisms for change. Those coming into a traditional society may maintain their principles and operate effectively in keeping with the totality of their sociocultural background and they are free to adapt to the new culture as need arises. Traditional societies, even as nontraditional societies, may have traditionalists within them. These members would focus on the form of the traditional society and seek to perpetuate it, even though the meaning of, or reason for, the form has changed.

The *relativist* or antinomian counts the relativity of individual behavior above all social controls over conduct. He thus abandons all that he is, in order to cater or pander to the other. He forfeits principle for the sake of the other. He may become a relativist by choice or through the pressures, however subtle, of the society of which he is a part.

Again, were the father in the opening case a relativist rather than a traditionalist, he would yield all principle and, catering to his son, would welcome him back on any terms. In fact, he might even abandon his own life-way in seeking acceptance by the youths. Were the youths relativists, they too might yield their emerging life-style and take on the form of the parents' life-style without really wanting to. Conforming in this way, for the sake of getting along, could cause serious loss of self-respect.

The relativist is to be distinguished from the *cultural relativist,* who holds that truth can be expressed through distinct cultural forms and that even though the form may differ across cultural boundaries, the truth remains the same. The cultural relativist encourages full responsibility of a member within his own sociocultural setting. If for some reason change is required because of some practice or belief that is contrary to humanitarian principles or is in violation of a universal norm or moral absolute, the cultural relativist will work in cooperation with the members of the society to *effect* the change rather than *dictating* the change. The cultural relativist encourages full maintenance of principle and responsibility, whereas the relativist abandons his principles in part or in whole.[2] The Christian, holding to the Word of God as his authority in ethical problems, is emphatically not an ethical relativist, but he should, equally emphatically, be a cultural relativist.

In *situation ethics,* espoused by Joseph Fletcher and other

2. For a fuller discussion of the problem of cultural relativism, see: Melville Herskovits, *Cultural Dynamics* (New York: Knopf, 1964).

David O. Moberg, "Cultural Relativity and Christian Faith," *Journal of the American Scientific Affiliation* (June, 1962), pp. 34-48.

Also refer to chapter 16.

writers, a person may abandon a certain amount of principle whenever necessary out of love for the other. In the words of Fletcher,

> The situationist enters into every decision-making situation fully armed with the ethical maxims of his community and its heritage, and he treats them with respect as illuminators of his problems. Just the same, he is prepared in any situation to compromise them or set them aside in the situation if love seems better served by doing so.[3]

If the participants in our opening case study were situation ethicists, they would yield any and every principle that would be necessary out of love for the others. This sounds very beautiful and can theoretically produce a "happy" home experience for all involved. However, working from the basis of willingness to abandon principle, someone may go too far and undermine trust. This arrangement will give the recipient of the favor a good feeling at first, but it could ultimately undermine the relationship.

The primary practical problem with situation ethics, as I see it, is that in any decision involving another, though the other may at first like what has been done in his behalf, he may later interpret the action as an abandonment of principle in some degree, and thus his trust is undermined. When the trust relationship is not affected and trust is not undermined, the result is much like the result expected of mutual respect. However, any undermining of trust that is not adjusted for, or any trust breech that is not closed, can serve to disrupt and is potential for destroying the relationship.

A more underlying philosophical problem with situation ethics arises in considering the decision-making process itself. Situation ethics suggests that, given the situation, out of the situation itself will arise the solution. "The situational factors are so primary that we may even say, 'Circumstances alter rules and principles.'" Or again, "Every man must decide for himself according to his own estimate of conditions and consequences; and no one can decide for him or impugn the decision to which he comes."[4] Rather, I would suggest, as an anthropologist, that everyone takes into every situation an elaborate value system with each of the values ranked in a hierarchy. (See chapter 14.) It is much the same with a computer program, with ordered rules instructing the computer. When the computer is given a prob-

---

3. Joseph Fletcher, *Situation Ethics* (Philadelphia: The Westminster Press, 1966), p. 26.
4. Ibid., pp. 29, 36.

lem, the solution will reflect the input or instructional matter. So the person, responding to the input of his socialization process however unique it is for himself as an individual in society, will make a decision in keeping with that input, or rank of values. His hierarchy of values is thus tested by the situation, but the situation itself is unable to bring decision. The decision lies in the intricate programming of values. The person responding, therefore, to his hierarchy of values may not like the choice he has made. It is at this time that he begins a careful and elaborate adjustment in his value ranking, a need that his response to a given situation has clarified for him. The adjustment in his hierarchy is thus ready for his next situational involvement and to be tested by that situation. His decisions in this new situation can clarify if in fact his hierarchy has been changed or not and will indicate to him further direction in the change process. *One's rank of values will always underlie and set up the decision within a given situation.* It is thus wise to investigate the value system one has rather than simply the situation one faces. The more the decision one makes is in keeping with the real value system, and not just the person's perception of his value system, the less tension he will encounter in interpersonal relations.

At times it would appear to the person involved that he does not respond in keeping with his value system. He falls into the trap of perceiving his values to be what they are not. As Paul commented in Romans 7:19: "When I try not to do wrong, I do it anyway." He wished that his life were pure in every way, but in reality it was not. He was responding in keeping with his true hierarchy of values whether he liked his response or not.

A fourth point of view leaves each of the participants in a relationship totally fulfilled as people and their lives integrated within a complete whole. This approach will be called *mutual respect* in that it involves a balanced, reciprocal relationship existing and developing between people — between a person and a group or between groups. Effective communication unites the parties, not necessarily in agreement, but rather, in trust development. The foundation for such a relationship is full and complete acceptance of one another as each one is, at any moment. Throughout the development of such a relationship, any reflection on the relationship or on any ingredient of the relationship will always result in building a trust, not undermining it. In the case of trust being undermined, both parties will extend every effort to restore the trust balance. Such a trust relationship between parties stems from and in turn reinforces mutual respect. Tournier speaks of it in this way: "He felt that he was understood. More than that, he felt also that he was understanding himself better and that I was understanding him just as he understood himself."[5]

In mutual respect, each person perceives that his point of view is worthy of being heard. He is not prejudged. He has a valid point of view. His point of view can be heard and responded to by another person or by a group. His point of view can become part of the consensual process by which all societies are maintained. The consensual process may involve a formal vote or a decree by a dictator, or it may involve simply a group willingness to be part of the "scene" at the place designated by someone uninvolved in the scene itself.

The consensual process is thus based on *negotiation*. All the parties involved in the decision-making process, whether leader or follower, whether dominator or subject, become part of the natural, ongoing negotiation process that insures the continual development of the consensual process within society. Each member or part of the society may enter through different roles or responsibilities to differing degrees of involvement and power. A child may enter by suggesting that the family go fishing. A subculture may enter by marching in public demonstration. Until consensus is reached, the negotiation process must and will continue. Any blockage of the negotiation within the consensual process limits individual and corporate development and produces disintegration to some degree. Where mutual respect is operating in the relationships set up by our case, the parents and children would talk over the past, present, and future, reaching consensus at each point along the way. Such consensus would concern the amount of money involved, if there were to be interest, when it was to be paid back, etc. Each agreement would be upheld by each member of the group.

RECIPROCITY

When people are working together in a trust relationship, a reciprocity of trust must follow. Trust is not built on a one-way basis; it must always be a reciprocating relationship. When a given person's trust is not reciprocated, it still must be considered potential for reciprocation. So long as it is potential, the person extending trust can proceed as if the relationship were

---

5. Paul Tournier, *The Meaning of Persons* (New York: Harper and Row, 1957).

complete. Some people weary after a few days, months, or years of trying to build a relationship with someone they feel is, or can be, meaningful to them in their lives. Parents whose child appears to ignore the trust bond may live for any number of years building toward an effective trust relationship, doing all the things necessary for laying a foundation for trust, yet not having their trust reciprocated. More and more, the child turns to his own way, and the parents tire. The reciprocating nature of trust is such that when it is reciprocated, it encourages trust; when it is not reciprocated, a rejection pattern sets in, leaving the interested party despairing of the effective development of trust.

Whenever a pattern of rejection has been expressed, it can be expected that final rapport will come about only after one works toward building rapport for as many days, months, or years as the rejection pattern was in effect. Any shortened period of time can be considered a bonus, something unusual. Acceptance of the person must therefore be deeply rooted within the attitude, or message-sending, component of one's life. It must be communicated as effectively as possible for as long as the message of rejection had been communicated, whether the acceptance is reciprocated or not; or whether the change of attitude is recognized or not.

Since mutual respect is a reciprocating relationship and must be carried on between at least two persons or groups, the persons or groups must stand on equal footing in terms of validity. One cannot force the other to do that which is untrue to himself. This means that both involved in a given relationship will learn, and both will change. The teacher learns from teaching students; the students learn from the teacher. If a teacher is not continuing to learn, the course readily dries up. Parents learn from children, even as the children learn from parents. A reciprocating learning experience will embrace both, such as may be found in the contemporary world of music. Parents learn from their children a new form of music and the children learn to put their sound into perspective in relation to other sounds of music.

Such a reciprocating learning experience can be illustrated in the form of a cooperative learning model. Reference will be made to the Balue people of Africa.

In the biblical story of the Ethiopian eunuch[6] witnessed to by Philip, we may ask the question: "What was the Ethiopian

_____
6. Acts 8:26-40.

eunuch doing out on the road? Was he on legitimate or illegitimate business?" The North American responds immediately by affirming that he was legitimately representing his government, for as a government representative he maintained his aura of representation while he was traveling, as illustrated in some of the conversation with Philip. A man from the Balue group would question the legitimacy of that trip immediately. His automatic response would be that since he was away from home, and quite a distance at that, he was up to no good. Anyone, whether on business or seeking pleasure, who is any distance from home would automatically be considered as being up to no good. The man from the Balue must learn more than the North American about the Ethiopian eunuch and about the trip. The North American can reinforce the Bible story through his automatic response to the conditions mentioned in the story.

However, when we read some other section of the Bible, as, for example, the account of the wedding of Cana, we ask the question, "Who paid for the reception?" The North American will automatically think the parents of the bride paid for the wedding reception, whereas the Balue will not question that it was the father of the groom. Just who paid really makes very little difference in the story of the wedding of Cana. But to be accurate, we must realize that probably the parents of the groom paid for it, or it may have been a third party of either relatives or friends. Thus, the North American has something more to learn from Near Eastern societies where lineage follows the male line quite rigorously and where the parents of the groom usually absorb the costs of such things as wedding receptions for their sons. The Balue thus has less to learn from us as representatives of societies where lineage follows either the male or female lines and where the parents of the bride generally pick up the tab for the reception.

Keith Miller is referring to this kind of reciprocal learning experience when he says,

> Now, in the soul of our marriage it was not my vision of what a marriage, of what a husband, should be against her vision, one of us always having to be wrong; but now together we began trying to find out Christ's vision of what our marriage should be. . . . At last we can relax and be children in the soul of our marriage and find peace together."[7]

---

7. Keith Miller, *A Taste of New Wine* (Waco, Texas: Word Books, 1965), p. 22.

SUMMARY

The traditionalist wants everyone to be as he is. The relativist doesn't care what the other is, or, for that matter, what he himself is. The proponent of situation ethics wants to give to the other that which he needs out of a motive of love; but there is little control to insure that the giver does not also yield principle. The one receiving may have liked the response but upon reflection, may realize the other went too far in serving him and a loss of respect may follow.

Mutual respect lets each participant in a relationship fully realize his own potential in terms of what he is. Each can be a whole, responsible person at the moment of encounter and continue throughout the relationship as a whole person. Neither need abandon his ethical and moral principles or give up what he really is. Both can learn from the other and contribute to the other for the good of each. Even upon reflection, one has no reason to lose even a small degree of respect for the other nor any degree of respect for himself. The relationship is always open and always potential for reciprocity. The two together are fully fulfilled, because each is fully fulfilled.

Questions for discussion:

1. How do the approaches of "mutual respect" and "situation ethics" differ?
2. How do "mutual respect" and the concept of Christian "love" compare?
3. How and when can a person practice mutual respect? Discuss.
4. In what ways does the average person "cop out" of the decision-making process?
5. What are the characteristic responses of a "traditionalist"?
6. What are the characteristic responses of an "ethical relativist"?
7. Could two people differ in opinion and still maintain mutual respect? How?

Group activities and exercises:

1. Behavioral observations:
    a. Observe to discover someone using situation ethics.
    b. Observe to discover someone using the traditionalist approach.
    c. Observe to discover someone using mutual respect.
2. Role play the case study of the California family. See explanation below.
3. Discussion in small groups: Have the group members select

three to five distinct situations: classroom, political campaign, church, etc., and discuss the differential balance of respect called for in each situation.

4. Discussion in small groups: Invite a member of a distinct culture or subculture to each small group. Have the group members discuss and compare the mutual respect demanded in this different culture or subculture in relation to their own.

5. Self-study: Have each group member write a statement or paper comparing the entire Acceptance-of-the-Person model with 1 Corinthians 13.

6. Research: Send the group members by two's to interview overseas students to discover if the relationship maintained by the missionaries in their homeland could be characterized by mutual respect.

CALIFORNIA FAMILY

PREBRIEFING:

Pass out copies of California Family case study found at the beginning of this chapter and tell the class to read it.

Then ask, "What models/tools/theories do we want to use in working with this case study?"

List all of the responses on the board (or overhead transparency). Be sure the final list includes all of the Acceptance-of the-Person models, including "mutual respect."

Review mutual respect by having them fill in the boxes to the following matrix:

1. Traditionalism or cultural absolutism

2. Ethical relativism

3. Situation ethics

4. Cultural relativity or mutual respect

OTHER

	SELF	
	Acc.	Rej.
Rej.	1	2
Acc.	4	3

SIMULATION:

First Grouping:

Divide the class into four equal groups and place each group in a different corner of the room.

Assign one group to play the role of the father; another group, the role of the mother; another, the role of the son; and the last, the role of the daughter-in-law.

F — father

M — mother

S — son

D — daughter-in-law

F F		M M
F F		M M
	Room	
S S		D D
S S		D D

Prepare questions for the various roles and have the groups discuss them.

Second Grouping:

When there is a lull in the discussion and you sense that they are "done," have half of the fathers go to the mothers' group and vice versa. Also, have half of the sons go to the daughters-in-law's group and vice versa. Each individual is to continue playing his original role in the new group.

Suggest that they again go through the discussion of the questions appropriate for their role — with two views being now represented in each group.

F M ⟷	F M
F M	F M
S D ⟷	S D
S D	S D

Third Grouping: (if there are fewer than sixteen students, skip this grouping)

When there is another lull in the noise volume, change the grouping again. Half of the sons and half of the daughters-in-law in each couple group will change places with half of the fathers and mothers in both parent groups. Now each is a "family" group with a father, mother, son, and daughter-in-law.

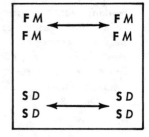

Set the scene for the class role plays: The center of the room is now an airport terminal where the parents are meeting the couple as they just return from England. Each group is to role-play this scene of the couple meeting and "breaking all the news" to the parents (see role play, below).

Give each group time to plan their role play which will be presented to the rest of the class.

Role Play:

The parents from one group will role play with the couple from another group (four plays; if there is a lack of time, do only no. 1 and no. 3).

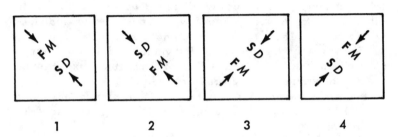

DEBRIEFING:

1. What were the different reactions taken (with reference to the mutual respect matrix discussed during the prebriefing)? Be as objective as possible.
   (Some students probably tried so hard to show mutual respect that they really acted like situation ethics persons. And there may have been other somewhat overdrawn efforts. Encourage the use of the *PQT* and self-acceptance models by those participating in the debriefing.)

2. What are some of the benefits of this type of simulation experience?
   (Preparation for real-life situation, seeing oneself, etc.)

3. Additional questions or comments.
   (Allow them to draw the conclusions on their own as much as possible. Don't allow yourself to be put in the role of "judge and jury.")

MODEL 2

THEORY OF NATURAL GROUPINGS

The model termed here *Theory of Natural Groupings* is the look taken at one's own sociocultural setting as well as that of the other, in order to really know what one is as an individual within society. There are seven submodels.

1. *The norm* of the group, or individual within the group, is the sum total of all the values, norms, rules, expectations, and aspirations of the group or individual.
2. *Hierarchy* refers to the network of social relations which structures a social system in which a given individual operates.
3. The *flow of truth* directly from higher levels of the social structure to the lower levels provides freedom; when it must be communicated through a second group on the same level of the hierarchy, the result is injustice or slavery.
4. *Item identification* of the group provides a scheme for recognizing groupings of formal or informal arrangement.
5. *Activities* of members help to further define a group.
6. *Values* underlie all arrangements and activities of groups. The value scheme utilized is a taxonomy of values called "basic values."
7. *Conflict of norm* is the disruptive tension within a person relating to both the ideal and the real; between a person and a group, resulting in culture shock; and between a group and group, resulting in "war."

Theory of Natural Groupings
The Norm
Hierarchy
Flow of Truth
The Group — Item Identification
— Activity
— Value
Conflict of Norm

6

the norm

YESTERDAY'S FOOL

Dear Ann:

I am 19, a sophomore in a midwestern university and considered good-looking and reasonably bright by my peers. I've been dating since I was 15 and, without boasting, I can truthfully say I've had more than my share of male attention.

During this summer, I met my ideal. We dated several times and I found myself saying "No" to others in the hope he would call. I loved being with him. On August 2 he was leaving for his vacation. We both hated to part and sat in the park two hours saying goodnight. For some mysterious reason all my will power and good intentions vanished and I gave in. I told myself, "This is love. Why should I deny him a true expression of my feelings?"

He sent a few postcards along the way but did not telephone me as I had hoped he would. Last night he returned — a changed man. He took me to supper and informed me that it would probably be our last date. These are his words: "You are not the girl I had hoped you were. Our last night together was a nightmare. You made me ashamed of myself. I could never marry you after that. I would always wonder if there had been others. This has been the greatest disappointment in my life."

So there's my story, Ann. I am trying to keep my chin up, but it isn't easy. I tell myself no decent man would treat a girl this way, but deep down I know it was my decision, not his — and all the rationalization in the world doesn't make it right.[1]

The term "norm" has many uses in scholarly literature.[2] It generally denotes what is normative, that which is the foundation for expectation within society. If someone acts in a way expected of him, given a certain stimulus within a given situation, he is carrying out that which is normative for the society. Any deviation from this expected or normative behavior is seen as abnormal in some way. The sum total of the expectations within a given society is the collection of norms of that society. Built into an individual is the sum total of the norms of that society, which in reality represents a composite of the norms of all the groups and all the subcultures in which he participates. Thus we can say that an individual has a "norm" which is the sum total of all the "norms" of his total experience. This total experience is in itself a composite of all the norms of all the groups of which he has been and is now a part. A social group that is a specific subculture within the society also has a composite of norms of all its components parts. It also has a composite norm for the entire corporate body or society.

Thus, the norm of any social group equals the sum total of its values, norms, expectations, rules, and aspirations.[3] The norm of the individual within the society or social group equals all of the norms of the groups of which he has been, or is, a part. A convenient way for the individual to determine his own norm is to ask himself questions such as these: How am I dressed? What am I doing? What am I thinking? What are my hopes and aspirations? What rules of the informal and formal nature are controlling my experience? What do I believe? What is normative for me? The convenient way to determine what is another's norm is to ask these questions about him while observing his behavior.[4]

---

1. From a column of Ann Landers.

2. References to norm:

Vilhelm Aubert, *Elements of Sociology* (New York: Charles Scribner's Sons, 1967).

Peter Berger, *The Sacred Canopy* (Garden City, New York: Doubleday, 1967). This book presents elements of a sociological theory of religion.

3. In one sense "norm" is synonymous with "culture" and can be used interchangeably once culture is understood as the whole of man's existence rather than just a part.

4. Refer to Model Three and the discussion of tools of research. Observation is more than just looking. It involves the utilization of conceptual models within the scientific method.

A person from a "supermarket subculture" will not automatically raise his hand to push open the door when approaching the entrance of a supermarket. He has the expectation that the door will open by means of some electronic device. A member of a subculture without supermarkets will automatically raise his hand to push open the door. When he sees the door open before him, he will simply drop his hand. When the door is not automatic, the former will be forced to raise his hand or suffer the consequences, i.e., bump his nose.

The automatic response to a stimulus is a clear indication that the person is a member of that given culture. The automatic raising of the hand indicates that the person is a member of a nonsupermarket culture. The automatic nonraising of the hand is indication of the person being part of a supermarket culture. Such automatic responses become part of every aspect of life and literally set up a given person to live fully within the culture without undue or destructive tension. The moment one has to think of his response within a given situation, he expends energy that can no longer be made available for creative extension or expression of one's life. Society is designed to make as many experiences of life as possible completely automatic, without the need for such thinking. This leaves the person "at peace" within his culture. In the case study for this chapter, the young woman was living within her norm until her "good intentions vanished" and she "gave in." She began to shift from automatic response to "think" response. This should have been a behavioral signal to her that she was approaching the "borders" of her norm. The thinking response was an energy consumer and occupied her thoughts then and possibly later also. Her "friend" apparently considered it a great deal after the experience as well.

When a person is unable to respond fully and completely within the habitual patterns of a culture, he must learn what he still lacks or he will be in conflict within that culture (see chapter 12). Irritation with practices within the culture thus provides a pragmatic indicator of cultural difference. When entering a new culture or subculture, one can very quickly isolate the cultural differences by being aware of his curiosity interest and irritation response. The sum total of these two responses is the degree of cultural difference existing between the norm of the individual and the norm of the new culture in which he finds himself.

Chart 7 presents a stylized means of representing an individual

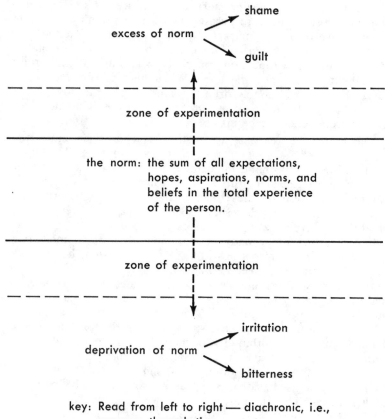

key: Read from left to right — diachronic, i.e.,
progress through time.
Read from "the norm" vertically —
synchronic, i.e., the here and now.

Chart 7. The Norm of the Person in Society (idealized)

norm. The norm as known at any one moment of experience is contained between the solid lines with the lived moment represented by the vertical broken line. The individual can be observed through time from left to right and any moment in the total experience he can be focused upon. The separation between the solid lines indicates variation of the norm. All of the allowable range of selection in response to a given stimulus is part of the norm. For example, a man who can select from a white or colored shirt in preparing for church has this range of selection as part of his norm. Thus any combination of potential responses becomes a part of the norm and is thus part of the automatic response behavior of the norm.

The practical outworking of the concept of norm for the agent of change is that he can encounter another person and by observing behavior begin to realize his norm. Through continued experience and association with the other person, it is possible by means of the scientific process, or the hypothesizing approach, to derive a working grasp of another's norm, increase the potential for the understanding of difference, and reduce the potential for adverse reaction to difference that will close opportunities for association and produce a breakdown in the communication process.

At this point, acceptance of the person teams up with the concept of norm to permit the agent of change to extend the foundation being built under the change program and to work with the person in terms of who and what he is without destroying him by making him over in keeping with the cultural demands of the agent of change.

VARIATION OF NORM

On the synchronic plane, i.e., the person or group at a given moment in time, the norm is not fixed or set in terms of one quality. The norm is a range of variation in relation to every aspect of the norm. It is not one unitary expectation a person has; it is a range of expectations. A given person can go to a college or a university. He can attend a local junior college for two years and transfer to a regular college for his last two years, or he can attend one college for all four years — without, in either instance, feeling he's had inferior education. Another person can attend one college and, by accelerating his pace, complete his course in three years, or he may continue for four years without feeling he is losing out, either way. A given person can wear a suit or sport combination to a formal event and not feel uncomfortable. In each of these cases, another person might feel shortchanged or uncomfortable, behavioral indication of a narrower variation of norm. Again, in each of these cases, some other person might be free to consider and carry out some other alternatives without any adverse effect.

Any person has potential for the infinite extension of the variation of his life-style. The fact that few extend their life-style in any extreme is testimony to the power of an individual's attitude, society's control over behavior, and the lack of opportunity granted any one person in his total experience. Multilingual and multiculture members of certain European societies give eloquent testimony to this principle. The ease with which the average North American has entered the "jet age" is further testimony to this process.

EXCESS AND DEPRIVATION OF NORM

In chart 7, above the lines encompassing the norm of the individual, *excess of norm* is indicated. Whenever anyone has more than that which is called for by the norm, he is living in excess of norm. The nonsupermarket person is living in excess of norm when he enters a supermarket door opened for him through an electronic device. A man who chooses a colored shirt from his collection to wear on Sunday when he has never before worn anything other than a white shirt is living in excess of norm. A teetotaler, when taking a drink of alcoholic beverage, is living in excess of norm. A new college coed accustomed to retire around eleven may readily begin living in excess of norm within a college community that permits her to stay out until one o'clock. A young couple, wanting to get settled before they really have the money for everything they want in their new experience of homemaking, may readily charge more than they can comfortably handle with their income and thus live in excess of norm. Students trained to expect examinations within a course find their response to a nonexamination course one of excess of norm, since it appears to them that they have greater freedom in reflecting their natural ability.

Excess of norm becomes a problem to the individual and the society of which he is a part whenever the behavior of shame or guilt is expressed.[5] Shame here means embarrassment before others and guilt means inward embarrassment. The embarrassment comes when there is excess of norm, causing the person to feel that he has no right to live as he does, but he is doing it whether he has the right to it or not. Shame and guilt will cause the person to act or behave in ways that are inconsistent within the total framework of the society and thus sow seeds of disorganization or disruption which may have an adverse effect on the individual and ultimately on the society. The mild embarrass-

---

5. Shame in the sense used here is discussed in:
Helen Merrell Lynd, *On Shame and the Search for Identity* (New York: Science Editions, Inc., 1958).
Julian Pitt-Rivers, *People of the Sierra* (Chicago: University of Chicago Press, 1961).
Guilt is discussed adequately in Paul Tournier, *Guilt and Grace* (New York: Harper and Row, 1962).

ment derived from wearing a colored shirt when one has been accustomed to wearing a white shirt is not potentially disruptive to the society that is flexible in its fashion operation, but it is potentially disruptive to the society that is nonflexible in this aspect of life. It further does not affect the individual with a proclivity for trying different fashions, but it is potentially disruptive to the one whose sense of security and well-being requires him to wear white shirts. A society permitting a degree of drunkenness within socially prescribed restrictions will not be affected by a given member who happens to get drunk for the first time in his life within such restrictions, e.g., at a Christmas office party. However, if he gets drunk on company time, he may be fired on the spot. The person who expresses himself in excess at the Christmas party is not in any trouble so long as there is no underlying sense of having let himself, another person, or a belief system down. He could have extreme guilt and shame within this experience were the drunkenness to go counter to a deeply ingrained sense of his responsibility to shun alcohol.

In the case study at the beginning of this chapter, whatever the precise degree of exceeding the norm occurred in the experience of the young woman who "gave in," the action her friend took caused him to so exceed his norm that he terminated the friendship. His guilt, or inward sense of embarrassment, was so great he feared it would affect him the rest of his life. He directed his sense of guilt toward the girl, suggesting that she was to blame: "You made me ashamed of myself."

Forgiveness in the Scriptures, when related to the concept of norm, permits the person to "snap back" to his norm whenever he has "sinned" by confessing his sin and being granted pardon. It is as if he had never sinned, as if he had never done that which caused him to feel guilty or ashamed.

Deprivation of norm occurs when an individual lives in such a way that he is unable to meet the expectations of his norm. There is no serious result either to the individual or his society if he makes the choice himself to live in deprivation, such as the pastor who agrees to take a pay cut when accepting the call to a mission church. However, deprivation of norm can be serious to the individual and his society if he is forced to live without that which he perceives to be his "right" by forces which he cannot control. Thus, the black American lives in deprivation of norm, or at least in perceived deprivation, and he expresses the behavior resulting from deprivation — behavior that is disruptive of American society. A child of parents who are more than able to pay his way through college but refuse to help him may have to work so hard that he is unable to get his expected grades, causing a continuing feeling of resentment towards his parents.

The behavior of deprivation of norm is that of mild irritation, resentment, or bitterness. An employee receiving a four percent pay increase when he has expected a five percent raise will feel mildly irritated and may work toward a more complete raise at the time of the next increment period. However, a person expecting a pay raise and not getting it when others, given the very same conditions of employment, receive it, may develop a bitterness which will seriously affect his work response within the institution of his employment.

Even though the young woman of the opening case study did not sense the same degree of guilt or embarrassment due to excess of norm as her friend did, she did sense deprivation of norm. She had come to the point of anticipation in sharing her friend's life. She had no expectation of losing the friendship but of seeing it develop into a deep and lasting relationship in marriage. Her irritation and disappointment, a mild reaction to deprivation, gradually developed into a more intense reaction, "I am trying to keep my chin up, but it isn't easy," and "I keep telling myself . . . , but deep down. . . ."

CHANGE OF NORM

Every norm, whether individual or corporate, has a built-in mechanism for its change: the buffer zone, or the zone of experimentation. One can live in excess of his norm or in deprivation of his norm for a period of time to test and see if this is in reality part of his norm, or compatible with his norm, or potentially new for his norm. Experimentation may be carried on in both directions, each with its own purpose: one to determine if the person is living up to the fullness of his norm or of his potential, and the other to see if he can include new things in his norm which he did not or could not encounter or try previously.

A student who has been accustomed to sleeping eight hours each night and achieving a *B* average in school, may choose to live in excess of this norm by cutting down on sleep and increase his proficiency in study to an *A* average. Such experimentation will leave the individual satisfied that he is living in the full potential of his norm, or he may find that he is constantly living in excess of his norm and revert to the eight hours of sleep, and thus be content with the *B* average.

People from a horse-and-buggy culture tried the automobile

and most found that they could live with the automobile and so made it part of the American norm. Individuals within American society at that time could choose between the horse and buggy and the auto and thus make the automobile part of their individual norm if they so chose. Members of the subculture who refused to make the auto part of their norm reinforced their society's norm of horse and buggy. By rejecting the auto they caused any member of their subculture to feel guilt when participating in automobile riding.

Generally speaking, no harm results from experimenting within the buffer zone of excess or deprivation of norm. No long-term effects will linger that will be adverse or unfortunate to the individual or group. However, in a small percentage of cases, such experimentation can be serious and have an adverse effect. A virgin, experimenting with sexual intercourse, will lose virginity, which can never be regained, and she may become pregnant. A person experimenting with drugs may have a bad trip the first time and die from the effects of the drug. A new driver experimenting with fast driving may blow a tire and be killed in the resulting crash or be seriously maimed. A young person experimenting with various ways to enter a social group may cause offense that may never be forgiven him and may retard his social adjustment throughout the rest of his life. A mission group may experiment with a new way of raising funds and alienate some of their most faithful contributors.

Anyone experimenting must be willing to pay the price of the experimentation. Youth experimenting with drugs must be willing to run the risk of going to jail. A mission feeling the need to experiment must be willing to adjust to a possible loss of funds.

Unfortunately, however, for those who are afraid of risking the adverse effects of the change process, progress and development will never come except through the route of experimentation. Without experimentation, the individual or social group remains stagnant or declines. The agent of change[6] will never be an effective one unless he comes to peace with the experimental or buffer zone of the change of norm permitting him to try different things in keeping with his sense of responsibility to meet the needs of the people he is hoping to serve.

The change of norm thus leaves one's norm "profile" through

6. George M. Foster, *A Cross-Cultural Anthropological Analysis of a Technical Aid Program* (Washington, D.C.: Smithsonian Institute of Social Anthropology, 1951); *Traditional Cultures and the Impact of Technological Change* (New York: Harper and Row, 1962); and *Applied Anthropology* (Boston: Little Brown and Co., 1969).

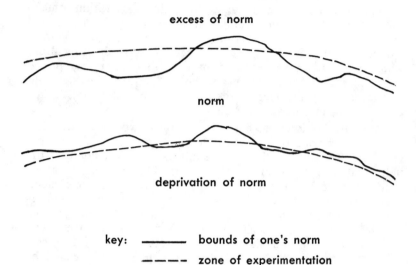

excess of norm

norm

deprivation of norm

key: ———— bounds of one's norm
        — — — zone of experimentation

Chart 8. The Norm of the Person in Society (actual)

time an irregular one. The idealized norm representation in chart 7 is simply to introduce one to the concept of norm. A more accurate profile would look similar to that in chart 8. One's norm is constantly changing moment by moment in significant ways that encourage the growth and development of the person or ways that ultimately will result in disorganization.

Within society, changes are programmed so that a person, enculturated effectively within his own society will naturally progress without strain through the various expressions of the program. He will thus be true to himself and also not offend the other. For example, the average American middle-class male is trained not to touch a member of the opposite sex until the "dating" period. Then he may hold hands or hug until a "going-steady agreement" is reached. From then on to the wedding, there is increased contact permitted, until the complete contact permitted by the wedding. A married man is trained not to touch a woman, other than his wife, in any sex-oriented way.

COMPARISON OF NORM

Since each norm is different, or at least potentially different, because of the different past, present, and future experiences and associations of each one within the corporate body, the comparison of norms becomes a challenge. Comparison-of-norm charts are useful in comparing those aspects of difference that are measurable or quantifiable.

When comparing a polygamous society with a monogamous society, we often condemn the former without seriously considering the situation. A more thoughtful approach would be a consideration of the norm of the polygamous society: adultery

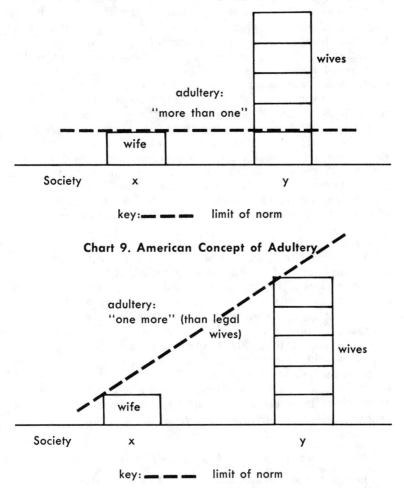

wives

adultery:

"more than one"

wife

Society x y

key: — — — limit of norm

Chart 9. American Concept of Adultery

adultery:
"one more" (than legal wives)

wives

wife

Society x y

key: — — — limit of norm

Chart 10. Polygamist Society's Concept of Adultery

is physical union *only* outside of marriage, regardless of the number of wives a man may have. In presenting the biblical ideal (norm) of monogamy, one should realize that existing multiple marriages are, in fact, legal and binding.[7]

THE PROCESS OF ENCULTURATION

The concept of socialization in sociology or enculturation in anthropology provides insight into the transmission of the norm of the group. Through this process a person learns what is expected of him in a given situation. The process of enculturation can bring an outsider (either through birth or through migration) into a comfortable relationship to the society within a period of two to five years. This does not mean that the individual must "buy" everything that he encounters, but he must know the proper way of doing things. He must respond correctly, both consciously and unconsciously, to the various stimuli within situations, permitting the other to see that he is adapting. Anything short of this dynamic, involving adaptation to the new society and its cultural ways, produces breakdown in communication.[8] The agent of change must know the system of the culture before he can effectively participate in its change. Otherwise he will introduce those ways that derive from his own way of life, but these may never meet the need of the target culture.

SUMMARY

The norm of the group or of any individual within the group is the sum total of all the values, norms, rules, expectations, and aspirations of the group or individual. Further, the norm of an individual within any group as well as the norm of a group included in some larger grouping equals all the norms of the groups and individuals of which he or the group is a part. That which an individual does completely automatically, without conscious thought, is part of his norm, and in essence defines the norm. If an individual must think about some action, it is likely that this is not part of his norm, but rather, part of another norm which he is being encouraged to learn and make part of his own, or from which he will turn as being incompatible with his norm.

7. Remi Clignet, *Many Wives, Many Powers* (Evanston, Illinois: Northwestern University Press, 1970).

8. Eugene A. Nida, *Message and Mission* (New York: Harper and Row, 1960); *Custom and Cultures* (New York: Harper and Row, 1954); and *Religion Across Cultures* (New York: Harper and Row, 1968).

Alfred G. Smith, *Communication and Culture* (New York: Holt, Rinehart and Winston, 1966).

Someone living in excess of his norm will find himself experiencing a sense of embarrassment that relates to his personal belief system as a sense of guilt and to others about him as a sense of shame. Someone living or being forced to live in deprivation of his norm will find a bitterness developing. This will become more intense with passing time or with each reinforcing action taken by those leaders of groups of which the deprived person is a part. The only chance of such bitterness not developing is when the person himself chooses to endure the deprivation by means of personal decision, rationalization, projection, or replacement of the right.

Every individual and corporate norm is expressed through a range of variation that is developed through time and in relation to millions of interpersonal contacts and associations. This range of variation permits change of norm in that some of the range becomes established and some is rejected. Experimentation continues within the range of variation and is a healthy response to life providing for a continual reevaluation and freshening of the norm.

Questions for discussion:

1. What other terms could be used to refer to the totality of one's life-way as Peter Berger uses *nomos* and the author uses *norm*?
2. How would you distinguish norm in this sense from "norm/norms" that refer to specific standards or moral and ethical prerogatives?
3. How might rejection of the person limit one's grasp of the norm of the host culture or subculture?
4. How might the biblical concept of "forgiveness" enable one to live within his norm?
5. In what ways do societies differ?
6. Does God intend that we live only within our norm?
7. What part does the supernatural play in relation to a person's norm? A group's corporate norm?
8. Is everything a group or society does approved by God?
9. Indicate some parts of your norm that have become clarified during the past month.

Group activities and exercises:

1. Behavioral observations:
   a. Observe someone living in excess of norm.
   b. Observe someone living in deprivation of norm.
   c. Observe one person over a period of time to determine his

"pattern" of behavior, i.e., what he does first, what he does second, what he does next, etc., or what he does most often.

d. Observe a number of persons over a period of time to determine their "pattern" of behavior.

2. Experimentation: Objectify your own norm, for example, in the area of "consistent use of uniform," i.e., the way you dress regularly. Live for a day or two in the zone of experimentation of norm by changing your dress, i.e., uniform, and observing behavioral responses to this change.

3. Group work: Spend a period of time either in the group or as work outside the group, defining the norm of the Hebrew society, particularly of the patriarchal period (up to the period of the Judges). Then compare this with the norm of the Jewish society of the New Testament period.

4. Written response: Indicate one way in which your norm has changed in the last month. Was tension associated with it? Has your norm changed in any way that has resulted in a sense of guilt? In bitterness? Explain.

Theory of Natural Groupings
The Norm
Hierarchy
Flow of Truth
The Group — Item Identification
— Activity
— Value
Conflict of Norm

7

hierarchy

THE KING AND QUEEN'S VISIT

In the far northwest province of Thailand the resident missionaries, a family and two single girls, had established good rapport with the provincial governor and his wife. The governor's wife had previously taught in a Christian school in Bangkok. She even volunteered as language teacher for one of the single missionaries for a short period of time. Mutual respect had resulted in genuinely cordial relations between them.

During the furlough of the missionary family, the king and queen of Thailand planned a royal visit to this provincial town. For months in advance, preparations were being made for this visit of the royal family. Houses and fences were repaired, streets were mended and swept clean. The king had never before visited this remote province. The anticipation, the preparation, and the wild joy of the people showed what a great occasion it was for them.

Shortly before the king and queen's visit, the governor's wife came to visit the missionary women. In the course of their conversation, she invited them to be present with her and the governor in order to welcome the royal couple. This was clearly a very high honor, since the king and the queen were the most important and prestigious people to the Thai.

At this invitation the missionaries found themselves in a state of conflict. A believers' conference had been previously scheduled.

The first day of the conference happened to be the day of the king's visit. With other missionaries to be entertained and preparations to be made for the conference, the two women politely refused the invitation to be present with the governor and his wife in order to welcome the royal party. With little to say, the governor's wife returned home.

The royal couple arrived on schedule. The missionaries too held their conference as scheduled and during the course of the day they caught a glimpse of the king and queen enroute from the local airstrip. . . .

A. R. Radcliffe-Brown defines social structure as a "network of social relations."[1] Social relations form through contact between two or more people or groups of people. Every addition of a person or a group increases the size and network of social relations. Every encounter with another unit of the network adds complexity to the network by establishing social relations not only with individual and individual, and group and group, but also with individual and group. The sum total of the network of social relations is the social structure of a given society. The sum total of all of the network of social relations of all the societies gives us the concept of world. Thus society is made up of larger groups containing smaller, less-complex groups of individuals.

The missionaries in our case study were involved in a network of social relations including the host state in which they were serving and their field conference, a part of a larger mission organization. Thus to the expected complexity of social relations of a person within a group within a nation, there was added the complexity of service to a second group responsible ultimately within a second nation.

NETWORK AS SYSTEM

A system is an assemblage of parts or objects united by some form of regular interaction or interdependence.[2] It forms an intricate whole; it is able to function, operate, or move in unison and in obedience to some kind of control. It is in balance when all the parts are functioning effectively together to produce the desired effect of the system. This means that all the parts or components or subsystems must also be functioning effectively

---

1. A. R. Radcliffe-Brown, *Structure and Function in Primitive Society* (London: Cohen and West, 1952).
2. C. W. Churchman, *The Systems Approach* (New York: Dell Publishing Co., 1968).

for the whole system to be running smoothly. Control mechanisms keep the system operating smoothly. The system is abused when it is taken advantage of by being used for selfish ends rather than for the purposes for which the system was established, or when some control is thwarted or overlooked, or when there is some attempt to ignore or to replace some part of control unnecessarily. The system must be "serviced" or recycled periodically, otherwise it will operate less efficiently than it was designed to.

The automobile is a system with component parts that operate as wholes within the larger whole.[3] The carburetor is a part of the whole and is itself a whole assemblage, any part of which may break down, causing the whole assemblage to need replacement. Or if a part fails, it may be economical to scrap the entire car and replace it. The automobile functions as a transportation aid. To use it as a bulldozer for moving earth or snow is to abuse it. To put regular gasoline into a high compression engine is to abuse the engine, resulting in carbon buildup that will shorten engine life. The entire system of a car needs servicing periodically, otherwise lubrication systems within the whole will dry up, producing irreparable damage.

The human body is a system with component parts that function in relation to the whole. The body can be abused by lack of sleep or improper diet. It is repaired by means of rest and food. The environment in which we live is also a system with component parts that can be abused through pollution and that needs replenishing through various means of fertilization or land-rest, for example.

Society is a system and can be analyzed even as any other systems operation can be analyzed and worked with. All the parts of the system relate to the whole and give it meaning. The whole in turn gives meaning to the parts. Without the whole, the parts would have no reason for existing and without any one of the parts, there is no whole. There are many models dealing with society as system.[4] Society can be described in terms of its social, political, economic, and religious systems and subsystems.[5] It can be described in terms of its institutions

---

3. Auto repair manuals are systems manuals as are some medical texts and some systematic theologies.

4. Talcott Parsons, *Essays in Sociological Theory: Pure and Applied* (Glencoe, Illinois: The Free Press, 1949); *The Social System* (Glencoe, Illinois, The Free Press, 1951).

Robert Merton, *Social Theory and Social Structure* (Glencoe, Illinois: The Free Press, 1956).

5. A series of case studies in cultural anthropology is available from

such as the family, the church, business, and political parties. The way society as a system will be worked with in the succeeding pages will be in terms of the item *identification of each group,* i.e., its identity observed; the *activities carried out by the group,* i.e., the actions that further define it; and the *values that underlie the group* and set up its activities and give it fullness of meaning.

Culture is everything with which an individual is concerned and involved in a society. This sounds like a very nonacademic definition of a very important concept. Culture can be defined in a couple hundred ways,[6] but the point is that every thought a person thinks, every hope he has, every step he takes, every belief he holds, and every interaction he undertakes is *controlled* by his culture. Every move he makes is trained into him by his culture.

The arena of this culture is the society: American society, Nigerian society, German society. These societies are not static but are themselves divided into many subdivisions, each of which has its own subculture, i.e., a unique blending of the various cultures making up the larger society. In turn, each of these societies is changing through time, and thus each culture and subculture is itself a dynamic process.

It is therefore appropriate to talk not just of culture, nor just of society, but rather of the *sociocultural setting* which combines these two concepts in one.

Further, it is not appropriate to talk of culture and society as unified, but as multiculture and multisociety. Each sociocultural setting is made up of many parts, each with its unique identity.

The sociocultural setting is further to be distinguished from the ecological setting, i.e., society's interaction with the environment, as well as from the products of the society or that which is produced as a result of sociocultural interaction and ecological involvement.

The socialization or enculturation process[7] is designed to pre-

Holt, Rinehart and Winston, Inc., 383 Madison Ave., New York, N.Y. 10017.

6. A. L. Kroeber and C. Kluckhohn, *Culture: A Critical Review of Concepts and Definitions* (New York: Random House, 1970).

Ely Chinoy, *Sociological Perspective: Basic Concepts and Their Application* (New York: Random House, n.d.).

See also chapter 1, note 20.

7. John J. Honigmann, *Culture and Personality* (New York: Harper and Row, 1954).

M. Mead and M. Wolfenstein, *Childhood in Contemporary Cultures* (Chicago: University of Chicago Press, 1955).

pare someone to live within his whole society and effectively maximizes the concept of society as one. This is necessary since it would be utterly impossible for someone to learn all the complexities of life in a given moment. The socialization process introduces to the learner only what he needs at the time. Thus, the perception continues to build that the person is growing up, living, learning with a single society. Differences are minimized or explained away; likenesses are maximized. Unfortunately, this is a false perception which society needs for certain purposes; but as one grows and matures, he learns to recognize and accept differences for what they are, and to that degree he can be fully mature.

A certain family has this saying: "Walk around the rug." By itself, this saying could mean many things. It could mean that a certain rug was white; therefore, one should walk around it so as not to get it dirty. It could mean that the rug was just washed. It could mean that this particular family had a game involving walking around a round rug but across a square one, for example. There are many possibilities, but the family that I am thinking of took this concept after a child became angry and walked around and around a rug to give vent to his feelings and frustrations. From that time on the saying developed that whenever a member of the family was angry or frustrated he should walk around the rug. You could get this meaning only by having someone within this particular subculture or social group explain it to you — in essence, teach you the rules of that particular subculture. This concept fits into the whole, that is, that family's subculture, and gives uniqueness to that particular subculture. To fully enter into the whole — the family — the part must have been learned. The part is that network of interpersonal relations which was expressed in walking around the rug.

I can enter three different kinds of restaurants in the United States. In one I am to sit and be served. In another I am to pick up some of the items of the meal and be served the others. In the last, I am to pick up everything and am served nothing. These are three distinct social groups. Many of their practices and many of the things they serve are the same. All serve American-style food, but each is set up differently to serve this food and thus they comprise distinct subcultures. Some members of the I-am-to-be-served-everything subculture refuse to enter the door of a smorgasbord or a cafeteria.

Within one ethnic-linguistic group in Central America, there are cultural and linguistic differences existing between villages just a few miles apart. In one village the men cut firewood and carry it home across their backs, i.e., in a horizontal position. In another village, the men carry it vertically along the length of their backs. In one village, the word *peren* is used for "rooster." In the neighboring town it is used as a vulgar term describing a dirty-minded old man. Even though these are parts of a larger ethnic-linguistic whole, they are distinct and unique within themselves and the outsider crossing the village "boundary" must learn the system, otherwise he will be related to only as an outsider and thus as a nonentity.

The missionaries in the case study of this chapter had entered an operating system. They were individuals with a team of four missionaries assigned to a given "station" within a network of stations within a larger mission emanating from the United States. This network was plugged into a community within a state within a nation. Each missionary thus had divided loyalties, but this ultimate response was toward the mission which was tied to the home board in the United States. This placed a strain on the network operating in Thailand. That network called for response to leadership at a time when this leadership and the attendant authority of leadership was being reinforced. It was being made visible by means of a reception for the royal couple. By undermining the authority, i.e., ignoring the function of the reception that was designed to bring to focus this authority, the missionaries abused the system that was operating and introduced a dysfunction within the system. One part of the whole was not operating in harmony with the whole. At this point the socialization process was breaking down, since the newcomers to the society were not learning the things they needed to know for the effective perpetuation of the society.

SYSTEM AS CONTROL

One way of defining the social system is to describe every social control mechanism involved within the whole.[8] For an automobile, every physical property becomes a means of control. The motor block can withstand only so much heat, and this limitation in turn limits the potential top speed of the automobile. Further, there are ecological limitations as to where the automobile can go. It cannot go up the rough side of a mountain, though some kinds of automobiles can travel over rougher terrain than others. Further, there are the sociocultural controls placed on the use of automobiles. Society's rules limit its speed,

8. H. C. Bredemeier and R. M. Stevenson, *The Analysis of Social Systems* (New York: Holt, Rinehart and Winston, 1962).

its performance, its right of way, etc. But there is another area of control by society that is informal but very real. A more economical turbine engine can be developed, but society, influenced by oil company interests and pressures, "drags its feet" in producing it, since this might limit gasoline sales. American Motors incorporated reclining seats in some of their automobiles, but other corporations did not follow the lead. In part this was due to expense, in part due to possible competition with camping units, but it was also in part due to our society's reluctance to permit any pair of youths from having an instant bed, thus controlling by extension, other aspects of the whole.

For a society, control mechanisms operate to control the immediate operation of the system, learn from its past, and perpetuate itself in the future. Societies differ as to the amount of the past they utilize in current operations and the degree to which they prepare for the future, but each aspect of life serves as control to immediate operations. Social control mechanisms operate in the social realm to regulate marriage and mating practices, for example; in the economic realm, to regulate flow and distribution of goods vital to the society's well-being; in the political realm, to control leadership and authority; and in the religious realm, to control belief and practice.

Money is a social control mechanism for the economic realm. A society not wanting to use money will use barter — payment "in kind." Another society will utilize ritual measures to insure distribution of goods. Pews in a·church regulate traffic flow in the place of worship; halls regulate it in the educational arena. Rituals that regulate and control behavior in worship are quite distinct from those that control behavior in a Sunday school.

NETWORK AS HIERARCHY

Society is organized to permit interpersonal relationships that are meaningful to each party involved. Were each individual and each group no different from any other, and were each one to be forced to relate to the other in the very same way, the energy available to the individual or group would be dissipated in meaningless pursuits. Thus society has the job of relating each of its members in an intimate way and each of the other members of other societies in ways that are less than intimate. This task calls for hierarchy,[9] for levels within a hierarchy, and for unit distinction within given levels within the hierarchy.

---

9. The concept of hierarchy utilized in this discussion is that discussed by Kenneth Lee Pike, *Language in Relation to a Unified Theory of the Structure of Human Behavior* (The Hague: Mouton, 1967).

Hierarchy is utilized to relate smaller, less complex parts or units within larger, more complex wholes. Every society can be seen to have some hierarchical structuring. The American society relates families within communities, communities within corporate communities such as cities and states, and these corporate communities within a corporation of communities that is called the nation. Latin society is organized around extended families that are embraced in name clans that in turn yield authority to a more or less loosely centralized government representing the "state." The Hebrew society grouped extended families together in name lineages, and these in clans, and the clans in tribes. Saul finally pulled the tribes together into a nation, which was later split into two nations.[10] Such hierarchical structuring can be called the sociopolitical profile of a nation.

Another way of viewing the American nation is socioeconomically. This involves the placement of individuals within departments within industries and businesses, as corporations, labor unions, guilds, etc. Another way is to consider the American within interest groups, and the interest groups within loosely structured power-prestige groups that become nothing less than a kind of "pressure" group within the larger society.

Some African societies have interlinked age-level groupings that bring together all the men of a given age as well as sociopolitical groupings such as councils within the larger tribal organization.

These various corporate "profiles" give one a quick, concise view of the structure of the society. No one profile is sufficient to describe the entire society, however. Various profiles of the corporate body need to be worked out to present the full operation of the society. (See chart 11 for the hierarchical structuring of Hebrew society.)

The individual is also caught up in a hierarchy of groups within the network of interpersonal relations. Such an individual hierarchy can be termed the sociocultural profile of the individual. Chart 12 presents one such personal profile and the groups of which that person is a part, and that thus influence his life in terms of the developing of subcultural uniqueness.

Units of the hierarchy on the highest level include units on the successively lower levels of the hierarchy; the latter can then be termed *included units* contained in *including units*. The smallest, least-complex units of society are *minimal units*. Whenever a given unit includes other units, we distinguish *levels*.

10. 1 Samuel 16-31.

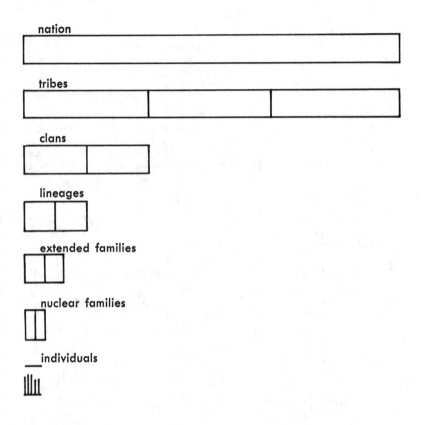

nation

tribes

clans

lineages

extended families

nuclear families

individuals

Chart 11. Hebrew Hierarchical Structuring

There are as many levels within the hierarchy as it takes to distinguish the included/including units within the society. Smaller, less complex societies have fewer levels and fewer units. Larger, more-complex societies, such as the Western societies, have more levels and more units on each level. What results in the larger, more-complex societies is greater complexity — not superiority, not completeness in dealing with life. The smaller, less-complex societies are totally adequate to work within the challenge of their ecological and sociocultural settings.

We distinguish units on the basis of contrast. Whenever two contrasting features of units are found, we have distinct units on a given level. Contrasting features may include distinctions

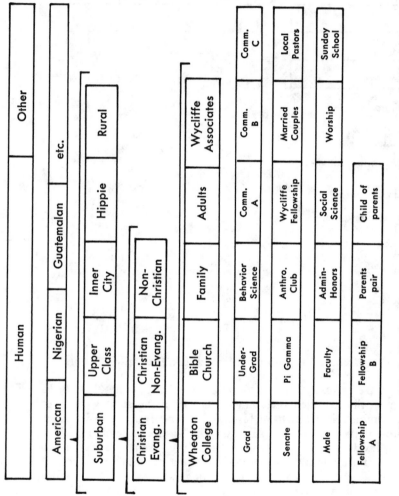

Chart 12. A Characteristic North-American Sociocultural Profile

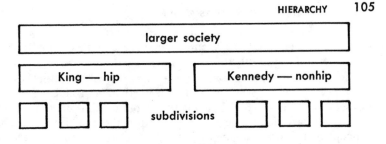

Chart 13. Comparable Subcultures Within a Society

of loyalty mechanisms, authority mechanisms, etc. Thus (chart 13) a person who looks more to Martin Luther King as a "hero" than to John F. Kennedy and who speaks "hip" English rather than "nonhip" English is part of a unit distinct from the Kennedy-as-hero, nonhip-language unit. These two units or subcultures thus fit into the multiculture hierarchy on the same level of the hierarchy, since they are comparable in terms of shared likeness-difference. Each subculture is likely to have comparable subdivisions and be included within the larger society.

The concept of units on a level within a hierarchy gives us a means of distinguishing groups while avoiding branding different groups as inferior or superior. The point of such analysis is not to provide a basis for value judgments. Rather, it provides a descriptive technique for knowing a society objectively. Change that is desired or needed can be effected in keeping with the true nature of society rather than being based on some false perception of the society as compared with another in terms of superior/inferior, or right/wrong evaluations. It is a means of understanding, of knowing, of recognizing difference. It provides a way for one to determine difference, recognize it as valid, and know what to do about it in effecting sound interpersonal relations. It also provides the sound foundation for knowing truly what is right or wrong within the sociocultural setting.

With the concept of hierarchy, levels of hierarchy, and units on a level, we now have the larger framework for understanding more completely the concept of network of social relations and the system of society built around this network. Social relations exist between individual and individual on an individual level within the hierarchy. Individuals group within larger more complex groupings either as individuals or as members of included groups, and finally, groups interact within groups within the hierarchy. The sum total of all the social relations in the network is the social structure which is systemic. The average

American, for example, is involved in one fantastic network of social relations and thus is part of a very complex social structure operating systemically.

The individual moves within the network of social relations in two ways: as a spectator and as a participant. As a spectator, he sees and observes what occurs around him in the social group. As participant, he fills roles within the social group. The concept of roles is a conceptual model that describes the pattern of responsibility assigned to an individual within a social group.[11] A given individual may have many different roles within the groups of which he is a part, such as father, manager, taxpayer, deacon, etc. He brings his personality, his uniquenesses, his idiosyncracies to the role, but in essence the society has already prescribed the extent of responsibility expected within the role.

A given individual filling an incompatible role, for some reason or other, may "play" the role and wear a mask to cover the basic incompatibility with the role. Such an individual lives in conflict within the society and may begin to evidence the behavior of conflict (see chapter 12).

SUMMARY

The average person looks at society as something that either is unitary or that ought to be so. Everyone must look alike, act alike, think alike, etc. Society is not built that way. Every society is distinct and every part of that society has its own expressions of the larger culture. The concept of "multiculture" is therefore a more accurate perspective when considering society.

Society can be conceived of as a hierarchy of groups, with the lowest level of groups being the simplest and least complex, and the largest level or highest level being the most all-inclusive and therefore the most complex. Thus we have the concepts of levels of structural units within a hierarchy of groups. The network of interpersonal relations that results is the web of society with the entire structure tied together through millions of strands of interpersonal associations.

Thus the concept of system is readily applied to the group, for it has a systems operation and the need for continual systems analysis and maintenance. The system is best discovered through the study of the behavior of the people operating within that system. Once the social control mechanisms are known

11. S. F. Nadel, *The Theory of Social Structure* (Glencoe, Illinois: The Free Press, 1957).

through the behavior of the participants, it is comparatively easy to define the system accurately. Once the system is grasped and obvious in its operations, it can be clearly seen which actions abuse the system.

Questions for discussion:

1. What types of behavior could clue one into status relationships within a given hierarchy of power; e.g., in the military, in the church setting, etc.?
2. In what ways does a local church exemplify a systems operation?
3. In what ways could an evangelistic campaign benefit by its leaders tuning into the sociocultural setting?
4. How does God work through the system of a society to reach men and accomplish His purposes?
5. How might our social system limit the effect of God on our lives?

Group activities and exercises:

1. Have each individual prepare his own sociocultural profile, indicating all the groups of which he is a part.
2. Have each member of a group enter a sociocultural setting new to him; e.g. a new office, a different store, a new church, etc. Seek to determine the network of social relations existing in this new context. Work with space relationships, verbal and nonverbal indicators of hierarchy, etc.
3. Experiment: Work through the system to accomplish some goal. Select any systems operation you wish to work with and establish some goal that you could accomplish without "rippling the waters." Work to keep from accomplishing some adverse effect; e.g., apply for a job and be successful.
4. Experiment: Have each person test the existing social control mechanisms operating in his subculture by breaking one purposely; e.g., stand very close to someone while talking, sit on the table to eat rather than on a chair, maintain more intensive eye contact than is normally called for.

Theory of Natural Groupings
The Norm
Hierarchy
Flow of Truth
The Group — Item Identification
— Activity
— Value
Conflict of Norm

8

flow of truth

THE DECISION-MAKING PROCESS IN JAPAN[1]

In Japan, decision making in organizations, large or small, is an extremely complex, diffuse process, in which everyone from top to bottom has a part. The views of all parties with an interest in the outcome are canvassed and an attempt is made to accommodate each view. A consensus must be reached before a decision may be made or put into effect.

Herman Kahn, in predicting that by the year 2000 Japan may well be the world's leading industrial state, describes the uniquely effective Japanese decision-making process. (*The Emerging Japanese Superstate: Challenge and Response*, Prism Paperback, 1971.)

There are, says Kahn, two methods of reaching a consensus: "ringi" and "matomari." "Ringi" is a process in which junior employees initiate and reach an agreement on an idea or problem within the company. They draft a paper on the subject for the department head's approval. Then the paper is circulated among other departments. There is much discussion and change in the paper as it passes back and forth.

After a broad consensus is reached within these lower and middle levels, the paper is presented to higher corporate authorities, who

---

1. From: S. I. Hayakawa, "The Decision-Making Process in Japan," *The Chicago Tribune* (April 23, 1972).

108

are then under serious pressure to approve the plan and forward it to the highest office for final decision.

"Ringi" being so diffuse a process, it is difficult to isolate the source of initiative behind an idea, since it may come from anyone, even quite low in the organization. It is also difficult to determine the actual decision-maker, since the decision has been made by all the interested parties.

"Matomari" is a meeting attended by representatives of all departments or levels within an organization. A problem is outlined by a senior officer, and each member offers his initial thoughts on the issue. No one discloses all his thinking for fear of offending colleagues, putting himself in a minority or, worse yet, in an isolated position.

Each person slowly presents his views, listens to the others, explores their feelings, backs off, and adjusts his own views. If there appears to be agreement, the leader sums up the group view and asks if everyone agrees. If consensus has not been reached, the leader does not press for one or even ask for a vote. He suggests that more time is needed to consider the matter.

A dissident party may, however, be placated by a concession on some totally unrelated issue or by acknowledging an obligation to make up any losses he may suffer by offering a generous concession on the matter at hand. Anyone who has been generous in conceding or who has gone out of his way to facilitate consensus is remembered — whether it be an individual or a corporation.

Such decision-making processes clearly differ profoundly from those of American business, in which decisions are either promulgated from the top, or a small group is selected to study the problem and report to higher authorities, who then make the decision. There then may be some attempt to explain the decision to employees — or even an internal debate on details. But there is rarely a chance to alter the decision.

Thus there is often a tendency for junior employees who have not been consulted and who do not understand the reasons for the decision to oppose it. And the more junior the employee, the greater the likelihood of misunderstanding and opposition.

In Japan it is unthinkable for a decision to come simply from the top down. The great virtue of the Japanese system is that the effort to keep all parties informed and satisfied prevents any demoralizing effect on junior employees.

While reading Herman Kahn on Japanese decision making and

on Japanese labor unions, I could not help thinking about the troubles General Motors is having with its highly sophisticated Vega plant in Lordstown, Ohio. Production lines are often shut down, there are bitter accusations of speed-up and counter-accusations of shabby workmanship and sabotage. What a mess!

Perhaps General Motors could use a management consultant team from Japan. Japan has learned much in the past 100 years from America. Perhaps she can begin to repay the debt.

One of the implications of hierarchy and the concept of social structure being a network of social relations within hierarchy is the challenge of effective communication within this hierarchical network. Dominance in hierarchy is a key concept in dealing with this challenge. If within hierarchy a higher level including group or a lower level included group dominates another, slavery or injustice can result. The dominating group, having more power of influence over the other, in effect forces that other group through the zone of mutual respect, hence the demoralization of employees at the Vega plant. If, however, communication is effected through the levels of the hierarchy in such a way that every lower level unit effectively communicates throughout the hierarchy, the result is freedom or justice. The dominance has now become part of balanced consensus, as in the case of the Japanese industry.

THE SLAVERY MODEL

The illustration (chart 14) utilizes a higher level unit and two lower level units. When the flow of truth, or that which concerns both the included groups within the including group, is from X to Z by way of Y, then Z must wait for Y to know what he should think, believe, or do in keeping with the expectations and requirements of X. This puts Z into a position of slavery or injustice (chart 15).

For example, when the blacks were brought from Africa to the southern United States, they had to depend on the whites of the South for a large percentage of their lived experience. Both whites and blacks were part of American society, and of that society specifically involving them in the southern state of which they were a part. Yet, before the black could move from place to place, select a job, form a belief, establish a standard, he had to consult with the white and follow to the detail the results of that consultation. He was a slave.

The political scientist also would call this slavery, thus reinforcing the idea of sociological slavery in this particular case. There are numerous other experiences of slavery that are not recognized in the political sense as slavery, but constitute sociological slavery nonetheless.

For example, the Central American Indian is not considered a slave of the Spanish overlords. He is free to move from job to job and from plantation to plantation, to request higher wages, and to work or not work. However, part of being an Indian, and thus a person, is seeing the earth produce. In this way, he is attached to the land that he has worked and is very reluctant to move elsewhere. The Spanish overlords, who view the land not as the Indians do but in terms of what they can realize as production from the land, make good use of the orientation of the Indian to the land and they reinforce his obligation to the land. The result is that the Indian perceives that he is not free — both because of his orientation to the land and because of the subtle influence of the Spanish to keep him there. It does

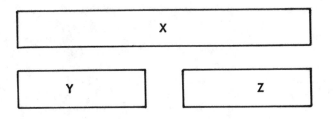

Chart 14. A Hierarchical Social Structure

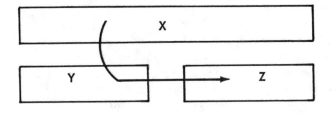

Chart 15. A Situation of Slavery

not need to be so, but the Spanish have continually interpreted the demands and obligations of the larger society to the Indian in this manner. It has not been difficult for them to do this, since they help maintain the illiteracy of the Indian by their educational processes. Injustice frequently results within this setting of virtual or perceived slavery.

A slavery experience of this kind occurs when parents meticulously force their children to abide by the standards and requirements of the adult generation. The natural process of socialization is designed to prepare a child for living within his total society. This process is totally adequate for communicating the moral and ethical principles of the adult generation to the youth generation. However, many adults, reacting to the process as not specific enough, add restrictions and rules that they feel will aid their children as they grow up. Many of these rules and restrictions and the punishments that accompany them fail many times in bringing the children to maturity, and in effect do the opposite of that intended by the well-meaning parents.

Consider, for example, the parents concerned with the strong influence of television beer commercials on their children. They may arbitrarily require that whenever a beer commercial comes on, the volume be turned down so no one can hear the words. The children have already heard the words, if not on their own sets, then on the sets of their friends. The turning down of the volume encourages the young person to commit the words to memory — the fewer times he can hear the words, the more confirmed the commercial becomes in his memory. When the volume is down, he is still letting the words go through his mind. The enslavement comes by way of restriction from the adult generation. The child, in seeking to be free from the restriction, takes steps that ultimately reinforce the advertisement and make him more aware of beer than he would normally have been in the course of discerning for himself the more suitable from the less suitable material entering his mind via television. The sum total of such arbitrary restrictions causes the youth to perceive himself, like Z in chart 15, as living in a slavery setting, obligating him to enter the larger world of X via the requirements and restrictions of Y.

Missionaries may enter a target nation and quickly reduce its members, as converts to Christianity, to a virtual slavery. Subsequent demands for national involvement, cries of nationalism, demands for national evaluation of pastors and missionaries, all indicate that the missionaries have enslaved the people to the

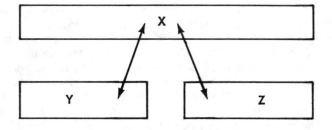

Chart 16. A Situation of Freedom

North American culture rather than freeing them to be true Christians in the bonds of Christ.[2]

THE FREEDOM MODEL

When the flow of truth is directly from the including group into the included group, i.e., from X directly into Y and directly into Z, then both Y and Z are living in a condition of freedom and justice. There is a voice for both Y and Z in the larger chambers of X (chart 16).

This, of course, was the cry of the American Revolution: "No taxation without representation." This is the hue and cry of the contemporary age: "I don't want to be prevoted," and again: "Let me have a voice in legislature, in administration! Let me control my own destiny. Place me in the councils of government, of education, of the church." Members of the adult generation who already have their authority established resist such change vigorously. They did not have such a place, they feel, so why should their children? Their children need such a place, since they perceive that they are living in a slavery setting, that they are being prevoted. They believe they are being taken advantage of by well-meaning people who have effectively protected them from the full experience of life — the right to make mistakes and to do things inefficiently because of lack of experience. Youth perceive themselves as living in slavery.

A refreshing freedom experience was related from the work of the Wycliffe Bible Translators in southern Mexico. Marianna Slocum and Florence Gerdel went to work among the Tzeltal

2. *Practical Anthropology* is a quarterly journal designed to limit the degree of enslavement of citizens of other nations by missionaries. Every missionary candidate would serve his own cause by subscribing to this journal and studying every issue carefully.

Indian peoples and, after learning the language and the culture, cooperated with their early converts to establish a program of worship and outreach that was in keeping with their way of life. A number of behavioral evidences for freedom came to light during the association of these workers with the Tzeltales. One was the length of service of three hours or more, rather than the more traditional Western hour-long service. The missionaries grew tired and bored, but the people, once started in an experience, did not want to end it until it was complete. When a man was to help the missionaries in their translation of the Bible program, the rest of the people took over his farming tasks so he would not suffer from lack of food. They also assumed his other responsibilities so he could give himself completely to the translation task. The young converts enthusiastically spread out into the entire Tzèltal region in their efforts to extend the outreach of the Gospel ministry to all their people. They organized churches, established local fellowships, carried out the discipline of the believers, fulfilled the obligations of the ordinances of the church, except those of baptism and marriage. The church grew tremendously in such a setting of freedom.

Scherer has described the growth of the church in Korea.[3] An interesting pattern emerges in his narration as he deals with the development of the church. When the missionaries lived in the villages with the people for an extended period of time and knew the people and their thought patterns intimately, *the church grew*. When the missionaries were withdrawn from the local areas — being required to stay in the larger cities, living in Japan during the war, or remaining in their missionary compounds for an extended period — yet continued to make decisions affecting the church, the church did not grow. Whenever the missionaries had to be out of the country for an extended period and did not make decisions affecting the church, the church grew. Apparently, when the missionaries were on the field, in the villages and towns with the people, living with them for an extended period of time, they absorbed the thought patterns of the people and knew what the people were thinking. They saw evidences of responsibility and dedication. They made decisions in keeping with the life-way of the people. When they were in the mission compound, however, or out of the country and still made decisions for the church, they let many of their decisions be affected by their own thought patterns and their

---

3. Roy Scherer, *Wildfire: Church Growth in Korea* (Grand Rapids: Wm. B. Eerdmans Publishing Co., 1966).

own American culture — not the Korean culture — and enslavement ensued, however subtly.

THE CONSENSUAL PROCESS

The consensual process underlies the freedom model. Every member of every group, whether an individual or corporate member, must perceive that he has a voice within the larger grouping, whether the Japanese type or the American type, for example. The consensual process operates informally when a class is assigned to a specific classroom and every member of the class, along with the teacher, shows up in that classroom. The process also operates more formally in a meeting calling for decision and operating by *Robert's Rules of Order*.

The consensual process is operating in one educational subculture when student body and faculty have separate organizations and neither feels the need for any change. It is operating in another educational subculture when both student body and faculty are representatives to a unified organization and neither group feels any need for change.

The consensual process is not operating, however, when there are two organizations and one or the other group feels that they are without a voice in the operation of the larger subculture which is the immediate arena for the interaction of both groups.

The consensual process does not undermine responsibility, rather, it reinforces and develops the sense of responsibility. It is when the consensual process breaks down that one of two groups interacting together perceives the other as irresponsible, when in fact the other is carrying out its obligations in the most responsible manner possible.

GOD AND THE FLOW OF TRUTH

The truth of God must come to each man completely and effectively in keeping with what he is socioculturally. Another man or group may interpret God in terms of the "good counselor" conceptual model discussed in model four, but no one has the right to communicate the "God truth" in terms of the slavery model. Any attempt to do so results in the individual member of a distinct culture or subculture being reduced to slavery, as well as the "God truth" being reduced to the limit of spiritual insight of a culture.

The reformers dealt with this when they spoke out for the priesthood of the believers.[4] The church had so reduced the be-

---

4. John Calvin, *Institutes of the Christian Religion* (Philadelphia: The Westminster Press, 1960).

lieving body to ecclesiastical slavery that no one could read or interpret the Scriptures for himself, thus limiting and restricting his grasp of the truth. The concept of the priesthood of believers restored each man to a freedom model of spiritual development and permitted him to share equally with all other men in the consensual process that allowed him immediate access to God.

The consensual process in this discussion in no way is to be interpreted as man dictating to God, or redoing "the God decision." It simply permits each man to be a valid person, a unique entity, and a fully responsible being in the sight of God, i.e., not a slave in an injustice conceptual model.

SYNOPSIS — THE FLOW OF TRUTH MODEL

Communication from group to group and from individual to individual is carried out throughout the hierarchy of groups. Means of communication vary in keeping with the structure of the group or groups. Telephones are useful in the more impersonal American society, but are of little value to a Pocomchi Indian in Central America who uses his children to maintain effective communication with members of his extended family.

Communication that comes through an including group to an included group via another included group produces the practice of slavery or of injustice. The other group defines the nature of truth as established through the larger including group. This is the point of the American revolutionary cry of "no taxation without representation." Today youth are grouped in ways distinct from the ways people were grouped when representation in the national government was established: their campus capers are one way of calling for representation and a voice in government.

Whenever the truth is communicated directly to each of the included groups from the including group, there is the situation of justice or freedom.

Questions for discussion:

1. List the periods of world history most associated with slavery. Indicate the nations involved.
2. How could a slavery setting develop within the typical North American family?
3. What kinds of things could a responsible member of a group do when he begins to sense the slavery model taking hold?
4. How many "freedom" settings can you name?
5. How can a slavery setting be changed to a freedom setting?

6. How could a missionary produce a slavery setting?
7. How many different methods of achieving consensus within a group can you name? E.g., voting, king's decree, etc.
8. What are the ways a teacher will use to achieve consensus? Do all help the group?
9. What are the ways a missionary will use to achieve consensus? Do all help the group?

Group activities and exercises:

1. Research: Have each member of the group interview an overseas student in order to discover to what degree the mission program in his homeland works with the slavery or the freedom model.
2. Simulation: A fairly common exercise called "Rumor Clinic" can be adapted to illustrate the slavery model. Variations are found in Pfeiffer and Jones.[5]
3. Observations:
   a. Observe someone using the slavery model.
   b. Observe someone using the freedom model.

5. J. William Pfeiffer and John E. Jones, *A Handbook of Structured Experiences for Human Relations Training* (Iowa City, Iowa: University Associates Press, 1971), Vol. 2, Experience No. 28.

Theory of Natural Groupings
The Norm
Hierarchy
Flow of Truth
The Group — Item Identification
— Activity
— Value
Conflict of Norm

9

the group: item identification

HER SISTER'S HUSBAND

I first met Tabarire when she ran away from home and came to the mission station asking us for protection. As we talked with her, we discovered that she was a Christian student at an outstation school about ten miles from us. Her parents were forcing her to marry an older heathen man who already had a wife. We gave her food and a place to stay that night.

In the morning her parents and a brother arrived, and we all sat out under a tree and talked. This is the story we heard: Tabarire's older sister — actually, a cousin perhaps — had been married to this man and borne him two children, then died while young. Since he had paid the *lobola* (bride price) for a wife and then was left without one, the family owed him a wife. Tabarire was the only girl in the family who could fill the position, so she was named as his wife. As she was just a child at the time, she had been left in her father's village. Now that she had developed breasts, her husband had come and demanded that his wife be given to him. In the intervening years he had taken another wife.

Tabarire asserted strongly that she did not want to go to him but wanted a young Christian husband. Her parents assured us that they would not force her to marry this man as it is against the law in Rhodesia to force someone into marriage. They agreed to raise the money to refund the *lobola* price and she went home with them.

Several weeks went by and we found Tabarire again at our door. This time she told us of having been locked in the man's hut, but said that she had broken out. We were on our way to town for several days on a shopping trip and took her with us. When the family heard this, they were frightened, thinking we were going to the European magistrate.

When we returned home, the family came again. They were having trouble raising the money and the man was impatient and wanted his wife. We suggested that they take the case to the magistrate to be judged. The father then showed us his arms and we saw the marks of leprosy. He feared that if he appeared before the magistrate, he would be forced to go to a leper camp. They were very afraid of the leper colonies because of stories they'd heard of lepers being thrown out to be eaten by lions. It was because of his leprosy also that he had been unable to get work to repay the lobola money. They decided to take the case to the African chief to be judged, and Tabarire went home with them again.

A few weeks later we got word that she had gone to be the man's wife. Surprised and disappointed, we asked what had happened at the chief's compound. We learned that the chief was the uncle of the man; therefore, there was really no hope for an impartial judgment. She had been offered freedom on the condition that she would go and work for the chief for a couple of years. This undoubtedly meant that she would also be one of his mistresses, as the chief is allowed to take any woman he wants at any time.

Finding no way out, Tabarire went to her husband. The last time I saw her, she had a baby and was also bringing up her sister's two children. Her husband did not allow her to attend church, but she said that she loved God and prayed and read her Bible. She seemed to have accepted her role.

Society is the name applied to interpersonal interaction or interrelationships.[1]

Society is distinct from environment.[2] The environment is the

1. Other definitions of society are found in:

A. L. Kroeber and C. Kluckhohn, *Culture: A Critical Review of Concepts and Definitions* (New York: Random House, 1970).

Peter L. Berger, *Invitation to Sociology: A Humanistic Perspective* (Garden City, New York: Doubleday, 1963).

2. Readings on the relationship of environment are:

Elman R. Service, *The Hunters* (New Jersey: Prentice-Hall, 1966). An ethnology in which the relationship between social organization and environment are studied.

Roger G. Baker, "On The Nature Of The Environment," *Current Perspectives in Social Psychology,* ed. E. P. Hollander and R. G. Hunt (New York: Oxford University Press, 1967).

arena in which interpersonal relations exist and are carried out. The environment is everything within the physical setting in which interpersonal relations are carried out. Whenever the interaction of environment with society is discussed it is termed *ecology.*

Society is distinct from culture. Culture results from the carrying out of interpersonal relations. Culture thus stands as the identifying mark of the society. Every society has a culture, a total life-way that characterizes it. This involves the way people think, live, and do things within the totality of the social relations.

Society and culture are so completely intertwined that it is impossible to determine where one begins and the other leaves off. For this reason we combine the two concepts into one and talk about the *sociocultural setting.* We have used two other terms synonymously with sociocultural setting: the norm and the system. These then are three ways of referring to the sum total of the life-way within a given grouping of people.

It is impossible to sort out the various details of the life-way without some conceptual model. The conceptual model utilized for the discussion of group will distinguish the ways people group, the activities they carry out within the group, and the values that underlie all that they are and do as a group. No one conceptual model is adequate to describe all of society; so numerous models can be called into use.[3] This crosscultural model does not therefore preclude the usage of other models that work with other aspects of the reality of society. This particular model, however, is maximally useful when encountering distinct societies.

A person caught up and controlled by his culture within his sociocultural setting is "at peace" within the culture. He is at home. This is "his way" of doing things. He is comfortable. He

---

3. For other models dealing with society, consult:

Herbert A. Simon, *Models of Man: Social and Rational* (New York: John Wiley and Sons, 1957). Mathematical essays on rational human behavior in a social setting.

Abraham Kaplan, *The Conduct of Inquiry* (San Francisco: Chandler, 1961).

William Davenport, "Jamaican Fishing: A Game Theory Analysis," *Yale University Publications in Anthropology.* Vol. 59:3 (1960), pp. 3-11.

Ferdinand Tonnies, *Community and Society (Gemeinschaft und Gesellschaft),* trans. and ed. Charles Loomis (New York: Harper and Row, n.d.)

Robert Redfield, "The Folk Society," *Human Nature and the Study of Society.* The papers of Robert Redfield ed. Margaret Park Redfield, Vol. I. (Chicago: The University of Chicago Press, 1962).

wouldn't want things any other way. He responds to each challenge of life in keeping with an elaborate code of reaction that is positively directed to protect him from tension and disruption. Anyone not controlled by his culture is in effect forming some new subculture that may ultimately only represent himself or may become the subcultural manifestation of many members of the larger society.

In our chapter case study, Tabarire was caught up in her sociocultural setting. This involved her as a marriage choice by a man who had established certain rights to her. The man was willing to work within the context of the culture as were the girl's parents. The parents further stood to lose a great deal were they to deal outside of their specific subculture, i.e., because of the father's leprosy. Tabarire, with the encouragement of the missionaries, was unwilling to work matters out in the context of her own subculture until she was given the choice of going with her "husband" or becoming a mistress to the chief. She discovered that she could remain within the context of her own sociocultural setting and continue as a Christian. It would be important for the missionaries to know thoroughly this sociocultural setting so they might counsel Tabarire in effective Christian growth and outreach within her own setting.

GROUPING

Society consists of a multiplicity of identity groups, each termed social groups or subcultures. Such groups may be informally designed with few rules and restrictions on the behavior of its members, or they may be formally designed with a multiplicity of rules and regulations. Each society has its own unique and distinctive ways of grouping its members and every grouping within the larger society has those uniquenesses that distinguish it from all other groups.

Society groups its members by age, sex, interests, status, friendships, blood and marital ties, skills and abilities, associations, and many other qualities.[4]

There is no known society that does not have some group division based on sexual criteria. Even the primitive Kaingang of Brazil, a group that assigns very few specific jobs for women within the division of labor, still permit them to select the site

4. For a more complete listing of ways people group, consult Philip K. Bock, *Culture Shock* (New York: Alfred A. Knopf, 1970). A reader in modern cultural anthropology. Bock's selected criteria of grouping tap one immediately into the dynamics of grouping within different societies.

of encampment and thus establish one of the basic distinctions of the male group versus the female group within the society.

In the highland Maya societies of Guatemala, when a meeting is held, the women sit on one side of a room and the men sit on the other. Such restrictions on the seating pattern separate and define groups, even though the group "women" is a less formal grouping in Mayan society and therefore subordinate as compared with the importance of the structured *cofradia* or religious brotherhood. It is easy to interpret the manifestations of such groups as meaning that the men and women do not want to sit together. This is not the point at all. The society has simply established men's and women's groups and one of the manifestations of this social reality is the pattern of seating people in a meeting, and another is the subordination of women to men.

Division of labor by sex defines male and female groups in many societies. In Iran, the Iranian men urge the Americans to pull the shade when the husband does the dishes. Dishwashing is one activity that defines a woman's group in Iran much more specifically than it does in the States. In many African societies as well as rural America, the woman will cultivate the garden where fresh produce is grown and the men will take care of the fields where the money crop is raised. Division of labor also determines who leads singing, who teaches, who keeps the money in a family. The man will lead singing in the States, the woman will lead it in Latin America. The man ushers in the church service in America; the wife of the pastor naturally takes this responsibility upon herself in the Philippines. Young women (e.g., teachers, baby-sitters, etc.) are the "good" storytellers in American society, whereas the old men are the storytellers in Thai society.

Language often reinforces the division of labor within the sex groupings when men's and women's speech differ. Men will speak a certain dialect of the language and though the women understand it, they will not speak it. The same holds for women's speech. A male outsider, for example, learning to speak a language from a member of the opposite sex may learn that person's dialect perfectly but still be considered "sick" or odd by members of his own sex because he does not talk like a "man."[5]

AGE

Age distinctions (chart 17) serve to divide other groups within

5. The Caribe or Moreno of the east coast of Central America have men's and women's speech established on historical antecedents and migration patterns.

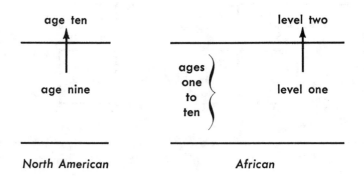

Chart 17. Age Distinctions and Groupings

society. In North American society, the educational process with its formal and informal extensions is based on age distinctions. School classes from kindergarten to college are divided by age. The expected age in any grade level is attained by ninety-five percent of the members of the class prior to entrance. Such age distinctions are maintained within the church program of education termed Sunday school, as well as the daily vacation Bible school and youth programs. Camping programs are age/grade programs, as are also boy scouts and equivalent training programs.

Another type of age division is that which characterizes certain African societies. Everyone born during a period of time, either months or years, depending on the system, is placed within an age level. Even though there are other kinds of groups such as kinship groupings and governmental councils, each member of the society relates primarily to his age level and then to other groups and attendant responsibilities within his wider sphere of life. Certain rules and restrictions apply only to the age level of the person, and correction of the member of a society in the case of such social deviance as theft must be handled first through the age level. The member of an age level remains with that level throughout his life, though the level itself moves through its levels of social existence successively, as each new age level is formed beneath it.[6] In African tribes that prac-

---

6. For a more complete discussion of age level systems, see:
A. H. J. Prins, *East African Age Class Systems* (Groningen and Djakarta, 1953).
R. H. Lowie, "Plains Indian Age Societies: Historical Summary," *American Museum of Natural History, Anthropological Papers.* Vol. 11 (1916), pp. 877-984.

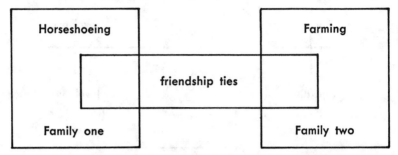

Chart 18. Friendship Ties Between Castes

tice cicatrization, "tribal markings" not only identify the tribe to which a person belongs, but also his age group, the markings being different for each successive age group. There are especially warm greetings exchanged between those who have identical markings.

INTEREST

Interest groups may be social, political, religious, or economic. Social groups are friendship groups that form some kind of identity through ongoing association. Economic groups draw together members of a society with the interest and ability to fulfill certain skills or obligations such as management or sales. Political groups form the basis for governmental supervision of a society. Religious groups oversee the religious and spiritual involvement of the members of society.

Among the citizens of Gopalpur of India (chart 18) two of these are linked in a total system of involvement.[7] Both families will remain as separate entities within separate "castes." The friendship ties relate them but also prescribe behavior.

Among the Pocomchi of Central America the social and religious are linked in a system of organization that is the primary training group, i.e., the university, for members within the society. Such a group is called a "cofradia" or religious brotherhood (chart 19). A member is elected to membership in one of eight to fifteen cofradias (depending on the size of the community). He enters on the lowest rank of responsibility and does everything that everyone else does. After two years, he rests a year and reenters for another stint of service on a higher rank. Everyone within the society is related or tied into one of these cofradias as an active member (men only), a resting member

7. Alan R. Beals, *Gopalpur: A South Indian Village* (New York: Holt, Rinehart, and Winston, 1962).

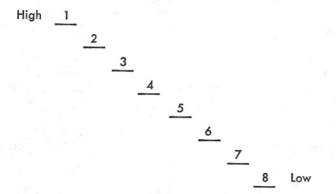

Chart 19. Cofradias and Members of Cofradias

(men only) or a member of a "shadow" cofradia consisting of women only.[8]

KINSHIP

Kinship groupings involve blood (consanguinal) or marriage (affinal) ties. A person is born into a nuclear family of father and mother but from that point on, society establishes just how he will relate to the rest of the society. American society, especially the middle class, stresses the nuclear family, and a member of a nuclear family may enter interest groups and may seldom if ever have anything further to do with blood relatives. In Philippine society, a person who has nothing to do with relatives is an ingrate and a snob. One essential aspect of living or existence in the Philippines is to be part of an extended family. Anyone not functioning within an extended family, termed an "alliance," is a nonentity in the Philippines' perception.[9] Iroquois society of Indian America stressed the community responsibility to the children, and each child, though he would know his biological mother, would refer to each of his mother's female peers as "mother." His responsibilities to his sociological mothers was equivalent to his responsibilities to his biological mother.[10]

STATUS AND STRATIFICATION

Status differences produce another type of grouping. These involve prestige relationships between people — those worthy of

8. Reuben Reina, *The Law of the Saints* (Indianapolis: Bobbs-Merrill Co., 1967).
9. Marvin K. Mayers, *Notes on Christian Outreach in a Philippine Community* (Pasadena, California: William Carey Library, 1970).
10. L. H. Morgan, *League of the Iroquois* (1851) (New York: Dodd, Mead and Co., 1904).

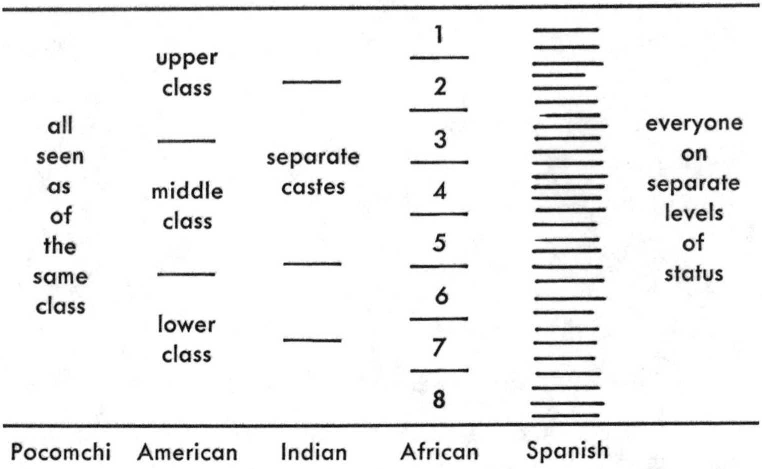

Chart 20. Class Distinctions of Various Cultures

higher prestige or standing and those worthy of lesser prestige and lower standing. Societies can establish a stratification system that causes everyone within the society to see everyone as the same, or to see everyone as different, or any combining of sameness or difference (chart 20).

Pocomchi society causes every member to see every other member in the same way — worthy of the same prestige, no one person being able to order another around. In reality, each member of Pocomchi society has more or less personal goods than another, but he is unable to see this in viewing another member. American society sees some people as worthy of more prestige and others less. It is called a class system with status considerations. Upper-class people have associations and develop comparable value systems as do middle-class and lower-class members. All the members of a given class can get together in a gathering and not feel uncomfortable when members of other classes are present. This is totally different from Latin American or Spanish society where everyone is seen on a rank level distinct from the next person. It is difficult if not impossible to get large groups of Latins together unless the concerns of status are specifically called off for that occasion. The Catholic church operating in Spanish communities controls this very effectively by having a variety of masses presented during the weekend, and having the front area of the church occupied by those of higher status, with increasingly lower levels of status being seated farther and farther toward the back. No one has to relate to any other person unless he chooses to. This is different from the Protestant service where efforts are made to have members interacting with one another during the course of religious activity. African societies with age-level organization relate everyone to the age distinctions, and the older one is, the greater his prestige and standing within the community.[11]

Tabarire was a member of a society with clearly defined status relationships. Her parents and her husband were on a higher level of status in relation to her own. This meant she must accede to their wishes within the context of her own culture. Her parents and her husband were lower in status, however, than the chief. They had to yield to his wishes if they wished to settle their problem without becoming involved with the "colonial" government, a still higher status level in that society.

ITEM IDENTIFICATION OF THE GROUP

Every group is identified not only by the primary mechanism of group formation by sex, age, interest, status, or kinship, but also by a complex of identificational features that give that group identity. Such identification features develop through association of its members but they nonetheless serve as very powerful constraints on the behavior of the members of the group.

Every social group needs to have all or at least a large part of the following characteristics in order to function effectively. Other characteristics can be added as they are found significant in other groupings.

Physical items:
- for example, an American family needs four walls to separate it from another family.

Sociological items:
- a name: either that which it calls itself or that which others call it, or both
- its own language
- greetings
- a place of meeting: its bounded area of meeting
- a time of meeting: or the composite times of meetings of the social group

---

11. For more thorough consideration of the parameters of status within society, consult:
Bernard Barber, *Social Stratification* (New York: Harcourt, Brace, 1957). A comparative analysis of structure and process.
Melvin M. Tumin, *Social Stratification* (Englewood Cliffs, New Jersey: Prentice-Hall, 1967). The forms and functions of inequality.

- membership: entrance requirements, severance of membership
- means of identifying members: uniform, odor, kinesics, or body movement
- leadership: The more natural to the group the leadership, the more effective the leadership.
- rules: either formal, i.e., written, or informal, i.e., unwritten, but known
- discipline: negative — by voice, by force, by withholding pleasures, by rejection
positive — criticism of others, evidence of pride, praise, reward
- mechanisms to induce loyalty: a mythology of sacred places and heroes; causes and issues unique to itself; memories that derive from shared experiences, e.g., here is where the peak of the festival cycle becomes significant.
- privacy: a right to have secrets
- authority: jurisdiction over all within the social group
- perpetuation: rules of inheritance, for example, election of leaders
- means of defense: to maintain the integrity of the group

LEADERSHIP WITHIN THE GROUP

The key to group involvement is the *nature of leadership* expected within the group. Every group has natural leaders — those who lead it in keeping with the group expectations. At times the leadership is unitary, with one person fulfilling all the obligations of leadership. At other times numerous members share the obligations, each doing that which is natural to him in terms of natural ability, or training. Among the Pocomchi, all eight members of the cofradia lead the cofradia by making consensual decisions in which all share, rather than one or a few deciding. There is no concept of the elite within the system. Within a college eating group, however informal, certain members take the responsibility of welcoming others as "visitors" or indicating that they are not welcome. Others take the responsibility of "conversation." Still others shape the belief patterns of the members as far as that group's interaction is concerned. In the United States Senate, the vice-president presides over the meeting, but other members distribute the responsibility for various aspects of lawmaking.

Tabarire's parents had a choice between two types of leadership: the "colonial" and the "tribal." They chose the latter, since they stood to lose too much were they to go to the colonial power's magistrate and run the risk of his discovering the father's leprosy. The tribal leadership, tied into family, in one sense did Tabarire a disservice, since the chief was more closely related to the husband's family than he was to the parent's family. In another sense, the tribal leadership did all concerned a service, since it reinforced society's rules and let the cultural problem be resolved in keeping with what the people actually were. The missionary leadership at no time was of consideration to any but Tabarire, and this only until the case was finally resolved.

Leaders receive their place and attendant prestige by having it ascribed to them by birth as in the divine-right-of-kings concept or by entering a role established within society or by achieving it by dint of hard work or by some specialized contribution.[12] Societies distinguish the two ways quite specifically; where leadership is ascribed, care must be taken that it is recognized and utilized; where achieved, the tools for achieving leadership need to be made available to all members on all levels of the society.

Who leads whom is one of the most critical problems that must be worked out when one crosses a societal boundary. People are led most effectively by their natural leaders. Young women can teach Sunday school in the United States, but are seen as inadequate teachers in the Philippines. Their inadequacy is not due to their inability to teach, rather to the fact that they are perceived to be of low status in relation to men and older women.

Another critical question is the way society utilizes the *primary and secondary leadership roles.* American society generally assigns one primary leader and makes use of secondary leaders. This is expressed in the community of the church where a pastor is primary leader and the boards, Sunday school teachers, and ushers fill secondary leadership roles. In the Philippines, where status/rank is so important, one of the means of achieving status is through higher education. It is assumed that part of the preparation of higher education is that of reading aloud. Every educated person can read aloud fluently. If someone stumbles or stutters while reading aloud, his education is questioned and thus his standing in the community is questioned. In the religious group Iglesia Ni Cristo, a quasi-protestant group, the primary leader never reads from the Scriptures aloud. There

---

12. For selection of leaders, see Edwin P. Hollander and Raymond G. Hunt, eds., "Leadership, Power, and Innovation," *Current Perspectives in Social Psychology* (New York: Oxford University Press, 1967).

is always a secondary leader who reads from the Scripture text. Whenever this secondary leader stutters or stumbles, he is reduced in standing in the perception of his hearers but the primary leader rises in comparison. Thus the primary leader never has to fear loss of status in fulfilling the obligations of his own leadership role.

Wherever there are primary and secondary leadership roles, the program or organization of a group must allow for them. Again, in the Philippines, due to the demands of the status system, the person of highest status in the group is recognized as the top leader. However, there may be another who perceives himself to be of equal or nearly equal status. He expects to have some leadership opportunity and if it is not given to him formally, he will take it informally. For example, during a Bible study held in the home of the highest prestige person in the group, if someone else in the group makes a long statement or dissertation on the subject of the study, or if he monopolizes the floor unduly, it is evident that he perceives his personal standing in the group as equal or nearly equal to that of the primary leader. For this reason, it is good to have two leadership spots available — one for the leader who introduces the study and another for someone to sum up the study. This brings another person into the proceedings in a nondisruptive way.

ABUSE OF LEADERSHIP — A CASE STUDY

Leadership roles and responsibilities can be abused as can any systems operation. There is a variety of ways to abuse leadership — by overextending one's responsibilities, by failing to live up to the expectations of the role assumed, by developing one aspect of the role while leaving other aspects neglected, or finally, by fulfilling only to the letter the demands of the role.

As an example of how leadership can be abused in the pastoral role, the following documented case is presented.

1. An individual is invited to serve either on a committee or board or as chairman of that committee or board.

2. He begins assuming leadership by calling a committee meeting. The pastor has already communicated the expectation that he will sit on the committee.

3. There is continual interruption of the meeting by the pastor. This is in the form of a conversation with another member, observing something out of place in the room, thinking out loud, or referring to some business handled previously or to be handled in the due course of the meeting.

4. There is further reaction by the pastor to statements, concepts, and ideas brought out during the meeting. These responses are negative in nature. They probably are not 100 percent negative, but all of them are perceived to be negative.

5. If an idea calls for work, the next question is "Who's going to do it?" The question is not "Who will we get to do it?" but rather, "I don't expect anyone will do that unless I do it, so who will get the work done?"

6. There is a growing frustration building in the life of the "leader."

7. The thoughts and accompanying feelings that develop from this frustration are dealt with, but before long they are of such a degree of intensity that the automatic reaction of the individual is to think of them as "sin."

8. The final straw comes when it becomes apparent that the frustration, along with the attendant feelings, is going to continue and thus, besides the sense of "sin," there is also a sense of failing God.

9. This is heightened when, in some way or another, the leader finds that the pastor says he "had nothing to do with it" and declares, "I didn't understand you at all."

10. Thus, this is made to be the leader's problem. He must resolve it in his own life and before God.

11. His reactions during this period, and especially during the time of crisis, are now turned back to himself by the implication that his response has some "sin" source. Now, he not only has a sense of sin within, but this is imputed to him from without.

12. The sermons during the next few weeks give him the message: "Shape up or ship out. If you want to have anything to do with this church, you must follow the pastor. He is the real leader. He is above you. He has this authority from God Himself. Any disagreement with the pastor is a disagreement with God Himself."

13. He begins withdrawing. There is further sin because of disagreeing with the pastor.

14. His defeat is complete. He withdraws more and more until he is finally out. This is the final sign and sure indication of "sin" in his life.

SUMMARY

Societies group people in many ways: age groups, sex groups, interest groups — such as religious, social, and political — economic groups, status groups, and kin groups.

Each of these groupings has physical and social characteristics that distinguish that specific group from any other. The physical characteristics grow out of the products that the society produces, such as buildings and emblems. The social characteristics are the result of interaction of the people in associational experiences. These involve name, language, rules of membership, loyalties, and many other distinctions.

Each group, no matter how subtle the distinctions, is a unique group and has certain characteristics that must be learned by anyone entering the group. Since culture is learned behavior, whenever a learning process is being undertaken, there is cultural or subcultural distinction. This is one of the behavioral approaches to people in understanding how they differ from others.

Perhaps the most significant relationship within the group processes is that of the leadership of the group. Leadership can be either appointed or elected, formal or informal.

Questions for discussion:

1. In what ways might women's liberation movements affect natural groupings in North American society?
2. Do characteristic North American groupings need to be changed?
3. Compare the age-grade groupings in the more typical North American church program with those in the secular educational program.
4. What problems might be encountered by grouping graduate students with undergrads in the educational setting?
5. Who are the heroes in your subculture?
6. Where are the sacred places of your subculture?
7. In what ways might prayer be used as "discipline"?

Group activities and exercises:

1. Observation: Observe examples of sex, age-level, and status groupings in your subculture.
2. Have each person do an item-identification description of a subculture available to him.
3. Group discussion: How many ways can prayer be used to reinforce the characteristics, traditions, or identity of a group? For example, how is prayer used for disciplinary purposes?

4. Simulation: "Broken Squares" game is available in Pfeiffer and Jones.[13]

5. Simulations as systems games: "Overpower," representative of the North American class system, and "Strata," representative of the Latin American strata-rank system of stratification, are available from the Associates of Urbanus. They can each be played with a group of thirty in about an hour, with a brief period of debriefing.

---

13. J. William Pfeiffer and John E. Jones, *A Handbook of Structured Experiences for Human Relations Training* (Iowa City, Iowa: University Associates Press, 1971), Vol. 1, Experience No. 7.

Theory of Natural Groupings
The Norm
Hierarchy
Flow of Truth
The Group — Item Identification
— **Activity**
— Value
Conflict of Norm

10

the group: activity

INITIATION RITES IN AFRICA[1]

Probably all the tribes of Central and South Africa have possessed from time immemorial initiatory rites which have been regarded as essential and obligatory on all young men and women of the tribe. . . . In the life of an African these rites have a paramount importance. . . . Each of these rites represents an elaborately devised portico by which one leaves all that is past to emerge a new being into a new life, with new untasted experiences and responsibilities before him.

The real meaning of the initiatory rite is that the boys are being freed from childhood and admitted to the full life of the tribe, with all the responsibilities and dangers and duties that belong to adult manhood. For example, only the initiated in the tribes with which I am familiar are allowed to take part in the burial of the dead; or to cut hair; or to take life (for instance, to kill a hen); or to attend the council of the grown men. Prior to initiation the boys are regarded as mere irresponsible children.

With the Yaos and Makuas in Tanzania, circumcision does in fact take place as part of the rite. Each boy is given a young man who will live with him, cook for him, look after him, sponsor him; in fact, behave as an ideal godparent might behave here at home. A period of seclusion in a forest camp usually lasts about three

1. W. Vincent Lucas, "The Educational Value of Initiatory Rites," *International Review of Missions*, Vol. XVI, No. 62 (April, 1972), pp. 192-198.

134

months. The teaching and training to which the boys are subjected stress manners and manliness. As an example of manners, I remember that an old chief told me that when he was a boy he was taught in the initiation to sit on the Council of the Elders; he had to be careful always to sit in the lowest place unless he was definitely invited to move up higher; and also whenever he ran along the forest paths, if he met any who were older than himself he had to slacken his pace and make a detour lest the dust raised by his feet should rest upon the clothes of his elders. The importance of not entering any room of the house without obtaining the permission of those within is stressed. The way to wear one's clothes modestly, the salutations proper to those whom he meets, the duties of a host — these and other points constitute the code of manners which is impressed on the initiates.

Their training in manliness includes endurance of heat and cold and pain, courage in meeting danger and what is fearful. Obedience is insisted upon almost unreasonably. Boys will be told that they will have no food until they have caught a particular bird visible on the bough of a tree, a task which may plainly be impossible. In the early hours of the morning before the dawn, when the air and water are as cold as they ever become, boys will be roused from their sleep and taken to stand in a pool or stream for an hour or two, and required at times to duck completely under the water. A bamboo will be split and their finger pinched in the opening and then brought close to a hot fire that they may endure heat. They will be taken out at night into a forest by their trainers or godparents, and then suddenly left alone in the pitch-black darkness, while their trainers imitate the roaring of lions and other dangerous animals and leave the boys to find their terrified way back to their camp alone. They are taught songs suitable to each occasion that may arise, and greetings to visitors, and woe betide them if they are slow in making correct response or in singing the allotted stanzas. Failure in any one of these trials is accounted as failure in all. The African proverb runs, "If one fish in the basket is bad, they all are bad," and beating and other penalties follow swiftly, and in some cases unmercifully.

The admission to this camp is preceded by careful and elaborate sacrifice, and interceding with the spirits of departed chiefs. When the three months of initiation are at length ending, the hair of their heads is shaved, new clothes are provided, finery up to the very limit of their parents' purse, and a new name is conferred, so that nothing that belonged to the past may be carried by the boy into the new life into which he is stepping.

The three months' initiation in the forest has been a time of strict training; the boy has probably grown in body; he has certainly grown in mind; and he looks upon his mother and sisters with a new awe, and they for their part recognize that he is not the child who left them, and regard him with unwonted respect. This helps to establish the desired new relationship proper to the new life.

Coupled with the teaching of much that is excellent there is an equal insistence on much that is immoral, and much that is, if not immoral, yet undesirable. Also the hardening process to which the boys are subjected becomes definitely cruel at times, at any rate from the European point of view.

When missionary work begins in an African tribe, what has happened in the past has been that at first the missionaries, knowing no details of these rites, have given them a vague benediction; then, when the passage of years has unlocked the doors of language and the confidence of some of their converts has been won, it has become revealed to them with a horror akin to revulsion that much that they have ignorantly allowed to go on is definitely contrary to Christian morals; and so the vague benediction is exchanged for an indignant campaign of suppression, and this campaign of suppression has in many instances ended in victory. The rites have been discredited and abandoned in many mission areas, though not in all. Now the purpose of this article is to beg that we consider whether the indignant suppression has not on the whole been as unfortunate and ill-considered as the general benediction which preceded it.

Horror at the immoral element has caused us to sweep away what in itself was of a definitely striking value. Where the suppression of the rites has been complete, we have cut the African loose from the old sanctions. He is in grave danger of becoming disinherited from the tradition of beautiful manners; loyalty and reverence for his chiefs and his past have been shaken; and have we really been able to put any adequate new sanctions into the place of what we have destroyed? Man is a social animal, says the old wisdom of the Greeks, and the African tribal rites stress this point and teach each boy to regard himself not as a mere individual but as the member of a tribe, with duties to all his brethren akin to him. By the suppression of the rites he has been in danger of regarding himself merely as an individual, selfish and self-regarding.

An experiment has been made, successfully, so far as can be seen, to take the old initiatory rite, purge it of its immoral elements, enrich it from the storehouse of Christian wisdom and experience, conduct it with as elaborate a ceremonial as belonged to it of old, and then offer it as the initiatory rite for all Christian or catechumen Africans. The measure of its success may be gauged from the fact that heathen chiefs have written asking that their heathen boys might be accepted into the Christian rite. The names of the old rites have been retained.

The activities of the social group cause it to have some significance within the larger society. The specific activities it carries out and the degree to which these are made significant within the larger society determine just how significant the group is or is to become. In this discussion, therefore, the focus is on behavior of activity rather than the institution; on what the people do and when they do it, rather than with whom they do it. The group is thus seen as a series of actions within activities, and every group develops a distinct lineup of activities. In the city of Wheaton, one social group conducts the Fourth of July fireworks display simply as a display of fireworks. The city of Ottawa, fifty miles southwest of Wheaton begins its display with a high school band concert. The American recreational or athletic activity of football is played with an oblong ball in a rectangular field measuring one hundred yards in length. The ball is primarily thrown or carried by hand. Latin American football is played in a field larger than the American field and a round ball is only kicked, never legitimately touching the hand or other parts of the body. (In Africa one may also use his head to propel a flying ball very effectively!) The North American calls the game the Latins play "soccer" and play it as a secondary sport, whereas the Latin Americans play it as their primary or national sport. In our case study, certain initiatory rites, leading young people into adulthood, are spelled out. These are certainly not like North American practices, nor those of Latin America, nor those of any other society. They are, however, what makes the Yaos and Makuas unique.

THE SCHEDULE CYCLE — CALENDAR

Every social group has some means of ordering or scheduling its activities. It would be futile to have an activity that the members of the social group knew nothing about. Since the socialization process is designed to minimize the amount of decisions that one has to make by making many of these decisions simply automatic, society builds the activities of the group into a calendar schedule. The schedule is thus set up with all activities in relation to other activities. In some societies they follow the simple rule "after 'a' comes 'b'." In other societies a specific time and place is established so there can be no question about precisely when something is going to happen. The first society needs some system of public announcement; the second needs clocks and watches.

One of the convenient schedule arrangements is that of the *cycle* includes the time from rising to retiring. It involves preparsonal cycle, the year cycle and the multiyear cycle. The *day cycle* includes the time from rising to retiring. It involves preparations of dress, of food, of work, of recreation and relaxation. The characteristic North American day schedule starts about six to seven o'clock and ends between ten-thirty and midnight. It includes time spent in the following activities: shaving, bathing, applying cosmetics, eating breakfast, going to work or to school, working, enjoying breaks for coffee and the noon meal, returning home for supper, resting or relaxing in the evening (which may or may not include a variety of social activities), and preparations for going to bed.

The Pocomchi day schedule starts considerably earlier — between four-thirty and five-thirty. A minimum of time is spent in the bath and a maximum of time is spent preparing the food and getting ready for the chores of the day, such as the farm activities or those things that must be done around the house. The Pocomchi man goes to work around seven and returns in the afternoon, between three and four. About eleven o'clock in the morning the women of the household bring food to him and his work mates, giving him a break that is as long or as short as he wishes to make it. After he returns home, he spends three to four hours relaxing, eats the evening meal about seven, and then goes to bed.

Conflicts in societies ensue when subcultures have different cycle orientations. American youths tend to arise later and retire later than do the adults. American blacks tend to start later in the morning than white youths and end later in the evening. Colleges find that black students choose later-scheduled courses and tend to retire later, demanding or expecting dorm hours to coincide with their day-schedule patterns.

The *week cycle* provides a pattern of work and rest. Every society has a period of work activity and then a period of relaxation. The North American society structures a five-day week (and may even change to a four-day week), with a weekend of relaxation. The North American pattern formerly consisted of a six-day work week with only Sunday as the day of rest. Certain of the Mayan-derived groups of Central America have a five-day week, working four days and going to market the fifth.

The *month cycle* is a cycle of bill-paying for the North American, and of watching the changing faces of the moon for the more primitive and folk people of the world. The British capitalize on a fortnightly concept and others emphasize the bimonthly cycle.

The physical *season changes* produce a scheduling of activities that generally have to do with planting and harvesting. There are also representative seasonal changes that have nothing to do, necessarily, with the changing phases of the moon that control society. For example, the "fall" season is the time for starting school, for the introduction of new automobile models, new television programs, new efforts at fund raising, etc. In some cultures, seasons also introduce fertility rites designed to cause the crops to grow better.

The *year cycle* is utilized in all societies for experiences of loyalty development, bringing the annual celebrations of "becoming a nation," religious festivals, and town and city festivals. These provide opportunity for remembering local and national heroes. Multiyear cycling of activities very frequently involves more the political than the economic or religious activities. Elections are held generally every two or four years. Yearly elections prove to be too frequent in the development of government within society.

Every society selects the patterns most useful to it from this total range of scheduling. The smaller, less complex society invokes fewer scheduling mechanisms; the larger, more complex society will have activities throughout the year. One must be in a society over an extended period in order to sort out the various calendar-scheduled events and their relative importance. Where two societies live in geographic proximity or are mixed, the number of activities will be greatly increased. The reason for this is that members of each society select from the activities of the other those which they wish to incorporate in their total lived experience.[2]

THE LIFE CYCLE — RITES OF PASSAGE

Societies also employ a means of advancing their members through the various stages of life in terms of life development

---

2. Refer to the Holt series for various descriptions and alternatives of scheduling.

or age development. The rituals that attend the passing from stage to stage are termed *rites of passage*.[3] Generally, rites of passage mark or signal four primary *life crises* within the life cycle: birth, the transition from childhood to adulthood, the transition from the unmarried state to the married, and the transition from life to death. The case study of this chapter selects the transition from childhood to adulthood and concentrates on it.

Each society will emphasize one or more of the life crises within the life cycle. This is signalled by the extent of complexity and significance of the rites of passage. Societies, such as the Black Carib of the east coast of Central America, practice *couvade*, where the husband goes to bed instead of the wife when a child is born. This practice tends to reinforce the importance of the *birth life crises* over other life crises such as marriage, where there is simply a taking of the bride into the household and a minimum of ritual attending this transition. When birth is not stressed, there is simply the attendance by a "midwife," and little more. In North American society a "shower" may be added, but little else is done at birth.

The North American tends to emphasize the *transition from childhood to adulthood* more than the other life crises, though a case can be made for either marriage or death to be the most significant during the contemporary period. The rites of passage involving the transition to adulthood are so varied and complex that a fifth life crisis has been established in the social structure of American society. It has been termed "teen" or "youth" and separates childhood from adulthood by an entire period of development.[4] Rites of passages involved in the transition to adulthood involve graduations, driving, voting, drinking alcohol, and numerous other practices. These so embellish the ritual of the transition that it exceeds all the other rites involved in life-crisis transitions. Very few societies stress the childhood-adulthood transition to the degree of adding a "youth period" and an entire rite of passage.

The second most significant of the North American life crises is that of *marriage*. More ritual accompanies marriage than birth and death and the attitudes toward marriage raise it to a

---

3. Arnold Van Gennep, *Rites of Passage* (Chicago: University of Chicago Press, 1960).

4. Eric Erikson, *Childhood and Society* (New York: Norton, 1965); *Identity, Youth and Crisis* (New York: Norton, 1965). Kenneth Keniston, *The Uncommitted* (New York: Harcourt, Brace and World, 1965).

primary position over the others, but it still remains a secondary rite of passage as compared to that of the childhood-adulthood transition.

Societies stressing marriage develop an elaborate ritual of wedding but also a careful set of rules regulating contact between the sexes prior to and following marriage. When marriage is not stressed, a man will simply take a woman to his home; and there will be a minimum of ritual and a maximum of corporate support for such a practice.[5]

Societies stressing *death* will develop the elaborate ritual around the death-life crisis and have a detailed death belief that will involve reincarnation, such as in some cultures of India. The ritual of death is so elaborate that some groups even call for the burning of the wife along with the corpse on the funeral pyre. In other societies that stress death, such as the Pocomam of the eastern region around San Luis Jilotopeque, corpses are placed on wooden platforms and allowed to lie there until decomposed. In other societies, large funerals are held, with the corpse being laid to rest in elaborate structures. In North America, the ritual of death has developed to such a degree that it is vying for second place in competition with marriage. The funeral is more elaborate than ever, with the undertaker handling details; the cost is also increasing, with even innerspring mattresses for the corpse often being included in the preparations for interment.

Some societies, such as the Latin American, stress a number of life crises equally, rather than just one. The transition to adulthood is attended by the ritual of godparenthood and confirmation. Marriage calls for an elaborate wedding, and death calls for the all-important wake and year wake held one year after the funeral. If one of the life crises stands out, perhaps the death crisis does. There is slightly more elaborate ritual attending the death and more is done following the funeral than following each of the other rites of passage. The post-funeral program is so elaborate that relatives may be involved with it for years following the death of a loved one, e.g., paying for his release from purgatory.

The Yaos and Makuas mentioned at the beginning of the chapter stress the transition to adulthood. The rites attending this life crisis are not only elaborate, they are made to be deeply

---

5. Behavioral evidence for the lessening place of the wedding (not marriage, however) in American youth culture is the committing in marriage with the wedding being held at the convenience of the family and friends.

meaningful by the isolation of the child, the assistance given him, the ritual upon his return as a young adult, etc.

FESTIVAL CYCLE — CELEBRATION

Tied in with the calendar cycle and rites of passage is the festival cycle which supplies every social group's need for *celebration*. The concept of celebration embraces a period of mundaneness followed by a period of excitement within the group. If every day, week, month, season, and year were the same, there would be very little interest in life. Boredom would result. If everything happened the same way, the group would suffer in loyalty building, as one group would not develop distinctions from others.

Within the day cycle, the Latin American siesta is a festival. The North American looks at it as merely a nap, at best unnecessary, if not a sign of laziness. To the Latin, it serves to reinforce a sense of family in a society where the family is more significant than any other unit of structure within the hierarchy. In North American society, "dinner" does what the siesta does in encouraging a sense of family. Everyone is together at dinner in the typical American family, whereas they are not usually together at any other meal nor at any other time. Thus, the dinner time is a time for celebration within the day schedule.

Within the week schedule, religious observance brings a sense of "something special" to a mundane work period. Thus, worship at its best is a celebration, not only with God, but also as a release from the normal everyday pressures of life.[6]

National holidays occurring yearly underscore the sense of loyalty to the larger society. The fourth of July in the United States is the date for the celebration of independence as a nation, while the fifteenth of September is the date on which Guatemalans celebrate their independence.

Every celebration has its plan or walking pattern associated with it, which, in turn, reinforces the celebration by the degree of detail and elaborateness. The Latin American procession is a vital part of celebration and the complexity of the march indicates the degree of importance a particular festival has in the lives of the people. Perhaps the most elaborate plan of march of a festival procession is that occurring around Good Friday. There is not only a variety of processions during this time, but each one is more elaborate than an equivalent march during any

---

6. Even societies, subcultures, and individuals that do not have a specific belief in God will still institute in their lives some worship replacement which has a similar effect in their corporate lives.

other festival, involving not only more people but more kinds of people within the society.

Societies focus on specific celebrations in every social group. Thus, the nation has its celebrations, the states their celebrations, the community its unique celebrations, the family its festal practices, and the individual his own birthday. In small, minimally complex societies, the matter of celebration is apparent because it tends to flow quite naturally within the activity cycle and not to be potential for conflict. In larger and more complex societies, celebrations may conflict with each other, and a ranked code of holidays and festival periods is developed to circumvent such conflict. Such a rank establishes which are more important and which are less important. For example, family celebrations which are more potential for conflict with community and national festivals are frequently held on the same day as the larger festival, thus averting such conflict in North America. In Latin America, however, a family festal responsibility will frequently result in a family member ignoring his social, economic, and religious obligations. One such conflict that is seldom satisfactorily resolved in American society is when the child's birthday falls on or near Christmas day. Many families resolve the conflict by giving both a Christmas and a birthday gift and celebrating both occasions at the same time. To the child, however, this is less than adequate, for he sees that children having birthdays at other times have two celebrations.

Within every social group, there will be one festival that is ranked as the major celebration of the group. It occurs at the *peak of the festival cycle* and is the most significant celebration within the social group. No social group will be without a series of celebrations; therefore, it is important to note the most important celebration and be able to distinguish this from the less important ones. Primary loyalties are focused on the peak, and lesser loyalties on the secondary festivals. In North America, Christmas time is the peak of the festal cycle, both in terms of national concern and personal concern. Even though the festival is concerned with the birth of Jesus Christ, that which is stressed is gift sharing, establishing a strong basis for object production and distribution. Thus the production cycle comes into sharper focus than does religious devotion. However, in Latin America, Christmas is one of the lesser celebrations, for the most significant festival of the year is that of Good Friday, with festivities being completed even before Easter.

THE RESPONSE CYCLE

Another cycling is termed here *response cycling*. This is the expected response of an individual to a stimulus of some kind. Responses involve greetings, acceptance of gifts and the giving of gifts and favors in return, acceptance of "office" or resignation from same, religious participation, and many others. Greetings are controlled both in degree of response and timing of response. Whereas the Filipino might simply raise his eyebrows in response to a verbal greeting, the North American would totally overlook such a response, expecting a verbal one in return. A North American would submit his resignation to public office and expect it to be accepted, whereas in Latin America, a resignation is simply a test of strength and is never intended to be picked up and accepted, at least not the first time it is presented. The response in religious services is so patterned and practiced that many adherents are able to "go through the motions" of the religious rituals without really paying attention to what is going on.

WALKING PATTERNS ACCRUING FROM ACTIVITY CYCLES

Every activity calls for its own unique *walking pattern* and the composite walking pattern is built from the composite of activities within the society. The typical North American walking pattern is established through the interaction of work and school. If work calls for a man to punch in at eight o'clock and leave at five, his walking pattern then involves getting to work before eight and leaving work at five. Such a walking pattern causes the freeways to be jammed at eight and five. Another pattern, the week pattern, with its weekend of heavy traveling, is graphically indicated by the offer of reduced fare for families during the off times, i.e., in the middle of the week. Resort areas feel the pressures of the yearly walking patterns during the slack times in resort activity. They have to make their money "during the three months of summer" if they are going to survive. Motels frequently have two charges — the vacation charge and the off-season charge.

In primitive or folk societies where the people have a market day, if that market day falls on a Sunday, the walking pattern calls for the Sunday morning period to be spent selling produce and buying staples for the week, and then attending church. This is in direct conflict with the walking pattern established from the North American or "Western" society where the late morning is a more effective time for the rural farmer to attend the weekly celebration of religion. He gets his chores completed by mid-morning and then must return home to complete others in the late afternoon. A church schedule in the Indian areas of Latin America having a Sunday market should be built around the market sequence, whereas the schedule in rural North America can follow the "chore" sequence.

In contemporary North American society, people are finding the recreational activities dominant over the religious interests and some churches are adjusting their schedule to the walking pattern of a recreation weekend by having their service prior to the weekend (e.g., on Thursday evening) or early Sunday morning.

SUMMARY — THE GROUP AS ACTIVITY

When studying any group, but especially one for which it is impossible to find written materials, the need is to focus on the behavior of the members of the society. The behavior is most clearly expressed in the activities of the group. Such activities encompass a wide variety of interests ranging across social, economic, political, and religious concerns.

One way to analyze the activities of a group is to take a look at the scheduling of these activities through the different time periods of life: the calendar, the life crises, the celebrations. It becomes obvious, quite quickly, just which are the most important activities of the group — those around which the most "ritual" develops. Working from the ritual activities, it is possible to determine the "peaks" and "troughs" of the festival cycle.

When the agent of change approaches the society he seeks to influence, he can study the walking patterns of the people to see if that which he wishes to introduce is compatible with the activity cycling of the group. A missionary does not introduce an 11:00 a.m. service in the Pocomchi area during the market time if he wishes to have any Pocomchi attending the service. This is the same principle that established the North American worship time, i.e., a time that would not interfere with the farmer's chores.

Questions for discussion:

1. What holidays are most important to the North American?
2. What is the most important holiday in North American society? What rites and rituals attend the celebration of this holiday?
3. How has the festival cycle been adapted to meet the demands of the work/recreation cycle? Which holidays have been changed and which have not been changed? Can you produce some gen-

eralization that is consistent with the changes as you see them?
4. How might the North American activity cycle be imposed upon Christians in some other society?
5. When might a missionary need the most encouragement and support in his stay in the host society?
6. What kinds of problems might a missionary's "kid" (MK) face upon returning to the United States after five years in another society?

Group activities and exercises:
1. Group discussion: In small groups probe the list of heroes, sacred places, primary and secondary holidays or celebrations, etc., of the subculture of which the members are a part, e.g., a local church, a college, etc.
2. Film: A film like "The Dead Birds," an ethnographic documentary from New Guinea, (83 min. color and sound, McGraw-Hill Contemporary Films Inc., $45.00 rental) is a valuable film to use as a discussion focus on this chapter.
3. Small group activity: Have the members of the group "generate" all the ways a "devotional" program could be developed in keeping with the schedule cycle of their subculture, i.e., for periods in the day, week, month, year, multiyear, etc.
4. Large group discussion: Introduce the four life crises that a typical society has and put them in order of rank in North American society according to the amount of rite and ritual attending the rites of passage. For example, of the four life crises — birth, puberty, marriage, and death — the North American society has most elaborated the puberty life crisis as evidenced by the variety of rites of passage that attend this crisis: graduations, voting, learning to drive, etc. In fact, this one has become so elaborated that an extra life crisis could be inserted in the list of four to make "teenage" a life crisis not shared by many other societies. Once this has been completed, compare the life crises of a second society with the North American practice.
5. Prepare a festival or celebration that is consistent with the group of which you are a part and adds to the sense of well-being of the members in the group.

Theory of Natural Groupings
The Norm
Hierarchy
Flow of Truth
The Group — Item Identification
— Activity
— **Value**
Conflict of Norm

11

the group: value

THE SEVEN-MONTH BABY

Phairote, a young Thai Christian, brought his bride with him to Bible school when he returned for his second year. He had lived previously in the boys' dorm but during vacation he had married a young nurses' aide at the Christian hospital where he was working.

They entered easily into Bible school life and continued their studies together. Before long it was announced that they were expecting their first child. Everyone looked forward happily with them to its arrival. They had talked of returning to Central Thailand for the birth of the child; then, as the time drew near, they decided to remain and have it in the government hospital nearby. The day came for the birth of the baby, and they proudly announced the arrival of a son.

The missionaries who were teaching on the staff of the school began to be uneasy. One of them had attended the wedding of the young couple some months before. When they compared the wedding date with the birth of the baby, it appeared that the child was born about six weeks earlier than they felt it should have been. Since the baby was above average size and weight and normal in every way, it seemed clear that he was not premature, and so the missionaries concluded that the newlyweds had lived together prior to their wedding day.

Before long the matter took on crisis proportions in the eyes of

147

the missionaries. As they gathered to discuss it, it was felt that since the purity of the church was at stake, the young couple must be faced with the issue. Since confrontation is the western method of solving conflicts, they decided to visit the young couple in their quarters and talk the matter over. One evening while the other students were studying, three men and two women visited Phairote and his wife. After prayer, one of the missionaries broached the subject, informing the proud parents that their behavior had been improper by Christian standards. Silence filled the room.

One of the aspects of the Thai value system is that of saving face. They will always approach things indirectly so that no one loses face in the situation. Without an intermediary which Thais would have used in such a case, the young couple somehow felt "naked" in the overpowering presence of the five missionaries. There was no one to remind the missionaries for them that the Thai betrothal is considered as binding as marriage and that sexual relations during the period covered by the betrothal are not considered particularly improper.

There was little that Phairote and his wife could say, so they listened while the missionaries proposed a solution. They suggested that the couple should stand up before the assembled Bible school students at one of their chapel meetings and confess their misdeed publicly. The young couple was not especially pleased at this suggestion, so they remained noncommittal. After considerable consultation, the missionaries departed and awaited the chapel hour when this confession would be made. It never came. The couple refused to comply, the missionaries were disappointed, and at the close of the term the couple returned to their home.

Values are whatever an individual within a group considers of importance. In each automatic or consciously made decision some value underlies the choice of one thing over against another. Since the socialization process is designed to make as much action as possible automatic in response, it thus is responsible for developing or underscoring values. The entire life of an individual can be plotted simply by indicating the values by which the individual lives. These values underlie the social groupings of which the individual is a part within a society, and they select out from the total range of activity those specific activities that a specific individual or group chooses to act out or engage in.

Every social group, every subculture, every community has its own pattern, or network, of values. In part, these are derived from the sum total of all the values of the members of the community. In part, they are in addition to any and all individually held values and become that which the community develops. These values are what make a community unique; they are the things that cause a community to grow and maintain interest in life. Without them, life would become ordinary and humdrum, boring and dull. Every community has its own patterns.

No community exists without values. A given community may have values that are distinct from those of some other society, but there is no real difficulty in finding values within every society or subculture. An outsider feels that a given society *should* have other values than those they do have, but this is due to an extreme focus on one's own way of life and becomes a negative expression of ethnocentrism.

THE BASIC VALUES

Besides a general consideration of values, in which we have seen that everything a person or group chooses above something else is of value to him, there are certain underlying values that form a taxonomy. I will call these *basic values*.[1] A taxonomy is a device utilizing categories of thought that permit the analyst or the one describing a culture to objectify that culture through the means of something other than a value judgment; e.g., something is better than something else. Value judgments applied to the known aid discernment. Value judgments applied to the unknown distort and confuse and ultimately result in falsehood and injustice.

The categories of thought utilized in the basic values model include the following patterns of behavior:

1. Dichotomizing
   a. A dichotomizing person will tend to polarize life in terms of black and white, here and there, myself and the other, right and wrong.
   b. It is relatively easy for a person to evaluate the other (person, program, or idea) on the basis of such dichotomies.
   c. The person must feel that he is right — that he is doing

---

1. There are numerous taxonomies of values including McLuhan's hot and cool media; DeBono's vertical vs. lateral thinking; Reich's consciousness I, II, and III, managerial grid, etc. Each of these is reduced to a pair of values with extended discussions. Basic values is a multicategory taxonomy which can further organize the other discussion as well as extend the application of the taxonomy itself.

the right thing and thinking the right thoughts — to be satisfied with himself.

d. A dichotomizing person adapts well to the computer, so much a part of modern society. However, for some, fear of the computer may result from seeing it in terms of "the other."

e. Such a person is highly systematized in terms of classifying and organizing experiences and ideas in his mind.

f. The ability of such a person to organize and to understand where he "fits" and where others "fit" gives him a sense of security.

2. Holistic
   a. The parts will have a vital function within the whole.
   b. No consideration can be given any part unless it is also considered within the whole. Situations in which one must consider one part without respect to the whole produce frustration for the holistic person. He sees it as "simplistic," not valid, an ineffectual insight.
   c. Such frustration will result likely in some defensive measures such as the mock. The mock strikes at the whole scene.
   d. A holistic person derives his satisfaction through integration of thought and life, whether planned or natural.
   e. The person feels very insecure whenever he is placed in a category.

3. Crisis or Declarative
   a. A crisis person seeks an expert (someone with extensive knowledge of a particular area) to advise him in a crisis.
   b. He tries to find the very best authority to use as his most important guide.
   c. He likes an authority which is easily accessible, to which he can return, and to which he can direct others seeking knowledge. Consequently, he reads a great deal and uses the best written authorities as the basis for his decisions.
   d. This person will have a keen interest in, and a deep respect for, history, since he believes that crises similar to his have been faced before and that he can find a solution through looking at past solutions.
   e. No crisis is entirely new, since there are bound to be

similar crises and answers conveyed through information given by an expert.

f. In a learning experience, much emphasis is placed on comprehending the instructor and being able to re-verbalize what one has been taught.

g. The responsibility for the learning experience primarily belongs to the instructor. He is expected to be stimulating and motivating.

h. The crisis person trusts the knowledge and advice of an expert. Following such advice gives him confidence in making decisions.

4. Noncrisis or Interrogative
   a. A noncrisis person will expect to have to select an answer to the question from various alternatives.
   b. Security and satisfaction will derive from selecting among alternatives. Frustration will come if no alternatives are available.
   c. Bitterness will develop later if one finds he has not been given opportunity to select from alternatives, or an alternative has not been suggested to him that might have been available.
   d. For this person, therefore, a new problem arises out of the alternatives selected.
   e. Personal satisfaction comes with the alternatives considered and the ones elected, as well as from the vitalness of questions or problems arising from the one selected.
   f. A noncrisis person can, through the events of life, be brought back to the same situation he faced earlier and then choose a different answer — another alternative.
   g. This person will be frustrated with a lecture situation in which an expert speaks.

5. Time oriented
   a. A time-oriented person will be concerned with the time period.
   b. The time period will be a certain length depending on what is the intent or purpose of the time spent.
   c. Concern will be given to the "range of punctuality" at the beginning and end of the time session.
   d. The time period will be carefully planned to accomplish the most possible in the time allotted.

    e. This person sets goals — long, middle, and short range — which are related to some type of time period, whether it be hours, days, weeks, months, or years. He feels most comfortable planning ahead in this particular manner.

    f. This person will attempt to condense into a given time period as much as he can of that which he considers worthwhile.

    g. There will likely be a time/dollar equivalence, or a time-spent/production equivalence in his way of life. If he spends a certain number of hours studying for a particular test, he expects a certain grade.

    h. He will not fear the unknown too greatly.

    i. He will remember and try to reinforce certain times and dates.

6. Event oriented
    a. An event-oriented person is not too concerned with the time period.

    b. He will bring people together without planning a detailed schedule and see what develops.

    c. He will work over a problem or idea until it is resolved or exhausted, regardless of time.

    d. He lives in the here-and-now and does not plan a detailed schedule for the future.

    e. He is not much interested in, or concerned with, history.

    f. He does not rely on the experience of others, but rather trusts his own experience implicitly. He will have little empathy with, and confidence in, the experience of another unless it is communicated to him through some form of "sharing."

7. Goal-conscious
    a. A goal-conscious person is concerned with a definite goal and with reaching that goal.

    b. Achieving the goal becomes a priority.

    c. He finds his deepest friendships with those who have goals similar to his.

    d. When necessary, he will go it alone.

    e. Depending upon his motivation in attaining his goals, he will even be willing to see his own body destroyed for the sake of the goal.

8. Interaction-conscious
   a. An interaction-conscious person is more interested in talking with others than achieving his goal.
   b. He derives his greatest satisfaction from talking with people.
   c. He will sacrifice a goal for the sake of conversation.
   d. He will break rules or appointments if they interfere with his involvement with another person.
   e. Security for him will come in the group — getting to know people in the group and being involved with them.

9. Prestige ascribed
   a. A person who feels that prestige is ascribed and then confirmed by the social group will show respect in keeping with the ascription of prestige determined by society.
   b. He expects others to respect his rank.
   c. He sees a person's formal credentials as important.
   d. He sacrifices to achieve the rank and prestige in society he desires.
   e. He plays the role his status demands.
   f. He tends to associate most with those of his own prestige or rank.

10. Prestige achieved
    a. A person who feels that prestige is achieved and must be achieved again and again will ignore formal credentials.
    b. He will consider rather what the person means to him.
    c. He will struggle constantly to achieve prestige in his own eyes and not seek to attain a particular status in society.
    d. He will work to prove himself.
    e. He will give as much consideration to statements made by those without formal credentials as to those with credentials.

11. Vulnerability as weakness
    a. A person who feels that vulnerability is a weakness will take every step possible to keep from error,
       1) double-checking everything he does, and
       2) being methodical and organized.
    b. He enjoys arguing a point to the end.
    c. He hates admitting mistakes.
    d. He tries to "cover up" his errors.

    e. He will not expose his weaknesses or tell stories about his mistakes.

    f. He has a tendency to speak vaguely about areas of his life that are personal.

    g. He is rather unwilling to become involved in a new experiment.

12. Vulnerability as strength

    a. A person who feels that vulnerability is a strength does not find it difficult to admit mistakes.

    b. He is not too concerned about making errors.

    c. He tells stories about himself exposing his own weaknesses.

    d. He is willing to talk freely about very personal areas of his life.

    e. He is willing to be involved in new experiments.

These twelve categories of thought are not the only ones that could be considered in such a taxonomy, but in the ongoing study of society these appear to be the most significant values for consideration of difference. If he grasps these, the analyst can then derive the primary motivational values of a society. Possibly eighty to ninety percent of behavior within a given society opens to understanding once the relationship of these values to the society is discovered.

APPLICATION OF THE BASIC VALUES

These individual categories of thought or conceptualizations within the basic values model can be applied to a society as *individual items*. In other words, for example, a society can be described in terms of its time orientation and its response within a time setting. Or, it can be described in terms of the ascription of prestige.

A study of individual categories as applied to the Filipino can be most enlightening when implications are drawn from these in understanding their life-style.

A Value Profile: Philippine (Tagalog) Society[2]

1. Schedule. The Filipino appears to like a schedule, but not one that is tied to a narrow time pattern. In other words, he likes to have something to do over a particular time period,

---

2. From Marvin K. Mayers, *Bicultural Evangelism: Philippine Focus* (South Pasadena, California: William Carey Library, 1974).

such as in the morning, but he doesn't have to appear at eight and leave at twelve to carry out his schedule. His schedule does not control his life. The North American is more tied to a time-clock pattern and hesitates to disrupt his schedule for fear that he won't get everything done.

2. Time. The following principles appear to guide the Filipino in range of punctuality: (1) The more important the individual, the narrower the time range of punctuality. (2) The business event demands a narrower range of punctuality than does the social event. (3) The more prestigious the social event, the wider the range of punctuality. Examples: An appointment with a V.I.P. meets at the time set; for mass lasting an hour, one can arrive within the first half hour and not be late; Rotary Club induction may have a one-to-one-and-a-half-hour range of punctuality. To the North American, the time stated is the time intended.

3. Event. In nearly every experience of life, the Filipino is more concerned with the event itself and what is going on than he is with the time the event begins and ends or whether it moves within a narrow time schedule. He expresses this in a variety of ways. If something does not get done today, he excuses it by talking about mañana. His making of a livelihood is built around an event; e.g., if he can make a living by selling one item, he does not need to be in the office from eight to five. The Filipino has what might be called a stoical approach to life: if something interferes with his schedule, he can patiently endure. Life is centered in the experience of the now, or the present moment, and the Filipino often is very good at starting something now but not continuing it later. Some refer to this as *ningas kogon;* i.e., things will start with a bang and then the enthusiasm will wane. For most North Americans, time and the timed program are more important than the event itself and to a large extent control the entire event.

4. Vulnerability is a weakness. In some instances the Filipino appears to value vulnerability as a strength and will readily admit to things that the North American never would, such as an illicit sexual involvement. However, through most of his life the Filipino is very sensitive to vulnerability, to any evidence of weakness or erring, and works within the society to cover all such evidence.

When someone stumbles, falls, or in any way harms himself,

Filipinos will stand around and laugh rather than aid the person injured. To the North American this appears to be crass insensitivity and an unwillingness to become involved. But the Filipino sees it differently. If someone has stumbled, the Filipino might feel this is an evidence of that person's vulnerability, and if he took the accident seriously, the injured one would be embarrassed because the seriousness would underscore his weakness in having fallen.

The society supports the individual in any evidence for vulnerability through the practice of the intermediary. One arranges for an intermediary in every situation in which he might be proven vulnerable; e.g., if he needs money and the person who could lend it to him has no obligation to him and thus could easily refuse the request, a third party to whom the potential lender might be under obligation is sent, so that the request will not be denied. The North American seldom works through an intermediary and feels that the best resolution of a problem is by face-to-face confrontation.

The Filipino appears to be a poor loser and will at times exert superhuman physical effort in his attempt to win; e.g., a basketball team winning against a Filipino team can be badly battered physically.

The Filipino does not want to put someone on the spot. The moment he does this he makes the other person vulnerable and potentially disrupts smooth interpersonal relations.

The North American adult also considers vulnerability as a weakness. His society, however, does not stand behind him in this value orientation, as does the Filipino's, to provide him with as many social mechanisms for covering up his vulnerability.

5. Personalness is valued highly. This is evidenced by certain attitudes and responses within the society.

An announcer of a basketball game may fail to announce the score because he is talking about the personal qualities of the basketball player making the score.

Much personal support of another is expressed through tactile or touch behavior, showing a dependence one upon another, e.g., men holding hands, one man laying hands upon the other's leg, women touching women in a crowd.

In certain respects the Filipino is very sensitive to the other person. He will respond to a request with a euphemism to keep from saying no.[3] You say no only to a person with whom you do not want to be associated.

The Filipino does not want anyone within the society to be alone, so he feels that it is his responsibility to be with the other person even though he may be ignoring some of his own responsibilities.

The Filipino likes a "personality," one who relates warmly to him, who builds a network of interpersonal obligations through a sense of interest in him and his needs.

The North American, on the other hand, is exceedingly impersonal in such interpersonal relationships with a patent insensitivity to others and a distaste for the "personality" type. He will attempt, by various means, to make the "personality" just one more of the crowd.

6. Noncrisis. The Filipino attempts to avoid crises. A crisis would disrupt smooth interpersonal relationships. Instead, he follows every avenue possible to feel someone out before taking a stand, making a request, extending a favor. The practice of using the intermediary is designed to eliminate the crisis experience. Noncrisis value might also explain the "permissive" child-rearing practices of the Philippines. The parents do not want to make a scene and so they yield to the demands of the child. This does not necessarily mean that the child grows up to be immature in his adult behavior, for at a certain point in life, he is expected to evidence mature behavior in spite of this more permissive early training. For the youngest child, especially a boy, this point is delayed indefinitely. The North American does not hesitate to precipitate a "crisis" if this furthers his own ends.

7. Prestige. When one is born into a family, he acquires prestige. An individual starts in the status system at the level of status of his family. However, he can achieve higher status through education or marriage or "luck." Thus, frequently, the motivation for education is not to gain knowledge but to gain a diploma, which enables him to strive for a higher status level. A person's family name causes those below the status of his family to expect good of him, to assume that he will succeed in maintaining the status of the family or improve it. The family name, however, is no guarantee that the status level will be maintained. The Filipino becomes a kind of "copycat," one who

---

3. If a person wishes to borrow your umbrella and you do not wish to lend it to him, instead of saying "No," say rather, "I don't think it is going to rain."

is quick to sense the demands of a higher status and fit in, whether he fully deserves this status or not.

8. Authority. The Filipino is very authoritarian. The higher status has authority over the lower, the leader of an alliance over the follower. The sense of authority is intense; e.g., a youth accepting Christ may reverse this decision if the leader in his alliance disapproves.

The Filipino will speak softly to the authoritarian. He will not answer or respond when asked to do something by this authority figure, deeming it neither necessary nor respectful to do so. Both practices irritate the North American.

The hold which the authority figure has over the follower is extremely frustrating to the average North American who feels that everyone must be free to make up his own mind as to the final decision, though he himself doesn't realize just how much this is controlled by his own culture.

9. Holism. The Filipino sees life as a whole, as a unity, with all parts being explainable within the whole. The North American tends to be more particularistic with greater attention to detail, to linear sequence, to a sequential type organization. In comparison, the Filipino appears to have an absence of logical thought and uses euphemism extensively to talk around a subject rather than speak directly to the point of a subject.

The North American is particularistic and usually pairs the particulars in dichotomies and is very linear; e.g., B must follow A, and C must follow B, or he is frustrated. Reading and writing, both based on linear sequence, come quite naturally to the North American. A society which is more holistic and non-sequential is attracted more to films and television rather than to books.

FURTHER APPLICATIONS

We can also use these individual categories of thought as contrasting items within a larger scheme which have *binary* considerations or *bipolar* relationships. In other words, we can select any two that appear to have relevance to each other and through contrast or bipolar relationships we can see that one society is more of one kind than it is of another. One society may be experience-oriented, whereas another society may be time-oriented. A visitor in the United States notes a great deal of time orientation, i.e., careful attention is paid to the clock; there is extreme concern for meetings held during a specific time period; these meetings are to start and end on time; there are clocks everywhere — on towers, on banks, on filling station walls, in every room of the house and on every wrist. Meetings and programs are established around a time concept — whatever is going on is set aside when the meeting is over, i.e., when the time limit for the meeting approaches or when the "bell" rings. In fact, the people with whom one has spent this time period are no longer of primary importance. The contrast is striking when one enters the Philippines. The people are more concerned with who is there and what is going on than when something starts and ends.

One drawback of such a binary or bipolar method of contrasting items or approaches to life is that the analysis tends to polarize, and in the process people are polarized, societies are polarized, and the value judgments slip in to support one category over another in very subtle ways.[4]

Therefore, a more significant means of utilizing the basic values than either through individual application of the categories or polar application of them is by means of *continua*. As with the polar approach, two categories are selected that appear to relate to each other, e.g., time vs. event, or two aspects of one category may be selected such as crisis-noncrisis. In this way, distinctions between societies can be noted, but there is less chance of applying value judgments that tend to be prejudicial. In other words, a given society can be seen to fall somewhere along a continuum, e.g., anywhere from an extreme time consciousness to an extreme event consciousness. Different aspects of the same society can be described by the use of a series of considerations involving the same continuum; e.g., American society would trend toward time orientation in economic aspects and toward event orientation in recreational aspects.

By taking two continua and placing them in a matrix with two axes in the matrix, one can compare individuals and societies by means of as many as four categories. In the "managerial grid" utilized in today's business and management world, the categories of person relatedness and production are considered, with axes representing a more person-oriented individual in comparison with a less person-oriented individual on a one-to-nine scale also. Thus, an individual who produces little and relates poorly to people is a one-one person and an individual who is tops in production and great with people is a nine-nine.

---

4. DeBono's vertical vs. lateral taxonomy is a binary pair and is susceptible to a dichotomizing value judgment being applied to one or the other poles of the binary pair.

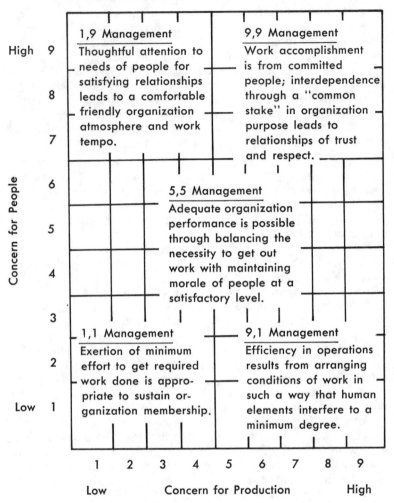

Chart 21. The Managerial Grid

All the other "boxes" formed by the intersection of columns and rows can also be filled with the types of individuals thus indicated or with the actual names of people representing these characteristics on the working staff. A person who is less than nine-nine in any way can theoretically be trained toward a nine-nine capability (see chart 21).

Another valuable matrix is that formed by the axes of time

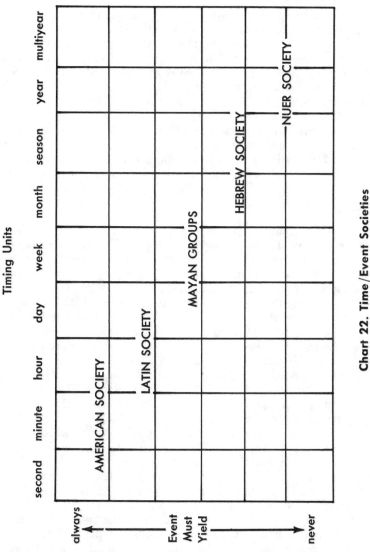

Chart 22. Time/Event Societies

and event. The various time units of second, minute, hour, day, week, month, season, year, and multiyear, are placed along one axis, and the event in maximum focus scaled to minimum focus is placed along the second axis. At the intersection of columns and rows, it is possible to place the names of societies that trend toward the dominance of time structuring over the event itself or toward the dominance of the event over the time structuring (see chart 22). For example, American society is so oriented toward the smaller time units of second, minute, and hour that the event, whether it is completed or not, must yield to the timed unit. When the time is up, the event is over. Where the season dominates the timing within the society, the event has a large enough time arena to complete itself.

A final way of handling the categories of thought termed "basic values" is through the use of *wholes* or *unities*. With wholes it doesn't matter where someone falls in relation to another. It is simply important that a category exists and that there is a way of developing the whole by means of concentric circles or "smear."

PROFILING

A composite of a series of evaluations derived from the basic values will give an *individual* or *corporate* profile. An individual can trend toward time orientation in his economic experience and toward event in his social experience; toward crisis when dealing with money matters and religious concerns, but noncrisis when it comes to educating his children; toward dichotomizing in every aspect of life where he is constantly distinguishing one thing from another, and to top it all off, where vulnerability is a weakness restraining him from ever referring personally to his personal existence, and the expression of these values.

Such an individual profile is useful, first, in understanding what makes this person "tick"; second, in planning any program of directed activity or involvement for him, and third, in developing a program of change.

A corporate profile can follow from the sum total of all of the individual members' profiles. This profile is generalized to a degree, but its value lies in the range of variation of the members' values within the corporate body. In a less complex society there is greater likelihood of homogeneity; i.e., more members would fall at certain points along the various continua of the profile or at some intersection of columns and rows in a matrix. In a highly complex society, such as that of the United States, there is greater likelihood that one would discover a scattering of points along the continua.

The profile approach is useful when developing educational programs for students living in the contemporary period.[5] A

5. See M. Mayers, L. Richards, and R. Webber, *Reshaping Evangelical Higher Education* (Grand Rapids: Zondervan Publishing House, 1972) for application of basic values to contemporary education.

Elements of a learning experience	Basic Values Time Dichotomy Crisis	Basic Values Event Holism Noncrisis
The classroom	Set. Four walls with blackboards, bulletin boards and windows. Plus "field trips."	Vary. In essence, one protracted field trip. World tours, city as classroom, professional quarter off-campus.
Assignments	Set units. Timed assignments, assigned in keeping with timed units of study.	Grow out of discussion, project, world concerns. Need for continual re-evaluation.
Class preparation	Units prepared beforehand and executed as planned. Lecture primary.	Total grasp needed at any moment. Material introduced where called for in class development.
Individual research	Careful detailed supervision. Little change from original plan.	General guidelines set. Plan changed as project develops.
Papers and projects	Assigned readings. Set length of paper.	General reading list; selection by cooperation of instructor and student. No set length.
Examinations	Primary basis for evaluation. Individual, objective, time limit.	One of many bases for evaluation. Individual or group, objective or essay, no time limit.
Role of professor	Carries full responsibility for learning experience. Has impersonal contact with students. Questions are of information type, not contradictory type.	Shares learning experience responsibility equally with student. Has personal contact with student. Questions are of all types and one expected answer is "I don't know; you find out."
Completion of course	At a set time, with all the material of the course completed.	Course ends only after demonstrated proficiency. The course is the beginning of learning.

Chart 23. Elements of a Learning Experience

student with profile A trending toward time, dichotomism, and crisis needs one kind of approach to education — one that is fact-oriented, where these facts can be tested by objective examination, and one that focuses on the teacher as authority (see chart 23). A student that trends toward event orientation and is more holistic and noncrisis learns best by experiencing personally the whole of that which he is learning. This has led to the "schools-without-walls" concept and the "tour-the-world" educational opportunities.

A society that is linear will develop a traffic pattern that is ordered in terms of lanes and assignment of lanes to distinct kinds of traffic; e.g., "Slow vehicles keep right." Filipino society is nonlinear and lanes are therefore somewhat meaningless as can be seen when a street gets crowded and people move freely into lanes of the opposite direction, onto the shoulders, and even onto the walks in an effort to pass. Gigantic traffic snarls ensue that take hours, at times, to disentangle. This would be quite serious for timed, goal-oriented people, but for the Filipino who reaches goals by event scheduling rather than time scheduling, there is a certain "fatalism" that attends his attempts to get free and on his way. He tends to wait patiently for things to straighten out.

In a time, linear, and dichotomistic society, corporate prayer usually takes place at regularly scheduled prayer meetings. The members of such a society present their lists of prayer requests and the items are prayed for, one by one, by those in attendance. In his individual praying also, the member of such a society tends to wait for specific times of prayer. Prayer in an event, nonlinear, and holistic society tends to be something more "spontaneous," happening whenever there is an impulse of a need to pray. A prayer could last a few seconds or indefinitely. "Pray without ceasing" then becomes a life-style where the channel of communication is never closed and prayer flows continually from the life even as all other expressions do. And this attitude towards prayer expresses itself also in communal prayer. It is interesting to read the book of Acts with the different value profiles in mind. It would appear that prayer in Acts grew from a society that was more event-oriented than timed, somewhat nonlinear and certainly holistic. Over ninety percent of the praying in the book of Acts followed an experience shared by the believers following which they were literally impulsed to pray. At times the praying was brief, and at times quite extensive as in the first chapter where an extensive (three-day) prayer session was held.

WORKING WITH THE THAI CASE STUDY

A taxonomy such as that of basic values gives one perspective in dealing with a case as emotionally charged as that of Phairote. Without such a tool, it is easy to be ethnocentric, thinking, *My way is right,* and to have each party take the matter personally, with each intrusion in the case becoming a personal affront. There is no need for such highly charged emotional response. Further, there is no need for making judgments about behavior until one has worked through the conflict of culture and seen the specifics of motivation and intent. When this has been done, there will be ample time to work out the moral problems involved and come to a conclusion of rightness and wrongness in the matter.

Since the Thai trend toward considering vulnerability a weakness, any direct confrontation would be in very bad taste. The North American is defensive when his personal integrity is called into question but is very open and direct in seeking to determine wrongness of social and public behavior. The sexual realm is something that is liable to this openness, since fornication and adultery in the experience of a member of a group is seen as reflecting on the group. The Thai is vulnerable in both personal integrity and social behavior, since the one brings reflection on the other. The direct intrusion into the Phairote case left the participants with no other recourse but to withdraw, since they had been shown publicly to be weak.

In North American society, marriage occurs at the time of the wedding — not at the time of engagement. Each step leading to marriage is part of a timed sequence which is ultimately fulfilled at the wedding. At this point in time, intercourse may take place, since the couple is married. They are neither fornicating nor adulterous if their physical contact is in keeping with the expectations of the timed sequence occasion we call "marriage."

The Thai has a different timed sequence in which marriage is completed at the time of engagement rather than at the wedding. The ancient Jews had this practice, as do numerous contemporary societies. Engagement to them is as binding as the wedding is to the North American. They are neither fornicating nor adulterous when their physical relations are carried out in keeping with *their* timed-sequence expectations.

Finally, the North American tends to be more crisis-oriented than the Thai, seeing one solution to a problem, rather than considering natural solutions, and seeing one way to resolve an issue, i.e., by confrontation, rather than considering alternate ways of reducing conflict. The North American, choosing his one way, offends, not realizing his goals could be met by alternate routes without being so highly offensive to those with whom he deals.

GENERATING SOCIETY

Another of the usages of the basic values is in generating society, or parts of society. The process is intricate but the results leave the analyst free to range widely through society and societies much as the linguist can range freely through language and languages.[6] The generation of societies is part of the larger development in anthropology called ethnoscience.[7] Ethnoscience seeks to apply the principles found useful in linguistic analysis to the wider considerations of culture. In effect, the generation of societies grows out of the application of generative linguistics to the whole of culture.[8]

Generating Societies Games in the Behavioral Sciences
(based on some theoretical principles developing with the behavioral sciences)

1. Ethnoscience — transformational grammar in linguistics and systems in communication theory

6. For the generative approach, consult:
N. Chomsky, *Syntactic Structures* (The Hague: Mouton, 1957).
E. Wagel, P. Suppes, and A. Tarski, eds., *Logic, Methodology, and Philosophy of Science* (Palo Alto, California: Stanford University Press, 1962), pp. 528-550.
J. A. Foder and J. J. Katz, *The Structure of Language* (Englewood Cliffs, New Jersey: Prentice-Hall, 1964).
7. For the application of ethnoscience, see Claude Levi-Strauss, *Structural Anthropology* (Garden City, New York: Doubleday, 1967).
8. Sociology: Leonard Broom and Philip Selznick, *Principles of Sociology*, 4th ed. (New York: Harper and Row, 1970).
Bruce J. Biddle and Edwin J. Thomas, eds., *Role Theory: Concepts and Research* (New York: John Wiley and Sons, 1966).
Charles H. Cooley, *Social Organization* (New York: Scribner's, 1909).
Edward T. Hall, *The Silent Language* (New York: Doubleday, 1959).
George C. Homans, *Social Behavior: Its Elementary Forms* (New York: Harcourt, Brace and World, 1961); *The Human Group* (New York: Harcourt, Brace and World, 1950).
Robert K. Merton, *Social Theory and Social Structure* (Glencoe, Illinois: The Free Press, 1956).
Robert A. Nisbet, *The Social Bond* (New York: Alfred A. Knopf, 1970).
Jean Piaget, *Language and Thought of the Child* (New York: Harcourt, Brace and World, 1926).
Talcott Parsons, *The Social System* (Glencoe, Illinois: The Free Press, 1951).
H. H. Turney-High, *Man and System: Foundations for the Study of Human Relations* (New York: Appleton-Century-Crofts, 1968).

2. Process:

Analyze the internal dynamics of a society.

Reduce this to a core system operating.

Test the operations with experiments.

Examine the system for internal consistencies and inconsistencies.

Evaluate the system for evidence of the various control mechanisms that keep the system operating effectively.

Become aware of the malfunctions within the system or abuses of the system that reduce its effectiveness.

Once the system is reduced to its minimum components, take these and generate all the rules, and only the rules, needed to operate the system.

Check the rules over against the original analysis of the system.

Correct the original analysis.

Become aware of malfunctions and abuses. The rules appearing to be part of the systems operation may be there only to correct the system also, where part is made to be the whole or abuse is made to be the whole system.

Observe these areas in comparing the logical construct with the more thorough analysis to see if there are ways that the control mechanism can be reinforced, corrected, or adjusted, or if the system needs modifications, or if there needs to be attention paid to the abuse — so that the system can function effectively again.

3. Yield of this type of approach:

It helps a society to analyze systems, evaluate existing rules, determine the extent of slavery or freedom, generate a "new" society, and train "doctors" of sociology through computer and game simulation.

Case 1

In building a societal system from three basic core value-motivations:

1. time (control mechanism),
2. production,
3. comfort,

the following rules are derived:

1. Everyone must work.
2. Everyone must begin work on time.

3. All must work a certain number of hours per week.
4. No one may undo the work another is doing or has done.
5. Everyone must achieve maximum production within a time period or schedule.
6. They must have this schedule, and they must produce.
7. There must be a basic unit, a measure of time, for all members of the society.
8. This basic unit must be stated.
9. Vocabulary must be limited to absolutes. There must be basic units of language with a 1:1 correlation of form and meaning for a minimum waste of time.
10. There will be no talking while working, except for production talk.
11. There should be centralized, dictatorial government to control the use of time.
12. Everything must be done in the shortest time possible.
13. Workers should produce only what can be produced rapidly (basics and/or variety items).

Now, compare this to a business or industrial system within American society.

The "child-labor laws" were designed to guard the members of the larger society from the extremes of efficiency of such a value-based subculture.

Case 2

In generating worship experience for this profile:

1. event oriented,
2. holistic,
3. noncrisis,

we have the following:

The experience of worship will take place in an outdoor setting. The participants will be asked to arrive around dawn, to see the sunrise over a distant mountain in the background. The event will be focused on God as the Creator; the splendor of the world awaking before these worshipers will allow them to see some of the magnitude of His power and glory. Hymns of praise will be suggested as they watch the sunrise. The participants will be asked to share God's revelation by reading from Scripture regarding the glories of God in His creation. The persons gathered will be given a choice of (1) meeting together for prayer in small groups, (2) going out in the woods alone for meditation, (3) or joining others in composing a psalm to be sung in praise of God.[9]

---

9. Acknowledgments to Lynda Ray for the worship experience.

SUMMARY

Underlying all activities of the group as well as the group structure itself is a web of intersecting and interrelating values. Values refer to that which a society and each member of a society values or holds as important as compared to something else. Were we to define all the values in American society, large volumes would be needed to explain each value, the place that each value has in relationship to another, the individual expressions and arrangements of the value, and the corporate expressions as well.

To cut incisively into the heart of the value system, certain basic values are useful in providing clues to the larger pattern of values that motivate any member or corporate body to action. These basic values are "ideal types" as they stand in individual considerations, continua, matrices, and wholes or unity. Such profiles are useful when studying either a society, any group within that society, or any individual member of that society. The basic values indicate relationship of one person or group to another.

Besides profiling for understanding individual or corporate terms, the whole of a society or any part can be generated from a core of basic values. Such an exercise can aid in developing new programs and new concepts and aid in applying and refining those that meet the felt need of the society and its members.

Questions for discussion:
1. Name as many different schemes for working with values that you can.
2. Which one of these appears to be most useful? Is it as useful as the basic values?
3. Distinguish between values and value judgments.
4. Can value judgments ever be objective or nonbiased? When? In what ways?
5. How might the basic values scheme be used in a judgmental way?
6. Why might the basic values model be referred to as a "radar" system (i.e., a system operating to keep two vehicles from colliding)?

Group activities and exercises:
1. Using the basic values model, profile a person or group in keeping with his observed behavior.

2. Using the basic values model, profile a program such as a church service, commencement, play, etc., as based on the behavior expressed within the program.

3. Small group involvement: Let a small group visit an art gallery or display, attend a musical concert, listen to records, become part of an experience such as a "rock" concert or a church service, etc., and then discuss the experience in light of the insights made available through application of the basic values.

4. Generative game: Prepare a dozen 3 x 5 cards with some program named on each (worship service, party, class, etc.) and another set of cards with one basic value on each. Have a student or a team of students select one card from the first set and three cards from the second set (let the order of selection become the rank order of dominance in the exercise) and then design a specific expression of the program consistent with the basic values selected. (Refer to the examples of such programs provided in the text.)

5. Discussion: Have the group members compare and contrast two of Charles Reich's "consciousnesses" or compare the Filipino profile with what they see in their own society. During the discussion period, have the members indicate or hypothesize the differential behavior of one person represented as he would enter the other subculture, e.g., a consciousness II person in consciousness I setting.

6. With a greater or lesser amount of adaptation, additional alternatives to the above may be found in the following sources:

   a. "Status-Interaction Study" from Pfeiffer and Jones.[10] This exercise illustrates status achieved vs. status ascribed.

   b. "The Five-Day Course in Thinking" illustrates the crisis-noncrisis continuum.[11]

   c. "The Managerial Grid" from Pfeiffer and Jones.[12] This exercise illustrates the goal-interaction orientation by placing these perspectives on two axes within a matrix.

---

10. William J. Pfeiffer and John E. Jones, *A Handbook of Structured Experiences for Human Relations Training*, Vol. 2, Experience No. 41 (Iowa City, Iowa: University Associates Press, 1971).
11. Edward De Bono, *The Five-Day Course in Thinking* (New York: Basic Books, Inc., 1967).
12. Pfeiffer and Jones, *Structured Experiences*, Vol. 1, Experience No. 3.

Theory of Natural Groupings
The Norm
Hierarchy
Flow of Truth
The Group — Item Identification
    — Activity
    — Value
Conflict of Norm

12

conflict of norm

DINNER DECISION

Helen's grandparents immigrated to America from continental Europe while their children were young. Since that time the family has lived near a large eastern city with a large group of other former Europeans who share many cultural similarities. Folk dances, food, drink, and dress are among several features of their older culture which survived, at least in part, the trans-Atlantic crossing earlier in the century.

Each person in Helen's community appreciates his heritage of distinctive traits from pre-American culture which has blended with the "American way." But Helen doesn't really feel any different from other American young people. During her childhood she experienced no conflicts between the two ways. She was raised in a Christian family and both she and her parents were eager for her to attend a Christian college. She considered many schools but finally narrowed the choice down to two. This was between a school which maintained a statement of expected standards of conduct concerning abstinence from dancing, drinking, smoking, etc., which a student was required to sign, and a school which left the student's behavior to his own discretion. She decided upon the one with the stipulated standards of conduct and signed the statement, fully intending to keep it.

One weekend in the early fall, she received an invitation to a dinner party which her aunt and uncle were giving. Several relatives and some friends from the "old country" were invited and she excitedly accepted the invitation. She eagerly awaited the day and was glad when it arrived.

The party was entertaining and Helen was enjoying herself. There were several relatives she hadn't seen recently and it was refreshing to hear the native tongue of her parents and ancestors. Cocktails were served, but she refrained from drinking, more from a dislike for the beverages than because of the standards of conduct pledge. In the back of her mind, however, was the wine which would be served with the meal. She had always enjoyed this. Then a handsome young cousin whom she adored asked her to join him in a traditional folk dance. . . .

Conflict is the result of tension that grows within an individual, between individuals, between individuals and groups, and between groups. It stems primarily from a relationship that goes awry. We will not be dealing in this chapter with personality conflict, which is the effect of this relationship breakdown on the person and the personality problems that result from this breakdown. Rather, we will be dealing with conflict resulting from tension within the sociocultural setting.[1] In our case study, tension arose from the contact between a drinking subculture and a pledged-not-to-drink subculture.

Where the individual alone is concerned, conflict involves the gap between what a person really is and all the ideals which he is forced, or seeks, to live up to. When individuals conflict because of underlying tensions, we talk about personality conflict or an inability to get along with others. When an individual conflicts with a group, we suggest that he lacks social graces, has not been effectively socialized, or — in the case of encounter with a distinct society — is in culture shock. When a group conflicts with a group, we say they are at war or in a cold war, in the case of nations; or competing, in the case of subcultures. Each case represents, in some way, the effect of tension within the interpersonal relationship or within the network of interpersonal relations.

CREATIVE TENSION

Tension can be constructive and useful, or it can be de-

---

1. The aspect of conflict as it deals with personality is dealt with in:
Marvin Kaufmann Opler, ed., *Culture and Mental Health* (New York: The Macmillan Company, 1959).
Lewis Coser, *The Functions of Social Conflict* (Glencoe, Illinois: The Free Press, 1956).

structive. Useful tension within the group can be called "creative tension." Malinowski calls this "aggressiveness."[2] Such creative tension has a number of valuable functions.

One function that creative tension fulfills within the group is to help it *achieve authenticity*.[3] Group identity is involved. This can be developed through loyalty mechanisms, through selection of heroes who are important to the group, through the delineation of issues significant to the group, and through the kinds of festival expressions that produce group solidarity. In one sense, Helen experienced creative tension that was helping her define her identity in her new context of life.

One way the group achieves its identity and authenticity is by extending its political control to the full limits of its cultural unity. Even though it was not immediately apparent to the respective thirteen colonies, there was a cultural unity that extended from north to south, and slowly political control extended throughout the cultural entity. On the other hand, social and religious values differed enough from those of the continent and Great Britain that the Revolutionary War allowed the separation of the two cultural entities and the development of separate political control over each.

In the Nigerian situation, a cultural entity known as "Biafra" with a tribal integration named "Ibo" attempted to establish its own political control over the people loyal to it (as well as over some who did not wish to be a part of it). This was a very similar situation to the colonies separating from Great Britain. In the contemporary case, however, Nigeria was able to maintain political control over the Ibos and the revolution was terminated. There was no place for a "George Washington" among the Ibos, nor for the successive heroes of a new struggling nation.

Creative tension is a constructive part of the ongoing *socialization process* within society. Education is effected when men of different classes and statuses train and fight side-by-side during a wartime setting. A different kind of information is conveyed than that in public school. Further, some of the men must be sent to schools of specialization. During the second

2. Bronislaw Malinowski, *Coral Gardens and Their Magic* (London: G. Allen and Unwin, Ltd., 1935).

3. W. G. Sumner, *The Challenge of Facts* (New Haven: Yale University Press, 1914). This is a classical work in sociology. It is quite valuable to the anthropologist, since it develops a field in which social anthropology has developed and also sets up comparative sociology which is of prime interest to the anthropologist dealing with change.

See also by the same author, *The Science of Society* (London: Oxford University Press, 1927); *Folkways* (Boston: Ginn and Co., 1907).

world war, for example, the field of linguistics became recognized as a full-grown, legitimate discipline, due to the challenges of war with a variety of non-English-speaking nations. Members of one society, also, learn about numerous others, either being based in those societies as friends or fighting as enemies. This is not to say that all war is constructive and creative. There are, however, benefits to any nation because of the tension, and these can have a creative impact within the society.

Industrialization or the economic base of any nation is also affected by conflict. The skill of artisans is increased significantly. New developments grow out of the extreme needs of warfare. Such developments are useful not only in the actual struggle itself, but they are ultimately useful to the civilian populace as well. Scientists are still unfolding the multitudinous uses of atomic power, the development of which was accelerated greatly because our nation was at war.

Through the effects of tension, social organization is developed that could prove beneficial to society. This does not imply necessarily the overthrow of the old, but significant changes are made that permit the group to surge ahead in progressive development. Japan is a good example of this. Prior to the second world war, Japan looked back many centuries for its traditions and its place in the world. The emperor ruling Japan was the primary symbol tying all of Japan to its deep-rooted traditions. However, following the war, with the emperor removed from the seat of power, enough changes in the social organization of the society were effected to allow the Japanese people to develop as one of the leading industrial nations of the world.

Along with change, however, comes no guarantee that the result will necessarily be better than before. The Philippine nation is an example of a people who may have lost a great deal because of a shift from a more Spanish type of social organization before the second world war to a more American postwar type. The Spanish authority was rooted in the extended family. The Philippine nation, to pursue national development, was forced to pay attention to the needs of the various families of the Philippines. The postwar American system placed greater power and authority in the hands of individual leaders to the detriment of the families and to the potential detriment of the total populace. The families and national leaders are in continual power struggles that leave the people torn and disorganized.

Tension effects a rude and imperfect selection from among leaders and organizations within society. This selection is made between those defeated and those made great by victory. The Crusades initiated a breaking up of the stagnation of the Dark Ages and an emancipation of the social forces of Europe. In American society we may perhaps never know the full effect of the rise of John L. Lewis to prominence in the labor unions. His more militant approach to union negotiations have not only been with us as prototypes of subsequent patterns of negotiations, but also spelled the virtual death knell of coal mining in the United States.

Sumner talks of a *peace bond*[4] between societies and groups. Tension serves to keep groups together that need to be together and to separate those that need to be separate. In effect, the peace bond keeps together but could not work effectively without the tension that keeps separate. It also determines in what manner groups are to be kept separate and the depth of involvement between those needing to be kept separate or together. Latin American nations have a long history within the contemporary world. Because the Spanish type of government is based primarily in the extended family, the smaller the national unit, the more likelihood there is of each family having its needs met by the government in power. If a number of national units were put together, certainly many families would suffer greater injustice than they do at present.

Nevertheless, Latin American countries need to cooperate with one another for the full development of their economies. No one Latin nation, with the possible exceptions of Brazil and Argentina, can fully develop without some kind of trade relationship with its neighbors. Yet, Latin nations dare not go beyond this cooperative trade arrangement to permit rule by an outside aggressor, for then the structure of the national government or alignment of national governments would be too restricting and could easily produce injustice to many family units as noted above.

Creative tension, therefore, can be said to play a vital role in society. It results in conscious effort to affirm the borders of the group, establish its unique identity, reinforce known rules, and cooperate with compatible groups in further progressive development.

THE MALFUNCTION OF TENSION

The malfunction of tension results when a group attempts to modify or to control another. This becomes then a manifestation of the slavery or injustice model.

---

4. Sumner, *The Challenge of Facts.*

War is classically defined as "an armed contest between two independent political units, by means of organized military force, in the pursuit of a tribal or national policy." Thus, war is the most extreme expression of the malfunction of tension on the national level of society.

Intergroup relations also on other levels of the society may result in a malfunction of tension. It is in these experiences that the members of the society train for their interaction on the national level. However, if interpersonal relations and intergroup relations on the lower levels result in outbreaks, mob action, rebellion, confrontation, resistance, and other violent and forceful practices, then there is little hope that international relations will be handled any differently.

On the local or community level within the society, any family that seeks to modify or control another family creates an undue tension between those families. A family has various means of accomplishing its wish. It can bring religious concepts and sanctions to bear on another family. It can dominate another by sheer personality. If the attempt is simply to modify the family, resistance to the dominant family will become manifest through the one ignoring the other. If the attempt is to control the other, legal means may be brought to bear on the dominant family.

In the expression of the malfunction of tension existing between youth and adult in American society, the youth is likely to contradict his parents in cases of attempts to modify behavior; whereas, in cases of all-out control, there will be more rebellious actions.

Within subcultures of the larger society, whenever there is a malfunction of tension, demonstrations or feuds break out if there is an attempt to modify one group by some other group. If the attempt is made to control the one, then riots and even blood feuds result. Such reactions have been evidenced between Indian and Latin peoples of Spanish America, black and white peoples of North America, and mountaineer clans of eastern United States. This same type of conflict is also observed between members of the same culture or subculture.[5]

Whether the conflict between groups results in one family taking another to court, in rebellion, rioting, feuding, or all-out war, these expressions are behavioral indications of one group *attempting to control some other group* in some way or

---

5. I have described one type of Indian feuding in "Two-Man Feud in the Guatemalan Church," *Practical Anthropology* (July-August, 1966), Vol. 13, pp. 115-125.

other. If one family ignores another, or if there is the contradiction process existing between parent and child, or demonstration or feuding between subcultures within society, or the expression of nationalism by some nation, there is reason to believe that one person or group is attempting to *modify the other.*

On the national and international levels of society, nations express nationalism whenever they sense an attempt at modification of their lives. This is the reaction that many Protestant and Catholic missionaries sense in certain countries of the world where they have worked. This is also the result in many programs of colonization.

Any malfunction of tension on any level within the society calls for the use of weapons in keeping with the level and with the type of malfunction, i.e., modification or control. On the family level, the door lock becomes a very effective defense weapon if a neighbor continually enters unannounced and seeks to influence the choice of furniture, fabrics, wall decorations, or paint color within the house. Social ostracism is another weapon in a neighborhood where the people are somewhat close and do many things together.

The surliness of a youth is a weapon he uses to defend himself against an overaggressive parent who is forever trying to make him "shape up." The "mock" is also a useful weapon turned against adults. The mock can be a devastating weapon when used selfishly, and a highly rewarding one when used to protect the young person from unreasonable control by an adult. In a noted Christian college, during a period of adult reaction against popular music — a reaction that caused jazz and rock music to be restricted in performance — student organists sometimes wove a jazz theme into the postlude following the chapel service. The "judgment" is the kind of weapon used by many adults to decide whether someone is "their kind" or not. The judgment can be used to discern between a good and a bad person, or it can be used to cut down someone who does not agree.

Demonstrations, petitions, breaking of laws, sit-ins, and other like weapons are utilized by members of different subcultures within a larger society to protect the group from injustice.

Finally, on the national level of society, guns and rocketry are used.

Two serious questions arise out of a discussion of weaponry in a war arising from the malfunction of tension. These are simply "What effect do these weapons have on the 'enemy'?" and "Is the effect of one worse than the effect of another?" The guns and rocketry of a nation kill the body, but the other

the person

Chart 24. The Person in a Tension Situation

weapons tend to kill the spirit. In other words, even though the one takes life, is not the effect of a "spirit killer" more serious to the person and his society in the long run? The breaking of fellowship and of communication between people produces alienation. This in effect is living death.

Taken one step further: "Don't be afraid of those who can kill only your bodies — but cannot touch your souls! Fear only God who can destroy both soul and body in hell." "There will always be temptations to sin . . . but woe to the man who does the tempting. If he were thrown into the sea with a huge rock tied to his neck, he would be far better off than facing the punishment in store for those who harm these little children's souls."[6]

TENSION AND THE INDIVIDUAL

The individual's central conflict involves the gap between the real person and the ideal that is held up, or that he holds up to himself. Discrepancies between the real and culturally defined ideals produce emotional unrest, a state of living in tension.[7] (See chart 24.)

An attitude or approach of rejection becomes extremely dangerous when it builds into a pattern of rejection. When someone rejects someone or something, that other person or thing will in turn reject him. Thus, when a person rejects what he really is (i.e., the real), the real rejects him. When a person strives to attain his ideal, and finds it elusive, he will get rejection feedback and will likely discard the ideal. What results is a *four-way flow of rejection* in which each stage in the rejection process reinforces each other stage and thrust of rejection which in turn produces a counterthrust (chart 25).

6. Matthew 10:28; Luke 17:1, 2.
7. For a fuller discussion of the results of tension in an individual's personal life, consult the materials of psychology, psychotherapy and social psychology.

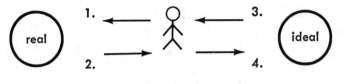

the person

1. The person rejects the real in striving for the ideal.
2. The real rejects in return.
3. The ideal is impossible of attainment.
4. The person rejects the ideal.

Chart 25. A Four-Way Flow of Rejection

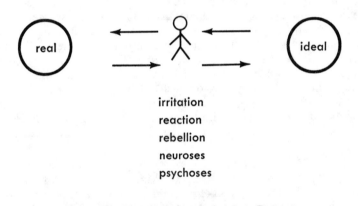

irritation
reaction
rebellion
neuroses
psychoses

Chart 26. Results of a Rejection Pattern

Within conflict situations among individuals and groups, the first step of rejection is almost impossible to overcome, for it yields a responding reaction of rejection. Once this pattern of rejection begins to build, a number of things begin to happen within the person. Irritation grows, ushering in further irritations. Eventually, given sufficient stimulus, there can be rebellion or reaction or neuroses of some kind or even psychoses. Such resistance to the ideal or to the other person within the rejection pattern can result in psychological or sociological anomy, where a reduction of standards and disintegration of life-way ensue. In time, the person will feel the tension building and seek to free himself from the burden of conflict (chart 26).

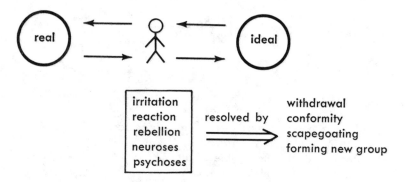

Chart 27. Resolution of Conflict

People will utilize a series of characteristic ways of breaking or resolving such conflict (chart 27). Some of these ways are therapeutic; others only increase or reinforce the tension. *Escape* or *withdrawal* is one of the immediate responses to the burden of tension. Suicide is the ultimate in escape. There are other means that one may use: entertainment, such as television, films, etc.; speed, either on the highway or in drugs; developing a friendship with a member of the opposite sex; eating or drinking, and not only the drinking of alcoholic beverages; losing oneself in a work responsibility; masturbation or other sexual deviance; and many others.

Conformity is a second way of getting out from under the burden of tension. There are two kinds of conformity: conformity for conformity's sake and adaptation to another's lifeway. The latter results in mutual respect and self-respect. The former undermines self-respect and thus undermines also the trust base in a relationship. Conformity for conformity's sake is the way a person modifies his behavior just to get along, just to be seen as a "good guy," just to "pull something off," to gain something selfishly from the relationship.

A third means of gaining release from the burden of conflict is by *seeking a scapegoat*. This lets the person place the blame for his conflict on another person or another thing, and thus perceive himself free of the conflict.

A fourth way is by *forming a new group*, i.e., a new identity group that is established around the ingredients of the conflict. This new group will be perceived as supporting and encouraging the individual in conflict and thus will reduce the strain of the conflict. Too frequently, however, the formation of another group reinforces other conflicts or introduces new ones.

Case 1: Forming a new group

The Indian peoples of Central America, descendants of the ancient Maya civilization, have lived under the pressure of forced conformity to a Spanish life-way. They have been impressed constantly with the fact that the Spanish way is the right way and that the Indian way must be abandoned and will be abandoned. Thus, for example, the Pocom cannot really be Pocom but are forced to be something that they are not. This naturally pushes them into the conflict model.

Many of the Pocom, along with others of the Central American Indian peoples, have chosen or have drifted into the alternative of the formation of a new group in resolving their conflict. These have even been given a name, *revestido,* or "change-of-dress people." They reject their Indianness and their Indianness in turn rejects them. Yet, at the same time, they can never become Spanish background people because of their appearance and because the Spanish-derived stratification system places the Indian at the bottom of the status hierarchy. Since there is very little social mobility permitted in the system, the Indian takes no less than three generations to move anywhere in the social hierarchy, and usually longer. Thus, with every step into Spanishness, the Indian is repulsed and feels the rejection and in turn rejects. This leaves the Indian neither Spanish nor Indian. His dress so reflects his being neither the one nor the other, that the name of "change of dress" has been that which has begun to characterize him and give him identity. The way of dressing is a cross between Spanish or more Western type dress and Indian "costume"; e.g., such a *revestido* might wear western-type work pants and shirt but no shoes.

The new group does much to help the person establish a new identity, but it does little to resolve the actual conflict. In fact, it introduces a new conflict involving getting established in those parts of the total life-way that can absorb such a "misfit."

Case 2: Conformity for conformity's sake

The missionary's child returning from the country of his parent's ministry to the North American society steps into a tremendously reinforced setting of conflict (chart 28). In the country in which he grew up, he knew adult American society, since he associated with his parents and their peers primarily. The

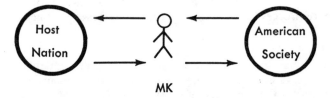

MK

1. The missionary's "kid" (MK) must leave his host nation and in essence "reject" it.
2. The host nation "rejects" the missionary's youngster, since they have nothing further to do with him.
3. The American culture which he enters is in reality youth culture rather than adult culture, and being less familiar with this, he is rejected by its members.
4. He in turn rejects members of American youth culture as "snobs."

Chart 28. An Example of the Four-Way Flow of Rejection

major youth culture of which he would become a part would likely be more of the host nation than his own (this would be true to a lesser degree if he attended a school established especially for missionaries' children). When he enters the United States, he enters American youth culture, and since he is likely not living with his parents during this period, his contact with American adult culture is minimal. Also, he has no further contact with the youth culture of his host nation.

An example of the reinforcement of conflicts arising from an MK's leaving Latin America to return "home" involves the flirtation pattern of each society. In Latin America, a Latin boy can be more aggressively flirtatious toward members of the opposite sex than can the American boy. The MK learns the flirtation pattern of the Latin, and without thinking, applies it in his approach to North American young ladies. They react to him as being too bold and aggressive, and it "turns them off." The MK is looked upon as a bit queer or odd and is refused dates and generally has a tough time with his social life. When the MK is a young woman returning to the States, the problem is compounded. The more aggressive flirtation she has learned through her contacts in Latin America has had no adverse effect when dealing with Latin fellows, for flirtation is just that and nothing more. When she returns to the States, she is seen by the North American men as an "easy mark" and can be taken advantage of.

The typical MK does not think of himself as different from his North American peers, and when the possibility of difference is raised in his mind, he tends to shut it out. In doing this, he goes along with everything he finds, merging into the total picture. As he does this, however, some of the things he feels pressured to do run counter either overtly or covertly with his established principles. Conforming for conformity's sake then tends to undermine his self-respect.

The formation of a new group possibility does not help the MK out as it did for the Central American Indian. Few MK's from the same host country wind up in the United States in the same place. Therefore, even though in general they have something in common with other MK's from other host countries, specific experiences differ greatly and they find when it comes to these specifics, they have little in common.

Case 3: Withdrawal

American youth are well-practiced in utilizing withdrawal to free them from conflict. They begin in the home, where they have their "place" and their "possessions." When there is something unpleasant to face, it is easier for them to go to their room and close the door and shut out the unpleasantness. This is further trained into them in the church where they attend Sunday school and then are encouraged to go to church, but they are not really mature enough to appreciate the adult type of service. They have their Sunday school papers, however, and from the first moment of unpleasantness due to lack of understanding, they can turn to the papers. As they grow older, more means of withdrawal are made available to them, including the automobile, drugs (frequently used regularly by their parents), eating, sleeping, and many more. Many parents are willing to make all kinds of excuses for their children to get them out of difficult spots. Even though withdrawal may be a very necessary route of escape due to the seriousness of the conflict, youth practice withdrawal as the first means of dealing with conflict, and their maturity is slowed by the process.

Case 4: Scapegoat

The classic example of scapegoating is found in the early chapters of the Bible. Adam blamed Eve for tempting him with the fruit: "It was the woman you gave me...." Eve in turn blamed the serpent: "The serpent tricked me." A society based on the value of vulnerability as a weakness, in which the members seek to avoid being wrong or in error, people will readily practice scapegoating. The Latins even build this scapegoating practice into their language when they blame the thing itself for getting lost rather than explaining that they lost the thing; e.g., *se perdió*, "it lost itself," as against the English, "I lost my pencil."

In reference to the opening case study, Helen is in an excellent position to work through her problem. It is in early stages of development and not reinforced, as yet, by other conflicts. She can accept herself *as she is*, i.e., a young person, pledged to a school culture where the drinking of alcoholic beverages and dancing are "frowned" upon, yet one who likes wine and dancing. Further, she can accept a setting and any person in the setting as he is, i.e., enjoying alcoholic beverages and dancing, with no external restriction on either. At this point she can begin seeking out and/or making use of cultural cues that leave her a valid autonomous person in a setting of potential cultural conflict. One such cue is "no thank you," a fully acceptable cue that leaves her principles intact and leaves her in good graces with her hostess. Another is "sip but don't drink." Another is "I've been bothered lately by alcoholic beverages." Whatever cue she utilizes, that is effective in leaving her as a person intact and permits an openness, i.e., building trust with those about her, has been a proper as well as useful cue. She can build on this opportunity for both further identity and further strength as a person.

However, if Helen proceeds to participate in wine drinking and dancing, she may find a series of conflicts reinforcing her original conflict. She can question herself as a person of integrity; she can question the school that "put her in such a bind," i.e., the scapegoating route; she can form a counterculture that turns against the school and its "pledge"; she can become more and more uncomfortable in the presence of her drinking and dancing friends, thus finding the association and the experience unpleasant.

A third route is available to her. She can "experiment" with the amount of participation in each cultural setting that leaves her intact as a person with no sense of guilt. Having achieved such balance, she will then need to moderate her life in such a way that one part brings no reflection on any other part. For this she must remain completely open to setting aside any aspect of any part of her total life that produces such an adverse effect.

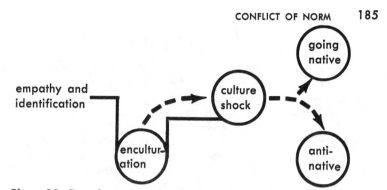

Chart 29. Development of Culture Shock and Reactions to It

CULTURE SHOCK

Kalervo Oberg states that culture shock is

> precipitated by the anxiety that results from losing all our familiar signs and symbols of social intercourse. These signs or cues include the thousand and one ways in which we orient ourselves to the situations of daily life: when to shake hands and what to say when we meet people, when and how to give tips, how to give orders to servants, how to make purchases, when to accept and when to refuse invitations, when to take statements seriously and when not. . . . These cues which may be words, gestures, facial expressions, customs or norms are acquired by all of us in the course of growing up and are as much a part of our culture as the language we speak or the beliefs we accept.[8]

William A. Smalley says that culture shock has been described "as that emotional disturbance which results from adjustments to new cultural environment."[9]

The person in culture shock takes flight in one of two directions: either he clings blindly or immovably to his original ways or he blindly and indiscriminately renounces his former ways and values in favor of the ways and values that are responsible for the culture shock to which he is falling prey (chart 29).

Those who cling to their original ways and values become more and more aggressively antinative, while those caught in the second current "go native."

An antinativist tends more and more to pull himself back into his shell of culturally acquired beliefs, attitudes, and behavior.

8. From Kalervo Oberg, "Culture Shock: Adjustment to New Cultural Environments," *Practical Anthropology.* Vol. 7, No. 4 (1960), p. 177.
9. William Smalley, "Culture Shock, Language Shock, and the Shock of Self-Discovery," *Practical Anthropology.* Vol. 10, No. 2 (1963), p. 49.

Thus, in his view, the local people must become like him rather than he become like them.[10]

Oberg gives two phases (chart 30) to the reactions of the antinativist — frustration, and anxiety. First, he rejects and then he regresses. He rejects the environment which causes the discomfort. Then regression follows with the home environment suddenly assuming a tremendous importance.[11]

Going native, on the other hand, is a neurotic longing for security and an exaggerated hunger for belonging. This unbalanced craving for acceptance drives the unwary individual to approve and to accept as his own, indiscriminately and blindly, any and all local ways and values.

Going native differs from identification in the following ways.[12]

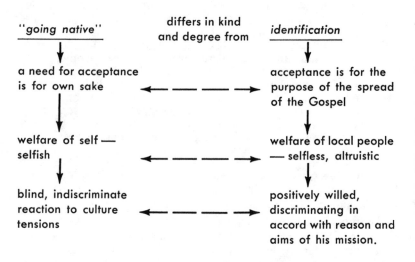

Chart 30. "Going Native" Versus Identification

SYMPTOMS OF CULTURE SHOCK

Rejection of the host country (antinative): Rejection is turned outward toward the host country and its people through endless complaining and faultfinding. Nothing seems to be going right and all reactions are tinged with bitterness. Rejection of the

10. Louis J. Luzbetak, *The Church and Cultures* (Techny, Illinois: Divine Word Publications, 1963), pp. 96-98.
11. Oberg, "Culture Shock," p. 177.
12. Luzbetak, *The Church and Cultures,* pp. 97-100.

host country leads to the development of a protective personal isolationism.

Rejection directed against the home country (going native): The complaint and criticism may be directed against the home country. They live a life of imitation and emotional dependence on their host country.

Rejection directed in a particular way against the mission board, the field executive committee, and the colleagues who put the newcomer in this intolerable situation. Bitter feelings about real or imagined injustice begin to arise. Field policies are bitterly attacked. Personal failures are blamed on a lack of proper orientation — on the fact that nobody had protected him from this suffering.

> If the person suffering from culture shock feels a sense of identification with the host country, he may lash out bitterly against the mission and his colleagues when he sees a lack of such identification in them. He projects the hostility arising out of culture shock against the symbols of authority over him.
>
> Rejection of the mission board and of missionary colleagues is often related to the shock which comes very forcibly to many missionaries when they find that with the development of 'indigenized' churches no new role for the foreign missionary has yet been established. He doesn't know what he is supposed to do, or what he does does not fit his image of himself or his understanding of his calling. This can be a bitter and frustrating experience, indeed.

Rejection turned inward against self: The person may feel he is a complete failure, that he had no business coming overseas in the first place, that he cannot possibly make good.

> He feels that all the money spent on him — his training, his outfit, and his transportation — has been wasted. He blames himself for every mistake and feels utterly defeated when he is not an instantaneous success in everything that he tries. His problem may be compounded by the fact that he feels guilty about his feelings of rejection and hostility in any direction.[13]

Rejection may even be focused on God: It was God who called him into missionary work and sent him to this place. Consequently, God is to blame for making such a terrible mistake.

Obsessiveness is the other symptom of culture shock. An excessive concern over germs and illness may be seen in the com-

---

13. William Smalley, "Culture Shock, Language Shock," p. 51.

pulsive handwasher or the person's refusal to eat food for fear of the germs he might ingest.

STAGES OF CULTURE SHOCK

Oberg discusses four stages through which an individual may go. The first stage is that of *fascination,* where the newcomer has no real contact with the country into which he has moved because friends or colleagues stand as buffers between him and the problems. He can communicate through his protective buffers.

The second stage is characterized by a *hostile and aggressive attitude towards the host country.* This hostility evidently grows out of the genuine difficulty which the individual experiences in the process of adjustment. There is maid trouble, school trouble, transportation trouble, shopping trouble, to mention only a few sources of irritation. This is the point where adjustment can go in either of two directions pointed out at the beginning of this section. If one can overcome this crisis and develop a sense of humor (the third stage), he is able to develop a healthy attitude and adjustment to his new environment. If not, he should leave before he reaches the stage of a nervous breakdown!

The third stage is the ability to develop a *sense of humor.* Instead of criticizing, one begins to joke about the people and even crack jokes about his or her own difficulties. He or she is now on the way to recovery. And there is also the person who is worse off than himself whom he can help, and this, in turn, gives him confidence in his ability to speak and get around.

The fourth stage denotes *adjustment* as complete as it can be. The individual accepts the customs of the country as just another way of living. He operates within the new milieu without a feeling of anxiety, although there are moments of strain. Only with a complete grasp of all the cues of social intercourse will this strain disappear. The individual will understand what the national is saying, but he is not always sure what the national means. With a complete adjustment, he not only accepts the foods, drinks, habits, and customs, but actually begins to enjoy them. When he leaves on furlough, he takes things back with him, and if he leaves for good, he generally misses the country and the people to whom he has become accustomed.[14]

Smalley adds an additional stage that is often forgotten by the secular world: the dimension of self-discovery, the frank facing of utter defeat. With the facing of failure, self-discovery can assist the individual to face reality. One can come to the

14. Oberg, "Culture Shock," pp. 178, 179.

determination to do one's best in spite of the difficulties, to study hard, to learn well, to refuse to give in to the symptoms of culture shock but to conquer them by developing a degree of bilingualism and biculturalism as fast as possible, even if the pace is slower than one would like.

A time of self-discovery is a time when the individual faces rationally and realistically what frustrations and problems he is going to encounter and learns how to deal with these situations whether they be learning the language, loneliness, uncertainty regarding the future, nationalism, or new physical, social, or ideational differences of his new culture. These are several areas where frustrations can easily lead to discouragement and utter defeat.

THE FRUSTRATION MODEL

When the conflict model is carried to an extreme of hopelessness, we have the frustration model. Within the conflict model, one can at least see a way out, or he can move in some way to reduce the effect of the conflict. He can withdraw, if not permanently, at least temporarily. He can form a new group which might ultimately be so therapeutic as to reduce the effect of conflict to a comfortable level. The frustration model applies when there is no conceivable hope of resolution. This appeared to be the model operating during the French Revolution where the intensity of the conflict within the person and within the subculture built up to such an extent that the French citizen saw no hope and finally lost all sense of the rational and logical. Such a model also operates within a church conflict, for example, when a group or a board seeks change and the pastor poses as the divine representative of God who is not to be opposed.

WORKING WITH CONFLICT

The mistake made in working with conflict is to attempt to eliminate it altogether, or, in doing the wrong things, to resolve it, to wind up reinforcing it. Neither of these alternatives is necessary. Tension can be creative within society and can help society accomplish its goals, for this accomplishment grows out of healthy interaction in working with people. When it malfunctions, however, it adds to the deterioration of the group and reinforces the conflict. Thus the task of the agent of change is to correctly observe and correct the malfunction of tension.

The place to begin is in correctly observing the response of irritation. Irritation is generally the first sign of crosscultural conflict whether within an individual or between individuals and groups. Verbal and nonverbal indicators of irritation can be read by the wise counselor who can take immediate steps to resolve the source of irritation. A missionary must constantly watch for this irritation in his contact with members of his host society. Being aware of his own irritation can help him focus on cultural difference and set up the learning process that he needs in adapting effectively to the new. Being aware of the irritation felt by members of the host nation can guide the missionary in effectively presenting the Gospel in such a way that cultural impositions are avoided. Unfortunately, so many missionaries are in culture shock during the period when they are needing to be aware of such irritation that the irritations develop into more serious types of reactions to their ministry. Such irritations caused by crosscultural contact are *frequently misinterpreted as spiritual conflict and valuable clues to effective presentation of the Gospel are lost.*

Nationalism and nationalistic movements in host nations are signs of conflict. When members of the host nation feel the effect of the narrow ethnocentrism of the guests, they resist and reinforce the boundaries of their own society. The first eight chapters of Romans share with us the way Paul dealt with conflict effectively and can become a model for the missionary in dealing with nationalism and other conflict problems in the mission field.

SUMMARY

Whenever there is culture contact or the contact of subdivisions within the larger culture, there is a potential for conflict. Such conflict is based on a flow of rejection that encompasses the association of the members of the diverse cultures.

Conflict can have numerous sources: the individual may be caught between an ideal held out to him and what he really is; an individual may be caught in conflict between himself and another individual or a group; a group may be in conflict with another group. Each of these expressions of conflict may have shared similarities, but each conflict develops in a slightly different way.

The individual in conflict between the real and the ideal finds irritation and reaction developing. In an effort to get out from under this burden, he seeks means of escape, or he will tend to conform for conformity's sake, or he will find a scapegoat or form a new group. Each of these means, when chosen carefully, may provide him with release. The danger of such outlets from conflict is that they may reinforce the conflict or add unwanted dimensions to the conflict. The support model is a healthy means of easing conflict (see chapter 17).

The individual in conflict with a group will find culture shock developing. A group in conflict with a group will find some expression of war developing.

Frustration develops when there is conflict, yet no means of resolving that conflict.

Questions for discussion:

1. What things have irritated you over the past twenty-four hours?
   a. List them.
   b. Rank them in importance to you.
   c. Determine which could be caused by cultural differences in *groupings* or in *activities* or in values.
2. In what ways are you thrown into conflict by the larger society?
3. In what ways do you put those about you into conflict?
4. What behavioral signs of conflict do you see expressed about you?
5. How might a well-meaning missionary throw a member of his host society into conflict?
6. In what situations might it be possible that Christianity must give first priority to resolving social conflict created by the missionaries rather than introducing Jesus Christ?

Group activities and exercises:

1. Role play: Select some situation involving family, class, or church and assign roles accordingly, e.g., father, mother, and child in a family setting. Assign two or three basic values, ranked in terms of dominance, to each of the roles, e.g., father: time, dichotomy; son: event, holism. Role play the family scene as the participants fulfill their assignments.
2. Simulation: Using the exercise entitled "Hidden Agenda" in the Pfeiffer and Jones series, develop a simulation that expresses conflict behavior and its resolution.
3. Panel discussion: Invite a group of missionaries to the group and ask that they share experiences of conflict they have had with members of their host society and with other missionaries. Especially note in the debriefing period their ways of dealing with the conflict.

MODEL 3

THE VALIDITY OF, AND ASSIMILATION INTO, DISTINCT SOCIETIES

The model termed *The Validity of, and Assimilation Into, Distinct Societies* suggests two main thoughts. First, each society is different and worthy of respect. Secondly, there are certain tools necessary to make assimilation into another society natural. Further, the model provides intercultural bridges that enable respect to be granted to the distinct society, along with tools of research which allow one to find and use these bridges. There are three submodels.

1. The form/meaning composite permits the agent of change entering a distinct society or subculture to distinguish between the meaning or significance and its expression.
2. The tools of research applied to each situation permit the agent of change to be aware of difference as well as of the effect of crosscultural contact.
3. The intercultural bridges cause one to start with the meaning and then find the different but proper form in the new society. These bridges will be called the tools of relationship.

The Validity of, and Assimilation Into, Distinct Societies
The Form/Meaning Composite
Tools of Research
Tools of Relationship

13

the form/meaning composite

PRAISE HIM WITH THE DANCE

One of the major forms of communication in Africa is the dance. Africans dance to gain power and to appease the dead, to celebrate, and to mourn. They seem to us to dance for any excuse whatsoever, and if there is no excuse they dance for the fun of it. Last April in the Camerouns I was riding . . . through a village in the evening just as the moon was coming up. We heard drumbeats — and believe me, I know of little else that has the fascination of the intricate, complicated rhythms of African drums on a moonlit night. We stopped and walked over to the open square where young men were tapping out the beat. A few others were beginning to get itchy in their feet. A couple of fellows were trying out a few steps (Africans dance individually, of course, and not in the Western manner of ballroom dancing). We asked what was going on. The bystanders were delighted with our interest and told us that a woman had been buried a year before, the period of mourning was over, and now the family was about to celebrate.

We did not stay to see the celebration because supper was waiting for us at home. But that evening we again heard drums, this time down over the hill from the mission station in the quarters where teachers and students lived. We rushed down, and this time the dance was a game. The fellows were in a circle, dancing and singing, while one in the center acted the fool to make the others

193

laugh. He would then point to someone in the circle who would take his place and try to outdo the previous dancer.

Along with these and many other functions of the dance in Africa is its relation to drama and to other forms of communication. The dance is a major instrument by which Africans transmit values, ideals, emotions, and even history. It is a medium which the African understands. But more than once the African has been rebuffed by the missionary when he has attempted to worship God in dance — or, for that matter, even to tell the Good News in this most natural form of communication.

For example, a foreigner, an important church lady, was visiting the mission and church. Because the visitor was a woman, the African women of the area wanted to put on something very special for her, and so they worked out a dance-drama in which they portrayed the history of their contacts with Christianity. This was to be an expression of their appreciation for the fact that the missionaries had come to them.

They started out by portraying themselves naked — a bunch of leaves in front and another behind as their only clothing. This is the way they often dress in the fields and in out-of-the-way places where they are not likely to be seen by outsiders. Then the missionaries came to their country. There was an elaborate, intricate story unfolding and a quickening in tempo until they ended up by going to church in their brightest-colored, new cotton finery.

But the sight of these African women — nearly naked — dancing so enthusiastically, their whole bodies bouncing with every violent step, and their breasts flapping, was too much for the visitor. She berated them for this "heathen" display, unworthy of Christians. The poor Christian women were stunned, hurt, crestfallen, ashamed. This offering of thanks, this testimony of their gratitude to God and to the missionaries, this act of worship — far more real, far more deeply felt than most of our perfunctory acts of worship — had been so cruelly rejected by the distinguished visitor.

Fortunately, this sort of thing has not always been the case. There have been instances of missionaries who have been perceptive to the power and function of African dance and drama in communication, and who have encouraged them to splendid advantage.[1]

---

1. From William A. Smalley, "The Cultures of Man and the Communication of the Gospel," a paper presented at the twelfth annual convention of the American Scientific Affiliation, August 27-29, at Gordon College, Beverly Farms, Massachusetts.

All structural units consist of some basic meaning or significance and a way of expressing that significance. We will call this combination of meaning and expression of meaning the *form/meaning composite* or f/m. The symbolic system of language utilizes certain verbal and written forms to express meaning. A person's life is the expression of a total culture and its values. These values are expressed in certain specific and obvious ways.

People respond to what they perceive as realities in life. For example, they will see something growing which is large and, by agreement with others with whom they interact, will call it a tree or an *arbol* depending on the sociogeographical association, i.e., either English-speaking association or Spanish-speaking association. Again, depending on association patterns, a large growing thing can be called *tree,* and something small, *bush.* Within a different pattern of association, both large and small are responded to with the word *che.* This pattern of association is Pocomchi and those interacting together have chosen to refer to both the large and small with the same linguistic term. They are responding to the same reality that the speaker of English responds to, but they have a distinct f/m or composite of form and meaning. Thus, for the person associating within an English-speaking community, it is tree vs. bush, and for the person associating within a Pocomchi-speaking community, it is *che.*

Were society not to use a symbolic system, we would be continually faced with one challenge after another to know how and what to say or do when confronted with a large growing thing or a smaller growing thing or, for that matter, any other aspect of reality. Language, as a symbolic system, is thus a convenience.

Culture, the larger frame of reference within which language exists, is also a convenience allowing the energies of man to be expended on the new and the creative.[2]

As in the case study, "Praise Him With the Dance," the

---

2. Refer to books on language and culture as symbolic:
E. T. Hall, *The Silent Language* (Garden City, New York: Doubleday, 1959).

Joyce Hertzler, *A Sociology of Language* (New York: Random House, 1965).

Eugene A. Nida, *Message and Mission* (New York: Harper and Row, 1960).

E. Sapir, *Selected Writings in Language, Culture, and Personality,* ed. D. G. Mandelbaum (Berkeley: University of California Press, 1949).

L. A. White, "The Symbol: The Origin and Basis of Human Behavior" in *The Science of Culture* (New York: Farrar, Straus and Company, 1949).

dominant symbolic system of the North American missionaries appeared to be the language system. For the Africans it appeared to be the drama/dance. Body movement, change of costume, the depiction of historical progression by dramatic representation, all communicated the same content of message, yet with greater impact on the lives of the African. The symbolic references of the drama/dance "hit home" in a way words and language were unable to.

White suggests that it is this symbolic system, or the ability to symbolize that distinguishes the primate from the non-primate.[3] It is the degree of sophistication of symbolization that distinguishes the human primate from the nonhuman one. Malinowski suggests that society is the result of the symbolization process operating to extend man's basic needs of food, shelter, protection, etc.[4] Thus, the symbolic system becomes so intricate that a person's entire life is caught up in some way in symbol and symbolic interaction. This could be unfortunate except for the fact that we can know the real only through some abstraction of the real, which is then represented by some symbol. It is not the actual process of symbolization and response to symbol that is potentially dangerous within society; rather, it is the artificial or negatively ethnocentric use of symbol to manipulate someone else within social interaction. The utilization of distinct symbolic systems in the African setting mentioned previously was no problem — the problem lay in the conflict of systems brought about by a unilateral decision on the part of a representative of *one* of the systems. By this means, she sought to control the behavior of the others, manipulating such behavior for her own ends rather than for the good of the others.

LANGUAGE AS A SYMBOLIC SYSTEM

In reality, language has two distinct symbolic systems operating: the verbal and the written. The two may or may not coincide, depending upon society's response to the spoken language and the degree of training its members have had in preparing scientific orthography for the writing of the language. For example, the Spanish language is controlled by a commission that makes orthographic changes whenever this is needed because of some phonological change in the structure of the

3. L. A. White, *The Evolution of Culture* (New York: McGraw-Hill, 1959).
4. Bronislaw Malinowski, *Coral Gardens and Their Magic* (London: G. Allen and Unwin, Ltd., 1935). A study of the Trobrianders.

language. The symbols of Spanish thus more closely coincide with the actual phonics of the language than do, say, English symbols. An English *a* can represent any number of different pronunciations phonetically such as "father," "rat," "share," "amount," etc.

All of language grows out of the lived experience and represents some aspect of that lived experience. The spoken language is the basic symbolic system that is then taken and formally symbolized by the writing technique or orthography. This symbolization passes from generation to generation and everyone entering the society either by birth or by migration is expected to learn that symbolic system.

Any given symbolic system is completely adequate for handling all the needs of the society. In the past, some have argued that certain languages were superior to others in terms of their symbolic representation. Categories of thought, represented by members of a society naturally divide the total spectrum of life into those divisions that can be grasped and symbolized. Such categories of thought are definitive for each society and permit that society to interact with the sum total of experiences confronting them. If two systems of representation do not coincide, they will appear to represent two different realities, but such is not necessarily the case — they are just different. For example, the North American distinguishes a proliferation of colors and shades, whereas the Pocomchi has five basic colors and one "no-color" which he uses to represent color reality, yet he has no lack in meeting any challenge of color put to him by either his environment or his society. Again, the North American looks at a corn field and talks about the experience with a very limited vocabulary, whereas the Pocomchi can use a full range of vocabulary in distinguishing the various parts of the corn field, the different stages of growth of the corn, and the various conditions of corn growth. The American system is not inferior because it uses fewer symbols for the same reality, nor is the Pocom system superior for its greater range of symbolic reference, even as the American system is not superior for its greater color differentiation. They are different but equally valid within their own culture setting.

CULTURE AS A SYMBOLIC SYSTEM

A person's life-way is symbolized very much as language is. The flag of a nation stands for its integrity and identity. Heroes are representative of the highest values of a society. A stop sign is a symbol of traffic control, as are yellow lines in the middle of the street. Uniforms are symbolic of a person's status or standing or role within a society. Book shelves placed horizontally are symbols of control, symbolic of a society's need for order in the arrangement of books and periodicals. Women's breasts uncovered in public are symbolic of loose, sensual living to the North American. To him, seeing this part of a woman's anatomy involved in movement signals vulgarity — a voluptuous sensualness. Contrarily, these actions and movements symbolize the old or former way to the African. Naked female breasts are part of the enduring identity of the African and have no vulgar or sexual connotation in such a context.

The question frequently arises: Which comes first, the symbol or the lived experience? The lived experience is prior to the representation of that experience and in essence gives it birth. Something within interpersonal relations in a society calls for an expression of those interpersonal relationships. This expression can be by language, by touch, by associations or relationships, or by any combinations of these.

There is no symbolic reference, however, unless both meaning and form are present. If the form exists without the meaning, then the form is sterile, and is referred to as a "survival" by Frazer.[5] If the meaning exists without the form, the members of the society run the risk of being miscued regarding the significance of the event. In certain Mayan areas in Central America small crosses adorn the peaks of the roofs of the houses. When asked about them, the people are at a loss to explain the meaning of the crosses. One can conjecture that they have something to do with the invasion of Catholic Christianity at the time of the discovery and exploration of the new world, but there is absolutely no remembrance of such among the people themselves. They are quick to admit frankly that they have no idea what they stand for — they just put them on their houses. Again, for example, as one reads the King James Version of the Scriptures, he encounters numerous survivals that need explanation. The dynamics of change have left many of the words of the King James Version devoid of vital meaning to the average speaker of contemporary English. Thus, these words have to be explained and one of the major roles of the minister has come to be that of explaining the words of Scripture. This occupies so much of the time of the average minister that little time is left to explain the concepts or truths of the Scripture as these relate to the everyday life of the Christian.

5. James G. Frazer, *The Golden Bough* (London: Macmillan and Co., Ltd., 1911-1915). A study of magic and religion.

Whenever a *literal translation,* i.e., a word-for-word translation, of the Bible is produced, the form is wholly present but the meaning is deficient and garbled. Even a *grammatical* translation is inadequate, since it does little more than extend the literalness throughout the grammatical system and not just to the words alone. A more vital translation is a *conceptual* one where the concepts are translated across cultural boundaries. But the most adequate is a *life-way,* or *impact, translation* in which not just the words nor just the concepts are true to the Scriptures, but in which the same impact is felt on the present hearer as was felt by the original hearer when the Word of God was first presented.

GENERATING LANGUAGE FROM THE LIVED EXPERIENCE

Most people living within society experience only the process of socialization that gives them a language to speak, or a total culture to live by. The language or culture is then experienced "after the fact" and the excitement of developing new forms to coincide with dynamic meaning is lost to the average person. Occasionally, within a person's life span, new forms do develop from the lived experience itself, and if he is able to recognize what is happening, he can get a small look into the development of the symbolic system. This occurred during the sixties with the generation of the word "happening." Life gained a new significance based on event orientation: people would be together in a social way and not be having a party (a party needs careful planning and organization), or in a political or a religious way and not be having a meeting (a meeting calls for a beginning and ending point and planned progression). "Party" and "meeting" are words coded to the time orientation. They are linguistic symbols that have grown out of time orientation to life, by which a party or a meeting is planned and scheduled, it starts and stops, its parts are timed so that so much time is spent doing one thing and so much time doing another. For people with event orientation, "party" or "meeting" would be totally inadequate as a symbolic representation, so the term "happening" developed to represent the event nature of their experience, i.e., just being, and being together. Prior to the application of this term to the experience itself, there was meaning and significance with the interpersonal relationship, but this was not formally represented. For a period of time, an uneasiness ensued that came from doing or being something that did not have symbolic expression. Once being or experience produced the formal, understood expression, the unease and the ambiguity diminished.

In the early stages of a social group, a club, or an informal grouping of people, there may be no name assigned to them and for a while they could be referred to by a description of what they were doing: "They are the ones who stand at the corner of such-and-such a street." Later they may be called "hippies," but initially there is only descriptive reference to these people who are different from others in the vicinity. Once they are named, the larger description is unnecessary, since the formal naming has done away with the need for description — so long as everyone using the name is agreed as to what the new term of reference describes.

In every language/culture setting, the society operates to see that the expression of what is significant corresponds to the meaning. A society operating efficiently continually adapts to the dynamic change, making symbolic adjustments, and thus keeping the form/meaning composite intact. A society that is traditionalist or a society with traditionalistic members will tend to thwart the change process and so forms become fixed and established. The vital flow of change is blocked or restricted, causing the society to become static or to "dry up." Such is the case in some conservative evangelical churches which are resistant to the idea of changing their official Bible translation. They have traditionally used the King James Version and, by nature, have difficulty changing to a newer version. Thus the flow of change has been blocked, forcing ministers to spend time translating the KJV rather than making application of the biblical truths.

SUMMARY

The form/meaning composite approaches structural units as a combination of significance or meaning and a dynamic way of expressing this meaning. Language is a symbolic system with two subsystems: The verbal and the written. A language maintaining the form/meaning composite forces change of form in keeping with the dynamic process of the society. Culture is the larger framework within which language operates and which, in fact, gives birth to language. Cultural expressions in which there is form without meaning are called survivals. Cultural expressions in which there is meaning, but with no formal symbolic expression, will in time develop until the unease and ambiguity resulting from a lack of form is corrected, as the form is generated in keeping with meaning — the normal process of flow and change within society.

Questions for discussion:

1. Indicate meanings you find difficult to express.
2. Indicate forms/expressions that don't seem to reflect the real meaning intended, e.g., "remnant."
3. Select one situation in your life when you were quite upset because of some misunderstanding. Discuss how a functioning form/meaning correlation could have averted some of your problem.
4. Forms that no longer express their original meaning are termed "survivals." Are there survivals in North American life?
5. Does the Scripture passage "Man looketh on the outward appearance but the Lord looketh on the heart" (1 Samuel 16:7) have any relevance to our discussion?

Group activities and exercises:

1. Take a setting quite common to the members of the group and go through the experience, using language characteristic of some other distinct setting, e.g., do a church service in street corner speech, or a weather forecast in "sacred" speech.
2. Let the members of the group participate in a "blind walk" during which time one serves as the "eyes" for another (ten minutes is adequate time for a walk). Then let the two reverse roles and the second serve now as the eyes for the first. Debrief the experience with such questions as: When did your eyes pop open? What did this tell you about your "eyes"? What kinds of cultural cues were needed to direct the one without the eyes? What did you do to compensate for lack of sight?
3. Let the members of the group participate in a "nonverbal" experience. By two's or three's, with at least one girl in each group, have the group members go somewhere nearby and attempt to purchase something or gain a favor. Permit them to arrange beforehand any nonverbal cues they will need for directions and other challenges they might anticipate. Then when they begin the experience, insist that they do not speak. During the debriefing session, probe the kinds and usages of cues they developed as they proceeded with the experience. What kinds of reactions did they encounter? How did they feel about the experience?

The Validity of, and Assimilation Into, Distinct Societies
The Form/Meaning Composite
Tools of Research
Tools of Relationship

14

tools of research

Most Americans are acquainted with library research for which one goes to a book and takes from it information relating to his area of interest. Fewer Americans are acquainted with the full scope of behavioral science research which involves primarily people, though books may also be utilized. Most Americans also know about scientific research where a hypothesis is made regarding some matter of scientific concern in the world of chemistry, physics, biology, or botany. A hypothesis is made and refined. When refined sufficiently, it becomes a working hypothesis which is confirmed by further experimentation. Fewer Americans know of behavioral science research that applies the techniques of science to the study of human behavior.[1]

The basis of behavioral science research is also the hypothesis. Scientists observe a certain behavior and assign it a scientific explanation. This hypothesis is not a fact or final opinion, it

1. John Madge, *Tools of the Social Sciences* (Garden City, New York: Doubleday, 1965).

Madge includes all the tools of the social sciences, but fails to indicate that certain tools are used more by specific discipline within the social sciences. For example, history relies more heavily on archiving than do other social sciences. The behavioral sciences within the social sciences rely more heavily on the other three according to the nature of their interests — sociology using interviewing, psychology using experimentation, and anthropology using participant observation.

Pertti J. Pelto, *Anthropological Research: The Structure of Inquiry* (New York: Harper and Row, 1970).

merely provides reference points to open up more and more insight into the behavior observed or experienced. It develops when greater insights and more information are acquired concerning the circumstances and behavior of the event. For example, one can observe a person walking down the street. He might then form a hypothesis that the people of that culture walk when they are on the street. However, this particular hypothesis for observing American society proves inadequate since he can later observe a person driving down the street in an automobile. The hypothesis therefore is refined to include Americans walking as part of a larger complexity of walking and driving. The hypothesis would likely not include, at least at this writing, an American flying down the street.

Now, observing one person walking doesn't imply that anyone else will walk. The original hypothesis involving one person walking is expanded upon seeing a second person walk, then a third. If one were to do a thoroughgoing statistical study based on this participant observation of the walking scene, he would take detailed records of all of those walking. He would then do the same for driving. Such a study, however, does not tell him "why" the persons were walking. Some may have been walking because they chose to; others may have had no other means of transportation; still others may not have had a license to operate a vehicle or the vehicle may have been in the shop. Participant observation has thus yielded to the interview technique to get a different kind of result.

The program of research would also investigate whether only lower-status people were walking while upper-status people did something else. Such research in the United States would likely find this particular point nonsignificant, for in American society anyone of any station in life can walk or ride. However, this particular question becomes quite significant in the Philippines which is strongly status oriented in its interpersonal relations. The Tagalog, for example, will own their own vehicle (whether they are able to afford it or not) if they are upper status, will never ride a motorcycle with sidecar (common means of transport and equivalent to our taxi), and will never wish to be seen walking. A lower-status person will not own his own vehicle, will ride a motorcycle with sidecar, and will not hesitate to walk. The fact that a person owns his own vehicle, however battered, is a validating sign of his higher status. If he rides a motorcycle with sidecar, then he is admitting to being of lower status than people may have perceived him to be. Status is tied in with influence, i.e., the higher one's status, the greater the influence.

Therefore, where one is perceived to be on the status ladder is crucial.

The researcher continues to refine his hypothesis until he has a complexity of hypotheses which open meaningful patterns of behavior within the society.

THE TOOLS

The tools of research in developing refined, working hypotheses are participant observation, interviewing, experimentation, and archiving. (See chart 31.)

Participant observation lies at the base of all sound behavioral science research.[2] One must observe the behavior of others in given situations in order to hypothesize anything about that behavior. Observation, in and of itself, can be carried out without participation in the society — one can just look in upon the members of the society. However, as we saw in the study of society as system, it is impossible to be truly objective in observation unless the person observing is also participating within the system. In this way, observation can provide a solid foundation to other kinds of research. By itself, however, it provides only beginning hypotheses. The outside observer in Central America sees many of the Indian people learning Spanish and attempting to change from "Indianness" to "Spanishness." Such an observer is therefore led to believe that it is only a matter of time before the Indian peoples make their transition fully into the Spanish background life-way. The participant observer, however, entering the dynamics of the Indian system as it operates and seeing all the ways the traditional culture draws the Indian back into its ways, knows the process will take decades if not many generations. One period of critical choice comes to the Indian at about the age of forty, when he makes his final choice as to whether he will enter the Spanish background society and give up his own Indian life-way. In thirteen years of contact with one such group, I did not find one Indian male who made the choice to go into the Spanish background society. Before the age of forty, he may have toyed with the idea, changed his clothes, operated with the "revistidos," but by the age of forty, he had become a confirmed Indian, leaving the choice now to his children.

2. For studies utilizing the technique of participant observation, see:
Jules Henry, *Jungle People: A Kiangang Tribe of the Highlands of Brazil* (New York: Random House [Vintage Books], 1964).
Bronislaw Malinowski, *Argonauts of the Western Pacific* (New York: E. P. Dutton, 1961).
Thomas Rhys Williams, *Field Methods in the Study of Culture* (New York: Holt, Rinehart and Winston, 1967).

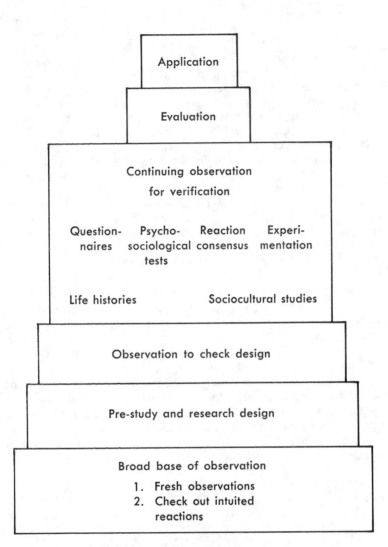

Chart 31. A Master Plan for Behavioral Science Research
(Begin at the bottom block and read upward)

A second, more intensive kind of research is that of *interviewing*.[3] In the interview process, the interviewer works with a subject in a way that elicits responses or answers to questions. The interviewer may choose a formal approach, utilizing a questionnaire, or an informal approach as in a verbal interview that is more like a conversation. The oral interview can proceed in a structured way or an unstructured way. In a structured interview the questions will be prepared in advance and posed to the respondent. In an unstructured interview, the interviewer simply lets the respondent talk as he wishes on a given subject, following his own chain of thought, and any questions posed to him arise out of the progression of the respondent's thought. Interviews can be conversational — a very natural, relaxed way of interviewing even to the point of the respondent not knowing he is being interviewed. Or, they can be direct and posed, giving the respondent a feeling of "being interviewed." Interviewing builds on the base of participant observation and grows out of what was found in the preliminary research of participant observation.

A third kind of behavioral science research is that of *experimentation*.[4] Experimentation takes the basic information provided and tests it. Such testing may take place on animals, as in certain psychological experimentations, and on persons in carefully controlled situations. The testing is designed to see if the information on which hypotheses are based is valid, correct, effective, and useful. In experimentation, one takes the step of proving in actual life that the research finds are valid. Careless applications of experimentation infringe on the human rights as the objects of the experimentation. Sound research will always honor the rights of the persons involved and, as much as possible, open to the persons the full expression of these rights.

---

3. For studies utilizing interviewing, see:
Oscar Lewis, *The Children of Sanchez: Autobiography of a Mexican Family* (New York: Random House, 1961).
Benjamin D. Paul, "Interview Techniques and Field Relationships." In A. L. Kroeber, ed. *Anthropology Today* (Chicago: University of Chicago Press, 1953).
J. R. Selley, R. A. Sim, and E. W. Loosley, *Crestwood Heights: A Study of the Culture of Suburban Life* (New York: John Wiley and Sons, 1967).
Frank W. and Ruth C. Young, "Key Informant Reliability in Rural Mexican Villages" in *Human Organization*, 20, 3 (1961), pp. 141-148.
4. For studies utilizing experimentation, see:
Gardner Lindzey, *Projective Techniques and Cross-Cultural Research* (New York: Appleton-Century-Crofts, 1961).
Evon Z. Vogt, "Navaho Veterans: A Study of Changing Values" in *Papers of the Peabody Museum of American Archaeology and Ethnology* (Cambridge, Mass.: Harvard University, 41, No. 1, 1951).

Archiving is a fourth kind of research available to the behavioral scientist. Archiving involves materials that are already produced, whether they are highly unstructured materials, such as bodies of records in some institution, or a book that has already thoroughly processed the data. The library is the center of the archiving research, though documents useful in such research can be found anywhere: in attics, in offices of businesses, or in personal letters. Archiving to the behavioral scientist is a means of reinforcing, correcting, or adding to his own research. It follows and expands field research, but is not to be used as the only or final word.

RESEARCH DESIGN

These tools of research can be especially useful and, in fact, vital to the new missionary in the field or a veteran missionary in a new field. Often a plan is drawn up before one arrives in the new culture so that it can be studied and learned in an orderly way. An example of such a plan follows:

1. Build a broad base of objective observation, seeing the people as they are, not as you think they should be. Be concerned with all the little things that go to make up the everyday life of the people. It is out of these observations that the sketches of your research will gain fullness.

2. You will be engaged in a sociocultural program of research. This involves the total man in his total society. Your "village" can be considered the total society and it would be wise to concentrate, especially in the early stages, on one or two individuals in that society. The others will all be there, but it is too confusing to try to extend detailed research beyond just a few. This extension can come later on in research. For this stage of research, you are interested in elicited materials. Such elicited materials should be gained by specific questioning, keeping the following possible sources in mind:

a. Make use of your own background. (If you recognize that the society will be basically different, there is no harm in assuming that some aspects of the society will be the same as yours, or somewhat like yours.) Start here, then, and see what responses you can derive from questions arising out of your own background; e.g., you can assume that there will be some institution surrounding the responsibilities of the education of children (the enculturation process). Probe to see what institution in the society is designed to handle this: Is it the family? an age-level? etc. Some have called these points of similarity in cultures "universals." You'll soon hit upon a number of these and from whatever material you get information in this way, you can go on to the specifics of that particular culture.

b. Get the individual to respond to specific questions about pictures you might show him.

c. Plan some simple tests to get reaction. E.g., prepare a food dish and ask the people to tell you what you did right and wrong. This will be quite a test.

d. Ask your informant to act out some aspect of the sociocultural setting that may not take place while you are there, or that you might not have the opportunity to see in its entirety.

3. As you let the above flow out like an ink blot — not trying to guide its particular direction at any one time — you will begin to get a feel for various aspects of the whole. Begin to sketch the various relationships between people and groupings of people, the activities they carry on, and any interrelationships of values discovered. This should not be complete nor sophisticated, just a simple sketch or outline. By this time you should have hit upon the aspect of the society that serves as a key to all the rest; e.g., the age-level groupings are typical of an African society. After this point, the whole of a given culture begins to make sense, since a point of focus has been discovered.

4. During this stage, you will concentrate on nonelicited material. Take a sampling of the following:

a. Select words or concepts that you meet in stages one to three and suggest one word or concept at a time to the informant and let him respond as he wishes. It is immaterial whether he talks at length or for only a brief time. As you get more and more information, you will continue selecting stimulus words and getting short texts in response to the stimuli.

b. Ask for the life history of the informant.

c. Secure ethnographic texts (as in *Pocomchi Texts*[5]).

---

5. Marvin K. Mayers, *Pocomchi Texts* (Oklahoma: The Summer Institute of Linguistics and the University of Oklahoma, 1958).

d. Learn as much as you can of folklore. This is of help more for the diachronic perspective than for the synchronic perspective, giving clues to the development of values in the society.

e. Ask the informant to make a map of his area.

f. Let the informant draw pictures of cultural items. He may emphasize some part of the item that will give you a clue as to the importance of that part in the whole society.

g. Have the informant write texts (if he is able to write).

5. Now, a critical step for you: Make a list of all the differences between your society and his. Use your imagination. Make an exhaustive list. Spare nothing. This is vitally important for the next step.

6. Begin a structured analysis:
Ecological setting — the physical world, demography, etc.
Sociocultural setting
    Natural grouping of individuals in institutions
    Activities carried out
    Values expressed, reasons for doing things, ways of looking at life, etc.
    Products of the culture: a tool, a house, a piece of clothing
Select a unit of focus, e.g., the family. Define it in terms of the tools of the family, names given the family, privacy expected and carried out, interests expressed, means of perpetuating the family and so forth. Consider variants of the unit, the varying sizes of families, the allowable variation in the tools of the family (we have the refrigerator and stove as obligatory tools in our society, but the freezer is optional). Contrast the family with an economic team and with a religious team of the same complexity. Then attempt to arrange your units (i.e., institutional units) on levels of complexity, those less complex on lower levels and those more complex on the higher levels.

Continue checking the distribution of the family in the society: the extent of distribution and the interaction with other families.

Select a complex of activities, e.g., burial activities. Seek to determine the beginning, the parts of continuation, and the close of the complex. Compare this with birth activities. See if you can find units of structure in the complex of activities that are the same. Identify the various units of structure of the activities in terms of unique parts, details of participation, and expression.

Select a pattern of values, again identify such a pattern in terms of its unique features and the variation of expression of the value and the extent of its acceptance in the social grouping.

You won't get very far in this particular study in a few months, but you should try for a sampling of each, then try to develop one aspect (e.g., institutions, activities, or values) more completely.

7. Do extensive reading in your selected field. Reading should be kept at this point in your research so that others' errors will not be perpetuated in your work. Malinowski warns that this is the reason he had to separate himself from the "whites,"[6] and the same holds true for reading material. So much is biased, you can't trust it. After some depth of involvement in the field, you will become more discerning and will be able to get some help from it.

8. Make applications in the field. It is expected that such a study will result in an extensive list of things to be careful about, things to watch for, things to expect, etc. In addition, there should be some definitive suggestions to someone going into the field regarding the introduction of the Gospel, the organization of the church program, and the setting up of the educational program. Each of these must be carried out in light of the uniqueness of the society studied. We respect differences and utilize differences as stepping-stones to truth. The sociocultural setting is our friend, not our enemy. Let's make it a good friend.

9. Check all findings and conclusions with the results of linguistic analysis. The two are vitally interrelated and one cannot be considered apart from the other.

Note: Record as much as possible on tape.

The following is a sample case study in which the tools of research were used.

Case Study in Research: Tagalog, Philippines

The investigator entered a distinct society, the Tagalog, in the Philippines.[7] To aid his participant observation, he moved into a Philippine home. After a few days of meeting people, a pattern began to emerge: about eighty percent of the people he met during the first few days were *members of the family,* i.e.,

---

6. Bronislaw Malinowski, *Coral Gardens and Their Magic* (London: G. Allen and Unwin, Ltd., 1935).

7. Taken from notes of the author during a period of field work in the Philippines.

relatives of the immediate family. The other twenty percent seemed to have some special relationship to the immediate family — something the investigator became aware of but could not resolve at the moment. All of the people met were not only individually named, but their *relationship to the family* was noted; e.g., "Maria Fernandez, my mother's brother's daughter's child." The intricacies of consanguinal and affinal relationship were always spelled out. Besides, another pattern was beginning to emerge that tied in with the more obvious one: different people were *encountered in different places in the home.* It appeared that the servant girls, the members of the immediate family and the parents had access to all parts of the house. The investigator, as a guest, had access to his room and the living and dining rooms. The brothers and sisters were "at home" in the living area of the first floor, but never went to the second floor where the bedrooms were. Those whom the investigator responded to as nonrelated but important to the family were comfortable in the living room and ventured cautiously into the dining room and office, but did not go further. Whenever they were in the house at all, they were polite, waiting for indication that they could go here or there, whereas the blood relatives did not have this restraint. Finally, there was a continual progression of other people, some reaching the porch, but most of them remaining at the gate.

Thus, participant observation suggested the beginning hypothesis: family, including both the nuclear and the extended families, was very important to the Tagalog Filipino; and further, the extended family was as important as, if not more important than, the nuclear family in the development of relationships. Related to this hypothesis was the observation that in some way there were friends that were more important than other people.

By the interview process, the investigator confirmed the initial observation. A series of more formal questions were prepared and administered to a number of Tagalogs. This bit of questionnaire/interview research confirmed that there were three categories of people: 1) family, 2) close friends tied into family, and 3) others. The kinds of questions used during this stage of research were as follows: With whom do you associate on social occasions? How frequently do you see your relatives? Are they considered important to you? In what order would you respond in an emergency: to a blood relative, a member of your "alliance," a friend, a stranger? A second type of questionnaire was used with questions such as this: Anyone who fails in a commitment to his relatives is a bad person (agree or disagree).

Simple, nonmanipulative experiments were conducted with these hypotheses in mind and each of the former developments in research results were confirmed. The family appeared to be a very important part of the Tagalog life. Then, with archiving, the full extent of the family influence began to emerge, and further research of the earlier types confirmed and corrected the reading material. The archiving produced a name for the extended family plus close friends brought into the family through the machinery of godparenthood: *the Alliance.* Continued work with the Alliance showed it to be the dominant institution of Filipino society influencing strongly all social, religious, economic, and especially political concerns.

SUMMARY

Someone studying a society unknown to him — or for that matter, even one in which he has participated — needs tools of research to enable him to observe objectively the experience of the culture. Such tools are archiving, interviewing, participant observation, and experimentation.

Archiving is the research tool most people are familiar with. It is used in perhaps ninety-eight percent of the American educational program to date. It involves books and other written materials. Archiving is the primary tool of the historian.

Interviewing through formal and informal means is the primary tool of the sociologist. Interviews may be verbal or written (questionnaires). They may be structured in such a way that all the questions are prepared beforehand, or unstructured in the sense that questions flow from the interview itself.

Participant observation is the primary tool of the social anthropologist. He enters the other society and keeps his eyes and ears open. By applying conceptual models, he "sees" things that others would tend to overlook. In this way, he puts together material available to him because of his objectivity. Others tend to ignore certain things, since they are involved subjectively in the experience.

Experimentation is a basic tool of the psychologist. A hypothesis yields certain conclusions and these are tested in a simulated experience. An agent of change must come to terms with the process of experimentation if he desires his purpose to be of impact on the people.

Questions for discussion:
1. How can effective research aid us in decision making?
2. How can research hinder sound decision making?
3. In what ways might effective research aid in our task of mission? Do any missions carry out sound research in their programs? Name some.
4. Does research necessarily detract from the work of the Holy Spirit?
5. How might effective, ongoing research aid the pastor in his work?
6. In what ways did Jesus carry out effective research? Paul? James?
7. How might the experience of Paul on Mar's Hill have been the result or outcome of an effective research program?

Group activities and exercises:
1. Simulation: "Koko Kolo," available from Associates of Urbanus, is a scientific hypothesizing game that permits one to develop a hypothesis and continue refining it during the progress of the game. Twenty to forty group members can play it during an hour.
2. Archiving research: Consult Louis Luzbetak, *The Church and Cultures* for some excellent ideas for library research as it relates to mission.
3. Participant behavior: Have each student become part of a new sociocultural setting and see how much they can determine of the system operating in that setting.
4. Interviewing: Have each group member try two or three unstructured interviews and from this experience have him construct from five to ten questions of the information type that he might administer to some other people to check his findings from the interviews. This does not need to be complex, but it does reveal something of the need for staging in research and gives the person doing the research the sense of discovery in research process.
5. Experimentation: Have each group member attempt some experiment that he can follow up by observing the behavior of the people involved; e.g., maintain excessive eye contact upon greeting, eat with the British method of filling one's inverted fork by pushing it against the knife, etc.

The Validity of, and Assimilation Into, Distinct Societies
The Form/Meaning Composite
Tools of Research
Tools of Relationship

15

tools of relationship

THE DEAD DOG

One day at the dormitory where we were houseparents in Congo, there was a dead dog in need of burying, as it was attracting flies and becoming a health hazard. I asked Sebuhire, one of our hired pagan Banyaruanda helpers to bury the dog, and then asked if he understood. He replied that he did and then he disappeared around the dorm, supposedly to fetch a shovel. Several hours passed and I happened upon the dead dog once again.

"Sebuhire! That dog hasn't been buried yet and every moment it remains unburied it represents a greater danger to the health of the children. Please bury him immediately! Unasikia? (You hear?)"

"Ndio, Bwana! (Yes, Sir!)," as he again made off around the corner of the dorm.

Later that afternoon, to my horror, the dog still lay unburied! About to find Sebuhire and read him the riot act, I was fortunately prompted to inquire first of Musakura, a Christian, Munyaruanda worker, as to why Sebuhire hadn't buried the dog.

"Bwana, he believes that if he buries that dog, he will be burying a member of his family within twenty-four hours!"

It was true that Sebuhire hadn't said, "Yes, I'll bury the dog." He only said, "Yes, I hear." Then, when he immediately withdrew, he was silently telling me, "I hear you, Bwana, but I can't do it."

214

And I, misreading the cue, thought he was saying, "I'll do it, and I'm going immediately to get a shovel." With my newly acquired understanding of the meaning of the dead dog in the total belief system of this pagan man, I then suggested, "Musakura, will you ask Sebuhire to relieve you at your present task so you will have time to bury the dog?"

"*Ndio,* Bwana."

And so the dog was buried.

Tools of relationship are needed when one crosses cultural or subcultural boundaries. They are the essence or foundation for crosscultural communication. Communication very quickly breaks down, at times with serious results, when one has no means of determining meaning from behavior. The missionary could have found himself in trouble by insisting that the person he considered "lazy" get at the job of burying the dog.

Without the tools of relationship, the new would be seen as the old, in terms of the form/meaning composite of the way of life of the foreign intruder. Thus, the tools of relationship permit the foreigner to see the culture as it has developed in keeping with its own need, its own challenge. They also permit the one entering a new life-way to maintain his full validity as a person within the new society.

Tools of relationship include the cultural cue, the functional equivalent, the principle of the adverse effect, the ranking of values, the abuse of system being made the whole, the part being made the whole, and the distinction between the real and the ideal and between the real and perceived. They are the elements of the working stage in crosscultural communication. Acceptance of the person is a starting point but it does not take one very far unless there is also an understanding of the systemic life-way of the person. The grasp of life-way takes a certain amount of effort and research, but the tools of relationship require a great deal more concentration and effort. It is not until the foreigner, the visitor, the agent of change begins to work consciously with the tools of relationship that he begins *validating the other society.* It is not until he works with all the tools consistently that members of the host society perceive themselves as fully human and their life-way valid, worthy of full respect.

Tools of relationship are quite distinct from tools of research. Both permit the full validation of each society in which operations or associations take place, but each is designed for a different purpose. Tools of research validate society by accurately and fully searching out the various elements and aspects of each society. Sound research technique must be carried out lest the investigator see only what he wants to see and hear only what he is pretuned to hear. *The tools of relationship, on the other hand, permit the actual association with people within the society and must be utilized in personal interaction.* They cannot be applied by observation alone (see chapter 14), but by participation also. They cannot be applied by interview alone, but by full and complete interaction in addition. Constant experimentation is necessary to make sure that the full kit of tools is available at any time, and the experience of others, recorded in archives, can help one carry out the discovery process effectively.

THE CULTURAL CUE

The concept of cue is taken from the acting profession: the cue indicating the correct point at which the actor makes his appearance. Extended into the crosscultural setting, the cue lets one do precisely what he wants to do, at the right time, and in the right way without manipulation. The cue may be verbal, as in "come in," or it may be nonverbal, such as a wave of greeting. It may be simply the placement of furniture in a room. As a verbal cue it is tied into the larger linguistic pattern within the framework of culture, and as a nonverbal cue it ties into the kinesics or body movements that are culturally established. As placement of object, it fits into that aspect of the culture termed "space relationships."[1] Society can be conceptualized as one vast, intricate network of cues.

One way of analyzing a society is to pattern the cues by which one responds to societies' stimuli. Our response pattern is based on millions of such cues that guide us in every social setting to do the proper or expected thing, to recover when the unexpected has been done, or to impulse some change in the way of doing things. Another way of looking at the socialization process is to see it as internalizing all the cues one needs for living within his own society. Culture shock may be devastating to someone who is monocultural because there is lack of correspondence between the cue responses of the two societies. For example, the occasional North American hand wave of goodbye with the fingers

1. E. T. Hall, *The Silent Language* (Garden City, New York: Doubleday, 1959). Also, *The Hidden Dimension* (Garden City, New York: Doubleday, 1969).

pointed down is just the opposite of the Latin American wave. The Latins extend their fingers up for "goodbye," but down for "come here." The discomfiture of North Americans is great when they wave goodbye to someone and that person approaches rather than departs, following the cue which meant to the Latin American "come here."

A knowledge of the cultural cue is needed by the agent of change so that he can adapt to the new society without losing his identity as a person and as a member of his own society. In other words, he must know the cue to remain a man of principle and to fulfill responsibly his role in life, in whatever culture. Well-meaning missionaries who are from nondrinking backgrounds may refuse alcoholic beverage with a curt refusal designed to protect them from the evils of drinking. This is perceived by the host as "a slap in the face." Each society has a way of effectively refusing an alcoholic beverage, and the host will always provide this cue, though it demands that the outsider seek it out, recognize it when he finds it, and act correctly in accordance with the cue. To the Central American Indian it is enough to say "It hurts my stomach," and alcoholic beverage is automatically recorded in the mind of the host as being in the same category as "chili," the spicy addition they use to make their food tasty and which not everyone can "stomach." He reads the message of refusal, therefore, in this way: "This person wants to remain my friend, but he just can't drink an alcoholic beverage." The curt refusal, on the other hand, signals to the host that one does not want to remain his friend. To the Filipino it is sufficient to request coca cola instead. (Or, one can seek out other nondrinkers at an occasion when alcoholic beverage is served and remain in their protective association.) Again the message communicated is that the guest is a fully responsible friend of the host.

THE FUNCTIONAL EQUIVALENT

Most people expect to find in another culture exactly what they have in their own. They expect it to look the same and have the same meaning. They assume that if the form is the same, the meaning must be the same, and if the form is different, the meaning is different also. In other words, they focus on the form of the communicated message, or the form of the cultural expression rather than on the significance of the message or the impact of the cultural expression. The direct equivalent or non-functional equivalent is then the carrying over from one culture to another the f/m of the first.

The *functional equivalent*,[2] to the contrary, is based on meaning out of which form grows and develops. Equivalence of meaning is therefore sought and from meaning one seeks out the form that is the means of expressing the significance intended. Wherever there is agreement to and knowledge of an f/m correlation, the hearer automatically comprehends the full and correct impact of the communicated message or deed. Within the crosscultural setting, complete agreement and knowledge of the f/m must be learned. The process of adaptation to the new is the process of learning the cues of the new and the functional equivalence of the parts of the new. It is to be expected in crosscultural settings that the meaning will remain intact, though the form will differ. When this is not the case, and the form is the same for two cultures, the agent of change can consider he has received a bonus. For example, the functional equivalence of the occasional goodbye greeting in English, with the fingers of the hand extended downward, is the fingers extended upward in Spanish-speaking areas. The functional equivalence of "It hurts my stomach" for the Pocomchi is "I'll have a coke, please" for the Filipino. The functional equivalence of bell ringing to dismiss classes in our society is the clapping of hands to dismiss classes in other societies. The functional equivalent for reading in the Philippines is to know the right people, for in that society it is more important to know someone in order to get ahead than it is to be able to read.

The functional equivalent for the King James Bible for speakers of American English living in the latter half of the twentieth century is *The Living Bible* or some other translation in modern English. The impact that the King James Version had in the day it was prepared is no longer possible, because of the process of language and culture change. The only way for a person to respond exactly as people responded in King James' day is to have someone explain not only what changes have transpired, but also how people in that day responded to the various stimuli provided in the Scriptures. In essence, this is the task of the translator. Unfortunately, not every person is prepared for the translation task, and so misunderstanding results. The producers of *The Living Bible* have done their work well, so that, although

---

2. Eugene Nida, *Message and Mission* (New York: Harper and Row, 1960).

Clyde Kluckhohn, *Navaho Witchcraft* (Cambridge, Mass.: Harvard University, Peabody Museum of American Archaeology and Ethnology, Papers, Vol. 22, No. 2, 1944).

Harry C. Bredemeier, "The Methodology of Functionalism," *American Sociological Review*, 20 (1955), pp. 173-180.

they have called their work a "paraphrase," it is a rendering of the original meaning and intent of Scripture in the total lived experience of the average American living today. The translation process goes beyond a literal translation, beyond a grammatical translation, beyond a conceptual translation to a total life-way translation that is perhaps as true not only to the intent of the original text as humans can make it but is also as true to the total life-way of the American as members of one subculture can make it.

No functional equivalent can be expected to equate across cultural boundaries one hundred percent. Thus, functional equivalence may involve a range of equivalent items that do in one culture what one of them alone does in another. For example, our word "carry" in English is joined with other separate words called prepositions to indicate the direction of carrying. In Pocomchi, four words form the functional equivalent of the English "carry": camlok, camje, cambeh, and cam.[3] Again, Calvin's *Institutes*,[4] a classic work on the theology of the Christian community, is impossible to match for its completeness and breadth in the contemporary period. Therefore, the functional equivalent of the *Institutes* is a series of volumes on the Christian responsibility to mankind in community.[5]

THE PRINCIPLE OF THE ADVERSE EFFECT

Behavioral signs can indicate to us whether we have achieved what we set out to do or whether we have accomplished just the opposite. Awareness that verbal and nonverbal indicators can alert us to errors in our approach to others opens up an entire study of how these errors are communicated and what such communication indicates in the way of adjusting our approach. Many parents punish their children immediately upon finding them in the wrong. With some children, this communicates the message "You have done wrong, shape up." In contemporary American society, it has been found that this communicates, rather, "You can never do anything right." The two messages are quite distinct and the American parent needs to be aware of the possibility of the two messages. The first develops positive response, the second generates negative and destructive

3. Marvin K. Mayers, *Pocomchi Texts* (Oklahoma: The Summer Institute of Linguistics and the University of Oklahoma, 1958).

4. John Calvin, *Institutes of the Christian Religion,* 2 vols., ed. by John T. McNeill (Philadelphia: Westminster Press, 1960).

5. Jacques Ellul, *The Meaning of the City* (Grand Rapids: Wm. B. Eerdmans Publishing Co., 1970). Also, *The Technological Society* (New York: [Vintage Books] Random House, 1964).

Harvey Cox, *The Secular City* (New York: The Macmillan Co., 1965).

responses. One must be sensitive to possible miscommunications through cultural cues and all forms of verbal and nonverbal communications. How easy it would have been for the missionary to have insisted that Sebuhire bury the dead dog and thereby to have lost for all time the opportunity of effective witness of the grace of God.

RANKING OF VALUES

Our value system is not a series of values all jumbled up together, causing erratic responses to stimuli. Order and arrangement exist, based on a hierarchy of value distinctions. Such a hierarchy of priority or rank[6] from greater importance to lesser importance determines our choice in any given situation. A person never makes a choice or decision apart from this ranking. A given situation allows one an opportunity to reevaluate his ranking — thus permitting certain adjustments to be made — but such adjustments never precede the ranking itself. This is one of the major fallacies of the approach to ethics termed "situation ethics."[7] Situation ethics suggests that the decision can be made in keeping with the situation, but one's rank of values is such a powerful control on the decision-making process that one is unable to make a decision apart from this control. Some people objectify their rank of values and so will make a decision that appears to go contrary to this rank. They have idealized what they are, or they have perceived themselves to be one thing when they are actually something else. Many American youths perceive themselves to be free from economic control and the drive to so-called "materialism." As they mature, their choices are more and more economic in nature, and the materialism they foster, though different in some ways from that of their parents, is still materialism. For example, though the clothes they wear are different from those of their parents, the studied approach to clothing is still there with the strong focus on fashion, correctness of dress, the totality of the uniform, etc.

American young men of the forties were willing to expend themselves in the service of their nation, whereas their counterparts of the sixties were reluctant to go to war. The behavior of the former was generated from a value ranking of nation over person, and the behavior of the latter from value ranking of

6. P. Drucker, "Rank, Wealth and Kinship in Northwest Coast Society," *American Anthropologist,* Vol. 41, 1939, pp. 55-65.
H. Kuper, "An African Aristocracy: Rank Among the Swazi" in *Royalty and Commoners in a South African Tribe* (London: Oxford. 1947).
7. Norman L. Geisler, *Ethics: Alternatives and Issues* (Grand Rapids: Zondervan Publishing House, 1971), pp. 60-78.

person over nation.[8] In other words, there has been a shift in values but not the way many people have interpreted this, i.e., from responsibility to irresponsibility, or from self-denial to selfishness. The shift has been in the person motivation moving above group interest. The men of the forties were responsible in terms of nation interest first and person second, whereas the men of the sixties were responsible in terms of person interest first and nation second. It is easy for members of the former subculture to call members of the latter irresponsible. There is difference of subculture that exists and each may be fully responsible in terms of his value ranking. If the members of the former do not like the expression of behavior of the latter, they need to effect a cultural change. If the larger society can operate in keeping with the justice model with both subcultures, then there is no reason for change.

When time and production units in timed periods are ranked highest within society, it is impossible to generate behavior that does other than recruit the largest work force available, unless machines can do all the work. The child-labor laws of the latter part of the nineteenth century were designed to limit the labor force to adults only. This social change was necessary because society was holding time production units to be of such high value that it was undermining the state by failing to educate its children effectively.

THE ABUSE OF SYSTEM SEEN AS THE WHOLE

As was indicated in chapter 7, society can be seen as a systems operation and thus lends itself to "systems analysis." Any system can and will be abused. There is no problem of social abuse to society's system if the abuse can be identified and dealt with effectively. When, however, the abuse of the system is seen to be the entire system, or when one perceives the abuse as the whole, it is possible that in regulating or destroying the abuse one regulates or destroys the entire system. Revolutionaries are often guilty of this. They strive to destroy the system and wind up putting the same system back into operation, since that is the system in which they have been trained. What they have accomplished is the possible elimination of what they saw as abuse. The French Revolution followed this pattern, but those who advocated overthrow were themselves destroyed. Fidel Castro sought to overthrow the system in Cuba and wound up subject to the very same system he sought to destroy. He de-

8. Charles A. Reich, *The Greening of America* (New York: Random House, 1970).

ported or destroyed all the higher strata members of the society, sensing that these were the ones blocking progress. This simply left a vacuum in the stratificational system operating in Cuba, and lower status people immediately moved in to fill the vacuum. At that time, however, people were not trained to operate on those status levels and were controlling those levels in erratic and unpredictable ways.

THE PART SEEN AS THE WHOLE

Every system consists of component parts that exist only because they are parts of a larger component within a larger system.[9] Any part gains significance only by being part of the whole. Christ used the grapevine in illustrating this principle. Paul referred to this principle when he was talking about the place of the hand in relation to the body. Any one part of society that sees itself as the sole recipient of truth can very quickly throw the system into imbalance and do a disservice to the other parts involved. The fundamentalist movement in American Protestantism claimed to be the sole recipient of the truth of God and developed an approach to other Christians that was so exclusivistic it ultimately resulted in a movement of separatistic groups none of which would have anything to do with another.[10]

THE REAL AS AGAINST THE IDEAL OR THE PERCEIVED

The real is known only through the process of abstraction from the real. These abstractions from the real are symbolized for and by society so there is some consensus as to what constitutes the real. During the process of crosscultural communication, consensus is being reached as to the recognition and representation of the real. If such consensus is not reached, conflict results that is destructive of the societies involved.

The process of abstraction is a healthy one that helps develop responsibility and responsible response to the society and the environment in which the society is set. Two extensions of this process may develop societal health or ill health. All societies through their ranking of values cause certain aspects of the real to be held up as ideals to the members of the society.[11] For

---

9. See Paul's discussion of the parts of the body in 1 Corinthians 12: 12-26.

Quinn McNemar, *Psychological Statistics* (New York: Wiley, 1962).

10. Millard Erickson, *The New Evangelical Theology* (Westwood, N.J.: Revell, 1968).

11. The "Ideal Type" is especially prominent in Max Weber's works. See for example, *On the Methodology of the Social Sciences* (Glencoe, Illinois: The Free Press, 1949).

example, for years the American populace was encouraged to see smoking as a rewarding experience. Many people began smoking because of this ideal. Later it was discovered that smoking produced cancer. By this time smoking had become so strong a habit with many people and made so much money for others that it became a source of individual and corporate tension.

A second extension of the symbolization process is the perception of the real.[12] Individuals or the corporate body can develop perceptions of the real that are in fact nothing like the real itself. The perception of smoking as a fulfilling habit was quite distinct from the real, so that it was in effect a self-destructing habit. The perception of the missionary in the case study at the beginning of this chapter was that the worker was lazy or that he procrastinated in failing to bury the dog. In reality, the worker was fully responsible to his family, though he did need a spokesman to make him fully responsible in his job.

SUMMARY

The tools of relationship are necessary in permitting a society to be fully valid and responsible. These include the cultural cue, the functional equivalent, the principle of the adverse effect, the abuse not being made the whole, the part not being made the whole, the difference between the real and ideal, and between the real and the perceived. The risk of failing to use these tools is the imposition of the sending culture on the receivers or host members through the injustice model. The challenge of the total validation of the host society is able to be met by the use of the form/meaning tools of relationship. This does not legislate against change; rather, it expedites effective change. Only if these tools are perceptively used is assimilation natural and smooth for both the foreigner and the host society. This complete assimilation also expedites effective change.

Questions for discussion:
1. How do tools of relationship differ from tools of research?
2. Can you name any other tools useful in developing and maintaining effective relationships that might be added to our list?
3. How might the person who trends toward dichotomism in value formation tend to take the part of a whole as the whole itself? Can you name instances of this?
4. Distinguish values and value rank. What other items do we use to express ranking of values?

12. Pertti J. Pelto, "Theory vs. Reality" in *Anthropological Research: The Structure of Inquiry* (New York: Harper and Row, 1970).

5. If a person values family over nation, how is he likely to respond to a military draft? What rank of values might a person have who is willing and eager to serve in the armed forces of his nation?
6. Compare and contrast the Fidel Castro type of revolutionary with the Jesus Christ type. In what sense was Christ the unique revolutionary?

Group activities and exercises:

1. Small group work: Have the members of a small group work out the various functional equivalents that provide adjustment between youth and adult subcultures, e.g., youth subculture — longer hair, adult subculture — shorter hair; youth subculture — grade as payment for effort, adult subculture — money as payment; etc.
2. If your group has members of distinct cultures and subcultures, have them demonstrate greeting patterns characteristic of their culture and then have other members of the group suggest the functional equivalent in their own culture. Hall's books can be consulted for examples.
3. Research: Have each member of the group spend a few days doing participant observation of: the system vs. its abuse, the part taken as the whole, the perceived taken as the real, and the ideal confused with the real. Let them report on their findings.
4. Translate the following into correct English. (The linguistic phrases were taken from Eugene Nida's book *God's Word in Man's Language* and adapted by Tim Black, Lisa Espinelli, Joyce Houggy, Paul Lewis, and Jim Savage.)

THE MESSAGE OF THE LARUTLUCIB TRIBESPEOPLE

We are the Larutlucib tribespeople from the country of Sreyam; we have come to you on a flying canoe. Our insides are sweet to be here. After the flying canoe came down, our heads were in the dirt because we had never been in a canoe that was not in the water — the water was so far below us. While we were in the flying canoe, we were shivering in our livers but now that we are in your country our livers are wide open for we have something that is very important for you to know and that you must accept.

But even though our heads are in the dirt, because we are here, our minds are killing us because we have found the only trail — the only right trail and you don't know about our trail. The jungle is so big and there are so many trails and this jungle grows so quickly and one can get lost very quickly. But we have found a trail that goes on and on. We haven't been to the end of the trail but someday we will be at the end of the trail where there is a place that is bigger than the big river that we crossed in the flying canoe. And in this place there will not be anything there to blacken our eyes but our eyes will be whitened. There our livers will sit down. Don't you want to know where this trail is? and how you can walk on this trail?

The one who is sufficient had a pain in his liver for the people which he had carved. These people were people with bad livers. But the one who is sufficient so hurt in his liver that he sent his Trailblazer into the jungle. And his Trailblazer blazed a trail for us through the jungle. But this Trailblazer died, but he isn't dead now. He's with the one who is sufficient. When he left to go with the one who is sufficient he sent one who ties up the thoughts.

You want to walk on our trail because the trails that you walk on are wrong. You are ones who chop water, you have unbent necks, you are people with bad livers. We used to have bad livers but now we have white livers and we want you to have white livers also.

In order to have white livers you have to begin to walk on this trail that we have found. You have to become like our Trailblazer. You must not put those pieces of bark on your feet because our Trailblazer didn't put bark on his feet. Then after you have done this you must pull out your livers.

You must ask the Trailblazer with your liver coming out. You must become untwisted and then you will retrace your steps and then you will be on the trail. The one who ties up the thoughts will help you to hurt in your livers for others who are not walking on the trail. As you walk on this trail, you will not be shivering in your livers because you will have one who ties up the thoughts. Your heads will be in the dirt because you are on the trail. The Trailblazer had been sent by the one who is sufficient to take us by the hand.

Perhaps your liver is made two right now. Pull out your livers, become untwisted and retrace your steps down the only trail. Who will be taken by the hand? If you want to be taken by the hand, take the bark off your feet and come to us. Our heads will be in the dirt and our Trailblazer will lead you on the trail. Then we will teach you how to cut your livers down before the one who is sufficient.

MODEL 4

EFFECTIVE MINISTRY

The model termed here *Effective Ministry* provides a variety of insights into interpersonal and intergroup relations, suggesting positive means of working with a person or group in keeping with what that person or group is, and effecting change in keeping with that reality. There are two submodels.

a. The discussion of absolutism and relativism opens the possibility that a Christian can be a cultural relativist and a biblical absolutist rather than negating the impact of biblical truth or absolutizing his own cultural ways.

b. The support model is reached by bridge from conflict. It involves the setting of goals and operations to meet those goals, a reevaluation of goals and operations, alternate sessions with debriefing sealing the learning experiences, and true creativity deriving from what a person or group is.

   The support person encourages the effective development and realization of each of the aspects of the support model.

If the models of crosscultural communication are to be effective, they must be applied. Suggestions are made in the final chapter of the book as to the implications of application.

Effective Ministry
Absolutism and Relativism
The Support Model
The Models Illustrated

16

absolutism and relativism

WHEN IN ROME

While working in Rome this past summer, I found myself in a very interesting dilemma. In the Italian culture, wine is normally served with the meal as a predinner "icebreaker" to guests one wishes to welcome courteously. The Italian does not associate use or nonuse of wine with Christian behavior as does the North American evangelical, who often uses it as a criterion for measuring the spirituality of a person.

I personally have no qualms about having wine with my meal while living in another culture that accepts this social norm, especially when I am a guest in the home of an Italian. I am also willing to limit my personal freedom for the welfare of another person.

One evening I was invited to dinner at the home of a friend named Carlo. Carlo was not a Christian and I had been introduced to him by his close friend Mario who was a Christian. Mario had been sharing his faith with Carlo for over a year.

To complicate the situation, Mr. Long, an American evangelical missionary, had also been invited. He was trained in the same Christian college in which I was serving as a Dean of Students. He totally abstained from drinking wine, feeling it is unbecoming of a Christian. He had been serving in Italy for three years and though I had met him previously, I knew very little else about him and his missionary organization.

227

Just about the time I was ready to ask Mr. Long some questions about his background, Carlo walked into the room with a tray of four glasses of wine. He served me first and I accepted. Then he served Mario and proceeded to Mr. Long. Mr. Long graciously refused.

So there I stood with my glass of wine. I didn't want to offend Carlo after having accepted the wine. Neither did I want to offend the missionary who totally abstained. Mr. Long, I was quite sure, knew I was Dean of Students at the college, further complicating the decision I had to make. This was no time for a letter to be sent to the college and the board of trustees.

What should I do? . . .

The average member of any society is likely to react to someone different from himself in the following way:

> What does this mean to me?
> How can it be said or done so that it *is* meaningful to me?
> How can others see life as I see it?
> Why shouldn't they see life as I see it?
> How can I make the other person be more like me?

We have called this a "monocultural" approach to interpersonal relations in that all other cultures are approached from the point of view of the person looking in. The process of enculturation, i.e., preparing one to live within his own sociocultural setting, though not necessarily designed to effect this monocultural response, may likely do so. The member of a society must be able to live fully and adequately within his own sociocultural setting, else it will not be perpetuated effectively, and the member will run the risk of being at odds with it. A crosscultural or bicultural approach is not necessarily antithetical to the enculturative process nor to the goals of society itself. It may, in fact, advance the purposes of the society. But it may need to be introduced, as a significant factor, into the enculturative process. Apparently, it is not always something that is developed naturally.

The bicultural point of view, thus introduced into society, would ask a different set of questions upon confronting difference:

> What am I really trying to say or do?
> What is the other person really trying to say or do?
> What is the other person like with whom I am communicating?

How can I say or do what I have to and know that there is complete understanding on the part of the other? Can I stand back and evaluate my communication and be sure that I have gotten across intact what I intended? Can we both stand back and evaluate the communication to be sure we have each fully understood the other?

The asking and answering of such questions does not in any way imply that we believe or "buy" all we hear; rather, it enables us to communicate with as full an understanding as possible.[1] The young man in Rome, in keeping with his own life-style of abstaining from wine in his own culture but partaking in a host culture communicated his respect for the host by partaking. The missionary, of a life-style characterized by abstaining in both cultures communicated his respect by a proper and courteous refusal. He had apparently discovered the effective cultural cue and did not seem to offend the host. The problem came in the conflict between the two life-styles of the Americans rather than in the communication process with the host.

The next step required of the young man in the case would be the effective communication to the missionary resulting in a trust bond developing there and thus averting the adverse-effect "letter" to the Board. He could attempt a verbal explanation on the side, sip once and drink no more, or hold the glass full to the end if any of these would maintain the balance of each trust relationship. It is not so much what one does initially that affects the relationship as what he does next. Effective cross-cultural communication must keep all parties in mind at all times.

The behavioral scientist works with human behavior. The question of meaning is asked first and then the form or expression of the meaning is discovered or determined. Once the question of meaning is resolved, the bicultural person is able to look for the way in which meaning is conveyed to others. Disciplines other than the behavioral sciences start from fact, theory, and concept and then ask the question of behavior. Only when we first get at the question of meaning do we have an adequate basis for understanding.[2]

When we are aware only of form, we run the risk of *ethical relativism*. We ourselves either abandon principle or we force

1. For additional depth in areas of communication refer to Everett Rogers' *Modernization Among Peasants: The Impact of Communication* (New York: Holt, Rinehart, and Winston, 1969); *Communication of Innovations: A Cross-Cultural Approach* (New York: Free Press, 1971).
2. Richard L. Means, *The Ethical Imperative* (Garden City, New York: Doubleday, 1969). Dr. Means is a philosopher dealing with a sociological approach to ethics. American society is his focus.

another to abandon principles on which his life is based. Such abandonment of principle causes a person to become an irresponsible member of his own society.[3]

CROSSCULTURAL THEFT

In the United States, property is divided into public and private property in the following ways:

1. What is purchased individually is individually owned and therefore private property.
2. What is purchased corporately, e.g., by an organization or a political entity, is corporately owned and therefore public property.

A responsible member of a certain other society maintains what he wants within his own land limits and may use and abuse that as he wishes. He is not allowed to use or abuse that which lies within the domain of another's land without express permission. However, anything found outside the stated boundaries of a property site is to be used, and may even be abused, by anyone. Thus anything found on trails, roads or properties not clearly marked as "owned" is available to all. These areas are perceived as "not owned by anyone."

A North American in that society had purchased a tricycle for his child. Later he found that his maid had taken it to her little girl for her to play with. On the basis of the North American division of property, he accused the maid of theft. She was scandalized and quit her job. She had acted responsibly within the laws and expectations of her own society by taking the tricycle. She had found it on a trail and so could take it home to let her daughter enjoy it for a while. She had a definite sense of moral obligation not to steal. She had not intended stealing. However, her action was perceived as stealing and thus she was judged irresponsible by the North American, who viewed her actions from his cultural point of view.

He had forced her into a setting of conflict of norm. For her to remain in his household, she would have had to admit to

---

3. The work of Peter L. Berger represents a sophisticated treatment of the sociological basis for religious and value commitments. See Peter L. Berger and Thomas Luckmann, *The Social Construction of Reality* (Garden City, New York: Doubleday, 1967); and Peter L. Berger, *The Sacred Canopy: Elements of a Sociological Theory of Religion* (Garden City, New York: Doubleday, 1968).

Eugene A. Nida works with this problem from the anthropological side in *Customs and Cultures* (New York: Harper and Bros., 1954); and *Message and Mission* (New York: Harper and Bros., 1960).

theft — which she had not intended — and thus abandon her cultural categories that give meaning to life. This would have produced confusion as to her ethical and moral responsibility. Such an admission and abandonment of principle is a step toward an ethical relativism and its accompanying irresponsibility. It is further part of the process of enslavement and injustice.

An outsider, seeking to be fully responsible within a society such as that of the Pocomchi, would first of all inquire into the distinctions of property maintained there. He would attempt to grasp them in their entirety and follow them pragmatically as fully as possible without abandoning any of his own ethical and moral principles. He would further instruct his household not to take any possessions outside the domain of their land or yard or patio which would be carefully marked, e.g., with a hedge, a fence, or some simple boundary markers. If something did inadvertently get outside this boundary and was taken by another, inquiry could be made and the item repossessed. If no admission was made and the item was not discovered, he would simply have to resign himself to its loss and be more careful in the next instance.

There are alternative possibilities, of course, but each would have to be checked out within the context of the host society. For example, if the North American had established a good relationship with a highly respected member of the society, he could share his plight with that person and allow him to work out the matter of the return of the possession.

ABSOLUTISM AND RELATIVISM

The question arises, is there any other kind of relativism than ethical relativism? *Cultural relativism* is distinct from *ethical relativism* and is to be carefully distinguished from it. Ethical relativism implies an abandonment of principle and the accompanying irresponsibility within one's own life experience. Cultural relativism implies, rather, the maintenance of principle, the development of such principle, and total responsibility within one's own life and experience.[4]

Cultural relativism permits the member of a society to experi-

---

4. "All men, regardless of who they are or where they are in history and geography are held response-able [sic] for the choices they must make as Persons in relation to Persons in the context of their particular culture and most important in relation to God the creator of their whole possibility of Response. Thus ethics is not dealing primarily with standards and absolutes but rather with whether or not man responds to God in faith and obedience." R. D.

Refer also to Melville Herskovits, *Cultural Dynamics* (New York: Alfred A. Knopf, 1964).

ence absolutes and to know their true significance. As in the case of crosscultural theft in Central America, each person could know the absolute, "Thou shalt not steal." Each could know, affirm, and practice the absolute within the rules and expectations of his own society, fulfilling his responsibility both individually and collectively. Neither has to abandon the absolute in accommodation to the other. The conflict of norm very readily resolves itself through mutual understanding and its resolution is maintained through wise adaptation to a given society. Confusion has thus resulted in monocultural settings because of the association of cultural relativism and ethical relativism.[5]

Confusion has also resulted because of the merging of biblical absolutism with a cultural absolutism. Many well-meaning people within the one-culture setting assume that the way they do things is not only the way God would have them do it but the way He would have everyone else do it also. They feel they are living in a way pleasing to God. If they were not, they would certainly change what they were doing so that it would be pleasing to God. If in fact there are biblical absolutes, they must be lived out in everything the Christian thinks, says, and does. Therefore, in their minds, absolutism extends from God's absolutes to man's expressions of these absolutes within the cultural setting. Any variation from this pattern to sociocultural nuance would result in abandonment of absolutes. Biblical absolutism thus becomes merged forever with cultural absolutism. Anyone not supporting such absolutism, they feel, must be a relativist and not believe in absolutes in any sense.

Any combination of two paired entities results in four possible combinations. Biblical/cultural and absolutism/relativism produces the following combinations:

1. Biblical absolutism and cultural absolutism.
2. Biblical absolutism and cultural relativism.
3. Biblical relativism and cultural absolutism.
4. Biblical relativism and cultural relativism.

Option number three has historically been of no particular concern to the church. If someone did not affirm number one, it was assumed automatically that he was abandoning all absolutes and espousing biblical relativism along with cultural relativism. Many professionals in fact do hold to number four, but this is not an inherent fault of the profession, rather of the professional. A given professional disturbed with the consequences

5. For a careful look at this problem from the point of view of the anthropologist, read the works of Clyde Kluckhohn, Margaret Mead and Ruth Benedict.

of a biblical and cultural relativism does not need to go to complete relativism. He may opt for possibility number two and aid members of any culture know God fully as a member of that culture without changing to the culture of the "missionary."

BIBLICAL ABSOLUTISM AND CULTURAL RELATIVISM

The approach of biblical absolutism and cultural relativism affirms that there is a supernatural intrusion. This involves act as well as precept. Even as Christ, through the incarnation, became flesh and dwelt among us, so precept or truth becomes expressed in culture. However, even as the Word made flesh lost none of His divineness, so precept loses no truth by its expression via human sociocultural forms.[6] It is always full and complete as truth. So long as the sociocultural expression is approached crossculturally it can be recognized as truth as well. The moment truth is wed to one cultural expression there is a high potential for "falsehood" in any other culture. More seriously, since any given culture is in the process of change, there is an even higher potential for falsehood within the culture that locks truth into one expression.

To refer once again to the illustration of crosscultural theft, the commandment "Thou shalt not steal," as a moral absolute and as the very truth communicated within culture, becomes expressed in North American sense. It is expressed in Pocomchi Maya culture equally fully and completely in terms of private vs. public property in the Pocomchi sense.

Four questions insuring validity of distinct societies

The question naturally arises as to which norm or life-way is correct. The problem is resolved in the very process of asking crosscultural questions like the following:

1. What is the norm?
2. Is the person living in keeping with his norm?
3. Does the norm need changing?
4. Who is responsible for changing the norm?

The average person operating within his own norm and approaching others from the point of view of his norm will likely

---

6. Edward J. Carnell in *The Theology of Reinhold Niebuhr* (Grand Rapids: Wm. B. Eerdmans Publishing Co., 1950) suggests that "Christ is a moral absolute which stands outside of history to exhaust the freedom of man but sufficiently in history to clarify history's possibilities and limitation" (p. 108). I suggest that Christ is God's act of supernatural intrusion and the nucleating factor of supernatural precept, i.e., always divine and always human with no dichotomies. See also H. M. Kuitert, *The Reality of Faith* (Grand Rapids: Wm. B. Eerdmans Publishing Co., 1968), p. 168.

begin the four questions at number three. Since the norm of the other person is seen from the perspective of his own, then the other's norm needs changing. If the norm of the other is seen to be in need of change, then the person deciding that it needs changing becomes responsible for changing it. This may involve the parent in relation to the child, one mate to another, a missionary in relation to the national, the pastor in response to the layman. The process of changing the norm of the other thus lies completely with the one deciding that the norm needs changing. No one else need be involved in the final decision. Thus the parent decides for the child, one mate for the other, the missionary council for the nationals, the faculty for the student body, the pastor for the layman. Within the Christian context, in case the one making the decision feels the need for support, he need only refer to the leading of the Spirit of God with whom he has counseled in the matter. Thus, no one is able to question the final decision.

The person approaching the action, thought, or belief of another from a crosscultural or bicultural point of view will start with question number one.[7] He will thus seek to understand fully the system on which the action, belief, or thought is based and then ask if the person is acting responsibly in keeping with that system; i.e., he will proceed to question number two on the solid base of system. He will have searched out the meaning by going to the basis of motivation.[8] He will be concerned with what the person intended in the first place, whether it was responsible or irresponsible action. Then, and only then, will he proceed to question number three. When the change agent asks this question, he will be doing so, not in terms of his own norm, but in terms of the norm of the other. This will immediately involve the other in the change process. But even more significantly, it will open the norm of the change agent to the possibility of change as well. Once the norm of each is open to change, there is a viable role for the Spirit of God to enter and guide either or both in the change process. In a dynamic way, three become responsible for the change of norm: the Spirit of God, the one whose norm needs changing as impulsed by the Spirit, and the support person. Thus, a true reciprocity of change develops, opening either or both to the effective change of norm (chart 32).

As the change agent, now open to the change of his own

---

7. Refer to A. Berkeley Mickelson, *Interpreting the Bible* (Grand Rapids: Wm. B. Eerdmans Publishing Co., 1963), p. 170.

8. Mickelson, *Interpreting the Bible*, p. 172.

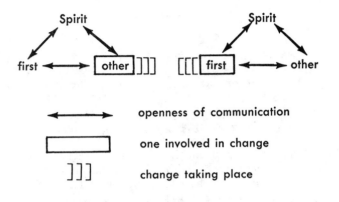

Chart 32. Reciprocity in Change

norm or that of the other (or for that matter, the change of both or neither) proceeds, he finds a new need arising. He now needs something other than the existential validation of behavioral change. He senses the need for some objective, external standard.[9]

The Scriptures (chart 33), in the form of the Bible, provide this standard. The first person, along with the other person, i.e., both the one whose norm needs changing and his support person, work with the Scriptures in the language they can *both* understand and respond to as "the very Word of God." For certain North Americans this will only and always be the King James Version of the Bible. For other North Americans this will only and always be some contemporary language version, depending on their dialect of English. For those of distinct ethnic and linguistic backgrounds, this will be the product of a translation program directed by an individual, by a Bible society, or by some other organization such as the Wycliffe Bible Translators and the Tyndale Living Bible translation program. Thus a new combination of resources and resource people in the change process develops:

---

9. Carnell, in *The Theology of Reinhold Niebuhr,* p. 69, distinguishes his point of view, namely "orthodoxy determines its view of the nature of man from propositional revelation," from the view of Niebuhr who Carnell says determines his view from the existential witness of the heart. I suggest that both are involved. There must be the existential validation of the religious experience, which indeed, when prior, gives tremendous motivation in the process of knowing God. But this drives one to propositional truth. When the reverse is true, one shapes experience by word/form application, which is not very exciting (it readily gets bogged down in a traditionalism), but more, it is not always truth.

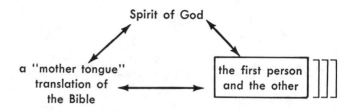

Chart 33. Resources in the Change Process

Within such a dynamic process, change demands from cross-cultural challenges, along with change demands within one society through time, can be effectively worked with.[10]

But a new problem may confront the agent of change once this process begins and the cooperative, reciprocal change process continues. Suppose neither norm needs changing? Or suppose a norm changes slowly over an extensive time period? Or suppose the norm of the first person changes while that of the other, seen previously as that which definitely needed changing, remains constant. This is perhaps the greatest challenge to be faced by the missionary or agent of change. He has gone to another people assuming that the norm will change with the entrance of the Gospel. After all, aren't they heathen? Certain things will likely change simply because of the demand of crosscultural contact, but there may be areas of resistance that seem to the outsider to involve aspects of the culture that *must* change.

Numerous considerations are possible at this point. It is possible that the other is *not* paying attention to the leading of the Spirit of God. The translation of the Bible being used among them may not be adequate. It is possible that the first person has interpreted either the sociocultural setting or the Bible incorrectly. It is also possible that the norm of the first must change before there can be a foundation for change in the other. It is also possible that change is taking place but at a slow pace, far slower than would otherwise be expected within the norm of the change agent, or far slower than what is actually beneficial for the people involved. Or it is even possible that the Gospel can enter a life and thus a society without any change — apart from spiritual change —being called for.

In such cases, careful attention must be paid to the effective ministries model presented in the next section. Any effort to

10. This is the more characteristic challenge facing the missionary moving at one point of time across cultural boundaries.

change one norm in keeping with the norm of another will likely result in the one whose norm is the subject of attention being thrown into conflict — a condition not conducive to spiritual growth. One must be careful not to introduce social conflict unnecessarily lest he confuse the spiritual conflict naturally taking place with the entrance of the biblical message of truth, i.e., the Gospel. Additional care must be taken that any progress in change be encouraged in keeping with the sociocultural system operating to ensure the cultural uniqueness that is necessary for spiritual growth. Finally, the support person in working with another can progress through the effective ministries model to encourage true creativity within the individual and corporate life experience of the Christian.

Consider the complex ethical-spiritual problem of the following case study:

SACRIFICIAL ADULTERY

As the Russian armies drove westward to meet the Americans and British at the Elbe, a Soviet patrol picked up a Mrs. Bergmeier foraging food for her three children. Unable even to get word to the children, and without any clear reason for it, she was taken off to a prison camp in the Ukraine. Her husband had been captured in the Battle of the Bulge and taken to a POW camp in Wales.

When he was returned to Berlin, he spent many weeks rounding up his children; two (Ilse, twelve, and Paul, ten) were found in a detention school run by the Russians, and the oldest, Hans, fifteen, was found hiding in a cellar near the Alexander Platz. Their mother's whereabouts remained a mystery, but they never stopped searching. She, more than anything else, was needed to reknit them as a family in that dire situation of hunger, chaos, and fear.

Meanwhile, in the Ukraine, Mrs. Bergmeier learned through a sympathetic commandant that her husband and family were trying to keep together and find her. But the rules allowed them to release her for either of only two reasons: (1) illness needing medical facilities beyond those in the camp, in which case she would be sent to a Soviet hospital elsewhere, or (2) pregnancy, for which she would be returned to Germany as a liability.

She turned things over in her mind and finally asked a friendly Volga German camp guard to impregnate her, which he did. Her condition being medically verified, she was sent back to Berlin and to her family. They welcomed her with open arms, even when she told them how she had managed it. When the child was born, they loved him more than all the rest, since little Dietrich had done more for them than anybody else.

When it was time for him to be christened, they took him to the pastor on a Sunday afternoon. After the ceremony they sent Dietrich home with the other children and sat down in the pastor's study to ask him whether they were right to feel as they did about Mrs. Bergmeier and Dietrich. Should they be grateful to the Volga German? Had Mrs. Bergmeier done a good and right thing?[11]

Applying the approach of biblical absolutism and cultural relativism to a case study, the following alternative solution reflects the critical distinctions that separate it from the traditionalist, the relativist, or the situation ethicist point of view. The value of the case study, as stated previously, lies not in the provision of "final" answers, but in providing a means of application of principles to test their validity and to provide experience in handling similar cases in "real" life.

The norm model suggests that there are certain norms at least represented in the case. These include the norm of Mrs. Bergmeier, the norm of the German guard, the norm of the husband, the norm of the pastor, the norm of the person reading the case, and the norm of Joseph Fletcher who has authored a book in which the case is set by way of example.

Fletcher's norm is expressed through the title as well as through the place given such a case in a discussion of *situation ethics*. He has already shared his norm with the readers by using the title "sacrificial adultery" implying that Mrs. Bergmeier committed adultery for the sake of something or someone other than herself since she acted out of "love" for another.

> The situationist enters into every decision-making situation fully armed with the ethical maxims of his community and its heritage, and he treats them with respect as illuminators of his problems. Just the same, he is prepared in any situation to compromise them or set them aside in the situation if love seems better served by doing so.[12]

The norm of the reader becomes expressed through agreement or disagreement with Fletcher. If there is disagreement, alternatives of norm become expressed in keeping with the way the person sees himself and thus sees Mrs. Bergmeier. It is easy, at this point in the case study, for the reader to respond that she

---

11. Joseph Fletcher, *Situation Ethics* (Philadelphia: Westminster Press, 1966), p. 164.
12. Ibid., p. 26.

did the wrong thing "biblically" and then proceed to state how she *should* have acted in keeping with the "objective standard" of the Bible. This is frequently expressed with the question "What is God's norm?" Were the person making such a response in contact with Mrs. Bergmeier at the time she was contemplating the solution to her problem, he would overtly or covertly begin the "self-directed" program of change — of Mrs. Bergmeier. She would feel the pressure to change and either conform to get along, or resist conformity, or possibly find reason to change in keeping with the pressures upon her to "shape up." There is the definite likelihood that any change thus introduced would come about through conflict, such conflict ultimately never being resolved.

The norm of the pastor, representing his church, was expressed in his noncritical response to Mr. and Mrs. Bergmeier. The norm of Mr. Bergmeier evidences itself in terms of both his positive response to his wife's return and the degree of tension leading them to seek out the pastor. The norm of Mrs. Bergmeier becomes clear in view of her action in the prison camp in seeking out a German guard and requesting the impregnation.[13]

The *ranking of values* within a norm and the generation of behavior as based on a core of ranked values provides an objective look at the behavior of a person.

If, for example, we concentrate on the two parts of Mrs. Bergmeier's norm that could be termed "concern for family" and "personal sexual purity" and rank these in alternate ways, we can predict behavior on the basis of a specific ranking.

Norm A

rank one — concern for family
rank two — concern for personal sexual purity

In keeping with the dominance of rank one value, other things being equal, personal sexual purity would yield to concern for family. Mrs. Bergmeier could have sought the impregnation as a fully responsible person. Whether she actually did seek it or not would not change her norm, rather, such a situation as indicated would only serve to give expression to the norm.

If, however, Mrs. Bergmeier's norm had the same two concerns in reverse rank:

13. A German viewing the case finds it significant that she sought out a German guard rather than a Russian. An American likely misses this nuance.

Norm B

rank one — concern for personal sexual purity
rank two — concern for family,

then in keeping with the dominance of rank one value, other things being equal, concern for family would yield to concern for personal sexual purity. She would have sought out the impregnation only in direct conflict to her norm; in other words, she would *not* have sought it.

Excess and deprivation of norm suggest alternatives of behavior and response to behavior involving guilt or bitterness. If we assume for the moment that Mrs. Bergmeier's norm was Norm A, she would be living fully and completely in her norm as a responsible person and would have no sense of guilt. If we assume for the moment that her norm was Norm B, not only would she have acted contrary to her norm, but it would also be expected that she would have a sense of guilt to the degree that she was living in excess of her norm.

Now, if for the moment we assume that her norm was Norm A, for her not to have sought the impregnation would have left her in deprivation of norm, unless some other way out was provided. Such deprivation would result in a sense of bitterness intense to the degree that she was living in deprivation of her norm. Had her husband's norm also been A, he would experience this bitterness as well to the extent of his knowledge of the situation. If we assume that Mrs. Bergmeier's norm was Norm B, then she would have no sense of deprivation were she to resist the impregnation route out of prison camp. She would then have "made the most" of the situation.

Conflict of norm suggests the possibility of a number of conflicts, some of which were resolved and others of which, insofar as this case is concerned, were not possible of resolution. Mrs. Bergmeier would have had conflict within herself if her norm was B; but no evidence of conflict would show if it was A. To the degree that there was ambiguity in rank, she would have had a degree of guilt or bitterness, whichever way the ambiguity revealed itself. She would have had conflict with her husband and those he represented, i.e., the children, if her norm was A and his B, or vice versa. She would have had conflict with the church to the degree that the norm of the pastor had been different from her own. She would have conflict with the reader had she operated on the basis of her valid norm and were that of the reader different from hers. She would have conflict with Fletcher if in fact she had operated on the basis of Norm A and there had been no place for the situation to set up her behavior in keeping with the love ethic.

It appears that Mrs. Bergmeier was not without a degree of tension, since she and her husband later approached the pastor. This conflict, insofar as this case is concerned, was resolved quickly with the decision of the pastor who apparently shared Norm A with her. Thus, it would appear that there was a degree of ambiguity of rank of values (though such ambiguity appears to have suggested a base of Norm A), with the ambiguity becoming resolved through consultation with the pastor.[14]

The *effective ministry* model suggests an approach to the case and to Mrs. Bergmeier that would have biblical absolutism as a foundation and let her experience absolutes within a valid culture. She would be in maximum conflict with one whose norm was B if hers was A. If such a person were to counsel her before her act, it would be necessary to effect the team or cooperative approach to change. Working with Mrs. Bergmeier with a Bible in her language, one might possibly introduce directed change into her life through the ministrations of the Spirit of God. Change would thus proceed, not in keeping with what the reader thinks the biblical absolutes are as seen through his own personal norm, but rather, in keeping with true biblical absolutes guided into distinct sociocultural settings by the Spirit.[15]

VARIATION OF NORM

Bicultural operations within the crosscultural challenge develop an ever-widening range of variation within the life-style of the individual. Anyone living for a period within a distinct culture, having approached that culture with a degree of acceptance, can witness to such increase of variation. If one is seeking to influence short-haired people, he can trim his hair; if long-haired people, he can let his hair grow. If one is approaching

---

14. In a later development of the case, it appears that certain doubts arose within the mind of the husband and tension increased. Such additions to the case would force a new study of the now "new case," yet they would not invalidate the insights gained from the above considerations, since these were provided in response to a now "different" case.

15. I personally feel, from my understanding of the Word of God, that her norm would change over time. At the same time, there is a great deal of insight I personally gain by leaving my own norm open to the Spirit in terms of my responsibility to my family. If her norm did not change over time, then I would be forced to reexamine my own understanding of Scripture, take a new look at her norm, take a fresh look at mine, examine the effectiveness of my agent of change operations and above all develop the patience of which James speaks in James 1. Compare this point of view with the five presented in H. Richard Niebuhr, *Christ and Culture* (New York: Harper and Row, n.d.).

time-oriented people, he can pay particular attention to time scheduling; if approaching event-oriented people, he can pay attention to those things that encourage eventing. If one is approaching families where the father is a strong figure, he can stress the father nature of God; if approaching families where the father is not a strong figure then some other teaching about God can be sought out and used. If one is a person with Norm B attempting to reach someone with Norm A, then he can both put into effect change potential and learn from the insights of the other in those areas where his life is needing such insight. Paul puts it this way: "I have become all things to all men, that I might by all means save some" (1 Cor. 9:22 RSV).

This is not an approach of compromise, but of enrichment. To compromise is to abandon principle, however little or much. To extend one's range of variation of life-style is to incorporate as many life-styles into his own as possible without producing destructive tension or cause abandonment of principle or absolute. One can therefore be "comfortable" or "at peace" when crossing cultural boundaries. He can also become maximally available to the members of the culture or subculture with whom the Gospel of Jesus Christ is shared. Christ did not condemn the woman taken in adultery. Rather, He opened the way for an effective change of norm and extension of norm that would leave her free to worship Him fully and completely.

SUMMARY

The monocultural approach to the behavior of others is to see in what ways that behavior is understandable to the one viewing it and how it can be changed to conform to the expectations of the one viewing it. The crosscultural or bicultural approach lets man be man and God be God in evaluating behavior. Thus, biblical absolutism is teamed with cultural relativism so that a Nigerian can be a Nigerian and be fully open to God; or a North American can be a valid North American and fully open to God. Such an approach effects maximum responsibility of the person and allows him to have those sociocultural uniquenesses that reinforce his identity and encourage mature growth in the Christian faith. Spiritual conflict is thus not intensified because of unnecessary social conflict. The sacrificial adultery of the Fletcher case study can be seen to be not so much sacrificial as the woman's living out her higher norm as a responsible individual; not just adultery, but the recognition of the precise nature of a norm that is potential for change by the Spirit of God through the Scriptures speaking to the heart of the person involved. It further opens to the same influence any distinct norm so that concern for family will not be totally dominated by other considerations of life-style. A truly bicultural individual can introduce the Gospel in any culture or subculture without the accompanying "cultural baggage" that is potential for enslavement of the person and falsification of precept or truth. His range of variation of life-style or norm is increased, so he is comfortable and at peace with peoples of diverse styles or norms, while at the same time he is protected from abandonment of his own principles. He gains perspective that objectively enables him as a wise counselor to aid another in effective change of norm in keeping with the expressed will of God. Four questions give one tools and flexibility to maintain the validity of a norm or culture or lifeway:

1. What is the norm?
2. Is he living in keeping with the norm, i.e., fully responsible?
3. Does the norm need changing?
4. Who is responsible for changing the norm?

Questions for discussion:

1. Is there anything that you do, which you notice no one else does, but which you feel is a very important part of your identity? Describe.
2. Can a person praying in an upright position be as close to God as one who is praying while kneeling?
3. Describe two distinct patterns of "hospitality" existing side by side in North American society.
4. Distinguish cultural relativism from ethical relativism. Which one intends total individual and corporate responsibility? (Consult chapter 5 if necessary.)

Group activities and exercises:

1. Small Group: Have the members discuss the cultural relativism evident in the progress of the Hebrews from the Old Testament period to the New Testament period. Is this bad? How did such development prepare more fully for the coming of Christ? How might Jesus have been introduced into the world had there been no culture change?
2. Panel discussion: Have three members of the group prepare a panel on the subject of biblical absolutes vs. cultural expressions as reflected in the Bible. Have each prepare a five-minute statement on a specific subject such as "The Bible says nothing

of dress styles except to indicate that one should be modest whatever his style." Then open the discussion to the larger group.

3. Have each group member respond again in writing to the case study "Sacrificial Adultery" and compare his new statement with his original response. This gives the members an opportunity to check their progress in the learning experience and it also gives the teacher the opportunity of working in greater depth with the case than would otherwise be possible.

4. Guest from a distinct society: Have a member of some society that practices a life-way distasteful to the average American (e.g., arranged marriage) come to the group and explain how his Christian life is enhanced by being fully responsible within the context of his own culture.

Effective Ministry
Absolutism and Relativism
The Support Model
The Models Illustrated

17

the support model

IF I FORBID KEN TO DRINK

When Ken Harris was a sophomore in college, he wrote home to his parents that he had begun to drink with the fellows. Ken's mother Ethel was frantic, and she said to her husband Sid, "Write and tell him to stop drinking at once."

After thinking about it a few moments, Sid replied, "No, I won't. If I forbid Ken to drink, he may stop, but it will be because I made the decision for him, not because he had come to a decision on his own."

Ethel found this reasoning very unsatisfactory. "Why shouldn't Ken have the benefit of our experience?" she protested. "Anyway, it's difficult enough these days to get through college *sober.*"

After some further discussion, the parents decided to make it possible for Ken to spend several weekends at home that fall. During those days together, Sid tried subtly to get close to Ken, not pressing for an abnormal intimacy but giving his son numerous opportunities to talk about whatever was on his mind.

Several times the two of them went hiking along mountain trails. As it turned out, very little was said about college social problems in general, or drinking in particular, but a new friendship developed between the father and son which eased communication.

One day Sid told Ken about a member of the family who had died of alcoholism. "I have quite an affinity for alcohol myself," he

245

admitted; "so I've decided to leave it strictly alone. Not only for my own sake, but for your mother's and yours."

Ken didn't comment on this. They resumed their climb up the mountain, and some hours passed in the deep silence characteristic of men who enjoy being in the woods. Occasionally one of them would make a comment, but what passed between them was largely unspoken.

Three months later, Ken again raised the question of drinking in one of his letters, but this time the emphasis had wholly changed. "I've decided not to drink," he wrote. "Some of the fellows in the dorm have been going off the deep end. I've come to the conclusion that drinking is wrong for me. I hope I can get some of my friends to take a good look at themselves, too."[1]

Rejection of the person for whatever reason produces a pattern of rejection likely resulting in conflict. Conflict serves to undermine interpersonal relations through the malfunction of tension. The behavioral response is inconsistency and unpredictability in interpersonal relations tending to undermine the trust base of those relationships. With the undermining of trust, relationships are terminated or, at the least, strained.

Given conflict, the resolution of conflict can be achieved only through the reversal of the rejection patterns, thus resulting in acceptance of the person. From the point that the message of acceptance gets through, acceptance or rejection of behavior can be worked with effectively.

THE BRIDGE FROM CONFLICT TO RAPPORT

Acceptance of the person as he is causes those involved in interpersonal and intergroup relationships to seek out a bridge (chart 34) that will lead the one(s) in conflict out of conflict into a basic rapport. The various means of resolving conflict utilized by the average person in conflict are one or more of the following: scapegoating, withdrawal, conformity for conformity's sake, formation of a new group, etc. They serve as a kind of therapy, but will just as likely reinforce the conflict as resolve it and may even lead the person or group into new patterns of conflict. The bridge or bridges sought for, therefore, must lead the person out of the conflict setting completely and not simply be therapeutic.

Bridges may be:

information   action apology

---

1. Lionel Whiston, *Are You Fun to Live With?* (Waco, Texas: Word Books, 1969).

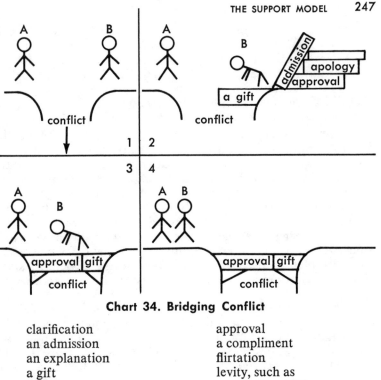

Chart 34. Bridging Conflict

clarification	approval
an admission	a compliment
an explanation	flirtation
a gift	levity, such as
a favor	punning, joking,
use of a metaphor	teasing, heckling
a show of power	a game or
correction	recreational activity
a counterstatement	acquiesence
verbal apology	

In Lionel Whiston's illustration of a college fellow who took up drinking alcoholic beverage much to the displeasure and disappointment of his parents, the mother kept after the father to order the boy to stop drinking. The father was aware that by ordering his son to stop drinking he would likely achieve the adverse effect — in essence driving the boy deeper into alcohol. When the father took his son on a camping trip, the father had a chance to share some of his earlier life with his son. Included in his sharing was the *admission* that he had once taken up drinking, but that after considering the effect of drinking on his personal health and considering that he had a wife and new child to care for, he had given it up. The sharing experience had quite an impact on the boy.

The Filipino uses the *apology* to end conflict. When there is tension between a mother and daughter, for example, and the daughter senses that the mother sees her as being in the wrong, no words will be said, but the girl will seek out some action that will communicate her apology to the mother, e.g., washing the dishes voluntarily. Nothing further is made of the event, but both know that the conflict is ended.[2]

At times, when working within the support model or the effective ministries model, it is necessary to throw someone back into conflict to achieve a greater rapport or a more firm base for interpersonal relations. A parent who senses that a child does not respect him, may eliminate certain privileges, e.g., the allowance, for a period in order for the child to have a greater appreciation for that privilege and greater respect for the one making it available. At times, when it appears that students perceive a professor to be an easy mark, it is necessary for the professor to "pour on the work" so the students, trained to expect a certain amount of work, restore full respect in him.

SUPPORT (Chart 35)

Once a bridge is built, those involved in interpersonal relations become support persons for one another. For the sake of this discussion, however, only two will be referred to — the one changing and the support person. The support person is increasingly cognizant of what the other is — his total socio-cultural involvement — and he begins to work with him in letting him progress in the change process in keeping with what he is, not in keeping with some external standard established by the first. The point of the support model within effective ministry is to have the person bring the real and the ideal together within himself and not have some external standard of an ideal held up to the degree that the person is caught between the ideal and the real, thus finding himself in conflict. This permits gradual, effectual change with what he thinks he is, or thinks he ought to be. The person involved with him is thus the one supporting him in this process of growth and development.

The support model involves the establishment of goals, setting operations to meet those goals, the ongoing evaluation of the goals and operations, resetting of each, the alternate session, and the impulsing to creativity. In other words, the support model encourages the full development and maturation of the

---

2. Marvin K. Mayers, *Notes on Christian Outreach in a Philippine Community* (Pasadena, California: William Carey Library, 1970).

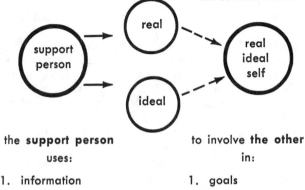

the **support person** uses:	to involve **the other** in:
1. information	1. goals
2. evaluation	2. operations
3. "counseling"	3. evaluation of goals and operations with resetting of each
4. moral support	4. alternate sessions
5. creative interaction	5. creativity

Chart 35. The Role of the Support Person During the Change Process

person to the corporate body. The support person has the delightful opportunity of seeing another develop fully in keeping with the fullest range of goals and opportunities available to him.

GOAL SETTING

Goals are anything toward which a person strives. They may be formal goals that are written down, sworn by, and carried out to the letter, or they may be hopes and aspirations that are nebulous in conception but nonetheless real. They may be short range, middle range, or long range. Time-oriented persons will establish timed goals involving timed periods of achievement; event-oriented persons will establish goals of being with people and embellishing the event. Though the two kinds of goals may differ in form, they are the same type of goal motivated by a distinct world and life view. Timed goals will throw an event person into conflict; eventing goals will frustrate the timed person. Long-range goals are likely more nebulous than shorter-range goals, and shorter-range goals more specific. A person needs both to enable him to move maturely through life.

Anyone who values one thing above another, a trait that is

characteristic of humans, will establish goals and strive for them. The support person has the opportunity to work with the person in establishing these goals and confirming their personal and ultimate value. He may suggest alternative goals in keeping with the person and his motivation. His task of providing information, however, is probably his greatest contribution in the goal-setting area: The person himself seldom has all the information he needs to set effective goals of any type. The support person extends the other person's objectivity and scope and opens the way to more effective goal setting.

A missionary may have a long-range goal of reaching men for Christ, but in his day-to-day goals he may not know exactly what to do. The Wycliffe Bible translator has the day-to-day goals built into his training so that he works from one aspect of the language to another until he is fluent within the whole. This then opens many doors to witness that become fruitful in accomplishing his ultimate goal of saving men in Christ's name. The nonlinguistic missionary needs day-to-day goals as well. Generally they are in terms of approaching men on the street, going from door to door and holding tent meetings. Such day-to-day goals are fine when the missionary knows the culture, but he also needs day-to-day goals that open to him the culture and the unique ways of working in that specific culture.

I have reported in another volume of the work being undertaken in the Philippines.[3] The long-range goal of winning men and women to Christ was established and each member of the team held firmly to the goal. Their day-to-day goals were made operational with the admission that "we really don't know just how to open Filipino society to the Gospel." They were doing numerous things such as holding tent meetings and conducting door-to-door evangelism, but these did not seem to be working as well as it appeared they could be. The Filipino was very receptive and responsive at first, but later on he turned cold to the message and to the missionary as well. Further, middle-range goals were almost nonexistent.

My work with the family and the Alliance opened to me a most critical area of the social structure and suggested some day-to-day goals that would effectively meet the long-range goals of the missionaries. It was suggested that, because of the centrality of the Alliance and the importance of the head of the Alliance (the highest status man in the Alliance), a short-range goal would be to get to know just who were the heads of Alli-

---

3. Ibid.

ances within a given community. Middle-range goals would be to know specific heads of Alliances within a two-year period and to have begun Bible studies in the homes of those who were most receptive. The long-range goal would continue as before, but a further long-range goal would be to let the Bible study in the home of the leader of an Alliance develop into the local church and become related to other local churches through a loose alignment of groups under a leader who was of higher status than any of the other Alliance leaders. In one area where such a program was tried out, five Bible studies were established within the space of two years, much to the encouragement of the missionary.

OPERATIONS TO MEET GOALS

Operations help the person achieve his goals and therefore they must be in keeping with both what the person is and the nature of the goal itself. The operations of a blind person must necessarily be different from the operations of a sighted person. The operations of a time person will differ from the operations of an event person. For example, in establishing a devotional program, a person who is blind and time oriented will concentrate on the use of thought forms rather than visible forms, and these will be scheduled according to some regularity of time sequence. A sighted person who is event oriented will be able to utilize visual as well as thought forms and build these into an experience of devotions that will not be controlled by time. The operations of a time person will be to effect schedule, whereas the operations of an event person will be to develop associations. The two types of operations are not mutually exclusive, for both together can be formed into a total pattern for either person. However, the time person is more likely to develop timed operations even as the event person is more likely to develop operations that extend personal association or that embellish the event.

THE ALTERNATE SESSION

There are times when a person in the change process needs to operate alone and there are times when he needs supervision. The concept of the alternate session permits both eventualities. Jesus would at times be with his disciples and at times they would be off alone doing that which was set up during their period of contact. The concept has come into contemporary usefulness through the program of social work and psychological counseling. The social worker and marriage counselor or the psychological counselor have a person for a work session or consultation; then they urge him to go out and put into practice the things he has learned during the insight session with the trained professional. In reality, church is one such alternate session, since a member is with the pastor for an hour or two and away from him until the same time the next week, applying (hopefully) what he has learned. School also has alternate sessions built into the educational program in that each holiday becomes a break from the learning process and the summer vacation permits a variety of experiences that can be debriefed at the beginning of the new school year.

That which makes the alternate session of maximal worth is the debriefing session. This involves talking through the experience away from the counselor. Everyone learns covertly from experiences. At times, however, it is necessary to make that learning overt. The person involved in the experience is too frequently caught up in it subjectively and is unable to see all the factors that are available to be learned and to be of help to him. The support person thus sets up the debriefing session either formally or informally to let the person himself see that which he has learned through the experience.

EVALUATION OF GOALS AND OPERATIONS

Part of the debriefing session also becomes a time for the evaluation and reevaluation of goals and operations. The time-oriented person will likely set scheduled times for the debriefing sessions. The event person will have to "be caught," ideally when he is between events. Scheduling for the event person cannot be time scheduled but it can be effectively carried out, nonetheless.

In working with departmental assistants and teaching assistants in my role as departmental chairman, I encounter numerous students who trend toward the event side of the time/event continuum. It is impossible to tie them down to a specific time schedule — any set appointment will be broken a large percentage of times. Therefore, it is necessary to look to other machinery to effect the evaluation of goals and operations. Whenever we meet, we are talking about the students' responsibilities. What results is an "ongoing conversation" that never ends; we simply take up where we left off. Naturally this is not possible for a large number of students, but where the program is small, such personal contact has effectively provided the alternate session as well as the evaluation of goals and operations.

If certain goals are not being met, they can be restated and reformed in keeping with all the new information and insight available at this contact session. When one approaches a new program, he idealistically sets up some goals. After experience, they can be limited, restricted, and reshaped more effectively.

FEEDBACK

Feedback is vital in any communication process because it provides a guide to the correction of message so that the message is received as intended. Every social group, every individual involved in interpersonal relations and thus in communication, needs feedback to make clear to him whether the "message" got through intact or was the bearer of falsehood.

Feedback is of special importance to determine the speed at which change is introduced. The support person's hands are not tied by adhering to a fixed scheduling. When there is feedback that shows him what change can transpire rapidly, he can move forward as rapidly as possible. When he senses verbal and nonverbal indicators of resistance, he can take a look at this resistance objectively, analyze the true message of the resistance, and gear his program and its speed of initiation to the new situation forming. Overall, in the process of change, that which takes a week to develop will take a week to change or resolve; that which takes a year to develop will take a year to change. Any change effected in a briefer period of time than that which is expected is like a "bonus" in the change process.

The missionary vitally needs to learn this lesson of feedback. He wants to introduce Jesus Christ, but so often he does this irrespective of the need-for-response of the person to whom he is witnessing. He does not realize that the person is frequently resisting on sociocultural grounds — not necessarily spiritual grounds — and until these are dealt with, the person will never be able to commit himself spiritually. The missionary can read the true message of resistance, back up, and establish a new relationship with the object of his witness. Later, when he reads the signs of response, he can move just as rapidly as that response indicates. Verbal and nonverbal cues provide red, green, and amber lights to the change process. Some people can grow rapidly in their Christian lives and others take a very long time. We don't have to insist on an identical or constant rate of growth for everyone in encouraging them in the Christian way and walk.

THE TRUE COUNSELOR

The true counselor (chart 36) is the support person who encourages the other to develop, change, and mature in keeping

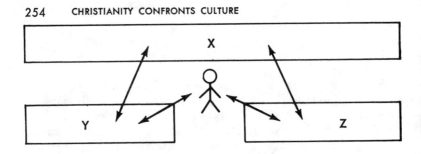

Chart 36. The True Counselor

with what he is personally. Such a counselor provides information and moral support so that the other person or group can be truly creative in keeping with his uniqueness as a person, within the total context of his sociocultural setting, i.e., fully responsible. He never dictates to himself, to his own group *(y)*, or to the other *(z)*. Rather, he permits each to tap into the "truth" of the larger group *(x)*, in keeping with the justice model (chapter 8). In this way each person or group develops uniquely and learns from the other, but does not become enslaved to the other.

Thus the true counselor needs objective knowledge of himself and the other through an understanding of distinctives in the sociocultural settings involved, accepting each as valid and worthy of respect. He will work with the various possibilities of bridges from conflict to rapport, attempting to release the other from the web of conflict. He will be one who provides information and thus will be available in the formation of goals and operations. His "feel" for the other and his true needs will involve him in the ongoing process of evaluation and reformulation of goals and operations. In being available in this way, he need never abandon his own principle and can thus encourage the other to be fully responsible individually and corporately. By becoming involved in the alternate session plan, he does not become a crutch but is there when needed to talk or work through a problem. This is most effectively set up through the debriefing process when opportunity is provided to let the covert learning of the lived experience become overt and specific. Debriefing provides the opportunity for the other person or group to feed back information that will show the true nature of the learning experience and effect change in the communicated "message" so it can get through correctly and not be laden with falsehood. Finally, the support person, creative himself, encourages the truly creative expression of the other.

One of the most difficult aspects of youth work is seeing the youth develop as youth and not thinking that they should be made over into adults before they can have the conversion and early growth experiences. The true conselor is one who lets the youth be youth and grow in Christ and lets the adults be adults and grow in Christ. He thus accepts each group as it is, letting the truth flow through the various levels of the hierarchy into each group so that each might maintain its true identity.

CREATIVITY[4]

Creativity grows out of what a person is and is shaped by what he is. Creativity can develop when a person lets all the various aspects of his life be integrated and blended in terms of his uniqueness and its forming. Everything that is involved in his internal, personal life experience and everything that is involved in the external life about him and yet that influences and shapes him .becomes part of that uniqueness. Uniqueness does not imply irresponsibility to the corporate body, rather it enhances responsibility. Since that which a person is, is his corporate nature and all the corporate entities and social groups of which he is a part, his uniqueness will feed out of their uniqueness and in return help form their uniqueness.

Note the following characteristics of a creative person:

PROFILE OF A CREATIVE PERSON

1. *Inherited sensitivity.* The creative person has a propensity for a greater sensitivity to certain types of experience: mathematical, artistic, musical, mechanical, literary. This appears to be well established by studies of families which exhibit high creativity in certain fields over several generations.

"Possibly," Seidel says, "the artist's apparently odd way of looking at things derives more from the inherited and developed sensitivity which makes him more readily attuned to the subtleties of various sensations and impressions, than from an asymmetrical viewpoint different from the ordinary man in the street. . . . The peculiar way the creative person may look at things derives from a physically based sensitivity toward sensations of a certain type."

4. For works dealing with creativity, see:

H. E. Gruber, G. Terrell, and M. Wertheimer, eds., *Contemporary Approaches to Creative Thinking* (New York: Atherton Press, 1962).

John W. Haefele, *Creativity and Innovation* (New York: Van Nostrand-Reinhold Publishing Co., 1962).

Jules Henry, "Spontaneity, Initiative, and Creativity in Suburban Classrooms" in *Education and Culture,* ed. George Spindler (New York: Holt, Rinehart and Winston, 1963).

2. *Early training.* The creative person, more likely than not, had his childhood in a home atmosphere that encouraged, rather than discouraged, inquisitiveness (although too rigid a home environment might drive him to seek new and original answers on his own). Creativity is as much a matter of attitude as anything else, and most human attitudes may be imprinted before the age of seven.

3. *Liberal education.* The creative person is more likely to express his creativity if he is exposed to teachers and curricula that place a premium on questions rather than answers, and which reward curiosity rather than learning by rote and conformity.

4. *Asymmetrical ways of thought.* The creative person finds an original kind of order in disorder; it is as if he stared at the reflection of nature in a distorted mirror, whereas "ordinary" people are able to see the image in a plain mirror only. Most highly intelligent people (as measured by tests) have symmetrical ways of thought, and for them, everything balances out in some logical way.

5. *Personal courage.* The creative person is not afraid of failure, or of being laughed at. He can afford this risk because what is important — to him — is not what others think of him, but what he thinks of himself.

6. *Sustained curiosity.* The creative person never stops asking questions, even about his most cherished ideas. "Those who have an excessive faith in their ideas," said Claude Bernard, "are not well fitted to make discoveries." A capacity for childlike wonder, carried into adult life, typifies the creative person.

7. *Not time-bound.* Morning, noon, and night are all the same to the creative person; he does not work by the clock. Problems may take years to solve, discovery may take decades. With his personal "window on infinity," time has a personal, not a social meaning. Truly creative persons seldom respond well to "deadlines" arbitrarily set by someone else.

8. *Dedication.* The creative person has an unswerving desire to do something, whatever it may be and whatever the obstacles to doing it. The problem will not be left unsolved; the feeling will not remain unexpressed.

9. *Willingness to work.* It is quite possible that no one in our society works harder than the artist; the same may be said for the creative scientist, inventor, composer, or

mathematician. This may not express itself in the number of hours put in on the job or in obvious physical labor, but in the fact that even in sleep or reverie the creative person is constantly working for a solution. The willingness to spend years simply accumulating data about which a creative question may be asked is characteristic of the creative person (Darwin is a good example; so is Edison).[5]

In working with many kinds of students, whether in the school system or the church system, I have found that they tend to minimize their strengths and abilities and feel that they can't really effectively develop them. I encourage them to branch out, to try new things, to be creative. In essence, I free them to create, to do something that only they can do, to do something even they have never done before. This encourages them; they know they can do it; they know they can achieve. The student then takes these lessons and applies them to the rest of his life experience. He is a new person. He is uniquely free. He personally gains and the social groups of which he is a part (and becomes a more vital part) gain also.

SYNOPSIS — THE SUPPORT MODEL DESCRIBED

Destructive tension or conflict is best worked with in a way that will reduce the tension effectively. A bridge is first sought from conflict to rapport. Such a bridge or bridges provide a means of moving from a setting of conflict to one in which the various individuals or groups are seen as valid, are cooperating with shared "voices," and are potential for mutual respect or are developing mutual respect.

Once a bridge is built, the individual or group needing the help is the center of focus and has the privilege of setting his own goals, setting up operations to meet those goals, evaluating the goals and resetting goals and operations accordingly, and developing true creativity. The other person, the one helping the individual or group, then becomes the support person or true counselor. He associates freely with the individual or group needing help and offers insight into goal setting, operations development, and reevaluation of goals and operations, and he encourages creativity. He is the moral support. He is the encourager, the provider of information, the interested one, the true friend. He provides the alternate session with the opportunity of debriefing the person involved so that learning can be overt.

[5] Don Fabun, *Three Roads to Awareness* (Beverly Hills, California: Glencoe Press, 1970), p. 64.

The result may not be exactly that which the support person seeks, but it will be a meaningful one to the other. Each will be a free man. Each will be a person growing toward maturity. When the cues indicate movement, the support person can move rapidly; when they indicate a need for slowing, the support person can slow. Verbal and nonverbal communication will develop to guide the support person.

Questions for discussion:

1. How can you serve as a support person and still maintain your own principles?

2. Are there times you might need to put a person into conflict to achieve effective rapport? Explain.

3. If I were to suggest to you that Jesus never put anyone into conflict without also providing a "bridge" to more effective rapport, could you discover some of those bridges? Indicate the bridges you discover.

4. How might a typical Sunday school class differ were it to be conceived as an "alternate session?" How might a church service differ? etc.

5. List your long-range, middle-range and short-range goals for your participation in the program in which you find yourself, e.g., educational, missionary, etc. Are your activities supporting your goals? Are the people with whom you associate aiding you in attaining your goals? Is your value orientation consonant with such goals? What kinds of changes in your life might be called for in view of your goal?

Group activities and exercises:

1. Simulation: "Bridges or Bombs" can be played by any number within the larger group. Each person is given a 3 x 5 card indicating a "bridge" for developing relationship, or a "bomb" for undermining relationship. (Consult the chapter list of bridges as well as chapter 4 for bombs.) This information is confidential and to be divulged only during the role play. With a specific setting in mind, e.g., family, the first person begins a conversation growing out of a specific situation, e.g., the son asks his father for the family car. The second person, in this case the father, responds in keeping with his bridge or bomb, and the first person responds in keeping with his. After a minute or two of such conversation, shift to the third person who may take the mother's role, for example, and respond in keeping with her bridge or

bomb assignment. The exercise is helpful in permitting the group to see how a "soft answer turns away wrath."

2. Role play, corporate: Prepare a series of two-minute skits in groups of four or five members. Assign specific roles, e.g., father, mother, son, and daughter in a family. Assign a specific situation, e.g., the daughter wanting to accept her first date. The situation and role assignments are to be shared within the group. Then assign each person two or three bridges or bombs (from which to make selection in response) — information the player divulges only within the role play.

3. Creative project: Let each member of the group prepare some project that grows out of his experience in the course. Let this be a full expression of the person and involve a paper, a creative-writing presentation, or something that captures the uniqueness of the person, e.g., pictoral or photographic essay, a simulation game, a painting, etc.

4. Creative project, corporate: Have the group members in small groups prepare an IMPACT presentation to the larger group. Use the formula: the principles of the course, some issue or concern, "married" or joined together via some art form (art, music, drama, etc.) or via electronic media (tape, TV, film). Let the presentations (allow 15 minutes for each group) function as "celebration" at the close of the course.

18

the models illustrated: two cases

The cultural models can be applied to life in a variety of ways. The following two cases illustrate their use in a dynamic and static way.

"In the Land of Ice and Snow" is Joe O'Hanlon's story of his experience of conflict of cultures in Vietnam and the resultant attitudes, until he began, almost without realizing it, to ask the prior question of trust. From this point on, he began to discover, through his changed attitude, the machinery that made this new and strange society run, those actions that revealed both the validity *and* the vitality of the culture, and finally ways of working with the people to accomplish goals as well as learn about life itself.

The second case study, on prayer, in a linear way takes the models one at a time and indicates a sampling of the kinds of insights that are available to us through the behavioral sciences. God could have given man "prayer" or the "behavioral sciences" to help man in his relationships to man and to Himself. He chose to give us prayer. Man took prayer and made it a doctrine, a verbal and conceptual control on behavior, e.g., he specified what times to pray; he prescribed the way to pray; he emphasized the "need" to pray, etc. Through the application of the behavioral sciences, prayer is freed from its verbal and cultural formulations and is allowed to become a guide to human behavior in the most significant aspects of one's life. Prayer becomes exciting — not done because we "have to" as Christians, or "to please God" so much as because it opens life afresh to us and what we learn in life, man to man, helps us tremendously as we approach God, who is person also.

CASE STUDY No. 1
TWO CULTURES MEET IN VIETNAM[1]

The date was 10 May 1967. The time — 2250 hours (10:50 p.m.) local time. The place — the U.S. Air Force runway at Cam Ranh Bay, Republic of South Vietnam. The big 707 Northwest jet had just touched down and already I was a "short-timer" — only 364 days to go on my one-year hitch as a volunteer.

I guess I'll never really know exactly why I had volunteered. Perhaps it was to "prove myself" as a man to my athletic father who served during World War II and had always been somewhat disappointed in his weakling son. Then again, perhaps I felt a need to prove to the girl who jilted me nine months previously that she had made a big mistake. Or perhaps I was trying to prove to myself that I really was a man and worthy of the respect of my peers, which I believed was my due.

Whatever the reason, I was, at last, there. All the months of self-doubt, anxiety, fear, rage, disgust, hope — everything melted in the intense gust of heat and humidity which surged into the aircraft as the ground crew opened the cabin door and our reception committee, consisting of two officers and several MP's, walked in to greet us. I heard nothing that was said. My mind was surrounded by the heat and humidity. All I could think was that if it was this hot at 11:30 p.m., what was it going to be like at noon?

In less than two weeks my feelings of sympathy and concern for the poor people of Vietnam were all but gone. They stank, understood little English except the curse words which they used in abundance when I refused to give them money, candy, cigarettes, etc., and they really didn't seem to care that I had *volunteered* to come from a soft life in America to their grubby little country to help them. Their sun scorched me during the day and their mosquitoes tormented me unmercifully during the night. And then I contracted *their* dysentery (which plagues me to this day). That was the last straw. I began to loathe them and the term "Gook" was a name which seemed to fit them perfectly.

I spent six months suffocating in the heat of Cam Ranh where the temperature averaged $110°$ F. in the shade (if there is any). Between the attitude of the local people, the heat, humidity, dysen-

---

1. A true narration from Joseph E. O'Hanlon, Jr.

tery, mosquitoes, and a battalion staff that was never at a loss to find work for my pipeline crew, I began to believe that *all* Vietnamese were shiftless, worthless to themselves and to the U.S.A., and that whatever they got in the way of misery, they more than deserved.

Then came an opportunity to transfer north — *out* of Cam Ranh and the oppressive heat. It was amazing what a three-hour trip by air could bring. I was dropped off on a little hole-in-the-wall airstrip by a twin-engine C-123, which took off again the moment I was clear of the aircraft. Two months later, during the Tet Offensive of January 1968, as I sorted through the wreckage of a similar plane that had crashed on the same runway because of mortar holes, I realized why the pilots were nervous about Duc Pho (which I later learned had been nicknamed "Rocket City").

Duc Pho was a terrible place. I landed there in the middle of the monsoon season and was constantly shuddering from the dampness and the cold. Nothing could dry out. My rifle and .45 pistol turned into rust. My leather jump boots rotted and fell apart and mold seemed to cover everything. The Viet Cong constantly harassed us with rifle and mortar fire. What work wasn't hampered by them was seriously impaired by the rain and mud.

The odds seemed to be against me. Out of nine 5000-gallon petroleum tankers, three had been totally destroyed by air burst artillery fire and two others had been damaged beyond repair in accidents on the treacherously slimy road. On top of all this, I had been assigned a major construction job of completing a 156,000-gallon bolted steel tank farm, a pump station, and a complete manifold system. When I learned that my "labor force" was to come from the local Vietnamese, my heart sank. How could I hope to accomplish so much with such lazy, useless people who might have been VC soldiers in disguise?

When they were first brought onto the compound by the MP's, I had my sergeant line them up so that I could get a good look at them. To say the least, I was disappointed. I had never seen such a sorry bunch of rag tags in all my life. They consisted of the very old and the very young — those who were not eligible for draft. And I was supposed to construct an entire petroleum complex to support at least one, perhaps two, infantry brigades. The task seemed impossible. I wished then that I would have gone to Germany with the majority of my fellow OCS graduates.

One of the younger Vietnamese could speak a little English. This was nothing short of amazing to me. My opinion of the Vietnamese was so low by this time that I had begun to think that they communicated like ants (with antennas) and that was how the VC could live underground for so long.

I explained to the little Vietnamese in short phrases and many gestures that they would be digging and constructing, and then I set them to the task.

It was the usual cold, damp, monsoon morning and after the Vietnamese "labor force" (all six of them, two of whom were twins) started working, I walked over to my jeep, "The O.D. Edsel," and dipped out some hot coffee from a mermite can into my canteen cup. I looked over towards the Vietnamese and for the first time since my arrival in Vietnam, I actually felt sorry for them. These men had a lot less (and thinner) clothing than I did and they looked miserable. I sent one of my troops with the jeep back to the main area and he returned in a few minutes with some paper cups. I yelled to the Vietnamese to stop working and to come over for some hot coffee. They looked dumbstruck, but then, led by the "interpreter," they smiled and walked over to the jeep. I handed each of them a cup of steaming hot coffee, which they immediately loaded with sugar packets. Since I was a smoker at the time, I gave each one a cigarette. The place turned into what sounded like a hen house! I had never heard a group of Vietnamese talking at one time and that's what it reminded me of. Regardless, they were happy and after about fifteen minutes, they went back to work of their own accord.

I forgot about them for awhile as my sergeant and I, plus several of my troops (I had a grand total of fourteen GI's) checked the selected construction site where the engineers had set up the fuel tanks and were making some preliminary recommendations. The morning hours flew by and soon it was time for noon chow. None of us knew what to do with the Vietnamese, as we were supposed to go back to the main area for some hot food. As I soon learned from the interpreter, whom we eventually called "Baby-san" since he was the youngest of the group, they didn't have enough food at their homes to bring a lunch and were content to eat only twice a day. (I later had an opportunity to check out this lack of food story and found it to be true.)

After deliberation, I decided to send my sergeant and the troops back to the main area with instructions to send the first man finished eating back with the jeep and some C-rations. I stayed to keep an eye on the Vietnamese.

The GI soon returned with the C's. When the Vietnamese discovered that I was offering them American food, they started that barnyard clucking again! They were especially pleased to find gum, cigarettes, and candy in the ration boxes. I had never seen people so happy to get greasy, cold C-rations before in my life! Even when I was hungry — really hungry — I was not enthused about eating cold C's. I guessed that the diet of these people "out in the sticks" left much to be desired.

It didn't take too many days before we knew all their names and could recognize them in the crowd which assembled at the main gate every morning. (Everyone *knows* that all "Gooks" look alike!) I was also delighted to learn that these "dumb Gooks" were expert carpenters. I even learned by watching them as they built a shack out of a stack of crate lumber for us. And they were absolutely tickled when I let them throw a huge stack of pallets over the fence while relatives (talk about extended families!) ran around gathering it all up. Now they would have huts made of real wood instead of thatching and cardboard. The entire camp sounded like a chicken barnyard that day!

As the petroleum officer, I was responsible for refueling the Task Force by ground. This meant that I organized and often led small tanker convoys. In spite of the danger of attacks and land mines, I enjoyed the scenery as we bounced along. I was shocked to discover delicate shrines (some destroyed by war), temples, and even an old fortress. These grubby little people actually had a "civilized" culture that went far beyond 1776!

Another discovery I made, quite by accident, was that the Vietnamese are a very strongly patriarchal and paternal society. I had noticed that although "Baby-san" was the interpreter, the eldest man was firmly in charge of the group. I really paid little attention to this until I started growing a Vietnamese-style moustache. I was also sprouting some "prematurely" gray hair which had not been noticeable up until this time due to my weekly military crop. However, without the benefit of a barber at Duc Pho, my hair began to grow out and the gray started to show.

The gray hair and moustache delighted the Vietnamese beyond belief. As I later learned, the average Vietnamese male is none too successful with any kind of facial hair until much later in life. The gray hair and moustache showed that I was not the "baby-san" second lieutenant they had thought, but that my wisdom came from age, which I had "kept hidden" from them until this time.

Suddenly, "Papa-san," the eldest, was talking directly through the interpreter to me instead of taking my orders *with* the rest of the group. I don't believe he considered himself a laborer after that and I quickly learned to help cultivate this image. I commanded *my* "team" of soldiers and he commanded *his* "team" of workers.

We now drank our morning coffee together, away from the Vietnamese and soldiers. All food, money, and further provisions which we gave to them later went from me to "Papa-san," who in turn doled it out to his workers. I also learned the art of making suggestions to "Papa-san" by telling him that I believed that if my father were doing something, he would no doubt do it thus and so. With all of these arrangements going for us, the construction progressed rapidly and smoothly.

As the months went by, we grew to like our Vietnamese workers and they responded in kind. I respected them because they seemed to be genuinely interested in accomplishing our task and took pride in their work. When we laid the cement floor of the little pump station and scribbled our names in the wet cement, I invited "Papa-san" to do likewise. He was delighted and scribbled his name next to mine. The other Vietnamese also wrote their names.

Once I was recalled to Cam Ranh for several days and "Papa-san" expressed great concern. However, when I returned a few days later as a first lieutenant, he was elated. Being identified as my "equal," he felt that he had also been promoted and clucked proudly.

I was making my first real attempt at learning Vietnamese and "Papa-san" made a habit of teaching me personally. At the end of the month I would give him a carton of his favorite cigarettes for his efforts and then drive him out past the main gate MP (who would have taken the carton from "Papa-san" had I not given him the personal escort). As the MP would salute (which aggravated me no end), "Papa-san" would sit stiffly at "attention" next to me as if to receive the salute!

Little by little we supplied our Vietnamese with necessary items such as boots, underwear, socks and even extra C-rations for their families. In return, they seemed to work at 200% efficiency. While other sections all over the new post had constant problems with "their Gooks," our workers (under the very capable eye of "Papa-san") outproduced themselves every day. And by the way, their set wage was 70 Piasters a day (about 67½ cents, U.S.).

When "Papa-san" suggested that they divert all labor for about one week in order to build larger and better bunkers than the ones we had hastily built, my faith and trust in him went up 100%. When we completed the fortifications — on schedule — I had them load some extra sandbags onto my 2½-ton truck and then had my sergeant drop the sandbags and the Vietnamese off in front of "Papa-san's" little hut. My sergeant told me later that evening that he was afraid "Papa-san" was going to kiss him and that the entire village sounded like a hen house!

Several days later, as I took a convoy south through the village on my way to Qui Nhon, I was pleased to see a bunker next to "Papa-san's" hut. What pleased me even more was the small Vietnamese flag that flew over it. That was the first sign of any type of national patriotism I had ever seen.

When the twins expressed, through "Papa-san," the desire to learn how to drive, I had one of my troops teach them. Then came the request, again through "Papa-san," that the twins be taught to fire a rifle. He explained that they were going to be eligible for the draft in several months and that they wanted the experience before they went into the Army. Although they gave me no reason to be suspicious, I told him I'd think it over because that type of training took much time, which I didn't believe we had. I was able to check into their backgrounds later and when I was sure that there was nothing to worry about regarding their being in any way tied with the local VC, I agreed to teach them some fundamentals. The twins were capable students and did well with the M-16 rifle. The .45 pistol was a little difficult for them but I couldn't hit anything with it myself, and told them so. They were pleased that I was honest with them.

All the while I was overseeing the twin's training, "Papa-san" was double checking the construction work. With some help from the army engineers, the bolted steel tank farm complex, pipeline, pump station, and manifold complex were all completed in five months — a month ahead of schedule.

We had also managed to set up a complete 55-gallon oil drum storage yard, build fortifications, office, and storage shacks for equipment, and string over a mile of concertine wire, complete with mines and flares. According to the Task Force commander, he thought the petroleum job would never be completed, and we were actually first!

With the major construction job completed, financial allocations were cut off, but we continued to pay our loyal Vietnamese out of our own pockets. (We did this without their knowledge, as "Papa-san" would have been indignant.) The twins eventually joined the Vietnamese Army, which was no surprise at all. We were all proud that they enlisted at a time when men were deserting.

The culmination of this relationship came to fruition just a few weeks prior to my rotation back to the States for a leave. "Papa-san" and I sat down one morning, as usual, and I offered him a cigarette. We didn't need "Baby-san," as by this time I was becoming fairly proficient in Vietnamese. As he took the cigarette, instead of beginning the conversation (I had learned the custom of waiting for the elder to begin or initiate any conversation) with the usual comments on the upcoming work, he looked at me for a few minutes and then told me that he knew the provisional (local) soldiers who were stealing rifles and selling them on the black market. They were giving the MP's and the local MACV officers ulcers. I was really surprised that "Papa-san" had decided to tell me about this I asked him what he thought would be the proper action to take with this information. He *told* me to contact the MP's and that *he* would arrange for me to "buy" some rifles. I then went to the Provost Marshal's office and explained the situation. They were elated! Later that afternoon, in an alley beside the orphanage in Duc Pho, my new jeep driver (who was an MP staff sergeant) and I were "arrested," along with four ring leaders, by several jeep loads of MP's. The rest of the "small-fry" were arrested later.

I was curious as to why "Papa-san" had told me about these black marketeers. He said that they were the local "tough guys" in the village and that he was especially disgusted that they had managed to stay in the provisional rifle company while the twins had bravely joined the South Vietnamese army. He had taken a risk in turning them in, but he said that he believed that I could handle the situation and that everything would work out all right. You can believe that I saw to it that "Papa-san" received *all* of the credit from both the MP's and the MACV officers.

I left Duc Pho, and then Vietnam, a short time after that. It wasn't easy to leave. I had grown up in that hole-in-the-wall place. And, ironic as it may seem, I received from a people I totally loathed at first (unjustly), the respect which I craved from others but had never received. And I didn't receive it until I gave it.

I would return to Vietnam for an additional six months of duty, and would eventually find myself Executive Officer of a Vietnamese Provisional Rifle Company which was made up of villagers like "Papa-san," "Baby-san," and the twins. And because of the respect I had learned to give, where others had failed, I, at last, succeeded.

CASE STUDY No. 2
PRAYER
Prayer is, by definition, conversing with God. The primary relationship in prayer is that of an individual or a group with God. The following is written with the recognition of the cultural overtones and interpersonal relationships that are also present in group praying.

Trust
1. When do you pray? when you have a selfish desire or a personal need? in a crisis?

2. Exercising the Prior Question of Trust in prayer to God is to ask, What now? What would you have me to do? This is the counting-to-ten prayer in which one first waits to listen. It prepares the way for clear thinking and level-headed action.
3. In stages of trust development, prayer is the adjustment factor in bringing trust in God apace. Meditation in prayer gives a clarity of vision that few other types of activities do. You get things straightened out in your own mind; you "get your head together."
4. In domains of interpersonal trust, prayer brings the principles together. An arena for openness operates. We are given an indication of how we are received beyond our immediate group.
5. The reciprocity of trust opens the way to effective dialogue. We pray with another to God and then let Him speak to us. What mechanisms do you provide to let Him reciprocate? We can verbalize things in prayer we never could in any other way — such honesty causes others to be honest also, giving them courage.

Acceptance

1. The prayer of confession is the acceptance-of-self prayer.
2. The prayers of thanksgiving, of forgiveness of the other, and of intercession are acceptance-of-the-other prayers.
3. Prayer permits an attitude of total acceptance on which a life of principle and infinite variety in life-style is based.
4. When rejecting others, prayer and even our ability to pray is limited.

Danger: Prayer can be used to legitimize nonreciprocative aid; e.g., "The Lord laid it on my heart. . . ."

Mutual respect

1. The "traditionalist" tends to use prayer to exert social pressure — a kind of preaching in prayer intended to legitimize his way and to make another feel he too must follow that way. E.g., "God has told me," or, "I prayed about this."
2. For the traditionalist, again, prayer can be a cause for inaction. E.g., "We prayed about it but the Lord didn't lead."
3. The ethical relativist (as distinct from a cultural relativist) uses prayer as a cover, a rationalization, an excuse, or an apology for abandoning principle. It tends to legitimize self-will.
4. The situation ethicist uses prayer to legitimize his acting in love and thus abandoning that which he is — if only in part.
5. Mutual-respect prayer draws out the deep inner feelings of man in the man-to-man and man-to-God relationships. Each

person is seen as valid before God and can know and be known fully.

The Norm

1. Background or sociocultural experience of the person lets prayer become (or not become) a part of the norm or sum total of a person's expectations. Prayer is thus carried out in keeping with this norm in terms of the form of prayer, the position of prayer, the length of prayer, who prays with whom, the audible/nonaudible nature of prayer, what part prayer plays in the total religious experience, and anything else involved in the expression of prayer.

2. A person whose norm incorporates prayer, and who does not pray or who is not permitted to pray, finds himself in deprivation of norm. He can find his spiritual life becoming sour, and bitterness can turn toward those who limit the prayer experience.

3. A person who has a quiet-based prayer norm and is drawn into some overt expression of prayer, or body movement in prayer, in extremes of audible prayer, may find himself living in excess of norm and will react in embarrassment, if not in guilt.

System

1. Prayer is a component of a larger system (more than even the religious component which itself is part of the larger system) and is an integral part of this larger system.

2. Prayer is also a process that operates within the system, aiding in achieving balance and in letting the various components inhere in the system. As usual, it is a control on the social controls of the system.

3. Prayer provides necessary cues for interpersonal relations within the system — guide to behavior, indication of leadership, instructions for gaining efficiency in operation.

Hierarchy

1. The style of prayer is different for each level of the hierarchy; e.g., intimate and informal in the small group of the lower, included units, and more stylized and formal for the larger group in keeping with the formal arrangements of the group.

2. Each unit on a given level has its own particular expression of prayer. One group will have one person pray and a second group will have audible group prayer.

3. At each level of the hierarchy, it takes distinct social mechanisms to have a prayer experience. At the lower levels prayer can be more spontaneous. With each successive increase in size and complexity, more refined means of getting

a group together and having effective control within the group experience are needed.

Multisociety

1. Prayer differs by occasion, place, group, intent, need, position, form, etc.
2. Prayer can be addressed to that Person of the Trinity indicated by the specific subculture.

Flow of truth

1. Prayer can be the means of effecting justice also by the human participants in that things spoken audibly in prayer can be heard by them when no other form of expression of the injustice is possible.
2. Prayer can be a powerful tool of social justice, bringing to the awareness of the corporate body needs of people and groups. The Spirit of God can lead them to fill those needs.
3. Prayer can also be used to enslave, in that a strong personality can create a climate of prayer in which there can be no possibility of disagreement. Prayer can then be used to rationalize the state of slavery.

Item identification of group

1. Every group has clear definition of who prays and when, the degree of authority as correlated with the experience of the prayer, the issues and concerns that are to be prayed for and about.
2. Prayer is a powerful means of developing the loyalty of the group.
3. Parents and church leaders tend to use prayer as a means of disciplining the group, whether family or church members.
4. Prayer is one means of making one's Christianity visible.

Activities of the group

1. Again, each group defines just how prayer will be used within the group process, answering such questions as these: Is it to be part of an experience or the total experience? What ingredients are to be included within the experience of prayer?
2. The degree of formality is defined in keeping with the occasion and the kinds of people present.
3. Each group also defines to what degree the event itself or the controls of the event are to dominate.

Basic values

1. The time/event continuum will set up the beginning and the end of the prayer event and the length of time for its fulfillment. It will determine whether there will be prolegomena and closure, the length of each of these, the order or sequence of the parts of the experience, the number of times

prayer is to be had within an experience or a time block, the degree of control of the event itself by the time schedule, the degree of embellishment of the event that will be permitted, etc.

2. The vulnerability continuum will set up the degree of openness in prayer, how much will be revealed in keeping with the size and complexity of the group, the nature of the confession, how a group will handle an individual's confession, who will be assigned the blame for problems and trials, etc.

3. The dichotomy/holism continuum will determine the degree of detail included in the prayer, the nature of the prayer experience as it is shared by the group as a whole or the group as individual entities, the degree to which "language smearing" phenomena will accompany prayer, the degree to which persons and issues are stressed or highlighted in the total experience, etc.

Conflict of norm

1. Prayer can highlight conflict and bring it into focus by way of summary statement debriefing.

2. Prayer can be one of the aids to recognizing conflict in light of the way a person prays. One can note the garbled utterance of a prayer or the evidence for withdrawal either from the immediate experience or from any occasion for prayer.

3. Types of prayer can be introduced to resolve conflict; e.g., conversational prayer to resolve, for the moment, the difference between time people and event people.

4. Prayer reflects the inability of one to pray because of conflict.

5. Prayer articulates conflict in times of trouble; for example, Hezekiah's prayer in 2 Kings 20.

6. The Holy Spirit should be looked to as a Resolver of conflict.

7. New groups are formed as people try to resolve conflict; e.g., certain Holy Spirit groups spring up; Christians are urged to conform to life-ways that are incompatible with their own, and to do this as a spiritual exercise; and scapegoating turns attention to perceived cause of conflict.

Frustration

This is reflected in the "cry aloud" to God.

Tools of research

1. The prayer experience is excellent for participant observation in getting to know people, their concerns, their challenges.

2. In essence, each prayer is a kind of interview in which a person is expressing to God and before others not only what is in his heart, but many specifics of his life-style or norm, as well.

3. Experimentation is often accomplished under the guise or direction of prayer. It can be legitimized by prayer.
4. The prayers of the saints are excellent material for archiving research to determine the behavior of Christians at different periods of the development of the church.

Tools of relationship

1. A prayer is one totality of cultural cues. Each cue, properly communicated and responded to leaves each prayer participant with the feeling of completeness.
2. The biblical source for our approach to, and manner of, praying comes via the functional equivalent. The prolegomena of the time-oriented person is the functional equivalent of the brief, direct, event-type opening of Jesus' prayer.
3. Well-meaning Christians can set up ideals within the context of prayer that other Christians are expected to follow. This is fine insofar as they derive from the biblical guidelines, but unfortunate if they produce a slavery setting.
4. When people pray they can leave a perception of their spiritual condition that is far from the real.
5. Prayer is one source to check out the adverse effect. A closing prayer by someone else can tell you if you accomplished your purpose in the session.
6. Prayer is one means of abusing the system. A person may pray and the words may be right, but his intent can be other than the content and context of prayer.
7. Prayer is frequently taken as the whole of spiritual life or assigned more value than was intended by God.

Biblical absolutes vs. cultural relativism

1. The content and context of prayer is totally cultural. Prayer is formed in the language of men. The order and arrangement of the thoughts as well as the concern for issues and concerns derive from the cultural context of the participant.
2. Prayer is one source for the supernatural intrusion — the most likely route into the cultural context.
3. When prayer is consistently and wholly of the person's culture, it is the most effective means of contact by the Spirit of God. The totality of prayer then makes the supernatural intrusion meaningful.
4. Prayer extends the variation of the life-style, for when you pray with someone you adapt most easily to his life-way.

Bridge

1. Prayer is a bridge from conflict to rapport. The prayer of confession uttered audibly communicates apology to the hearer and makes rapport more effective.

2. Prayer brings the principles together so that conflict can be resolved.

Support
1. Prayer is one of the most effective means of encouraging another: through promise of prayer, through the actual praying experience, or through the post-experience indication of your prayer support.
2. The Holy Spirit is our prime "support Person" and He is contacted most effectively via prayer.
3. The prayer of someone who has "strayed" from the path of Christian growth is effective in the restoration process.

Alternate session
1. When someone is out doing, following one session and preceding another, the sustaining nature of prayer is helpful.
2. The prayer session upon leaving and upon return is useful in orientation and in debriefing the experience.
3. The second coming is the prime example of the alternate session and Jesus encouraged His own to "pray till I come."
4. Prayer is a source of comfort to the believer who has been "in the world" for six days and worships with other believers on the Lord's Day.

Goals and mechanisms to reach goals
1. These can be defined and redefined in prayer sessions.
2. The prayer session provides the opportunity to muse over action and its results and plan anew for the future.
3. Prayer can itself be a mechanism to accomplish goals, for it provides the "counting to ten" before action or the "what's next" in the process of goaling.
4. The response of God to man's prayers is frequently that extra factor that makes things work.
5. Answers man receives in prayer may indicate the success or failure of the project, if not of the praying process. Even negative answers indicate success in praying (see 2 Corinthians 12:8, 9).

Feedback
1. Again and again in prayer a person indicates how person or program is perceived and this is excellent feedback if used to correct communication and not used against the person praying.
2. The 25-word (more or less) summary statement, a most useful tool in certain stages of the debriefing process, is one kind of prayer. Frequently, after a training or learning session, the first ones to pray sum up the session and can tell the leader a great deal about the session's effectiveness.

3. The person in tune with the Spirit of God can get feedback from that source through the prayer process.

Case study methodology

1. Each prayer, each prayer session, each experience of prayer provides a useful case study for consideration. The prayer will tell a great deal about the person, his attitudes, his interests, his abilities, etc., and used wisely, it can be a great aid to a pastor or Christian worker in encouraging Christian growth and maturity.

2. Prayer is one means of considering alternatives to a case. Anything considered through the prayer process is "legitimate" to the group meeting in prayer.

Creativity

1. Since creativity is the expression of the totality of fulfillment of a person and his uniqueness, prayer lets a person be himself, accept himself, progress in maturity of the self and thus provides a solid foundation for creative experience.

2. A person is not totally human until he is in fellowship with God, and prayer lets him become a total self, totally human, totally fulfilled in the creating process.

3. Prayer is also one kind of thing to be creative about.

Good counselor

1. The good counselor makes use of every means to effect learning and insight. Prayer provides one effective means.

2. Jesus was the good counselor model. He taught His disciples how to pray.

Questions for discussion:

1. How has your life changed during this course?

2. What effect might this program have on your effectiveness in witness?

3. Had the principles taught herein been applied a hundred years ago, what might Christian mission look like today?

4. What aspects of your life will hinder the consistent application of these principles and thus hinder your mission in life? What might be done to avoid such pitfalls?

5. In the story by Joe O'Hanlon, focus on one point in the narration and indicate what might have happened had rejection been the basis for action.

6. What new insights have you received about prayer from applying the principles of the behavioral sciences to prayer? What is still missing?

7. Could God be called "the Master Behavioral Scientist"? Discuss.

8. How might that which you have learned apply to the training of others in effective crosscultural communication?

Group activities and exercises:
- New course: Draw together a small group seminar and build the course around the reading of novels, the viewing of movies or plays, or the discussion and study of contemporary issues. These books might start the list: Elisabeth Elliott, *No Graven Image* (New York: Harper and Row, 1966); Juan Isaias, *The Other Side of the Coin* (Grand Rapids: Wm. B. Eerdmans Publishing Co., 1966); and Catherine Marshall, *Christie* (Old Tappan, New Jersey: Fleming H. Revell Co., 1968). Movies such as "A Man for All Seasons" or "Fiddler on the Roof" are full of insight for effective crosscultural communication. Contemporary issues that are productive for in-depth study are abortion, sexual morality, the church, the contemporary family, communal living, war, education in this half of the twentieth century, the computer, etc.

CASE STUDIES IN BICULTURALISM

contents

279

preface to case studies

No human society or organization is exempt from change. The encouragement of change itself is not a bad thing but is inherent in the idea of progress toward which the teacher, pastor, social worker, missionary, and sanitation officer are working.

The life of the primitive — the "noble savage" — or the twentieth-century urban "cave dweller" for that matter, is not *per se* satisfying, joyful, and beautiful. It is often, in fact, filthy, cruel, sordid — giving very little encouragement to its members to achieve their potential. Is this of any concern to the one who wants to follow in the steps of Christ, his Master? Can the Christian see himself as legitimately encouraging change without the necessity of feeling self-conscious about it?

The missionary admittedly sees himself as an agent of change. Because he's been told so often that effecting change is not his prerogative, he may feel guilty about his role, but he needn't be, because without contributing to change there can be no fulfilling of the Great Commission.

There are, however, certain principles which he should observe. He must first of all see the society he is entering as composed of persons organized into an intricate system of human relationships, interacting through that society's institutions. Each society is a valid, integrated whole, organized according to a system of hierarchical levels. To change behavior on any one level of such a system will result in reverberating consequences throughout the entire society-as-system and will result in the necessity for related and reinforcing changes above and below the actual level of the hierarchy initially changed, if disintegration throughout the entire society is to be avoided.

Therefore, the missionary who undertakes to initiate change should realize that this is a tremendous responsibility. Consider, for example, any change involving the institution of the family. "When an agent of change interferes with the structure of the family, he involves himself in cultural change in every aspect of society, and is therefore responsible for economic factors and personal problems at a very deep level.... Some things in a

281

society can be changed with ease, but the family is *not* one of them."[1]

Throughout the world societies are experiencing change, often so violent and disruptive that persons are thrown into confusion because they are no longer sure of what are the norms which are pertinent to them.

This is particularly true of the rural masses who have flocked to the cities in the developing countries, lured by excitement and a supposedly higher standard of living. They are cut loose from tribal cultural patterns and the old niceties of the social mechanisms governing interpersonal behavior and, in many cases, they have not yet assimilated new behavioral patterns to allow them to move freely and happily in their present milieu. As a result, they may be seen to act as barbarians even to their peers.

Take, for example, a large reception being offered by the mayor of an inland city of 100,000 people in West Africa. The occasion is the visit of the president of a nearby republic. A thousand people have been invited, including all the elite in the local government and the educational system, heads of the major business houses, Catholic and Protestant mission directors, and wealthy notables and tribal chiefs.

It is a fascinating gathering of many races and a veritable dress parade. One sees everything from a Dior just arrived from Paris, to a gold-plated cow's tail — a scepter of authority — being carried by a powerful canton chief.

Enclosing the vast area where the dinner is to be eaten are buffet tables groaning under whole roast lambs, fish, chickens, and huge piles of rice, *cous-cous* (the favorite food of North Africa), and pounded yams. Costly liquors cover another long table.

After the arrival of the honored guest, a signal is given and the buffet tables are literally attacked. Those who can run the fastest or shove the hardest, pile their plates high, grab armfuls of bottles of liquor and begin to gorge themselves. The startled European decides it's a question of "go thou and do likewise" or starve.

The thing which amazes him is seeing those all about him who represent the very highest status in the country, acting in a way which is lacking in all courtesy according to European standards, and which, if he knows the etiquette of the local Africans, he will recognize as being equally shocking to them.

---

1. Alan Tippett, "Polygamy as a Missionary Problem: The Anthropological Issues," *Practical Anthropology*, 17, No. 2 (March-April, 1970), p. 76.

He knows that even the Africans out in the bush observe intricate protocol in eating that would make the behavior of these elite shameful in the eyes of their grandparents. And so, much of the world today is caught in the process of change. The case "Conflict" portrays some of the confusion which can follow in the wake of change. The case "Blood of a White Chicken" reminds us of the four pertinent questions which may be asked when meeting a person or people who seem to evidence a real need for change in their behavioral norms: (a) What is the norm? (b) Is the person or society living in keeping with the norm? (c) Does the norm need changing? (d) Who is responsible for changing the norm?

Acknowledgment

The following persons have contributed to the collection of case studies: Helen Dunkeld, Lisa Espineli, Harry Johnson, Douglas Kell, Dave Kornfield, Dick Muzik, Gene Olsen, Roy Prester, Roland Raucholz, L. E. Read, and Suann Strickland.

introduction

There were two men in a certain city, one very rich, owning many flocks of sheep and herds of goats; and the other very poor, owning nothing but a little lamb he had managed to buy. It was his children's pet and he fed it from his own plate and let it drink from his own cup. He cuddled it in his arms like a baby daughter. Recently a guest arrived at the home of the rich man. But instead of killing a lamb from his own flocks for food for the traveler, he took the poor man's lamb and roasted it and served it.

So runs an ancient case study. And if we should wonder whether it were effective or not as a stimulus to thought and action, we have only to continue reading to discover that the person to whom this anecdote was addressed became furious. "I swear by the living God," he vowed, "any man who would do a thing like that should be put to death..." (See 2 Samuel 12:1-6, *The Living Bible*).

PURPOSE OF THIS MANUAL

So case studies have been used from ancient times. But what do we hope to achieve with this collection of cases dealing specifically with crosscultural problems? Our goal is simply this: to make people think through and live vicariously a wider range of experiences than it is possible for any one of us to live in reality. "Even the longest-lived among us need a wider range of experience. But time waits for no one! We need some way to crowd more experience into our short lives."[1] We feel this is particularly true of the student who is preparing to work with people — in North America or overseas — and who, from the beginning of his work, will be expected to have the ability to think through problems which only many years of actual experience normally bring.

John Dewey tells us, "The origin of thinking is some perplexity, confusion, or doubt. Thinking is not a case of spontaneous combustion...."[2] Certainly every one of us has sufficient per-

1. Leroy Ford, *Using the Case Study in Teaching and Training* (Nashville: Broadman Press, 1969), p. 9.
2. John Dewey, *How We Think* (New York: D. C. Heath and Company, 1933), p. 15.

plexities, confusions, and doubts to make us all great thinkers, but these alone do not necessarily assure us the ability to think our situation through to satisfactory solutions, for Dewey continues,

> If the person has had some acquaintance with similar situations, if he has dealt with material of the same sort before, suggestions more or less apt and helpful are likely to arise. But unless there has been experience in some degree analogous, which may now be represented in imagination, confusion remains mere confusion.... Even when a child (or a grownup) has a problem, to urge him to think when he has no prior experiences involving some of the same conditions, is wholly futile.[3]

More than half a century ago the Harvard Business School began using discussion based on case studies drawn from the fields of medicine and law. Since that time, the technique has been widely included in the curricula of schools giving training in business administration, politics, psychology, counseling, and management. "The use of the case method is more than a technique or an instrument for teaching ... it has realism and problem solving as its core."[4]

These cases have been organized to present problems coordinated with the units of this book in order to extend the student's thinking and problem-solving abilities.

We suggest that the cases may be used in a number of ways:

a. To extend by discussion the learning experience of a class using this book.

b. To teach a course entirely through the use of case studies.

c. To integrate classroom teaching with laboratory sessions, using cases for discussion.

d. To extend classroom teaching by assigning cases to be written up outside of the classroom.

e. To provide material for workshops where small groups may put into practice what they have learned in seminars.

We foresee these two parts of the book as being particularly relevant to pastors, teachers, and those responsible for the training of missionaries, whether in colleges, Bible institutes, or missionary conferences.

While the cases should be divided, perhaps, between those of particular interest to persons planning to work within the context of the North American culture and those planning to work abroad, we find that the problems of interpersonal relationships,

3. Ibid., pp. 15, 16.
4. Ibid., p. 8.

whether at home or abroad, are basically the same, and the same principles are applicable to both situations. Therefore, we have mixed the cases as to their location. A teacher may choose to work with those cases which best meet the need of his teaching at any particular time.

When a teacher uses a case study, he wants it to cause personal identification and to provoke an application of the principles to be learned within it. He wants to encourage a stretching of the imagination and a sharpening of the mental abilities of those who participate in case discussion.

A good case study should bring into focus a "real-to-life" situation so that others may identify with it. "How can people show greater acceptance to minority groups?" becomes "How shall the Johnsons act in such a way as to build trust between them and the foreign family who has moved next door to them?" It should illustrate principles which may by extension be applicable to a large number of similar circumstances; e.g., "John was delighted to learn he'd been named Salesman-of-the-Year until he found his prize was a weekend at the Playboy resort hotel. What should he do about it?"

A case study may have as its purpose a lesson to be learned. This may involve the changing of one's behavior or thought processes; e.g., "Does the wearing of ragged jeans and T-shirt to church mean the same thing to Linda who is a member of the local Jesus People as it does to her grandmother?"

At times the main objective of a case may be to initiate group interaction and a sharing of related experiences which may ultimately add more to the learning experience than was originally intended by the use of the case. "Case method can do most for anyone if . . . he uses it to help himself live through events alertly, objectively, imaginatively, and appreciatively."[5]

PREPARATION OF NEW CASE STUDIES

Any teacher, pastor, or missionary faced with the problem of getting those with whom he works vitally interested in discussing personal problems and reacting with one another, should seriously consider using cases to open up discussion. He may start with the cases in this volume but, hopefully, he will go on to become a case "addict" who will develop his own cases suitable for creating the type of interaction he desires. Once he becomes case-minded, he will find material for cases all about him — in conversations, in the chatter of children, in the daily paper, in

---

5. Paul and Faith Pigors, *Case Method in Human Relations: The Indirect Process* (New York: McGraw-Hill Book Co., 1961), viii.

the news on TV, in the advice columns in the papers, etc. "As soon as a person gets the knack of seeing and treating as a case any situation in which he is immediately involved, then case method has become — for him — far more than mere mental gymnastics. . . . He can learn from everything he lives through."[6]

A good case study may be very limited, including only the information needed for understanding the conflict involved. It should be assumed by those working with it that this information is complete. It should usually be limited to one or two problems or principles to be illustrated. If the case is longer and more intricately involved in a number of types of conflict (as many in this manual are), it may be broken down into several case studies, or may be looked at in a number of different ways in relation to various models.

One should always have a purpose in working with a case study. Then the type and amount of data to be included will depend on the time there will be to work on it, the background and experience of those involved in solving it, and how one intends to apply the learning material built into the case.

In preparing a case, for example, one might state his *purpose* or educational objective as: a discussion of whether or not one is responsible for what others may think of his actions. Subsequently he could present a *situation* using some or all of the following facts. He could add new information as he desires and thus give a new focus to the discussion from time to time.

Situation:

a. Mr. Thomas, a professor in a Christian college, was seen entering a liquor store in a neighboring town.

b. The one who saw him enter the store was a neighbor who made no profession of being a Christian. He conveyed his observations to another neighbor, Mr. Brown, a Christian, in a jovial over-the-backyard-fence chat. He was hoping to get a "rise" out of Mr. Brown because he knew both Mr. Thomas and Mr. Brown professed to be teetotalers.

c. Mrs. Thomas mentioned to Mrs. Brown one evening that her husband always stopped at the liquor store on his way home because the price of milk there was the cheapest in town.

d. One day as Mr. Thomas entered the liquor store to get his milk, he met the wife of a fellow professor hurrying out of the store. He hardly recognized her — disguised as she was by a large floppy hat and huge dark sunglasses. She

---

6. Ibid., p. 294.

greeted him, giggling nervously and hastened to assure him she had just been in the store to buy some wine to make cheese fondue "and wouldn't you know I'd be caught in the act!"

DEBRIEFING

Once the case has been presented, the debriefing process may involve a number of steps. The following is a suggested format for working with the problem in a group discussion:

a. *Discover* the problem, the source of the conflict or confusion.

b. *Define* the basic issues in relation to the models of crosscultural communication, as given in the text.

c. *Discuss* the problem for feedback from others.

d. *Dissolve* the problem — or attempt to — making use of general principles that might be extended to similar circumstances.

Some persons working with case studies feel that such studies should be presented without questions because the questions themselves may reflect the prejudices of the leader or predispose the group to a certain line of thought. For this reason a number of the cases are not followed by questions and even when they are, the questions should never be used as a crutch.

If the discussion leader wishes to use questions, he may form his own to guide the discussion as he desires. The following kinds of questions may be useful:

1. Insights gained from which models of crosscultural communication help us in working with this case?

2. How did you react or feel as you read the case?

3. With whom do you identify in the case? With whom do you find it hard to identify?

4. If you were so and so, how would you resolve the problem?

5. How might the problem have been avoided?

6. How did (or did not) various persons act responsibly in the case?

7. How could you look at the case from the viewpoint of systems, conflict resolution, hierarchy, program development, sequence of activities, etc.?

8. What questions would you like to ask the characters in the case?

9. What kind of orientation program would prepare a person to encounter problems such as this case presents?

To illustrate the suggested steps used in debriefing and to show how questions may be used in guiding discussion, a typical case study is presented below followed by questions and responses which members of a group might give. It will be given as a two-stage case. With the presentation of the first data, the group would assume this to be complete and work with the information as given.

Case:

Miss Y, a young Thai Christian, had recently graduated from the mission Bible school and had associated herself with a mission hospital in Central Thailand. Since it was the policy of the mission not to hire nationals for evangelistic or church-related work, an arrangement had been worked out whereby Miss Y would be employed by the Thai church for a half day, and by the hospital for the other half day. She was keen to enter into the church work. Soon she realized that she would be teamed with an experienced single lady missionary for visitation to the homes of believers and other interested people in the vicinity.

The missionary, Miss Anders, was extremely time-oriented and dichotomistic in her world and life view. Miss Y, as an Asian, was event-oriented and holistic in her approach to life. Thus it was not long before serious tensions arose between the two. Under the terms of the work agreement, Miss Y was to work in the hospital from 8-12 and then work for the church from 1-5, or vice versa as the situation demanded. Sometimes she rigidly followed this schedule while at other times she arrived a bit late or left a few minutes early, depending on existing demands of the work or other circumstances.

One day she was working at her job as seamstress for the hospital, and the clock was approaching 11:30 AM. Realizing that she had a Bible study for which she was responsible at 1:00 PM, she left early to prepare for that meeting. When her missionary co-worker observed her leaving ahead of time, she became very upset and reprimanded her for being unfaithful in fulfilling her responsibilities to the hospital which was paying her a wage for working a certain number of hours. Miss Y found it difficult to understand the importance of the time element in this situation, but she quickly realized that the missionary considered her in the wrong, and that she would never be convinced otherwise.

Other similar and extremely difficult situations arose and Miss Y was kept continually in a state of tension. This state of affairs began to wear on her until other personal relationships began to be affected. She began to withdraw into herself; often she would leave work in tears and retire to her room. She didn't want to eat very much or have time for social relationships. As a result, she became thin, worn, and irritable. She felt rejected by the missionaries at the hospital. Her condition became so serious that she was advised by the hospital doctor to see a psychiatrist. Accompanying her to Bangkok to visit a psychiatrist was a single lady, a new missionary who told Miss Y that she "should get right with the Lord." This suggestion merely upset her more.

Debriefing:

Discover the problem, the source of the conflict or confusion.

Q. What is the basic problem here?

A. "The conflict between event-oriented Asians and time-oriented Westerners and their rejection of each other because of their differences."

Q. With whom do you identify?

A. "With Miss Y because she was living according to her norm in her own country."

A. "Yes, I identify with Miss Y, but since I hold many of the same basic values as Miss Anders, I feel for her, too. I worked for ten years overseas with a committee which seldom arrived at work on time, but was perfectly time-oriented at five o'clock quitting time. If Miss Y were event-oriented, why did her work in the hospital always fill her working hours *or less?* Why didn't an event ever carry her into overtime?"

A. "If I were the doctor and needed some work finished only to see Miss Y going off across the yard half an hour early, I'm afraid I would feel quite justified in criticizing her, too."

Q. How do you think Miss Anders would have described her relationship with Miss Y?

A. "I'm afraid she might have made some pretty derogatory generalizations about Thais being irresponsible, or lazy, or not very dependable."

A. "If she were like most of us, she would have balanced what she felt were her good points — and reinforced her own rigidity in the process — with what she considered Miss Y's weak points."

A. "I think she would have justified her actions as part of the training process which she was obliged to give Miss Y."

Define the basic issues in relation to the models of biculturalism.

Q. Which models of biculturalism may be applied to this case?

A. "I see this as a conflict involving the basic values model, especially the difference between the time orientation of Miss Anders and the event orientation of Miss Y."

A. "We could look at it as a conflict of norm leading to frustration. We've learned that 'the individual in conflict with a group will find culture shock developing.' And then 'frustration develops when there is conflict, yet no end is in view of resolving that conflict.' We can see Miss Y going through four stages which result from conflict: (1) irritation — Serious tensions arose between her and Miss Anders; (2) reaction — It began to wear on her; she withdrew into herself; she would leave work in tears and didn't want to eat. (3) neurosis — She became thin, worn, and irritable. (4) psychosis — She was advised to see a psychiatrist, so apparently others felt she was developing a psychosis."

A. "Certainly the model, Acceptance of the Person, with each of its submodels, is applicable too. I don't believe that any of Miss Y's co-workers had asked the prior question of trust, and certainly Miss Anders and Miss Y both needed to accept themselves as they were (admitting their basic value differences) before they could accept each other and build mutual trust."

Discuss the problem for feedback from others.

Q. How did you feel as you read the case?

A. "I felt very sorry for Miss Y and longed to befriend her and build a relationship of mutual trust, accepting her just as she was. I felt Miss Anders, the mission doctor, and the new missionary who accompanied her to Bangkok, all overlooked the important prior question of trust."

A. "I felt really scared that I might go thousands of miles to minister to a people, and then be rejectant even to a fellow Christian, as in this case, when it came right down to one-to-one interpersonal relationships."

Q. How might the problem have been avoided?

A. "All the conflict and frustration might have been avoided if Miss Y and Miss Anders had realized that they were two people having very different life-styles, particularly in relation to time. Starting from there, each should have accepted her own way as being perfectly normal, and likewise the other's way as being equally valid. Then each might have chosen to endure some deprivation of her norm in order to accommodate herself to the other. In mutual love and respect their life-styles could have drawn closer together."

A. "I would like to see Miss Anders come to realize that all the world needn't revolve around her schedule. Single missionaries — and others, too — can get into terrible ruts from which they won't budge for anything. I'm willing to guess that if Miss Y were having a profitable time out visiting, she might continue for hours oblivious to time, while Miss Anders would dash home right on time to feed her cat or write her weekly letter to her mother."

Dissolve the problem.

Q. If you were the mission director and understood the whole situation, what would you do to better the situation for both Miss Y and Miss Anders?

A. "I might suggest that they would work better and each would be happier if they could work separately."

A. "If Miss Y were to continue to work in the hospital, I might suggest that she be given specific tasks to do which would take more or less time than the four hours a day."

A. "I would feel that the entire mission personnel needed some training in biculturalism. If they treated Miss Y as they did, they must surely act in a rejectant manner toward others, too."

A. "Yes, but I feel that it is most important that someone be encouraged to become a support person for Miss Y right away so that she may be restored to complete physical and mental health."

Additional Case Data:

At this juncture, a new missionary couple who were experienced workers, came to live and work at the hospital. Miss Y was living at the time in a room of the same house where they were assigned to live. For the first week after their arrival, Miss Y remained in her room most of the time. She complained of headaches and inability to sleep without the aid of sleeping pills. Slowly she began to talk to the missionary wife who tried to accept her just as she was. A friendship developed and Miss Y was then able to share her difficult experiences with someone who tried to understand her complex situation. Shortly after this, she found relief from her headaches and was able to sleep at night without sleeping pills. Then she resumed some of her work responsibilities while still living in the same house with the missionaries.

One day she remarked to the missionary wife, "Until you came, I had forgotten how to laugh!" Gradually she regained her composure, and with some measure of self-assurance she returned to a useful ministry in the hospital and in extended church outreach.

Shortly before the missionaries were to leave the hospital for the United States, Miss Y decided to move into the nurses' dorm with the other Thai girls. The missionary wife assured her that she could stay longer if she wished. Miss Y replied, "No, I want to try moving back to the dorm while you are still here." She did, and was able to settle in happily. She was again able to cope with life, although she found her work relationship with Miss Anders an extremely difficult one.

Debriefing:

This additional data could be discussed comparing the early rejection Miss Y had received with the acceptance the new couple showed her.

It may be discussed also in light of the support model, or used to stimulate thought concerning what sort of orientation program would have fitted the missionaries for the situation in which they found themselves.

In debriefing, do not feel that there has to be one correct solution. There may be several alternative — and equally good — solutions. Or perhaps all the alternatives seem wrong. Much of life is like that.

> One can think reflectively only when one is willing to endure suspense and to undergo the trouble of searching. To many persons both suspense of judgment and intellectual search are disagreeable; they want to get them ended as soon as possible. They cultivate an overpositive and dogmatic habit of mind, or feel perhaps that a condition of doubt will be regarded as evidence of mental inferiority.[7]

Some will say, "Well, if you can't come to any conclusion, what is the good of all the discussion? You're just pooling your ignorance!"

The interaction, the application of models and principles, the self-revelation of one's inner feelings in group discussion may be sufficiently rewarding goals in themselves. And always for the Christian there can be the searching of the Bible to find

---

7. Dewey, *How We Think,* p. 16.

which revealed principles give guidelines for arriving at a satisfying solution.

WAYS OF WORKING CASES

These case studies may be worked with in a number of different ways:

a. Role-playing, which is one of the most effective means of learning or bringing about attitude change because the player gains insights into how the others see him and how he might behave. (Try role-playing "The California Family," pp. 77-79.)

b. Symposium, in which a group of experts in a field present their analyses of the case. (Get a group of missionaries to discuss "Praise Him With the Dance," pp. 193, 194).

c. Debate, in which two suggested solutions are debated by group members.

d. Small study groups working on different aspects of a case.

e. Brainstorming, in which group members suspend all value judgment for a time to give rapid-fire suggestions, often "piggybacking" on one another's ideas.

THE DISCUSSION LEADER

The leader of a group discussion is not to dominate the discussion. He should try to get the participants interacting among themselves without referring everything through him. He should try not to ask a question which has an obviously right answer, especially "yes" or "no." To keep them probing and thinking, it is often good for his attitude to be, "You're not wrong, but I'm not sure you're right either." And finally, it is usually best to leave the situation open-ended and *not make a summary,* since this can be deadly to continued thinking and learning, which could continue long after the discussion is over. "Quit while the going is strong" is a good principle.

> Of a good leader, who talks little
> When his work is done, his aim fulfilled,
> They will all say, we did this ourselves![8]

It will soon become obvious that there are divergent points of view. This need be no problem either to the group itself or to any individual within the group so long as friendships can be maintained in spite of honest differences of opinion. *The Christian experience can embrace differences of opinion;* some individual Christians may not be able to.

---

8. Witter Bynner, *The Way of Life According to Laotzu: An American Version* (New York: John Day Company, 1944), pp. 34, 35.

NOT ALWAYS BUNGLING

As missionaries (Marvin Mayers in Guatemala and Gene Olsen in Ivory Coast) we can look back on a large part of our missionary experience and see how it falls into what might be called case studies. Many other missionaries have had the same feeling, and from the gathered accounts of what we have seen or lived, have come much of the material in this manual. As we have assembled these glimpses of missionary life, we have been troubled with a growing sense of how often the missionary has "blown" it. How often we've bungled opportunities and offended those we've most wanted to influence. All too frequently our best intentions to show acceptance to those of another culture have only resulted in conveying rejection and driving them farther from the knowledge of God in Christ which we'd hoped to witness to.

But we don't want to give the impression that all missionaries are inept and insensitive or that most of their activities have been ineffectual. This just isn't true. It seems somehow that the conflicts and confusions and errors we have made make better case studies than do the accounts of ideal helping relationships which we have been able to establish because they present the "perplexity, confusion, or doubt" which Dewey said we needed for thinking.

MISSIONARIES' USE OF THE CASE STUDY

It is our hope that the missionary who has been bitten by the case study bug will probe to see if its use can be an effectual medium for teaching. One of the favorite forms of amusement among the Baoulés of Ivory Coast is the telling of riddle stories such as the following:

Three small boys went for a walk. As they were going along a path through a yam field, they noticed a beautiful vine which gave promise of a nice big yam just under the ground. The first boy kicked the hill of earth where it was growing, loosening the yam — but he didn't take it! The second boy picked it up and shook off the dirt — but he didn't take it either! The third boy seeing the yam just lying there, picked it up and all three ran off together, roasted it and ate it. Accosted by the owner of the field, each boy denied responsibility for having stolen the yam.

Who do you think stole it?

When presented with such a riddle, the Baoulés launch into a long and highly entertaining discussion. Couldn't an imaginative missionary with a thorough understanding of this art form, use it to present Gospel teaching in an interesting way?

CHRIST'S USE OF THE CASE STUDY

Every parable Jesus taught was a case study. We are told "he taught them his message with many parables *such as their minds could take in.* He did not speak to them at all without using parables, although in private he explained everything to his disciples" (Mark 4:33, 34, *Phillips*).

The debriefing process of explaining everything to His disciples led to clarifications, additional stories, and the giving of further insights which were not possible in the presence of the masses. Feedback from His disciples showed Jesus when His teaching wasn't clear, and then He enlarged His teaching according to their needs. Their feedback seemed to draw it from Him, and at times it was rather reluctantly given, but He gave it because His disciples were so obviously dense.

After He told an immense crowd the story of the sower, His disciples came to Him when He was alone and asked, "What does your story mean?" He said, "If you can't understand *this* simple illustration, what will you do about all the others I am going to tell?" But after this comment on their dullness, He proceeded to retell the entire allegory, explaining it carefully. (See Luke 4:1-20 *The Living Bible.*)

On another occasion He presented the case of the compassionate Samaritan in reply to a hostile questioner. After telling the story, He began debriefing with that famous question, "Which now of these three was neighbor unto him that fell among the thieves?" (See Luke 10:30-37.) When the man's answer to this question showed he had received the lesson intended, Jesus told him to go and act immediately on the insights which he had gained.

By the process of debriefing, the disciples' own feelings and experiences, Jesus drew from them lessons and insights which could enrich the comprehension of the group as a whole. Starting with the question, "Whom do men say that I the Son of man am?" (Matthew 16:13), He engaged them in a conversation which drew from Peter his magnificent confession, "Thou art the Christ, the Son of the Living God."

When His seventy disciples returned from their first witnessing tour to declare jubilantly to Him that even the demons obeyed them when they used His name, Jesus used the occasion to launch into deeper teaching about the surpassing wonder of having their names enrolled in heaven. At the same time He shared their joy, saying how fortunate they were to see what they were seeing. (See Luke 10:17-23.)

Thus by debriefing the illustrations which He Himself had given or the experiences His disciples had lived through, Jesus prepared them in three years to carry on the teaching He had begun. He felt He could leave them now. His last words to them were to go and make disciples everywhere, teaching them to obey all the commands He had given them (Matthew 28:19, 20). *Only His disciples* had His full teaching which they had received in their debriefing sessions together, and if they were to pass these teachings on to others as they themselves had been given them, it would seem that the use of parables — or case studies — would be their method, too (Mark 4:33, 34).

MODEL ONE

ACCEPTANCE OF THE PERSON

Isn't the person who acknowledges himself to be an agent of change admitting a certain rejection of the persons or culture he hopes to see changed? Some people feel this to be true, for Gibbs says, "Implicit in all attempts to alter another person is the assumption by the change agent that the person to be altered is inadequate."[1]

This then is ever the dilemma of the agent of change: how to desire and work toward an amelioration of the other's situation and at the same time manifest toward him an attitude of acceptance and not rejection.

Carl Rogers conceptualizes the legitimate change agent's role as that of one attempting to form a helping relationship — "a relationship in which at least one of the parties has the intent of promoting the growth, development, maturity, improved functioning, improved coping with life of the other."[2]

Before I dare contemplate initiating a helping relationship with another, I must fully accept myself. When I accept myself at a given point, e.g., "I'm jealous of my brother," at that moment I am able to admit to God my jealousy (He's known it all along, of course), and then God can enter my life and work with me on my problem of jealousy. But that which I refuse to

1. Jack R. Gibb, "Defensive Communication," *Journal of Communication,* 11, No. 3 (September, 1961), p. 144.
2. Carl R. Rogers, *On Becoming a Person* (Cambridge, Massachusetts: The Riverside Press, 1961), pp. 39, 40.

accept, I cling to and the effect remains with me. John put it like this, "If we confess . . . He is faithful and just to forgive."

As a psychologist, Rogers sees it this way, "The curious paradox is that when I accept myself as I am, then I change. . . . We cannot move away from what we are until we thoroughly *accept* what we are. Then change seems to come about almost unnoticed."[3]

From one's acceptance of himself, the logical progression is to an acceptance of others. Rogers continues,

> The more I am open to the realities in me and in the other person, the less do I find myself wishing to rush in to 'fix things.' . . . The more I am willing to understand and accept the realities in myself and in the other person, the more change seems to be stirred up. It is a very paradoxical thing — that to the degree that each one of us is willing to be himself, then he finds not only himself changing but he finds that other people to whom he relates are also changing.[4]

Irwin Ruben tells us that one way to change a person's ethnic attitudes is somehow to alter his attitude toward himself, and change in self-acceptance is associated with changes in prejudice.[5]

We North Americans are taught to be rejectors. Faced with new ideas or acquaintances, we almost automatically seek first to disqualify them by one means or another, and then, if this fails, we may have to accept them. We have come to value the attitude which rejects in a would-be sophisticated, disinterested way.

Reyburn writes, "Every human relationship balances delicately between acceptance and rejection but rejection is accomplished with less effort."[6]

The attitude, therefore, with which I approach another human being will determine to a large extent how effective a relationship I can have with him. Do I see him as all wrong in every way, his language inadequate, his religion hopelessly unworthy of even being considered, his social relationships inferior? Or do I see him as a man made in God's image worthy of respect as

---

3. Ibid., p. 17.
4. Ibid., pp. 21, 22.
5. Irwin Rubin, "Increased Self-Acceptance: A Means of Reducing Prejudice," *Journal of Personality and Social Psychology,* 5 (1967), pp. 233-239.
6. William D. Reyburn, "The Helping Relationship in Missionary Work," *Practical Anthropology,* 17, No. 2 (March-April, 1970), p. 50.

a person. "If I think of the other as a heathen, as a polygamist, or a 'soul to be saved' I tend, as Martin Buber says, to confirm him in that state.... If at least one of us sees us as created in God's image, then the possibility of our becoming what we are potentially is vastly extended."[7]

If our sincere desire is to build toward a relationship of mutual respect with all men, we must be alert to the implications of our attitudes and behavior. *Is what I am doing, thinking, or saying potential for building trust or potential for undermining trust?* Asking ourselves this prior question of trust should become as natural as breathing.

Rejection of others would seem to be no stranger to the evangelical milieu if we read the message in "My Hippie Brother." It can be practiced anywhere: within the family — "Jane Steinback" — and even on the mission field toward those to whom we hope to minister — "Whose Church Is It?"

On the other hand, acceptance and the building of mutual respect may be a beautiful, growing thing between two people whether one is a dirty old wino or the king of a nation.

whose church is it?

While working as a missionary in Thailand, I became associated with a small Christian hospital where I acted as pastor-evangelist while my wife helped as an operating room nurse. This hospital had been established by the mission in a remote area in the midst of rice farming country, about twenty miles from the railhead.

The layout of the hospital grounds had been planned by medical missionary personnel and mission leaders. The compound, circled by a barbed wire fence, consisted of a main hospital building, a nurses' dormitory, two doctors' houses, utility buildings, and a plot of land designated for a church. On this rectangular-shaped lot, the hospital building occupied the central place toward the front with the nurses' dorm and the doctors' houses in the background. The plot of land designated for the church building was located on the corner of the compound farthest removed from the entrance. The nearest building to the church property, not more than twenty-five yards away, was the leprosy patients' house.

A short distance from the leprosy accommodation was the hos-

---

7. Ibid., p. 56.

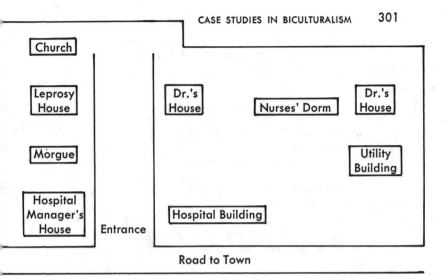

pital morgue. When a patient died at the hospital, the corpse was stored temporarily in this small building until relatives could arrange for the funeral proceedings. Thai people are naturally very much afraid of the spirits of the deceased. In order to reach the location of the church, one had to come along the road that entered the compound near the hospital and to pass directly in front of the morgue and very close to the leprosy building.

For some years the missionaries had been concerned that a church building should be erected, but there were not sufficient funds. The small group of Thai believers — consisting mainly of the hospital staff — had been meeting together on Sunday and Wednesday evenings in a basement room in the nurses' dorm. During the week daily prayers were conducted there and the staff was required to attend.

Then a gift of money was received from abroad for the church building, so it was decided to erect a simple structure consisting of eight main posts and a corrugated metal roof. After this much was accomplished, the money ran out. So nothing more was done for a long period of time.

The missionaries complained that the Thai believers didn't seem to have any interest in the development of the church. No one showed any desire to use the new building for church meetings. Later on, simple wooden benches were constructed, and with much insistence from the missionaries, services were conducted in it. Yet it seemed that the believers were ill at ease and unhappy about meeting there. Tension seemed to be building up between the Thai church leaders and the missionaries. This development was a hindrance to fellowship and a detriment to normal church growth. Something was wrong and a remedy was needed.

Questions:

To be used with chapter 2:

1. Without trying to display 20-20 hindsight and blame former missionaries for what they had done wrong, where do you feel the planners of the original compound should have asked the Prior Question of Trust?

2. What indications of respect or lack of respect for others do you see in this situation?

3. How many cultural values of the Thais have been ignored?

4. If the building of a new church building were to become a possibility, what questions should be asked of whom concerning its location?

5. From thinking on this case, can you formulate any principles concerning where churches should be located?

To be used with chapter 12:

1. What norms are in conflict here?

2. Can you find an example of withdrawal and scapegoating in this case?

3. If malfunction of tension results when one group attempts to modify or to control the other, who has caused the malfunction of tension in this case?

4. Do you think non-Christian Thais would readily attend church meetings on the hospital compound? Why?

To be used with chapter 15:

1. What do you think of the missionaries' perception that the Thai believers didn't seem to have any interest in the development of the church?

2. How do we see the principle of the adverse effect operating here?

3. Are North Americans totally devoid of influence from things similar to that which the presence of the morgue and leprosy house have had on the Thais? Give examples.

4. Rank some of the values of the Thais and of the hospital personnel as you see them evidenced in this case.

5. Imagine that the original planners of the compound and the Thai Christians are meeting together with you to try to improve the present situation. What would you do if you were (a) the leader of the local Thai believers? (b) a respected mission executive?

black and white

— Elliot Jones speaks in chapel

Coming here to college as a freshman four years ago was a big experience for me because it was something altogether new. I didn't know quite what to expect. But I did know that I should expect things to be different, because I went to a high school in Chicago that was all black. And I knew that when I came here, the situation would not be the same in that here it is predominantly white. When I came, my roommate was probably shocked, because he didn't know what he was getting. I knew what to expect, but he didn't. I was the only black person in my room; I was the only black person in my wing in the dorm; I was the only black person in my dorm; I was the only black person in most of my classes. This was really a different situation for me.

There's one verse that I want to emphasize in the things I'll be saying: "Let love be without hypocrisy."

One of the first things I noticed when I came here to college and walked into a room, was that I was obvious, and I felt obvious because I was different. It was something I had never felt before, because you don't really feel that you're different until you get into a situation where you really are different. You know, of course, in a way when you're different, it's because society says you are. In all my experience before I came here, I didn't feel obvious because I blended in with everybody — I was just part of the whole. But here, just walking into a room made me feel eyes everywhere. And they seemed just to look on me, making me feel obvious. The eyes seemed to say that I didn't belong, like, "Are you lost?" "Can I help you?" "Which way are you going?" or "Are you sure you're in the right place?"

This wore off pretty much after awhile, thank goodness, because it was a pretty rough experience, being obvious. I don't think very many of you have ever experienced that, and you may never experience it, unless you're in a situation where you're the only white person in an all-black group. It's really a weird experience, and I was glad that people finally got used to seeing me.

Everybody seems to think that all black people look alike. For three years I was called Rick Dudley. But the thing is, we don't all look alike. We all have different personalities, and we're different in every way. We're real people, and every way that you are different from each other, we're different also.

Another thing that I experienced was a lot of kids coming up to me and asking me what country I was from. My answer would usually be, "I'm from Chicago, Illinois; what country are you from?" Then a lot of people have seemed to be really interested in my social life. I always get questions like, "I bet your social life is really rough." "I bet you have a real frustrating time." These things made me feel obvious, or made me feel different because my blackness was always reemphasized. And it is still emphasized every day through just such comments as these.

One of the questions people always ask me after first meeting me is if I play any sports. No, I don't play any sports, because I wasn't any good. Not all black people are athletes, especially me.

Some people tell me, "I bet you were a good dancer once." No, I wasn't because my feet were so big that I was kind of clumsy.

Or I'd get a question like this: "Does sunburn hurt? Oh, I forgot, I'm sorry." The next question would be, "Do negroes sunburn?" And my answer is, "I don't know; I never had one." Or I may be walking down the street one evening from the library back to the dorm, and I see a friend and he says, "Smile, Jonesy, so I can see you." So I smile. These are things which make me feel obvious, and which make me constantly aware of my blackness.

Another "good time" for me is usually on Parents' Weekends. I've been through four of them now, and every time that parents come, I really get a kick out of watching their reaction at seeing me. It's usually one of two reactions. Usually fear, because they might be afraid that I'm taking out their daughter, or I might be rooming with their son. Or the other reaction is one of interest. They come up, shake my hand, and say, "How are you? Pleased to meet you. Where are you from?" You know, extreme interest. And I know they don't just walk up to any kid and react to him this way. And so this too makes me conscious constantly of my blackness.

I think one of the reasons that parents react the way they do, especially parents with kids here, is because everybody comes from middle-class suburbia which reeks! The whole atmosphere, I think. And I have come to dislike it quite a bit after having been here. I really didn't know too much about it while I was at home in Chicago where I lived. Middle-class suburbia to me is so stifling, and people don't seem to me to be free. Everyone is in a box, in a system where they follow through with certain norms and certain things which they just feel they have to do in order to survive within the system. And I reject this because the people don't seem real. They seem like artificial mannequins.

I went to a high school a couple of weeks ago to speak to some English classes on race relations. And it was very interesting to me to note how ignorant most of the students there were of what was going on in the world, just because of the fact that they live in suburbia. They were so sheltered from the realities of life they had no idea, no concept of what was really going on in the world. And this was really surprising to me.

Another thing I noticed was that there were two types of students there. The students classified themselves as "greasers" and "rahs." The "rahs" were students much like you — clean-cut, good dressers, worked hard at school. I would say they were probably conservative compared to the other kids. The "greasers" were the kids that were, I guess, the hoods, sort of. You know, slick heads and leather jackets — stuff like this. One class I talked to was predominately the "greasers" and the other class I talked to was predominately "rahs." I found that within the group of "greasers" there was a lot more freedom of expression, and I felt more free to express myself. They seemed to be more alive and able to react to me more quickly than the other kids did, because the other kids seemed to be out of it. I think the "system" had become so much a part of them because of their living where they lived, and their wanting to follow through with it and its norms. And because I've been here at college, I've come to reject all of these.

Being here at school has helped me tremendously to know myself — I've been forced to. Being black can be an exciting and challenging thing, especially in a place like this. The situation here has helped me to assert my blackness like never before, because I was definitely different from everyone else. Being here I became initially very conscious of my blackness. So I was forced to think more about me, about what and who I was, why I was here, and how I was to relate to everybody around me.

But that caused somewhat of a problem at first, because I'd always been taught to be proud of the fact that I was black. And at the same time, I was supposed to look at myself as equal to everybody else. But at first this was hard for me because me being black at first connoted that I had to be superior to be proud of it. But I learned through experience that it didn't mean that. It meant that I shouldn't be ashamed of my blackness, but I should accept it as part of me, and hopefully that you should accept it as part of me.

There were times when I wanted to forget my blackness; I wanted to throw it away, because its presence became a nuisance to me, because I was a part of the whole, but then again, I wasn't. I thought that my blackness would be a barrier at first to my acceptance in the group, especially in relationship to females. So I wanted to throw it away; I wanted to reject it. But actually what I really wanted to do was to throw off the implication that came with being black, rather than throwing off being black itself. I wanted to be accepted as a man who happens to be black, rather than a man whose blackness means that he should be treated in a certain way.

What's important, I think, is to realize that I am black and you're white, and be realistic about it. Look at me as an individual just as Christ looks at you and me as individuals. My blackness does not cloud my relationship with Jesus Christ. He doesn't attach any special connotations or conditions because I'm black. He accepts me for what I am as a man.

I was going to speak at a youth meeting once, and a lot of problems arose because they usually had the meeting in a lady's house, but she didn't want to have it when I was coming because she was afraid of what the neighbors might say. Okay, that was fine. So then they were going to have it in a church. But she didn't want to have it in the church because she was afraid of the reaction the pastor might get from the neighborhood. So finally we had to have it in a high school in a different community. That was exciting to me because I'd never caused so much trouble before.

"Let love be without hypocrisy." When you say you love, do you really love? Or are you just saying it? How would you react, or how do you think Christ would react? Suppose you were on a new job and your boss was black, how would you react? Or you arrived at grad school to find that your roommate was black? Or you see an interracial couple walking down the street? Or your brother or sister falls in love with a beautiful black person? Will your reaction be "What will the neighbors think?" Or "What about the children?" Or how will you react when a black child wants to join your lily-white Sunday school? How will you react when social pressure says, "Stay away from him because he's black. If you don't, we will ostracize you." Are you willing to put some teeth into your commitment to Christ? Are you really willing to let Christ's love be expressed through you to others in a real, sincere, and genuine way? He wants us to be able to love a person for *who* he is and not because of *what* he is.

pig food and missions

My wife and I were asked to work at a small Bible school where several ethnic groups were represented in the student body. There were Thai, Northern Thai, Lao, Meo, Yao — all manifesting distinct subcultures and valid value systems.

My wife is a nurse and I was involved in Bible teaching and practical Christian work with the students. From the start we made it our purpose to accept each student just as he or she was. There were six Meo families living on the Bible school premises because they had been forced out of their mountain home by Communist infiltration. One of these families consisted of Mark and his wife Cho and their two children. Mark was quiet, meek, and small of stature, but strong in faith and a good student. It was delightful to know him and to learn of his home in the hills, his background, his family, and his burdens and desires for the future.

All of the Meo families were raising pigs to supplement their meager resources and provide a limited means of support. The men took turns gathering a green underwater plant for pig food from the nearby lake. One morning I volunteered to go with Mark in the long dugout canoe to gather this pig food. We enjoyed good fellowship together and we talked about Meo ways, especially about Meo courting and marriage procedures as we worked pulling in the slimy, green pig food.

My wife had been helping the Meo families medically for some months, and she had grown to appreciate these industrious and resourceful mountain people. One day Mark came to visit at our house. As we sat on our front porch overlooking the lake, Mark said to my wife, "Cho will soon give birth to our child. It is our Meo custom to have the mother of the husband deliver the child. My mother is not here; she is still in the hills. Will you please take the place of my mother in the delivery of our child?"

We considered this a great honor. There was a local government hospital nearby, and my wife had encouraged the Meo women to have their babies there. This was new to them and they didn't trust the Thai anyway. They could have asked one of the Meo wives to assist, but they requested that my wife fulfill the role of mother-in-law midwife on this important occasion. Although my wife is not a trained midwife, she is a qualified registered nurse. She has assisted with deliveries in the past, but always with a doctor present. When the day arrived, she accepted her new role with a bit of trepidation and a prayer to the Lord for His help. All went well and Cho gave birth to a lovely baby daughter. Mark, of course, was delighted and our bond of fellowship with the family was greatly deepened. As a result, our ministry of teaching the Word of God became more meaningful to Mark and to the other Meo students.

Questions:

1. In what ways is acceptance of the other person demonstrated in this case?

2. Could we speak of a flow of acceptance here which ultimately reached out to a group considerably larger than the group of principles involved in this incident?

3. Why do you think Mark felt at liberty to invite the missionary nurse to function in his mother's place?

4. How might the missionaries have "botched up" this unique opportunity?

5. How did the missionaries put into practice Roger's ten principles for creating a helping relationship?

my hippie brother

I pushed open the door of Luigi's Pizza Parlor and entered another world — a world in which I was an alien, marked by short-cropped hair, tweed sports coat and shined shoes as identifiable with the Establishment. Funny how uncomfortable I felt as I walked to a back table, followed all the way by suspicious eyes. It was 10:30. My wife, Anne, had been late coming home from prayer meeting, but by the time she came in I was certain that I had to go out. If my information was correct, my kid brother was back in town and I had to see him.

As I sat down and scanned the room for a familiar face, I wondered for the thousandth time if I was being wise. Would I know Jim? Could my brother be like the rest of these young people, with their strange garb and incomprehensible lingo? Would I be able to communicate with him when I did see him? And how would he feel about this unrequested rendezvous? Would he resent his big brother's interest in his life?

But it was too late to worry about those things. I was here now, in the one spot in town where I might be reasonably sure of seeing him. And the waitress was tapping her pad, waiting for my order. "Black coffee," I ordered, and studied the room, table by table, once more. I sipped my coffee slowly, and thought back over the events that had led to my sitting here in this coffee house.

Jim and I had grown up together — a couple of years between our ages — in a comfortable, middleclass, Christian home. We went together to an evangelical church, and what we learned there was reinforced by teaching at home. If my parents had been a bit too concerned about making money, who was to criticize? Surely they were not more materialistic than the average Christian family. They faithfully tithed what they had and gave generously to missions. As we grew older, I became interested in the many enterprises which my father undertook — from house construction to crop spraying, while Jim merely scorned the drive that pushed my family to work.

After he completed high school, Jim got a good job but soon dissolved his connections and disappeared from town. The haunting question — "Why?" — broke my mother's health, and subtly transformed my dad from an outgoing and confident businessman to one who was tense, nervous, and introspective. And yet we knew that even by answering that question, by assigning the blame to one or the other thing in our lives, we would never solve the problem of the Jim we didn't know, the vanished son and brother.

It was this enigmatic Jim whom I was waiting to see. My parents did not know that he was back in town — a friend had phoned me that afternoon to confide the news.

And then I saw him enter the room. His brown wavy hair was shoulder-length and neatly combed. His beard was clipped short and topped by a long, flowing moustache. A coarsely woven poncho, handmade pants and moccasins comprised his outfit. But in spite of this garb, he was unmistakably my brother and I found it hard to keep myself from rising in greeting. Would he acknowledge me? I wondered.

But I didn't have to wait long. Jim had obviously seen me before I had seen him and without hesitation he walked toward my table, calling greetings to his friends as he passed.

He sat down without a word. "Have a coffee?" I invited. He nodded. "Thanks." I ordered another cup for myself and one for Jim.

As we drank our coffee, we made small talk about our lives. I tried not to ask the questions that were burning in my mind: What have you been doing? Where have you been? When are you going to come back to us? Instead, I finally asked, "Can I give you a lift to your pad?" He grinned at my self-conscious handling of hippie lingo. "Sure," he said. And we walked out to the car.

Near the river, where we could look across at the skyline our city was gradually piling up, we parked the car and talked. Jim didn't need many questions — he seemed more than anxious to pour out to me his complaints and bitternesses; a little less anxious, perhaps, to inform me about his activities. It was past midnight now and I was a working man, so when the flow of talk ebbed, I offered to take him around to where he slept. As I pulled up to the flophouse where he directed me, I reached for my pen and scribbled a number on a card. "Here's my phone number, Jim," I said. "If you want to visit more, give me a call."

Next afternoon the phone rang at 5:10 — not a minute after I had come in from work. "Jim here," my brother's voice said. "Got an hour or two?" I picked him up and brought him up to the house for supper. It was strange to have so other-worldly a visitor at our table and to know he was my brother. He was at his courteous and pleasant best — even helped Anne with the dishes before we went out for another drive and talk.

As we sat parked at the end of an unused runway at the abandoned air force base, I began to ask some questions. Not the ones of particular family interest, but ones which I felt might give me some clues to this hippie brother of mine. "Do you remember that Sunday night about 15 years ago — when I was 11? While Pastor Thom was speaking, I suddenly realized my need to accept Jesus Christ as my own Lord and Savior."

Jim looked at me for a minute. I could see he didn't care to remember that night. Then he looked away. "I remember it, man."

"Remember how I stayed to pray with the pastor after the service? And when we got home, remember how Mom and Dad turned to you?"

Jim looked out the window. "Yeah, I remember. They said, 'Don't you think you should do this, too?'"

"You do remember, then."

"Yeah."

"Jim — is that the only experience of 'salvation' you ever had?"

There was a long silence. "What are you getting to?" he asked defensively.

"Did you really become a Christian that night?"

Jim shrugged under his poncho. He seemed resentful of my question. "Do I look like a Christian?" he taunted.

"That's not the point," I said. "It's what you are — not how you look."

"No," Jim said finally. "No, I'm not a Christian." There was a momentary silence, and then his tone was bitter again. "Any reason why I would be? So I can get a holy feeling by going to church on Sundays? And get God to help me make a pile? No. From all I've seen, this Christianity kick is just not where it's at."

"Then 'where is it at'?" I queried.

"Don't know. But I'm going to find out. That's what all this (he indicated his clothes and hair with a sweeping gesture) is about.

This is the first time I've done anything that is me; the first time I've been a person apart from the rest of you."

"Ever read your Bible anymore?" I tried to sound casual as I pursued my quest.

"Sure. All the time. Along with the sacred writings of every other religion I can get my hands on." He became reflective. "You know, I met a very cool guy. He's a lama. When I'm down at the gulf I take instruction from him once in awhile. Sometimes I think that I might just find the truth and be free. . . ."

A red light suddenly pulsated in the night sky behind us and Jim snapped from his reverie. "The fuzz again," he spat. "They'll nail me for something just because I am the way I am."

"They're just checking us out," I consoled, and stepped out of the car to meet the police officer. Routine check of license, registration, insurance — and we were alone again. But Jim was bitter and launched into a tirade against police that gradually widened to include invectives against all authority. When at last he had spilled out his bitterness, we sat in silence together looking out into the spring darkness. Finally he turned to me.

"Think I should go see the folks?"

"If you want to. I think they would like it if you did."

"Think so?"

"Yeah, I'm quite sure."

"Let's go around to the house."

And so we went. I didn't really expect a replay of the gospel account of the prodigal's homecoming. But I was as unprepared as Jim was for the barrage of questions that Mother and Dad launched.

"Do you have to look so . . . so grotesque?" Mother asked, surveying Jim with disfavor.

"Planning a stop at the barber's sometime?" My Dad tried to be jocular but there was no laughter.

"I'll get that tweed coat you left hanging in your closet—" Mom suggested.

"How could you do this to us?" was the unspoken question behind every question. And all the questions were asked — the where's, and what's and why's? There were more.

Finally Jim turned to me and snapped, "Let's get out of here."

"Thought you said they'd like to see me," he snarled as we drove down the street toward his place.

"I thought they would," I said, feeling as betrayed as he.

"It's just like I thought it would be. Just like it always has been. Like it always will be. They don't really care about me. They care about my clothes, the impression I'll make on others, the way I've ruined their reputation. They won't accept me as I really am. Well, that's just too bad for them." He paused for a long minute. "And for me, I guess," he added, disappointment choking his words. And so my vanishing brother vanished again.

That was a year ago, and I haven't seen Jim to talk with him again. He is back in our state these days, with short hair and clipped moustache. He is a young man with a purpose. He tours with another young fellow, holding pacifist rallies. Just where and how he got involved in New Left activity, I don't know. Just how much he understands of his involvement I am not sure either.

But I am haunted by questions. In a New Left cell somewhere did he find acceptance which he failed to find in his own Christian home? Did some older organizer show Jim the attention his Christian Dad had always been too busy to evidence? Will my brother ever find his way to the Truth that will set him free from this new entrapment? And will I ever again answer my phone to hear my kid brother say, "Jim here. Got an hour or two?"[1]

wine but not tobacco

While visiting Geneva, Switzerland, I had the opportunity of staying with the European director of a well-known evangelical mission. This is a personal experience that he shared with me.

While living in the European culture, he did not feel that there was anything wrong with having wine with his meals at home with his family and with other European evangelicals. He would not have wine with his meals if this would offend another person with him who totally abstained. He was willing to limit his personal freedom out of respect for another.

The director who had preceded this man was a "traditionalist." He desired to totally abstain from having wine served with his meals in Europe or in the United States. This, of course, was his personal prerogative. But now the complications begin.

Upon retiring from the position of European director, the former director returned to his home in Atlanta, but his daughter came back to Geneva to be the new director's secretary. As she began to experience cultural differences and new social norms, her rigidity toward American, evangelical, social "taboos" seemed to lessen. For the first time in her life, she experienced the great New Testa-

---

1. Anonymous, as told to Maxine L. Hancock, *Moody Monthly* (October, 1969).

ment truth of 1 Corinthians 6:12: " 'All things are lawful for me,' but not all things are helpful. 'All things are lawful for me,' but I will not be enslaved by anything" (RSV). Her attitudes began to change so that she was willing to restrain her personal freedom — not because she had to, but because she wanted to. Thus, when she made her own personal decision to have wine with her meals while living in the European culture, this conviction was not based on a particular subcultural pressure, but established in a relationship with Jesus Christ.

The discovery of this new truth and the appreciation of other cultural and social norms was soon shared via letter with her folks back in Georgia. You can imagine the subcultural shock! Her father thought that the new European director was behind all of his daughter's "spiritual complacency." He called the home mission office in the States and told the general director that he would cut off financial support from his southern constituency and would also excite a few people to publicly question the biblical validity of their organization.

Incidentally, the former European director owns a huge tobacco farm and supplies the major cigarette firms in the South. . . .

the seven-month baby

Phairote, a young Thai Christian, brought his bride with him to Bible school when he returned for his second term. He had lived previously in the boys' dorm, but during vacation he had married a young nurses' aide at the Christian hospital where he was working.

They entered easily into Bible school life and continued their studies together. Before long it was announced that they were expecting their first child. Everyone looked forward happily with them to its arrival. They had talked of returning to Central Thailand for the birth of the child; then, as the time drew near, they decided to remain and have it in the government hospital nearby. The day came for the birth of the baby, and they proudly announced the arrival of a son.

The missionaries who were teaching on the staff of the school began to be uneasy. One of them had attended the wedding of the young couple some months before. When they compared the wedding date with the birth date of the baby, it appeared that the child was born about six weeks earlier than they felt it should have been. Since the baby was above average size and weight and normal in every way, it seemed clear that he was not premature, and so the missionaries concluded that the newlyweds had lived together prior to their wedding day.

Before long the matter took on crisis proportions in the eyes of the missionaries. As they gathered to discuss it, it was felt that since the purity of the church was at stake, the young couple must be faced with the issue. Since confrontation is the western method of solving conflicts, they decided to visit the young couple in their quarters and talk the matter over. One evening while the other students were studying, three men and two women visited Phairote and his wife. After prayer, one of the missionaries broached the subject, informing the proud parents that their behavior had been improper by Christian standards. Silence filled the room.

One of the aspects of the Thai value system is that of saving face. They will always approach things indirectly so that no one loses face in the situation. Without an intermediary which Thais would have used in such a case, the young couple somehow felt "naked" in the overpowering presence of the five missionaries. There was no one to remind the missionaries for them that the Thai betrothal is considered as binding as marriage and that sexual relations during the period covered by the betrothal are not considered particularly improper.

There was little that Phairote and his wife could say, so they listened while the missionaries proposed a solution. They suggested that the couple should stand up before the assembled Bible school students at one of their chapel meetings and confess their misdeed publicly. The young couple was not especially pleased at this suggestion, so they remained noncommittal. After considerable consultation, the missionaries departed and awaited the chapel hour when this confession would be made. It never came. The couple refused to comply, the missionaries were disappointed, and at the close of the term, the couple returned to their home.

MODEL TWO

THEORY OF NATURAL GROUPINGS

Just as one must first accept himself before he can extend acceptance to the other, so the responsible agent of change must look at and accept his own sociocultural behavioral norms before he can look at the norms of others and realize they are distinct from his own but equally valid.

Each member of the human race finds himself fitting somewhere in the hierarchy of all groups of which he is a member. Activities (see "Blood of a White Chicken") and values (see "The Seven-Month Baby") which are determined by his society's norms will largely determine how he will act in any situation.

Sherif tells us that norms which are expected modes of behavior and belief develop whenever people interact. They are necessary to reduce uncertainty and confusion so that each individual will not have to seek to determine for himself in every situation what would be appropriate behavior. Once formed, norms are binding on individuals even when they are absent from their group.[1]

Norms last until they produce unclarity, interfere with interaction, or create burdens for the majority of the group or society. They are maintained through social sanctions,

---

1. Muzafer Sherif, *The Psychology of Social Norms* (New York: Harper and Row, 1963), p. iii.

315

punishment for those who disregard them and reward for them who obey them.[2]

The person who lives at peace within his own culture and then moves with equal smoothness into another culture is comparable to one who speaks two languages fluently. If one enters a society not his own and is unable to respond fully and completely according to the norms of that society, he must learn what he still lacks in the way of a fluid use of that culture's norms, or he will be in conflict until he does. Extreme frustration to himself and offense to others can result.

No doubt many... can illustrate from their own experience the anguish and near paralysis felt when they found themselves in a strange situation with no clear understanding of how to act. If the situation is one which in fact has a structure, although the individual in question does not know it, the remedy is the fairly simple one (however painful it might be) of learning it.[3]

Norms of individuals and societies change and this is often a painful, disruptive process. Acting in excess of one's norm too often brings guilt, whereas a deprivation of one's norm tends to foster bitterness unless voluntarily embraced. But there can be very constructive experimentation in extending a norm. This commonly occurs when an individual or society turns to Christ as C. S. Lewis reminds us in "Thick and Clear Soups."

The truth of God must come to each man completely and effectively in keeping with what he is socioculturally. No one has the right to enslave another by posing as the administrator of God's truth to him (see "Marriage Will Solve It All"). This is the prerogative of the Holy Spirit speaking through the Word of God to every man.

A number of cases have been chosen to illustrate the taxonomy of values called the basic values. These may be illustrated in the behavior of individuals — "The Leper," "Please, Jim, Do Something!" — or whole societies — "The Decision-Making Process in Japan."

An understanding of one's own value profile is often a first step in self-acceptance, just as the knowledge of how another person differs from you in the basic values dichotomies may facilitate enormously your acceptance of him, although he is vastly different from yourself.

---

2. Ladd Wheeler, *Interpersonal Influence* (Boston: Allyn and Bacon, Inc., 1970), p. 12.

3. Harry C. Bredemeier and Richard M. Stephenson, *The Analysis of Social Systems* (New York: Holt, Rinehart, and Winston, Inc., 1962), pp. 24-26.

add onions

In the mountains of North Thailand and Laos there is a group of tribal people known as the Meo. For hundreds of years they have lived in the mountain forests sustaining themselves on a slash-and-burn type of agriculture and the growing of opium. In recent years some of these Meo have turned to Christ from their animistic ways. Many have been uprooted from their mountain villages and forced down into the plains by the Communists.

On one occasion a group of Meo Christians were gathered for a short-term Bible school. Periods of Bible study were arranged. There were also times for recreation and for meals taken together as a large family. Some of the wives of the believers shared in the cooking.

The local missionary who was doing some of the teaching, joined the Meo for a noon meal. They were all happily enjoying the food and conversation together until the missionary tasted one of the dishes and grimaced openly, remarking in a loud voice, "This food tastes flat. Didn't you put any onions in it?" A hush fell over the group and reluctantly one of those working in the kitchen replied, "Nzoe doesn't care for onions, so rather than offend him, the cooks refrained from putting onions in the food." Nzoe was a gifted young Meo with a keen mind and a deep desire to follow the Lord. Although quiet and reserved as a person, he was faithful and well respected by his peers. When the missionary heard this explanation, he bristled and said loudly for all, including Nzoe, to hear, "Next time put in the onions. If Nzoe doesn't like it, he can go without. The rest of us want onions in the food." A few daring glances were exchanged among the Meo, and then everyone went back to eating.

The teaching sessions continued with the missionary taking part. The Meo appreciated the opportunity to study the Word of God; to fellowship with one another, and to be together for the short-term Bible school.

Questions:

For use with chapter 6:

1. With whom do you identify, Nzoe or the missionary?
2. In this case, who willingly accepted deprivation of norm?
3. What do you think of the Meo cooks' method of handling the "onion" problem as an act having significance for interpersonal relationships?
4. Imagine yourself as Nzoe in the missionary's Bible class fol-

lowing the meal. What possible attitudes might he have toward the teacher and his teaching?

For use with chapter 2:

1. Who asked the PQT and who did not?

2. If you were the missionary and later realized your error, how would you go about restoring a trust relationship with Nzoe?

an m.k. goes to college

I'm a missionary kid. I grew up in Burundi, Central Africa. I can recall the early time when "everything was the same as it always was." After dinner at noon, Mother *always* read to us out of the big blue Bible-study book. The daily bath was as regular as dusk, and our dear African cook was eternal.

But after all, things do change, and I started going to the Belgian colonial school. Even my sister's left-handedness was soon overcome by the regimentation there, and she was made to write *comme tout le monde* ('like everyone else').

As time went by I saw some change and a certain variety in life, but basically things moved slowly and obeyed the Swahili axiom, "Bado kidogo ('Wait a while'). The third grade arrived out of the dim future and with it came a shocking change: My two oldest sisters and my older brother left Dad and Mom and us four younger kids, and flew away to some place called America to go to high school.

Then the next year we went to America too! The imprint left by that year's furlough wasn't quite erased when we came home to Africa again. Even it had changed with the fever of independence. But the ageless blue mountains across the lake in Congo seemed to belie any change. Wasn't it the familiar old roosters who still roused the same Africans to just another day of hoeing on the family plot?

Another year-long furlough with its timid forays into American life split my high school years which were spent at an American missionary boarding school in Kenya. Here, despite our khaki school uniforms, I began to understand the diversity in life. This school acted as a bridge to the accelerated life awaiting me in America.

Too soon the happy days with friends, familiar scenery, wildlife, and rugby games was ended and suddenly I found myself in the registration hassle at college, ID no. 435685.

I thought I could comprehend variety and change, but now I couldn't take it. There was too much, too fast! The host of churches in town all clamored for my attendance. The immensity of the chapel engulfed me. "That whole book read by next week!" "I'll try to remember, but you're the eighth Bill I've met today!" I imprudently ventured into the library and blew my mind just browsing through the magazine rack.

To a guy who'd had the same breakfast all his life, the choices in the dining hall were a pleasant problem. ("Move it! How long does it take you to make up your mind?") Freshman guys and dollies were already going steady and I hadn't even thought about a date yet!

Everything seemed to blare out, "Do, taste, experience, buy, absorb, read, feel, be — and quick, before it's too late!" I was being swept away by the philosophy lying behind Howard Johnson's thirty-four flavors of ice cream and Evelyn Wood's speed-reading course.

Questions:

1. How was the missionary child both deprived of his norm and induced to live in excess of his norm at the same time?

2. How does this case illustrate the words of T. S. Eliot, "We cannot step twice into the same river, not merely because the water has flowed by, but because we have become different persons in the meantime."[1]

3. Do you imagine experimentation will result in a change in the M.K.'s norm?

4. How might he become bitter and then reject himself and others?

thick and clear soups

For my own part, I have sometimes told my audience that the only two things really worth considering are Christianity and Hinduism. (Islam is only the greatest of the Christian heresies, Buddhism only the greatest of the Hindu heresies. Real Paganism is dead. All that was best in Judaism and Platonism survives in Christianity.) There isn't really, for an adult mind, this infinite variety of religions

1. T. S. Eliot, The Cocktail Party (New York: Harcourt, Brace, Jovanovich, n.d.).

to consider. We may *salva reverentia* ('Without outraging reverence') divide religions, as we do soups, into 'thick' and 'clear.' By Thick I mean those which have orgies and ecstasies and mysteries and local attachments: Africa is full of Thick religions. By Clear I mean those which are philosophical, ethical and universalizing: Stoicism, Buddhism, and the Ethical Society are Clear religions. Now if there is a true religion it must be both Thick and Clear; for the true God must have made both the child and the man, both the savage and the citizen, both the head and the belly. And the only two religions that fulfill this condition are Hinduism and Christianity. But Hinduism fulfills it imperfectly. The Clear religion of the Brahmin hermit in the jungle and the Thick religion of the neighbouring temple go *side by side.* The Brahmin hermit doesn't bother about the temple prostitution nor the worshipper in the temple about the hermit's metaphysics. But Christianity really breaks down the middle wall of the partition. It takes a convert from Central Africa and tells him to obey an enlightened universalist ethic; it takes a twentieth-century academic prig like me and tells me to go fasting to a Mystery, to drink the blood of the Lord. The savage convert has to be Clear; I have to be Thick. That is how one knows one has come to the real religion.[1]

deprivation

Seeing Clarise's immaculately groomed figure with its shining auburn hair bent over the old leper woman's extended feet as she carefully debrided the ulcerating sores, Paul was struck by the amazing contrast and stopped to reflect a moment. Clarise was chatting fluently in old Luala's language, trying to calm her fears. And perhaps, Paul thought, trying to keep her own mind off the stench, the flies, the heat.

Paul respected Clarise as a very capable fellow doctor. She could have had an exclusive practice in America. And just before coming to Africa, she had inherited from her father nearly a quarter of a million dollars, but few people even knew of this. From the time she had given her life to Christ as a teen-ager, she had looked forward to working among the lepers of Central Africa.

Paul never ceased to be amazed at her total acceptance of this

---

1. C. S. Lewis, *God in the Dock: Essays on Theology and Ethics* (Grand Rapids: Wm. B. Eerdmans Publishing Co., 1970), pp. 102, 103.

land and its people with seemingly no sense of deprivation. It was an acceptance with joy as she spread a contagious thankfulness to God in all circumstances. It made the routine and drudgery in the hospital easier for them all. What a contrast with Miriam!

Miriam. This morning had brought another scene which had left Paul feeling helpless and wondering if his whole ministry in this country was futile. She had wanted them to take the day off to go to the beach with the children. She felt he owed it to his family and let him know he was failing her and the children. She seemed incapable of understanding his enjoyment of his work. As for the children, Judy and John, Paul was certain he didn't neglect them. Through long evening hours they had been growing closer together as their parents' estrangement increased.

Miriam had never been happy since they moved to Dempala to direct the hospital. On the coast they had lived in the capital city. There had been a circle of French friends with whom she could always spend an afternoon. Here in Dempala her days were made up of drinking iced tea, visiting with the other missionary women when they were not too busy with their classes or hospital work, and reading the women's magazines. Redbook was her favorite.

Miriam had been beauty queen the year Paul was a senior in college. He'd felt himself the luckiest fellow on campus when a short courtship brought a June wedding soon after graduation. It had seemed so wonderful to him that she was a Christian from a good, though not well-to-do, family, and she seemed to be delighted at the thought of going anywhere in the world that he went. Now she never passed up an opportunity to say, as though it were a great joke, that she had married a doctor, not a missionary, and see what she'd gotten stuck with!

Looking at her this morning, he had found it hard to understand how her beauty had coarsened so in just sixteen years. Her bitterness and discontent had brought a permanent drooping sullenness to her face, a face from which all delicateness had been blurred by weight which had been creeping on over the years. Although she only stepped on the scales behind locked doors, one guessed that she was carrying at least eighty excess pounds. With this addition had gone all interest in dressing carefully. A drooping slip or a safety-pin anchored hem gave the final picture.

And perhaps hardest for Paul to bear was her antipathy to the nationals, whom he had come to sincerely love. Serving the Lord in this land was his whole life. Bringing his mind back to today's problems, he decided he would try to take the afternoon off. He'd try to appease Miriam once more.

pentecostalism in italy

In the early part of this century Pentecostalism was carried from Chicago to Italy where it has had a phenomenal growth so that there are more than twice as many Pentecostals in Italy today — over 100,000 members of the Assemblies of God alone — as there are all other Protestants combined.

"What made Pentecostal growth possible in this Roman Catholic land?" asks Roger E. Hedlund, Conservative Baptist missionary to Italy. He then explains that Southern Italy is a disintegrating society. He feels that identification with the Pentecostals has given a vital functional equivalent to formerly meaningful forms of worship lost through disillusionment with the Catholic church. The following excerpts from his article[1] show how Pentecostalism entered the void and offered a meaningful option to the disoriented people of Italy:

1. Recovery of "community" — a sense of caring and sharing. Conversion results in membership in a fellowship of loving concern.

2. A new dignity. In a disintegrating society the convert finds himself "belonging" in a community where he is "somebody," where he is important as a person.

3. A new interest. Life is drab, but now it takes on color. It is exciting to belong to an ongoing, aggressive body.

4. Replacement for Catholicism. Southern Italians are generally anticlerical, but they still are Catholics for the saving of their souls. The convert, however, finds salvation through another channel. Moreover, he is liberated from many fears and binding beliefs. Rather than merely sweeping these away, however, Pentecostalism replaces many of the old features with functional substitutes. At first glance Pentecostalism appears a complete negation of Catholicism. But it is more — a complete replacement. The disciplined way of life, the many meetings, the drive to witness — all these tend to replace the old system. Local house church services and Bible studies replace the old parish church. Activities in a larger, central "mother" church replace the cathedral function The characteristic change of life style brings a dignity and respect (despite persecution) — a replacement of the monastic system of the Catholic Church. The mass is replaced by the fervent Pentecostal worship in which everyone participates together. Catholic sacraments are replaced by crisis experience and by believer's baptism and the occasional celebration of the Lord's Supper. A doctrine of bodily healing is substituted for pilgrimages to Catholic healing shrines, and the

1. Roger E. Hedlund, "Why Pentecostal Churches Are Growing Faster in Italy," *Evangelical Missions Quarterly* 8, No. 3 (Spring 1972), pp. 129-136.

Holy Spirit takes the place of the emotions of Roman Catholic pomp and ceremony and procession.

Growth among Pentecostals follows family lines. Stress on witnessing compels the convert to share his faith, and his most natural contacts are members of his family. Italian family closeness is reinforced by the utilization of house churches.

It is difficult to isolate any one element as the key to Pentecostal victory. "The first reason for the growth of Pentecostal churches is that when a forgotten human being comes to one of them, he feels himself loved and understood."[2]

A simplicity of approach is no doubt one important reason for Pentecostal success. Christianity is not dogma so much as spiritual experience. It is therefore a living reality, and as such brings meaning to life and victory over unseen powers (which is important in spiritistic Southern Italy).

Pentecostalism brings, therefore, newness of life and a new dignity to the individual . . . within the context of a church . . . within the framework of the Italian family.

pilate the slave

The most complex case I ever dealt with during my term as governor of Judea involved the leader of a religious protest group who was feared by the Jewish leaders, because of his rising political popularity.

The Jews, who have never accepted Roman rule, were growing extremely restless around this time. Demonstrations against enforced taxation and compulsory government service were growing more and more frequent. Soldiers in the occupational forces were having to quell riots and marches at the risk of their lives. The secretary of the Bureau for Territorial Development had been putting increasing pressure on me because of this seething turmoil. Only the week before this trial, he had informed me that if this trend of riots and demonstrations continued, I would lose my job and my position within the governmental hierarchy. With the Passover bringing its hordes of tourists and Jewish pilgrims the next week, I expected the growing tension to explode.

All was relatively controlled, however, until the Jewish leaders brought this man to me claiming he was spreading anti-Roman

2. D. J. O'Hanlon, "Pentecostals and Pope John's New Pentecost," *America,* 108:634, 635.

propaganda and stirring up political opposition among the people. This amazed me because I knew that the Jewish local leaders had been encouraging anti-Roman sentiment themselves. I was convinced therefore, that this was a trumped-up charge, but I was forced to conduct a court trial because they had already bound him over for trial in a municipal council hearing.

I am ashamed to have had a part in such an outrageous mockery of justice. These same municipal officers who had convicted the defendant were the witnesses for the prosecuting attorney. The profanity and outright perjury these men used . . . !

The atmosphere in the courtroom became so heated that tension spilled over in loud outbursts from the audience At this point, I began to question the defendant myself. I was taken aback by his poise and calmness in the situation. He answered me calmly and directly. He claimed indeed to be the deliverer of the Jews, but he said that he brought spiritual deliverance — that he was king of a heavenly empire. He was bringing Truth to all people. . . . Well, we all could use a little truth right now, and if he thinks he's got it, who am I to say he doesn't? After all, who knows what truth is anyway? I didn't exactly follow all his ideas, but I sure couldn't find anything wrong with him. So he had a few big ideas about himself. Everybody has a few weird ideas.

I adjourned court to consider the verdict, although I had nothing for which to convict the man. While I was gone, the Jewish officials stirred up the audience (which by the way, was huge because of the defendant's renown) so that the courtroom was in an uproar when the session reconvened.

I quieted the people and told them that I couldn't find anything wrong with the man. . . . The clamor in the courtroom was deafening! Everyone began yelling at once! I told them I could release this man as innocent, based on a custom of their Passover celebration. But they all began clamoring for the release of a convicted thief and murderer, and the crucifixion of the defendant.

As the incensed crowd began chanting, "Crucify him, crucify him!" I began to resent intensely my forced loyalty to Caesar and his Rome. I felt as though I were in a box which was fast closing in around me.

The Jewish officials calmly informed me that acquitting the defendant constituted treason against Caesar. I realized suddenly that I had no defense whatever against any reports these men might choose to spread.

I had to get the people out of there before violence erupted. What could I do? Not only my job, but my very life was at stake. . . .

I had *never* sentenced anyone to death of whose guilt I was not unequivocably convinced. I would not pass a death penalty if any doubt existed....

But I had the welfare of the people to protect as well as the code of the Roman law. If revolution broke loose, and it was my fault....! I cannot forget that man who claimed to have Truth.... I can no longer live with myself....

marriage will solve it all

Dear Phil:

Greetings from out Ivory Coast way. It surely sounds like you're enjoying your graduate work, though I still don't quite understand why you're doing all that work in Anthropology. I personally never felt the need of it. You know the Baoulés have a proverb, "He who really knows ten will never be deceived with nine." If you really know your Bible and teach it just like it is, you won't need to worry about the culture that the anthropologists are always talking about.

You asked about conference. We had a good one. As usual, the first three days were given to the missionaries' reports of their work. The delegation from the church which had been invited seemed too busy with other things to attend. One wonders sometimes if they really care.

Oh yes, some of the younger missionaries brought up the idea again of changing the conference in order to present papers pertinent to the work instead of having the reports which have always been such a blessing down through the years. One of the young women — I won't tell you who — even suggested that we assign someone to study the etiquette of the Baoulés during the coming year and then present his findings at next conference. I vetoed that quickly enough. Imagine what a waste of missionary time! None of us is an authority in this field. And since the rest of us would not be prepared to refute anything which might be presented, it didn't seem fair to operate in that way. Nothing more was said, so I hope that will be the end of that.

You mentioned André Tanoh. He is still troubled by pains in his stomach — or so he says. The doctor can't find a thing wrong with him. You remember when he was converted about six years ago and came to work in the bookstore as accountant? He was doing such fine work and we were all so pleased until we found out one day that Aya, the "little sister" who had been living with him for several months doing his cooking, was not his sister at all, but his cousin — and she was pregnant.

Well, I surely didn't waste any time. I piled them in the car the same afternoon and took them out to their village to arrange for them to get married. I told him not to come back to the bookstore until the matter was regulated, though we needed him so badly. He tried to make all sorts of protests — his old pagan uncle who had raised him and paid for his education was opposed to the marriage. Aya, as a first cousin, was not acceptable as a wife to his family. He really didn't think he loved her, etc., etc. He even brought up their pagan ways, saying that according to their customs what they had done was normal, and would lead to marriage only if both parties agreed and the two families were in accord. Well, I knew he was only a new Christian and so I read to him what the Bible says about fornication and adultery and told him that before he could come back to his job, the marriage would have to be arranged.

He was away from work about a month but finally came and said he and Aya had decided to consider their marriage as final, though they would still have to work at getting the old folks' consent. As far as I know, they never have been able to move that hard old character of an uncle of his.

It was surely good I took a strong stand at that time on this matter because I can see now it served as an example for the church to follow when similar disciplinary cases came up. Funny isn't it, that after thirty-five years the Christians in this land have never really learned God's pattern for courtship and marriage. Our finest young people — raised right in the church — will go along until they reach that age when they want to get a wife and then they invariably revert to the old custom of *soman bole* which, at best, can only be regarded as trial marriage. I've seen it happen again and again in the Bible school. If the girl is pregnant, we usually urge them to drop out a semester while they make their relation official, and then, if we feel they are repentant, they may return as a married couple.

But I started to tell you why it was so good I had insisted that André and Aya go through with their marriage at once. Several years ago a similar case came up with a student in the seminary. He was one of our first students at the intermission seminary, and had been quite a ladies' man before his conversion. Then during his first vacation from seminary he had an affair with a real "bush" girl back in his village. When it was found out, the church leaders talked the palaver and insisted they be married if he wanted to continue in seminary. So they were, and now they have three beautiful children.

It's just too bad his wife has had no interest in even learning to read or in bettering herself in any way so that she could fit into the milieu for which his seminary training has prepared him. She will always be a drag on him, I'm afraid, and some people feel he is friendlier than he ought to be with one of the girls from the normal school. Oh why won't these fellows think about the kind of wife they need before they dash into an affair?

Some have criticized the church's decision to insist on marriage in such cases. They say that forcing people into a marriage which would bring a number of children into the world without love is a greater crime than the original affair. But what can the church do under the circumstances? Its purity has to be maintained.

Things are going along fine as usual out here. Have a good time with your studies and don't forget to put first things first.

Yours in His service,
Andrew

P.S. Phew! Before I got this mailed, I was called out for a palaver about André. It's funny that I had just been writing to you about him so I'll clue you in. It seems that he has been in the process of taking another wife for several months and none of us knew it. Aya has taken the children and gone back to their village. In fact, some of the Africans feel he has just done this to get rid of her. He makes no bones about the fact that he doesn't love her. Guess we're out a good accountant. And after all the hours I wasted on him, trying to teach him what a Christian marriage is all about...!

A. S.

Questions:

To be used with chapter 8:

1. How did Andrew, the missionary, unknowingly show rejection and lack of respect both to his fellow missionaries and to the nationals with whom he worked?

2. Was the use of the consensual process natural and easy to Andrew? How is this seen?

3. How does this case illustrate the model which speaks of the flow of truth and slavery?

4. How do you react to Andrew?

To be used with chapter 11:

1. From what this case reveals of their personalities, make value profiles of Andrew and André Tanoh

2. In how many ways might Andrew have changed if there had been a change along the vulnerability-is-a-weakness/strength continuum in his values?

To be used with chapter 15:

1. Did Andrew have a good understanding of Baoulé culture as a system operation?

2. Consider Andrew's behavior in light of the statement, "When the abuse of the system is seen to be the entire system, or when one perceives the abuse as the whole, it is possible that in regulating or destroying the abuse one regulates and destroys the entire system."

3. From what do you think Andrew's frustration and discouragement — which are evident throughout his letter — stem?

that experience

Drew came to a Christian college from a small town in Minnesota where his father was a minister at the First Covenant Church. His evangelical upbringing was very similar to that of many of the other students. Church was a sacred place to attend with reverence, but the sobriety often seemed stifling. He could well remember one Sunday morning the startled response and disapproving stares given to a certain visitor from North Carolina who shattered the service's monotone with a loud and emphatic "Amen, Brother!" "Hallelujah!" "Glory be!"

Drew had learned to worship quietly and reverently. The atmosphere at school was quite similar to that back home. Then he met a group of fellows who really seemed to be "on fire for the Lord," as Drew put it. They spoke of being "turned on to Jesus." Drew felt he could see real "power" in their lives and in an attempt to find this power for himself, he joined their group.

These fellows had their own get-togethers. The loose informality of the unstructured sharing times was strange to Drew. The group kept urging him to have the same experience with Jesus as they had had, and to beg the Holy Spirit to fill him completely. This was the only way, they said, that he could have a powerful Christian life.

Drew felt a little frightened, but decided that if this was the way to do it, then he wanted this experience. The group prayed over him as he sought for this experience, but it didn't come. Surely there was some obstacle, some unconfessed sin holding him back. Drew began to confess things before this group that he would have never dared to tell even his father — but still no experience. "You've got to want it real bad," they told him. He agonized on his knees for hours, but still no experience. Where was the power? What was wrong?

the surf-riders

One of the groupings most natural to Hawaii is that of the surf-riders. Three of the regulars in our Young Peoples' group were surfers. Had I understood them better before my church planting experience in Hawaii, much more could have been attempted in acknowledging the validity of their group, and in accepting the powerful restraints which membership in the group afforded. And with this understanding, perhaps a greater influence could have been exerted on them.

The following is a summary of the identification features of a Hawaiian surfers' group:

I. *Physical items*
   a. A beach
   b. A surf
   c. A surfboard
II. *Sociological items*
   a. A name — Surfers
   b. Its own language — This is basic surfer terminology with added flavor from Pidgin English, e.g., nose, tail, skeg, hang five, hang ten, going through the tube, wipe out
   c. A meeting place — the beach
   d. A time of meeting — when the surf's up
   e. Membership — A surfer must be a surfing Kamaaina (Old Timer) as over against a surfing Malihini (Newcomer)
   f. Means of identifying members — surfboard, surfers' cross, bleached hair worn long, surfers' knots (calluses on knees and across toes), uke
   g. Leadership — the most skilled surfer; in case there are two, the biggest one!
   h. Rules — Surfer riding wave has the right of way; don't surf without wearing surfers' cross

i. Discipline — continuous waxing of board for better toe grip, training for international meet at Makaha

j. Mechanisms to induce loyalty — Stories of group heroes, previous group winners at Makaha, guys who braved waves at most dangerous Sunset Beach

k. Privacy — Group is usually limited to twenty or fewer because of limited good surfing areas and danger of overcrowding

l. Authority — Leader selects surfer sites.

m. Perpetuation — no off season in Hawaii; skill continues to determine group leader; surfers' cross serves as protecting charm

n. Means of defense — fist fights for best surfing areas

blood of a white chicken

Among the Tagbanwa people of the Philippines, rice is the staple food, but only a small percentage of the total amount of rice consumed is actually produced by the people on their own land. This is of the upland variety, sometimes referred to as dry rice. The fields are carved out of secondary forest growth on the sides of mountains by the slash-and-burn technique. The seed is planted by hand in small holes dug by means of a dibble stick. Because the growth of the rice depends upon the rainfall, only one crop a year can be grown during the rainy season. Such fields are usually quite small and the yield ration is quite low compared to other methods which depend upon the use of the plow. Even when there is a good harvest, which is rare, the longest the supply has been observed to last is about two months.

Outsiders who visit the village of Banwang Daan, a Tagbanwa settlement located on Coron Island, are often struck with the fact that most of the arable land in the valley is not cultivated. Instead it is given over to the tough, resistant cogon grass. Furthermore, no water buffalo can be seen anywhere in the village, and there are no plows.

If the visitor should inquire from the people why the land is not put to better use, they will likely reply that they are too poor to own a buffalo. If one knows a bit about the Tagbanwas, he might proceed to remind them of the very lucrative trade in edible birds' nests which they engage in during five months of the year. In response, the people would probably pose the problem of social conflict should one's water buffalo get loose and wander over into a neighbor's garden. If the outsider should point out that there are ways to handle the problem of straying buffalos, and suggest that the introduction of plowing with them could help the people to make economic progress, the Tagbanwas would respond with silence. Why are the Tagbanwas reluctant to plow their own land? Traditionally, they have never been plowers of the soil. This agricultural technique has come into the area with other ethnic groups who have migrated and taken over land formerly used by Tagbanwas. This is not to say that present-day Tagbanwa men do not know how to plow. Most of them have had experience in the construction of rice paddies through hiring out to Cuyonon and Tagalog landowners on the large, adjacent island. However, despite their knowhow, rarely, if ever, have they been known to employ it on land which they themselves intended to utilize. This has been true even when water buffaloes have been available to them. There was one man who obtained two of these animals, but he never used them for plowing and within a year he had sold them to non-Tagbanwas.

There is also a deep-seated Tagbanwa belief that owning and utilizing objects which have not been contemporaneous with one's childhood experience, is very dangerous and will likely lead to one's death or the death of a member of his family. There is also a very close association between a person and the land he utilizes so that his use of the land is hedged about with many taboos and rituals designed not only to insure productivity, but also to maintain his health and that of his family.

The act of plowing is fraught with danger because it is perceived as an offense against the ground and is compared to wounding a person. Unless placated by a sacrifice, the ground will exact payment in retaliation for the offense by inflicting death upon the person or upon some member of his family. Through contact with Cuyonons, the Tagbanwas have knowledge of a certain ritual which could be used to protect themselves from such danger in the event they took up plowing. But there is a hitch when it comes to performing this ritual. The ability to perform it is a matter of inheritance — one's father must have performed this ritual and have passed it on to him. This is done by the son holding on the father's shoulders as the father performs it.

Apparently no Tagbanwa has inherited this ability. The only other known alternative would be to hire a qualified Cuyonon to perform the ritual. However, this seems highly unlikely. Perhaps the history of land-grabbing on the part of this ethnic group may account for the reluctance of the Tagbanwas to hire them for this service. Thus it is that most of the arable land in the valley is not being utilized for the production of rice.

As for the ritual itself, two intersecting lines must first be plowed in the field in the form of a cross, making sure that the intersection is at the approximate center of the area to be plowed. After this pattern has been formed, the plow is detached and placed at the intersection. Then a white chicken is sacrificed by severing its jugular vein and its blood is made to drip on the plowshare. Simultaneously, a chanted prayer is addressed to the ground. The gist of the prayer is that the debt incurred by opening up the ground is now being paid by means of the sacrifice. The ground is implored to accept this payment instead of retaliating against the family. No more plowing is done until the next day.

Questions:

To be used with chapter 10:

1. How does the activity of rice planting have social, economic, and religious significance to the Tagbanwa?

2. Why would an agent of change insisting on the Tagbanwa's using the plow cause deep disruption in the society?

3. Does this mean there is no possibility of encouraging a more productive rice culture here? Why do you think so?

4. Why may a change of activity amount to a change of norm?

5. Can you suggest how a functional equivalent (see chapter 15) for the blood sacrifice might be encouraged as a part of the people's festival cycle?

To be used with chapter 15:

1. How do each of the tools of relationship give insight into a study of this case?

2. Imagine you are (a) a government-sponsored agriculturalist, (b) a missionary. Present possible solutions to the problem which is hindering beneficial change among the Tagbanwa.

3. What is the missionary likely to suggest as a functional substitute for the sacrifice of the chicken?

4. In what way is the casual outsider likely to confuse form and meaning in this case?

the headman's hidden agenda

There were more people in Kiziza village early on that bright Sunday morning than I had ever seen there before. I was quite sure they hadn't been attracted by the prospect of hearing me preach, and I was right. They were having a cattle auction that morning, but they were perfectly content to delay their auction for a time to listen to the missionary. At that time, I am sure that I would not have delayed my service for the auction, had I been requested to do so.

I preached on John 14:6 and afterward chatted with the village headman. Latching on to the gist of my message proclaiming Christ to be the way or road, and apparently in all innocence, he said, "You know, Bwana, if we had a road between here and the mission, we could get to church each Sunday."

I realized that he was testing me. Some time before this, the Congo Administration, in an effort to get the population out of the boondocks and along the roads, had agreed to advance the price of a cement block house to any working man who would move out to the road. I could see that our headman, with this take-off on the word "road," was testing my gullibility with the idea in mind that perhaps the missionary would naively consider extending the mission road a quarter of a mile to Kiziza. His goal was to give the local Kizizites the possibility of having permanent houses without moving their village. I smiled, winked, and casually reminded him how admirably he had made the twelve kilometre walk to the Djomba market the preceding Friday without the aid of a road. "And besides," I said, "I am not here to prepare roads on earth but roads to heaven."

We laughed together and understood each other perfectly. Consequently he was always on hand for those early Sunday morning messages in his village, and he even managed to get to church occasionally.

Questions:

1. Where do you find each of the following illustrated in the case?
    a. cultural cue
    b. time orientation
    c. mutual respect
    d. acceptance of the other
    e. event orientation
    f. situation ethics

g. p.q.t.
h. vulnerability-is-a-weakness/strength
i. hierarchy
j. conflict of norm

2. Explain why you think the missionary would have accomplished more — or less — by a frontal attack on the "dishonesty" implied by the headman's suggestion.

3. Would extending the road as suggested have built trust?

"please, jim, do something!"

"If he'd only do something!" Karen wailed to herself. "Why *must* I be the only one to face the unpleasant situations? If only he'd help to carry the load." Then, realizing how self-pitying she sounded, she just gave up trying to understand and felt again the old frustration that enveloped her so often.

She could hear her missionary husband, Jim, in the kitchen laughing with Pierre who helped her with the cooking and housework. Today she had finally caught Pierre in the act of stealing part of the meat she had laid out for dinner. Long suspicious of how the portions of meat seemed to shrink between the time they were given to Pierre to cook and their appearance on the table, she had taken to counting the pieces. This morning when she had found three fewer Swiss steaks cooking than she had given him to prepare, she had searched until she found the missing ones carefully hidden under the sink, ready to be carried off to Pierre's yard after work.

Over their after-dinner coffee Karen had explained to Jim what she had found, and asked him if he would handle the situation by having a talk with Pierre and telling him once and for all that if this happened again, they would have to consider dismissing him. Now she could hear Jim chatting with Pierre, asking him how his farm was doing and if his oldest boy had passed his exams last week. Disgusted, Karen decided to take a walk so she wouldn't hear them talking. She was sure Jim would never face him with the ultimatum.

Jim was such a wonderful guy, why did he seem so "weak," so incapable of taking a strong position which involved any confrontation with other people? There was the matter of the Johnsons' chickens which had been ruining her garden. She'd asked Jim to speak to Bill Johnson about it, but somehow he always "forgot" to do it. Then there was the shirt which he'd bought last week only to find an ugly fault in the fabric when he'd unwrapped it. She was sure that if it were to be returned to the store, she'd have to do it. Perhaps the hardest of his "do nothing" way was his reluctance to take an authoritative hand in disciplining the children. Why must she always fill the role of the disciplinarian while he could be the "good guy," the father the children loved and respected, but who could be gotten around in almost any situation? Again a voice which she would have been ashamed to call her own whispered, "If he really cared for me as he says he does, wouldn't he take his share of the unpleasant jobs to be done? I'll bet if he saw me being robbed, he'd be a perfect gentleman and look the other way...."

But inwardly Karen envied Jim in a way. How often he attained his goal without the hurt feelings that her abrasive and abrupt actions brought in their wake. Now she could hear Pierre whistling as he got on his bicycle to go home. Apparently his talk with Jim had left him feeling self-confident and happy. He wouldn't be whistling if *she'd* talked to him!

Karen glanced at her watch and turned back to the house with a sigh of futility. It was time for her to take her medication for that ulcer which seemed to be threatening.

Questions:

1. Jim and Karen's difference exemplifies a conflict between what two basic values?

2. Can you think of characters in the Bible who reacted to situations as Karen did? As Jim did?

3. Describe what an entire society might be like if it were motivated by each of the above basic values.

4. What sort of student do you think Karen was in college? What makes you think so?

the leper

Mr. Glab is a smiling, energetic young Asian from the Central Province of Thailand. Early in life he was afflicted with leprosy, which left its mark in the form of claw hands and difficult-to-heal sores on his feet. Through the ministry of missionaries who early became concerned for leprosy sufferers in the Central Provinces, Mr. Glab found medical help and heard of Christ. During his long stay at the Christian Hospital he received treatment for his leprosy, which was arrested. His general health improved and he professed to believe in Christ.

Mr. Glab had been a carpenter. As he regained his strength, he became able to help in small carpentry jobs around the hospital and in the workshop of the leprosy rehabilitation center. A new hospital was being planned in another province, and a carpenter was needed to become a part of the full-time staff. Mr. Glab was asked about serving in this capacity. He was pleased about the prospect and eagerly took up his new assignment. At the new hospital he became active in the small group of believers and continued growing into a mature Christian.

A separate building was erected to house leprosy patients who came to the hospital for treatment — some staying for a number of weeks at a time. Mr. Glab was put in charge of this house, and this arrangement provided him with many opportunities to share the Gospel with patients from far and near. As a leprosy sufferer himself, he could identify with them wholeheartedly. Each year a leprosy believers' conference was held on the hospital compound and many gathered for this time of teaching and fellowship.

As one of these conferences approached, Mr. Glab was busy preparing the house to receive the guests from neighboring districts. The hospital director informed him that if he attended the conference, it would be without pay. Immediately Mr. Glab was thrown into a state of turmoil. He found it difficult — even impossible — to understand the doctor's reasoning in this decision. After considering this decision, he announced that he would not attend the conference if it meant losing his pay for those days.

There was a sense in which it was essential that he attend the conference since he was functioning in the role of host to the leprosy guests who were coming. Another missionary who was present at the hospital tried to help the doctor to see the importance of Mr. Glab's being there. They also discussed the matter of docking his pay. The doctor insisted that since other hospital personnel were required to work, Mr. Glab would have to work or attend the conference without pay.

Mr. Glab failed to see the situation as the doctor saw it. Since he was a valid member of the hospital staff and of the church, he saw no dichotomistic breakdown of categories. He could not understand why he should be penalized by loss of pay while performing his expected role in the total hospital program.

Through the mediation of the other missionary, an arrangement was worked out whereby Mr. Glab might attend the conference and continue on the payroll. However, the time consumed by the conference would be considered part of his regular vacation time. Mr. Glab agreed to this solution. A serious conflict between the doctor and Mr. Glab was averted, and the leprosy believers' conference proceeded with Mr. Glab playing his expected role in the community.

Questions:
1. How many of the basic values do you find in evidence here?
2. Do you understand why the doctor imposed the loss of pay control in this situation?
3. Do you think Mr. Glab was justified in refusing to attend the conference if his pay was to be docked?
4. Without some form of mediation in this situation, what might have happened? Would this have improved or hindered fellowship between Mr. Glab and the doctor?
5. Is there any evidence of acceptance/rejection in this episode?
6. Do you find yourself identifying with Mr. Glab or the doctor?

furlough

Lois Smith was a skillful missionary nurse working in a mission hospital in Southeast Asia. The hospital administration was planning to establish a nursing school to train national nurses to serve their own people. The government had set up rather stringent requirements regarding the educational standards of teaching personnel. A Master of Science degree in nursing was required of the nursing school director and of other key personnel. Among the nurses no one had that degree.

Lois was asked by the hospital superintendent and the field council to spend her forthcoming furlough in procuring her M.S. in nursing in order to be prepared to head up the nursing education program. She was pleased with this prospect and so were the mission leaders.

As time for furlough drew near, Lois realized that there was a little conflict. According to mission policy, no one was to go home for furlough early except for valid health reasons. Lois realized that she must plan to leave the field in August so as to be prepared to enter the fall term at the university in mid-September; however, her four-year term was not complete until mid-October.

She decided to write a personal letter to a mission director requesting early furlough — early by a scant two months out of forty-eight. The reply she received from headquarters was "No. Early furloughs are granted only for health reasons." Feeling this was a bit unreasonable under the circumstances, she felt constrained to write again. This time she was told that mission funds would not be expended unless she waited until her full four years were up. If she must go early, it would be at personal expense.

After carefully praying about the decision, Lois made plans to leave in mid-August and arranged for personal payment for an air ticket — costing $639.00 economy fare! Her furlough was a busy one and demands upon her were great. However, she earned her degree and returned to her post at mission expense.

their translation

Ray and Joyce Downer had been the first missionaries to enter the tribe twenty-five years ago. They had started at once to learn and write the language, and launched into translation and literacy work. They were considered by those who came later as the authorities in all matters of language and translation. Their goal was to translate the New Testament before their second furlough. Working rapidly with one informant, they were able to see it finished. The manuscript was hurriedly sent off to the publisher and when the New Testaments arrived, they were hailed with great joy.

However, as younger missionaries arrived on the field and started to use the New Testament, they came to realize that it was a literal, wooden translation, often wholly incomprehensible to the nationals if they were not taught its special language.

Those who attempted to suggest changes to the Downers found their suggestions taken as a personal affront to them. It was as if Ray and Joyce's integrity were at stake each time anything in "their" translation was questioned.

As the years went by, the Indian Christians spoke often of the need for revision and the Bible Society urged that work be started on a new translation, but the Downers' defensive attitude stalemated all hope of having an improved version. It seemed unlikely that anything could be done until their retirement which was still ten to fifteen years away.

Soon after John and Marge Carlsen began work in a neighboring tribe, they learned of this situation. John saw the temptation to become "the authority" in the language and wondered how the translation he was working on could belong to all the Christians and not be considered his alone.

From the beginning of language study, he sought correction from nationals or his fellow workers. He decided the translation should be a committee effort. Then as each book was finished he mimeographed it and sent it to all his fellow missionaries and the leading literates of his tribe — both Christians and non-Christians — asking them to read it critically and send in to him all corrections or suggestions for improvement which they might have. He was always happy when someone would come to him with an idea, for that person would feel he had had a part in putting God's Word into his own language.

Most of all John was glad to find he never needed to defend his work or feel hurt when it was criticized, since he constantly sought constructive criticism.

The younger missionaries working with the Downers envied John's program, and chafed at the frustration they felt in their own situation. They wondered what they could do to help Ray and Joyce have a change of attitude; or should they just "sit it out" until the day the Downers would no longer be on the field?

one house, or is it two?

Peruvian custom is such that there are essentially two laws governing behavior, one which is written and the other which is practiced. The reality of these distinctions came to our full understanding when the following incident happened involving fellow missionaries.

They were renting a three-bedroom house which was the lower level of a building. The owner lived upstairs where she also had three bedrooms. As one looked at the building from the street, it appeared as though it were only one house. It had a garage door, a front door, a picture window on the lower level (the missionaries') and one on the upper level (the landlady's). The landlady would enter through the front door which led directly upstairs to her "house" only. The missionaries would enter their "house" through the garage door. Since they were first-term missionaries, they did not understand at first the reason for the odd arrangement, but they soon found out.

It seems that in Peru real estate taxes are computed on the basis of the number of dwellings in a particular building. In this case there were two separate apartments which the written law says should be counted as two houses. Since from all outward appearances the house was used by one family, the owner was paying half the legally required amount of taxes.

The landlady began attending the church which the missionaries had begun, and before long she was converted. Soon afterwards the missionaries discovered the real reason for the unusual architecture of the building. They promptly confronted the landlady with the matter because they termed it deception and tax evasion. They knew that nearly every owner in Peru practiced this, and they knew also that in actual practice written laws were not binding on any level of society, but, to them, that was no excuse. "A Christian must not be involved in such corrupt practices," they said.

The landlady politely listened to their words of admonition but seemed completely unmoved by them. They continued to speak to her about the matter, using biblical references, but with no favorable results. They finally moved away.

"but, mom and dad, you don't understand!"

Collin, a sophomore at Northern Illinois University, grew up in a typical middle-class, evangelical home. He was a good student in high school, was active in extracurricular activities, and was well prepared for college. He enjoyed being with people and was involved in helping others.

Collin's father is a hard-working, conscientious person who is very loyal to his country's ideals. He experienced a depression, fought in World War II, and has worked hard to give his family the material things he never had as a young man.

His mother is a devout woman who is very concerned with the spiritual welfare of her family. She has had to sacrifice personal enjoyments for the sake of her children.

His younger sister, Mary, is a freshman in high school. She idolizes her big brother and has always been influenced by his opinions. She is beginning to rebel outwardly against her parents' religious views that all behavior should "conform to the Bible" as they understand it. Her frustration has driven her to succumb to peer group pressure to use drugs and experiment with free love.

Collin is very concerned about his sister's feelings and behavior.

He thinks her actions are wrong on the basis of what his parents taught him, but since he has been at the university, he is also questioning his family's value system and the principles of the religious training he was taught in church.

He has discovered at N. I. U. that if a person wants to be accepted, he must tolerate the views of everyone else. Thus, if another person seems sincere in his views toward life, it is right for him. Truth becomes relative and subjective. As circumstances and time change, truth will also change in order to keep pace with its environmental setting. Collin has learned that the only things that really count are those things that are happening now. His professors tell him that the criterion for evaluating life issues is "that whatever we do, it should be done for the immediate good of people — man will work out the reactions later. This is what really counts."

But this philosophy bothers Collin. If this criterion is good and true, he wonders, why doesn't mankind naturally practice this value system? Why do the outward manifestations of hate, strife, selfishness, greed, war, sickness, prejudice, pollution, and anarchy still exist? Why do the humanitarian teachings he has received seem so ineffectual?

These honest doubts have caused Collin to question the meaning of life and of his own existence. This is affecting his attitudes in other social relationships. He finds himself asking: What constitutes friendship or love? Why not free sex if the other person agrees? Is homosexuality wrong? Some of these thoughts have caused a tension between Collin and his girl friend. He has less desire to share his faith with others. He is preoccupied with questions like: Is the Bible the relevant, objective criterion for evaluating contemporary life issues? Was Christ really God in the flesh? Am I playing "church" games? Is there really a hell or a heaven? Is man born with a sin nature or does society make him that way?

Collin has lost much of his purpose and direction for his future goals. His moral judgments have become cloudy and he has a hard time making decisions. He sees people around him being manipulated and used for selfish reasons, but his cries are not heard above the noise of the political machinery. The teaching/learning process at the university has lost its effectiveness and he is wondering why he should even be in school.

Questions:

1. What are the subcultural differences at home and at the university that are causing Collin's conflict?

2. How did Collin's sister try to resolve the tension?

3. With the information you have, do you feel that she was justified for her behavior? Why?

4. If you were in Collin's place, how would you attempt to maintain a helping relationship with your sister who idolized you?

5. Do you think he would be successful in helping her?

6. What principles of biculturalism would you use in this situation if you were trying to be a supportive person to Collin? To Mary? (chapter 17).

conflict

An unmarried Chulupi girl, a member of the church, was seeking a husband. Under the old standard, she had to take the initiative and give herself sexually to a series of young men until one of them became her husband. According to popular belief she avoided becoming pregnant by sleeping with a different male each night. Once a young man sought her out for repeated visits, he was actually declaring that he wanted her for his wife and that he would also assume the responsibility of sociological father should she be with child. Now, however, with the new Christian standards, the possibility of sexual contacts has been greatly diminished and a girl often becomes pregnant before she has found a husband. Once her pregnancy becomes visible, she usually stays away from church services until she has given birth to her child in some hospital removed from the mission station.

Let us now look at the experience of a specific girl. On the day following the delivery, her sister called for her and the baby, but on the way home from the hospital the new mother strangled her baby and buried it beside the trail. It was not until the hospital called to confirm the news of the baby's death that the missionary became aware of what had actually happened. He called on the girl, but she denied all guilt, saying the baby had not liked her milk; it had cried all night and then in the morning it had died. However, the date of the death was the day of her discharge from the hospital. The missionary spoke to the Chulupi church leadership asking them to investigate the facts and impressing them with the seriousness of the crime of killing one's own baby. The church elders followed his instructions and reported that the girl herself had indeed killed her child and that the council had now decided to kill her — they were just waiting for the missionary's permission.

The missionary, of course, refused to permit such drastic action, and a public discussion resulted. At this meeting the girl told the whole truth, but justified her action by saying that the child had no (sociological) father. The girl's father, an older Chulupi, supported her, saying: "Her older sister already has two children without fathers and I am very deeply ashamed. I could not bear to have another bastard in the family." However, the church leadership, operating on the new standards, decided to punish the girl by making an announcement that nobody should marry her until she honestly repented for the murder of her child.[1]

The preceding example illustrates the conflicts between systems of standards in a changing society. Not only the young people are torn between two sets of ideals; the very tribal leadership is divided as to what values are primary (the father's counsel flatly contradicts the proposals of the church leaders) and how these values are to be enforced (if strangling an infant — which was standard pre-Christian procedure — is really as serious a crime as the missionary says, then they as leaders are responsible for applying the maximum penalty).

---

1. Jacob A. Loewen, "The Social Context of Guilt and Forgiveness," *Practical Anthropology*, 17, No. 2 (March-April 1970), pp. 85, 86.

MODEL THREE

THE VALIDITY OF DISTINCT SOCIETIES

Each distinct society, as well as every person, is valid and worthy of respect. Man may be fallen and in need of redemption, but he is still a "magnificent ruin." A society may also be in need of encountering Christ and changing what is dysfunctional in its behavioral patterns, but each society is nevertheless functioning as a system and must be regarded as such although it may be a vastly different system from that to which we are accustomed.

To know a language or a people deeply is to respect them for their amazing intricacies, and to appreciate their functional competence.

We who have been Bible translators, while admitting that Greek seemed to be the perfect vehicle for the original New Testament writing, are always amazed at how every other language can become a marvelously effective vehicle for expressing God's message to man. God's Word lives in all its power in any man's language.

And so each society can be the background against which the Christian life is lived.

There are dangers to the outsider who enters a society he doesn't understand in depth. He will give the same meaning to an item in the new culture as he gives it in his own.

Cultural cues are like traffic lights which enable one to move

344

smoothly and happily (if he knows them) within a society different from his own just as a car moves through heavy traffic. These cues must be learned and may often be misread at first. Reyburn tells of learning from such an experience:

I recall my own misinterpretations best. Once while traveling with a West African pastor, we entered the house of his maternal aunt, an old grey-haired lady. To my amusement, my African colleague walked across the room and sat down lightly in the old lady's lap. What struck me as a very informal gesture turned out to communicate *to them* just the contrary. He was by this act greeting her in most formal terms. He was expressing symbolically his status in relation to her. She said, "Greetings, child," and he, a man of thirty-five years, now an ambassador to the United Nations, stood up.[1]

Only as we grasp the concept of how values may be legitimately ranked differently by two different persons can we understand whole areas of conflict between subcultures in our own nation, or differences in other cultures. "It's More Blessed to Give" presents a picture of missionaries and nationals risking misunderstanding because of differing evaluations of behavior.

The belief in biblical absolutism and cultural relativism is often a misunderstood concept but, once fully internalized, it allows a person to move and minister freely within a society without abandoning any scriptural principles. "When in Rome . . ." (p. 227) is an example of mutual respect struggling with both legalism and "situation ethics."

The four questions insuring the validity of distinct societies embody, we feel, one of the most important teachings in biculturalism. "The Black Beads" and "One House, or Is It Two?" present situations where these questions should certainly be asked before one rushes in to present his own norms as the only legitimate ones.

should the left hand know?

One of the first pastors of the Baoulé church had died and the leading Christians of the Ivory Coast tribe of nearly a million had

---

1. William D. Reyburn, *The Toba Indians of the Argentine Chaco* (Elkhart, Indiana: Mennonite Board of Missions and Charities, 1954), p. 56.

gathered with a number of missionaries to participate in his funeral. As is customary at Baoulé funerals, a table was arranged to display the gifts of cloth which were given to the family. When a gift of money was placed on the table, the name of the donor and the amount was called out in a loud voice.

The missionaries, feeling they wanted their giving to follow the injunction "Do not let your left hand know what your right hand is doing," told the church president they preferred to offer their condolences to the widow and quietly slip her a gift of money later. In this way it would not be announced publicly. A sizeable collection was taken up and the mission director made a special trip to see her and present it.

About eight months after the funeral a large memorial wake was held at which time even larger gifts were given publicly. Realizing they should make some public presentation, and not just sit there as though totally unconcerned, the missionaries present took up a collection. Because they had already given in their own unobtrusive way, the gift was not as large as the Baoulé church president thought it should be. He nearly refused it as refusing a gift is a perfectly acceptable and often practiced privilege among the Baoulés. As it was, he accepted the token gift, but he let the incident rankle bitterly in his mind for months.

The missionaries see this sort of public giving as an ostentatious display. The Baoulés say, "This is our way of showing esteem for the deceased and consolation for the family." The missionaries say they like to give personally and without fanfare (forgetting the wreaths they send to funerals in America). The Baoulés say that things done secretly are suspect, as honest people want their actions to be open and known to all. The missionaries feel that by their example they can teach what is the correct way to give. The Baoulés feel the missionaries are miserly and terribly ungracious in their rejecting of their customs.

I corinthians 8

Setting: Filipino girl whose norm is not holding hands until engagement, begins dating American boy for whom holding hands is part of his norm during the pre-engagement period as well as during the engagement period.

1. In this situation, everyone feels that only the American boy's

custom is the right one! But, although being a "know-it-all" makes us feel important, what is really needed to build the church is love.

2. If anyone thinks he knows all the answers, he is just showing his ignorance.

3. But the person who truly loves God is the one who is open to God's knowledge.

4. So now, what about it? Should the Filipino girl hold hands with the American boy? Well, we all know that holding hands is amoral (neither here nor there).

5. According to some people, there are a great many alternatives as far as showing affection is concerned.

6. But we know that there is only one God, the Father, who created all things and made us to be his own (allowing for holding hands or not holding hands); and one Lord Jesus Christ, who made everything and gives us life, i.e. giving each one the choice of holding hands or not doing so.

7. However, some Filipino Christians don't realize this. All their lives they have been used to thinking that holding hands before engagement is wrong, and they have believed that it is wrong. So when they do hold hands, it bothers them and hurts their tender conscience.

8. Just remember that God doesn't care whether we hold hands or not. We are not worse off if we don't hold hands and no better off if we do.

9. But be careful, American boy, not to use your freedom to hold hands lest you cause some Filipino Christian sister to sin whose conscience is weaker than yours.

10. You see, this is what may happen: A Filipino girl who thinks that holding hands is a sin will accept a date from you, and you will try to hold her hand, since you know there is no harm in it. Then, she will become bold enough to hold hands even though she still feels it is wrong.

11. So, because you "know it is all right to do it," you will be responsible for causing great spiritual damage to a sister with a tender conscience for whom Christ died.

12. And it is a sin against Christ to sin against your sister by encouraging her to do something she thinks is wrong.

13. So if holding hands before engagement is going to make your sister sin, don't hold hands if you don't want to do this to her.

it's more blessed to give

Give to every man that asketh of thee . . . (Luke 6:30 KJV).
Lend, hoping for nothing again . . . (Luke 6:35 KJV).

If a person on the island of Truk has a need and goes to a friend who, he knows, has what he is in need of, the friend is required by custom to give it without any hesitation. Trukese hearing a missionary preach on Luke 6:30 and not practice it fully as they naturally do in their culture, are puzzled. They often come to the missionary and find their requests are refused even though they know he possesses what they need.

Once a fellow who owned an outboard motor asked me to give him some gasoline. I had only one drum left and didn't know when the next shipment would arrive. There was no other gasoline on the whole island. I wanted to keep this one drum for an emergency. Sometimes accidents happened and we would have to go to another island to call for help. Without any gasoline at all we might be stranded.

I tried to explain this to the Trukese. I reminded him that he used to go fishing without an outboard motor, and I felt he should do it again until there was more gasoline available. Of course he considered me stingy.

Not only I, but Trukese Christians have felt the effect of practicing this Scripture passage literally. Each church has a treasurer who keeps the books and the money. One treasurer was keeping about $250 in his house, to them, a very large sum. Some people who knew about this money found themselves in need, and so went to the treasurer to ask for help. To have refused them would have meant loss of face for him. So he gave (according to Scripture?) the church's money to all those who came and asked for it.

Finally the amount dropped down to about $80 and the treasurer decided to spend the rest himself before anyone else came asking for it. He resented the others' benefiting from the church's money when he, who had done the hard work of keeping the books and hiding the money, should go empty-handed. Of course no one ever brought the money back, since to the Trukese borrowing implies no obligation to return an object borrowed.

When the Christians found out what had happened to their church funds, they elected a new treasurer. He agreed to accept his duties under the condition that he would only keep the books and the missionary would keep the money.

reciprocity

On one occasion I, a missionary, had irked one of the Shan families in the town where we lived by kicking their young son in the seat of his pants for breaking a toy and then spanking him because he threw a stone at me. After realizing the mistake I had made, I looked for a mediator to resolve this delicate situation. Since the mayor was a nearby neighbor, I called upon him, explaining my dilemma and asking for his intercession as a mediator.

The mayor and I went to the house of the family involved, and the consultative process began. The mayor talked with the father on the porch of the house while I listened and looked on. The mother was crying inside the house, claiming the child's spirit was broken. The mayor then went inside to talk with her. After considerable deliberation, he returned to me on the porch. He said local custom required the payment of a fine since the child's spirit had been broken. This fine would be 300 baht ($15.00). I balked at this high fine but later yielded and paid the fine to the family. This eased the tension and cleared up the conflict.

Later on another set of circumstances brought me into contact with the mayor. I had been invited by the governor of the province to accompany him and his party on a trek to a distant district which was reachable on foot, a distance of about sixty-five miles which normally took five days of walking. I was going to this area for an evangelistic trip, so I agreed to travel with the governor.

At the camp sites each night I accepted the governor's hospitality and mingled freely with the lesser officials in the party. The mayor of the town was in the group. The governor, the mayor, and one other official rode horses while the rest of us walked. Since the governor's party was traveling rather slowly, I determined on the fourth day to go ahead alone so as to be at our destination for Sunday. Later I joined the governor's party as they returned home via another route using a truck.

A month or two later I found myself summoned to appear before a government investigator from Bangkok. It seems the governor had submitted a padded expense account for this trip and had collected money far in excess of what was actually spent. The vice-governor had evidently reported this to Bangkok authorities; hence the investigation. On the evening prior to my appearance before the investigator, the mayor paid me a visit. He had never before been to my house. After I invited him in for a chat, he approached the subject of the investigation, saying he heard I had been called to testify. I nodded agreement and wondered what was coming next.

He went on to say, "When they ask you questions, just tell them you don't know anything."

Immediately I recognized the bind I was in. Earlier he had done me a favor by acting as mediator with the family I had offended by my behavior. Now I felt he was expecting me to reciprocate by conceding to his request. I felt that I could not do it, and then explained to the mayor that as a Christian I could not willfully lie. However, I added that if I did not know the answer to any question, that I would say so. The mayor made his departure disappointedly. The next day I went before the investigator who asked about the various aspects of the journey in which I had taken part. The questions were simple, direct, and were designed to ascertain the what, when, and how many aspects of the journey. I tried to be honest and proffered as brief answers as possible. Later on I learned that the governor had been suspended from government service.

Questions:

1. Which biculturalism models do you feel are relevant to this case study?

2. By accepting the mayor's mediatorship, did the missionary necessarily obligate himself to reciprocity?

3. Can you identify with the mayor in this situation? With the missionary?

4. How might the missionary have handled the situation more effectively?

5. Could the missionary be true to himself as a person and agree to the mayor's request?

6. Do you feel there is a basic discrepancy in the way the author and the mayor rank values? If so, illustrate by ranking several values as each of them would.

the black beads

Suina and her husband were young Christians, both young in years and in their Christian life, when an accident took the life of her husband. Suina carried on in the believers' class where converts were prepared for baptism, and seemed to be growing in Christ. The class was completed and the date for baptism set. Then Suina came to us and, holding out the string of black beads she was wearing, said, "I can't be baptized."

As we talked to her and to the African evangelist, we came to understand that the beads had been put on her by her husband's family to show that she belonged to the spirit of her departed husband. The ceremony to free the spirit of the dead man had not yet been held, so she was considered married to his spirit. At the time of this ceremony, the beads would be removed and she would be given her husband's brother, at which time she could refuse to be the brother's wife, but would stay in his village and be cared for by him until another man paid the *lobola* (bride price) for her to her husband's brother.

Suina felt that she could not be baptized as long as she was wearing the black beads, and her in-laws had refused to take them off. We asked the evangelist if he could talk to the in-laws about removing the beads, and he said that would be asking to take her for his wife.

Suina waited two years until after the ceremony and then was baptized.

Questions:

To be used with chapter 15:

   1. Where in the case are you reminded of:
      a. the cultural cue
      b. the time-event dichotomy
      c. the ranking of values
      d. family as system
      e. the principle of the adverse effect?

   2. How do you know that respect for others ranked high in Suina's values?

   3. The fact that baptism and wearing the beads are incongruent in Suina's mind gives us a clue to what?

   4. What further questions would you want to ask Suina and the evangelist in order to fully understand this situation?

To be used with chapter 16:

   1. Suppose you find that the wearing of the beads and the ceremony to release the spirit of the dead husband are part of the spirit worship of Suina's pagan relatives. How would you advise Suina?

   2. Are the four questions insuring the validity of distinct societies pertinent to this problem?

   3. If Suina were to decide that she must remove the beads at once to be consistent in her Christian life, what steps would you advise her to take in order not to reject her relatives and cause distrust?

a kiss for the preacher's daughter

If men define situations as real, they are real in their consequences.[1]

Dear Ann Landers: I am a fifteen-year-old girl who is awfully mixed up. The first problem is that I am a preacher's daughter and everybody expects me to be perfect. My parents are very strict. They keep reminding me that I have to live up to my station in life. I hate feeling that I am different from other girls my age, but that's the way it is, and I have accepted it. Two weeks ago a very nice boy walked me home from choir practice. Just before we reached our block he kissed me. I felt so guilty I couldn't sleep. A week later it happened again. Although I have prayed forgiveness, I feel I should tell my parents, but I can't bring myself to do it. I'm afraid I would be restricted for life. This morning I was so nervous I couldn't go to school. I told my mother I had a stomach ache (which was true), but I'm sure my worries caused it. Can you help? — *Ashamed of Myself.*[2]

Questions:

1. Describe the conflict between the real and the perceived in this case.

2. What has gone wrong with the flow of truth in this family?

3. Can you foresee the possibility of bitterness developing in this girl's life? If so, what principle of biculturalism would this illustrate?

4. If this girl sought out a teacher to confide in, what steps would the teacher take to become an effective support person to her?

5. How would a healthy acceptance of self be helpful in this case?

1. William I. Thomas and Florian Znaniecki, *The Polish Peasant in Europe and America* (Boston: Richard G. Badger, 1918-20), p. 81.

2. Ann Landers, *Ann Landers Says Truth Is Stranger...* (Englewood Cliffs, New Jersey: Prentice-Hall, Inc., 1968), p. 198.

MODEL FOUR

EFFECTIVE MINISTRY

The true counselor — and we all fill the role of counselor at one time or another in relation to our family, pupils, friends, business associates, or congregation — is the support person who encourages the other to develop, change, mature in keeping with what he is personally. Some persons such as pastors, missionaries, and psychologists have chosen as their vocation a life of ministry to others. If they have not learned to accept themselves and others, and to appreciate their own culture and that of the persons to whom they hope to minister, they will encounter times of great frustration and discouragement.

And though they should endure great sacrifice and personal hardship in fulfilling their chosen calling, their work will not be accepted. They will be seen as making an unwelcome intrusion into lives of people who will feel only annoyance at what Shusaku Endo calls the "persistent affection of an ugly woman."[1]

But when one acting as a true counselor "communicates a desire to collaborate in defining a mutual problem and in seeking its solution, he tends to create the same problem orientation in the listener, and, of greater importance, he implies that he has no predetermined solution, attitude, or method to impose. ... It allows the receiver to set his own goals, make his own decisions, and evaluate his own progress."[2]

---

1. Shusaku Endo, *Silence* (Tokyo: The Voyagers' Press, 1969), p. 200.
2. Jack R. Gibb, "Defensive Communication," *Journal of Communication,* 11, No. 3 (Sept. 1961), p. 144.

Christ spent an afternoon with a miserable little cheat, and Zacchaeus was a changed man. From the records we have, it would seem that Jesus' words were few, but his acceptance of this man on the fringe of his society was great.

Paul showed respect for a culture utterly alien to his own when he stood on Mars' Hill. He used his audience's interest in gods and poetry to open the way to preach the message of Christ which burned in his heart. Paul yearned to see the Athenians change, but always he acknowledged them as valid in their distinctness and knew that the Holy Spirit alone could reveal to them the change which would be right for them.

"The Foreigner's Dilemma" takes us through the sad experience of a missionary who found himself defeating his own purpose for being thousands of miles from home. By small acts of ignorance and rejection he offended a child, a family, and a community. Because he was able to honestly and frankly tell us of his errors in the words of the offended child, we may be cautioned to avoid acting in the same way.

the foreigner's dilemma

My name is Noi which means "little one." I am eight years old and I live in a remote northern province of Thailand. Our town is a provincial capital. It isn't very large, but we enjoy life. I live with my parents and four brothers and sisters. My father is a barber.

A family of white foreigners came to live in our town and they rented a small house just down the street from my house. I liked to visit their house, especially on Saturday nights. They let us come inside for a children's meeting where we sat on the floor, sang songs, played games, and then listened to stories about the white man's religion. Lots and lots of my friends came to the meeting each week.

Sometimes during the week I would visit the foreigner's house. His children had many toys. One day I stopped to play with the toys and somehow I broke the wheels off of one of the trucks. The foreign teacher was at home that afternoon and he saw me with the broken toy in my hands. He yelled at me, "What are you doing breaking Jamrut's toys like that?"

He started down the stairs of the house after me. I was afraid. He grabbed the toy and gave me a boot in the seat and told me to go home. This made me angry, so I picked up a stone and heaved it at him. He started to chase me, so I ran under a neighbor's house, but he came right after me. My heart began to pound as he dragged me out and spanked my bottom with his hand. I wailed with fright and ran home to tell my father.

"Father, the foreigner kicked me and then he beat me." (To point with the foot or to kick anyone is extremely impolite among our people because feet are despised but the head is highly honored.) This made my father angry, so he went immediately to the man's house and, standing in the street in front of the house, he said, "Why did you kick and beat my son? If he did something wrong, why didn't you come and tell me?"

The teacher replied, "Please come up in the house and we'll talk it over together." My father was too disturbed and refused to go into the house. Later I guess the foreigner must have felt sorry. Suddenly I saw him heading toward my house accompanied by the District Officer who is the highest official of the area. They came up on our porch and the District Officer explained that he had come with the foreign teacher to make amends for upsetting the peace. My father and a group of neighbor men sat on the porch talking softly. My father suggested that the D. O. talk with my mother who was sitting inside the house wailing her eyes out. Leaving the white man on the porch with the men, the D. O. came inside to talk with mother.

It is our practice to have a middle man help talk over important matters. The foreign teacher looked sad and didn't seem to know what to say. He tried apologizing to my father, but my father just nodded and agreed with him. Soon the D.O. returned to the porch and spoke with the foreign teacher. He said, "Ahjan (Teacher), the boy's mother says the spanking caused her son's spirit to break. You must pay a fine of 300 baht ($15.00) in order to bring healing for this offense."

"But that's too much money!" replied the teacher. "There is nothing wrong with the boy; the spanking likely did him good."

The D.O. tried to explain how my people handle an affair like this. The foreigner didn't understand very well. He had never been in trouble before. After almost two hours or so of conversation, he consented and paid the 300 baht to the D. O. who gave it to my father. He in turn assured the teacher that all was well now. Farewells were exchanged as the D. O. and the teacher descended the porch stairs. It was now dark. Many people had gathered. The foreigner appeared perplexed but much relieved and grateful that the official had served as a friend and mediator.

After that I didn't feel like playing with the foreigner's children any more. In fact, I don't think I went to any more Saturday night children's meetings either.

Questions:

1. Which models of biculturalism give help in understanding this episode?
2. With whom do you identify in this incident?
3. Do you think the missionary should have gone alone to apologize? Why or why not?
4. If you were the foreign teacher, how would you have handled this unpleasant situation?
5. Could the missionary have done anything differently in order to reduce crosscultural conflict?
6. What steps might he take in order to try to rebuild trust and mutual respect?

soni

It was a typical warm, muggy morning when we first made our acquaintance with Soni. She came to our home primarily in search of help to obtain food, medicine, and possibly clothing for herself and her children. Soni and three of her preschool-age children, one an infant, were received into our salla — an area of the house where guests are received. They were dirty, unkempt, lice-infested, sickly, undernourished specimens of humanity. The children, particularly, were covered from head to toe with running ulcerous sores. After opening remarks, we asked her what was the purpose of her visit. We had, however, surmised the reason why she had come when we first saw her and her children. We, nevertheless, did not have the heart to send them on their way without first giving them refreshments, a customary practice when guests are received, and hearing her out. For the next hour and a half or so we mostly listened as she poured out her woes. After she left, we made inquiries about her. This information, together with that which we had learned from talking with Soni herself over a period of time, shaped into the following story of tragedy, hardship, and struggle to survive.

At an early age in life, Soni was made an orphan. She was adopted by a middle-aged couple who had no children of their own. They also had adopted a son about the same age as Soni but not related to her. These foster parents were both public school teachers and were well able to care for themselves and their two adopted children.

Up until the time that Soni was in high school, she was the favorite in the family. However, instead of completing her high school training as desired by her foster parents, she eloped with one of her classmates. Soni's foster parents, particularly the mother, were very much offended and put to shame by her rash action. However, she and her husband were received into the home and lived with the foster parents for several years. In the course of time three children were born into the family.

Soni's husband had been having difficulty getting regular employment to take care of his family. Jobs were scarce. He then decided to return to his home area which was located on another island several hundred miles away. Soni's foster mother refused to let Soni and the three children go. As a result, her husband left by himself. After a year or so had passed, word was received that he had "remarried" in his home area.

Beginning with Soni's elopement, the affection which her foster parents had had for her was transferred to her adopted brother. This was especially true of the affections of the mother. A new will was made out and all of the inheritance and property rights which were previously Soni's were given over to the son. Soni's name was left out entirely from the new will.

Soni's foster father had loved her before her marriage, and she felt that he continued to love her even though he was hurt by her marriage. As she reported, he was always sympathetic and kind to her and her children. After Soni's husband left to his home area, her foster mother became, in Soni's words, "jealous of her." She felt that the reason behind it was the attention and affection which her foster father continued to show towards her and her children. The situation in the home became unbearable and Soni, looking for an escape, remarried. Her new husband was a Moslem; and, as it turned out, he already had a wife and several children.

When Soni left her foster parent's home, her mother refused to let her take her first-born child, a girl, with her. From that time on Soni was never granted admittance to the home whenever her foster mother was present. She was, to her, counted as one dead. Her foster father, however, continued to help Soni on occasion. But then, after several years had lapsed they retired from the teaching profession and moved to another part of the country where they had invested in land. They took with them Soni's eldest child.

Soni was brought up in a Christian or Roman Catholic culture. When she remarried, she married into a Moslem culture. She had an inferior status as a second wife but a greater problem to her acceptance in the new culture was her being a "Christian." For the first year or more Soni lived in the city where there were also a large number of "Christian" people but the predominant group was still Moslem. Their home was a simple one-room dwelling about 10' x 10', constructed from native (thatch) materials with a split bamboo floor. Her husband's first wife lived in a similar type house but somewhat larger and located in the country among his people. His relatives did not own the land on which they lived. They were sharecroppers and their livelihood was quite meager.

When Soni's husband lost his job in the city, he, together with Soni and the children moved into the country to be among his own people. Soni had with her two of her children from her first marriage and an infant fathered by her Moslem husband. All were undernourished and sickly. The difference between Soni's way of life in the home of her foster parents was in great contrast to that which she experienced since her remarriage. The kind of house she lived in was different; the food was different; how and where they slept was different; the system of values was different; the religion was different; the language was different; and there were many more differences. In their new surroundings in the country, the children became afflicted with ulcerous sores. Native remedies were used to try to rid the children of the sores and other illnesses which they had, but to no avail. Soni and her children experienced great hardship.

The day came when Soni began her break from this situation. Without informing her husband or his relatives the true purpose of her trip, she made her way into the city to work, beg, or steal to get food and medicine for herself and her children. If they could have known what she was up to, they would not have allowed her to go; for, if she were to beg, it would bring shame upon her husband and his people. It was during one of these first trips of Soni to the city that we met her.

As time went by, Soni's practices were found out and she suffered for it. She was put under the guard of an elderly lady and lived together with her in a small hut. During this time one of Soni's children by her first husband died. Several months later she gave birth to another son. After that the old lady prohibited Soni's husband from sleeping with her. Later, Soni made treks back into the city and was able to get a job as a waitress in a small cafe. She worked about a week before her husband found out about it. In a rage he came to the cafe, threatened the life of the owner, beat up Soni, and took her back to the country.

Soni was fearful of cohabiting again with her husband lest she became pregnant once more. After awhile she "escaped" and together with an old lady began living in the city. The old lady cooked and watched over the children while Soni went out to try to get something for them to eat each day. It has been and perhaps still is a difficult and constant fight for existence for Soni and her children. She contracted T.B. and at least one of her children has also. She and her family need help but the kind of help and how it should be given so that she can maintain her own authenticity as a person needs deep and thoughtful consideration. In our efforts to help, we have often been both baffled and frustrated by the problem.

In our efforts to help her, we have fed her and her children when they came to our home; we washed off their sores and bandaged them; we accompanied them on occasion to doctors; we purchased medicines; we gave them vitamins and rice; we gave her a small start in selling vegetables in the market to earn a living; we gave her suitable clothes so that she would look clean when she looked for a waitress job; we prayed with her and for her; yet, we often felt frustrated over her situation as to how we could really help her.

On the other hand, we felt that she respected us and did deeply appreciate the help that we gave to her, feeble though it may have been. She felt that we at least cared for her to some extent and would listen to her. When we met her on the street or in the market, we recognized and greeted her. From her reactions she seemed to appreciate this very much; her face would always light up into a bright smile. On one occasion, with tears in her eyes, she shocked my wife by suddenly kneeling down and kissing her feet because of something that my wife had done for her and her children. Before we left for furlough she came over to our home alone just to say "goodbye" and then kissed our hands in departure.

addendum to case study:

Elopement

Elopement, as far as I know of Philippine culture, is frowned upon by all of the subcultures in the Islands: Christian (Roman Catholic and Protestant), Moslem, Buddhist, and pagan. To curb young women from getting married without their parents' permission, at least until they are of age, the government has enacted a law stating that until a young woman is twenty-one years of age she cannot get married without the signed consent of her parents or guardians. When a young couple elopes, they often do not go to a justice of the peace immediately and get married unless the girl is of age (21) and prior arrangements have been made for the wedding in a municipality away from their home area. What is commonly done in some areas of the Philippines is for the couple to cohabit with one another for a short period. If they have been together intimately, consent for the girl to marry is usually given quickly by the parents; however, and understandably so, there is a great amount of shame experienced by the parents in this kind of a situation. There often may be an attempt to lessen the shame by saying that the girl was abducted. The couple is separated and arrangements for the wedding are negotiated between the parents or guardians. Preliminary negotiations are often made through a third party.

Among Moslems, when a couple elopes, they try to get to the boy's relatives or to the person entitled "sara" — religious court — as fast as they can. If they are overtaken by the girl's relatives, the young man may lose his life.

Employment

For non-high school graduates it can be difficult to get regular employment. This is especially true if the person has no particular skill or craft — carpentry, mechanic, etc. In Jolo there are a number of unskilled, laboring jobs available, but the number of job seekers greatly exceeds the number of job openings

Soni's husband was not born and raised in Jolo. How he came to go to school there, I do not know but I can venture an opinion. He probably was brought there by one of his relatives to help out in their home. It is a common practice in the Islands for a brother or sister to take one of their younger siblings into their own home to help with household tasks and other jobs. They in turn provide his food, clothing, and shelter, and often help him through school as well.

When Soni and her husband got married, they moved into the home of her foster parents. It is also a very common practice for young couples to live with their parents or in-laws for a time after their marriage or until they can financially take care of themselves. After several years went by and Soni's husband was still having difficulty getting regular employment, he decided to return to his home area near Dadiangas, Cotobato, where employment was then more readily available.

Family

It often happens when a husband leaves his wife and family behind to seek employment and live in another area separated from his wife that he remarries. This is particularly true if his wife refuses to go or if her family refuses to let her go with him. A man may precede his family, with his family joining him after he has obtained employment and a place to live. If a man's family does not join him, the man commonly takes another wife. In the Philippines the government does not grant divorce, so that in circumstances such as that above, the man's second wife is in reality a concubine. Before the law his first wife remains his legal spouse.

Inheritance

I am not certain concerning the inheritance laws of the subculture to which Soni's parents belonged. However, the writing of wills is not commonly done except among business people, professionals (doctors, teachers, etc.), and landowners. Where there is no formal will drawn up, there is, nevertheless, an understanding among the heirs as to who gets what and how much. Adopted children may or may not receive any inheritance, depending upon their inclusion in a will and/or their good standing with the other heirs. Soni, by her behavior, lost the favored position she held in the family, and with it her inheritance.

Polygamy Implications and Requirements of the Wife in This Relationship

Plurality of wives is an accepted part of Islamic culture but not of the Christian culture in which Soni had been raised. She was married in accordance with Islamic wedding regulations. She could not be married before a judge nor have her wedding registered with the government, for she already had a husband who was still living.

From what we were made to understand, she did not know at first that the Moslem fellow whom she married already had a wife when she married him. There are a number of instances where a girl from a Christian culture marries a Moslem only to find out later that he already has a wife. Some women are really deceived, while others suspect or know the real situation beforehand, but nevertheless marry crossculturally anyway.

Usually, the second wife will be subservient to the first wife, particularly if they live in the same house. If they have separate dwellings, each can do pretty much what she likes in her own home. There is, of course, competition for the husband's affection and for the money he earns.

Illness Remedy

I am not sure what was used in these instances, but the Moslems have a number of "quack doctors." They brew medicines from herbs, roots, etc., which may be drunk or applied directly to the sores. The sores may be left open or may be covered with leaves. When the medicine is administered, it is accompanied with sacred sayings (utterances) in Arabic. There are others who present food offerings and perform certain rituals at holy places to placate "spirits" or devils that have caused the illnesses.

Moslem Male

The Tausug Moslem male is proud of his Tausugness and his religious heritage. He is very quick to fight and will fight till death when he feels his honor, or that of his family, tribe, or religion has been offended. In regard to his wife or wives, he has a strong sense of their belonging to him, and will not tolerate any other male giving flirtatious attention to them.

the marriage vow

While my wife and I were in language study, we lived for six months on a small Micronesian island called Oneop. A mission station has been there for about thirty years, and now the church is in the care of a national minister and two assistants. Before the influence of the Gospel came, the inhabitants fought with the neighboring islanders, killing and robbing each other.

One day the minister excitedly told us of an event which had happened the night before. The whole island was talking about it. A young man had been found sleeping in the house of his fiancée. The minister asked me if I would be willing to pray with the two young people involved. Before doing so, I set out to ask some questions.

After careful inquiry, we found an unwritten law was operative in such cases: If a young man had sexual relations with his fiancée before the marriage ceremony, they could not speak their vows and have a marriage celebration in the church. It was customary in such cases for the minister or missionary to have a brief prayer with the couple and the new marriage would be considered established. Many couples, we were told, got married that way. We felt there must be some reason for this behavior and so we continued to ask questions.

We found that the main reason seems to be the fear of making a vow before God who is to them a righteous judge. He would take account of their vow and it would be dangerous to incur His wrath by not keeping it. But they also know their own weakness which is in a sense stronger than their fear of God.

The Trukese custom used to be that a man would live with his wife until she no longer pleased him. Then he would send her away and live with another woman. But now a binding vow complicates the process, and threatens punishment from God. The perfect solution seemed to be to avoid making a vow and still receive the blessing of the minister.

We were not willing to accept this view. After receiving permission, we set to work to find a better solution in this case. We called the young couple for several counseling sessions in our home. We also talked with their parents about their responsibilities. Both families were of high rank and hesitated at first to listen.

Since the marriage vow was highly respected, we set out to convince them that it would be a blessing for them and would help them to stay together rather than divorcing in an easy way. After the counseling session, when I felt they understood what a Christian marriage should be, I performed an official marriage celebration with sermon and vow. I didn't perform it in the church building, however, but chose a classroom. It would have greatly offended the minister and the congregation if I had conducted the ceremony in the church. The close relatives on both sides attended, and after the service, everyone seemed happy.

We found there is also a financial reason for not getting married in the church. An unwritten rule says that the family of a couple married in the church must feed all the people who attend the wedding. If a couple is from a lower social rank, they cannot make a big feast because they just do not have enough money to feed a few hundred people. Often those from higher ranks do not want such a big feast either. I occasionally met this problem by conducting weddings in private homes where I could show them the importance of a Christian marriage and the vow regardless of the place where the ceremony was performed.

films

AUTUMN RIVER CAMP, PARTS I AND II
30 min each part, $9 rental (3 days), $270 purchase,
Universal Education and Visual Arts.
Subsistence technology, transport, and housebuilding among the Netsilik Eskimo, with emphasis upon the relationship of the Netsilik to their harsh habitat.

DEAD BIRDS
83 min, color/sound, $45 rental, $450 purchase,
McGraw-Hill/Contemporary Films, Inc.
Cultural ecology, pig raising, horticulture, raiding, and death are the major themes of this classic film on the Dani of the Baliem Valley of New Guinea.

EMU RITUAL AT RUGURI
35 min, sound, $22.50 rental, $430 purchase,
University of California.
Kinship rituals among the Walbiri, Australian Aborigines, shows the relationship between patrimoieties, and the preparation of totemic emblems; ceremonial singing and dancing.

FOUR FAMILIES
60 min, $12 rental, New York University.
A comparison of patterns of family life in India, France, Japan, and Canada.

HADZA, THE FOOD QUEST OF A HUNTING AND GATHERING TRIBE OF TANZANIA
40 min, b/w, James Woodburn.
Depicts the life of the Eastern Hadza of Tanzania, a small group of hunter-gatherers living in an unusually rich natural setting; emphasis upon the food quest.

HOLY GHOST PEOPLE
53 min, b/w, $30 rental, $300 purchase, McGraw-Hill/Contemporary Films, Inc. (can be rented from University of California for $21).
Worship among a white Pentecostal religious group in Appalachia, snake handling, poison-drinking, speaking in tongues, trance; leader of the group is bitten by a rattlesnake.

THE HUNTERS
73 min, color/sound, $40 rental, $400 purchase,
McGraw-Hill/Contemporary Films
Kung Bushmen on a 13-day giraffe hunt in the northern Kalahari Desert; excellent on subsistence technology in a difficult natural setting.

AN IXIL CALENDRICAL DIVINATION
32 min, color/sound, $20 rental, $350 purchase, Zia Cine, Inc.
A complete record of an Indian couple's consultation with a Maya day-diviner at Nebaj, Guatemala. Includes a clear and uncut recording of the prayers and advice of the diviner.

THE LOON'S NECKLACE
11 min, $4 rental, University of California.
Re-creation of a Salish legend using ceremonial masks; how the loon acquired his necklace; emphasis on man's relationship to nature.

MATJEMOSH
27 min, color/sound, $16 rental, University of California.
An Asmat woodcarver at work in southwest New Guinea, ancestor figures, musical instruments; the creative artist at work in the context of his traditional culture.

NORTH INDIAN VILLAGE
30 min, color, $13.50 rental, University of California, $300 purchase, International Film Bureau.
On the role of caste and kinship in the structuring of social and economic relationships in Rajput, a village in Uttar Pradesh.

OKAN, SUN DANCE OF THE BLACKFOOT
64 min, color/sound, write the Glenbow Foundation for current price.
Preparations for the buffalo-oriented sun dance, Old Woman's Society, face painting, construction of a sweat lodge.

WALBIRI RITUAL AT GUNADJARI
28 min, color/sound, $20 one day rental ($10 for each additional day), $365 purchase, University of California.
Australian aborigines in a three-day ceremony in a huge rock shelter, ritual body painting, song, dance, and drama depict heroes of Walbiri legend; excellent spoken commentary.

bibliography

*1. Books that deal with trust, acceptance
and mutual respect*

Bonthius, Robert H. *Christian Paths to Self-Acceptance.* New York: King's Crown Press, 1948.

Fletcher, Joseph. *Situation Ethics.* Philadelphia: The Westminster Press, 1966.
Many insights involving acceptance of the other. His case studies are classics.

Gatheru, R. Mugo. *Child of Two Worlds.* Garden City, New York: Doubleday and Company, Inc., 1964.

Goffman, Erving. *The Presentation of Self in Everyday Life.* Garden City, New York: Doubleday and Co., 1959.
A good starting point for reading on the subject of the self in interpersonal relationships.

Howard, Thomas. *Christ the Tiger.* New York: J. B. Lippincott Co., 1967.

Lakin, Martin. *Interpersonal Encounter: Theory and Practice in Sensitivity Training.* New York: McGraw-Hill Book Co., 1972.

Little, Paul. *How to Give Away Your Faith.* Downers Grove, Illinois: Inter-Varsity Press, 1966.
Discussion of the place of communicating acceptance, trust and mutual respect in the witnessing situation.

Mayers, Marvin K. *Notes on Christian Outreach in a Philippine Community.* Pasadena, Calif.: William Carey Library, 1970.
A practical example of mutual respect in cross-cultural witness.

Miller, Keith. *A Taste of New Wine.* Waco, Texas: Word Books, 1965, and *The Second Touch.* Waco, Texas: Word Books, 1967.
Intensely personal books that deal with the preoccupation of the self which often follows a reorientation of life. Miller is incredibly honest. He talks about a new freedom to love which comes from being able to see people as Christ saw them.

Rogers, Carl. *Freedom to Learn.* Charles E. Merrill Publishing Co., 1969, and *On Becoming a Person.* New York: Houghton Mifflin Co., 1970.
Rogers has many things to say about interpersonal relationships and the freedom to be oneself, primarily within an educational setting.

Schaeffer, Francis A. *True Spirituality.* Wheaton: Tyndale House Publishers, 1971.
In section two Schaeffer discusses how one can have freedom

from conscience and from the thought life, and how the whole person can be healed.

Simons, Joseph and Reidy, Jeanne. *The Risk of Loving.* New York: Herder and Herder, 1968.

Strauss, Anselm L. *Mirrors and Masks.* Glencoe, Illinois: The Free Press, 1959.

Tournier, Paul, *The Meaning of Persons.* New York: Harper and Row, 1957.
An excellent treatment of the nature of Christian interpersonal relationships.

Trobisch, Walter. *I Married You.* New York: Harper and Row, 1971.

Wilson, Kenneth L. *Angel at her Shoulder.* New York: Pyramid Books, 1970.
Good for acceptance-based living and discernment.

2. *Books that deal with the group: its definition, its activities and its values; conceptual models that aid in understanding the social group; and comparative cultures*

Aubert, Vilhelm. *Elements of Sociology.* New York: Charles Scribner's Sons, 1967.

Barber, Bernard. *Social Stratification.* New York: Harcourt, Brace and World, 1957.
A comparative analysis of structure and process.

Berger, Peter. *Noise of Solemn Assemblies.* Garden City, New York: Doubleday and Co., 1961.

————. *The Sacred Canopy: Elements of a Sociological Theory of Religion.* Garden City, New York: Doubleday and Co., 1967.

Biddle, Bruce J. *Role Theory: Concepts and Research.* New York: John Wiley and Sons, 1966.

Birdwhistell, Ray L. *Kinesics and Context.* Philadelphia: The University of Pennsylvania Press, 1970.
An academic treatment of body movement based on linguistic and kinesic research.

Blake, Robert. *The Managerial Grid.* Houston, Texas: Gulf Publishing Co., 1964.
Matrix theory applied to personal and production developments in management.

Bredemier, Harry C. and Stevenson, Richard M. *The Analysis of Social Systems.* New York: Holt, Rinehart and Winston, 1967.
Eclectic collection of information and insight on group life, the process of socialization, the structure of socialization, deviance, social control, adaptation to nonsocial environment, marriage, the family, kinship, belief systems, social stratification, and politics.

Broom, Leonard and Selznick, Philip. *Principles of Sociology: a Text with Adapted Readings,* 4th ed. New York: Harper and Row, 1970.

A standard textbook on sociological theory. Stresses the extreme importance of the group in daily life.

Buckley, Walter. *Sociology and Modern Systems Theory.* Englewood Cliffs, New Jersey: Prentice-Hall, 1967.
A systems approach to society, for the advanced student.

Casteel, John L. *The Creative Role of Interpersonal Groups in the Church Today.* New York: Association Press, 1968.

Churchman, C. West. *The Systems Approach.* New York: Dell Publishing Co., 1968.
A good guide to the "systems" approach. Application is made to industrial problems.

Clausen, John. *Socialization and Society.* Boston: Little, Brown and Co., 1968.

Cooley, Charles. *Social Organization.* Glencoe, Illinois: The Free Press, 1902.
An older but standard discussion of social organization. Considers primary aspects of organization, communication, the "democratic mind," and social classes.

Coser, Lewis. *The Functions of Social Conflict.* Glencoe, Illinois: Free Press, 1966.
Applies to the conflict of norm and frustration models.

De Bono, Edward. *The Five-Day Course in Thinking.* New York: Basic Books, Inc., 1967.
A useful series of exercises to train someone to be flexible in his thinking, i.e., to move from crisis to noncrisis in his thinking.

Fast, Julius. *Body Language.* New York: Simon and Schuster, 1971.
A popular treatment of the subject of body movement.

Hall, Edward T. *The Hidden Dimension.* Garden City, New York: Doubleday and Co., 1969, and *The Silent Language.* Garden City, New York: Doubleday and Co., 1959.
Provocative treatments of space relationships and the larger considerations of nonverbal behavior respectively.

Hall, Edward T. and Whyte, William Foote. "Intercultural Communication: A Guide to Men of Action" in Human Organization, Vol. 19, No. 1, Spring, 1960.

Hertzler, Joyce O. *A Sociology of Language.* New York: Random House, 1965.
The relationship between language and society is presented.

Hinde, R. A. *Non-Verbal Communication.* Cambridge: The University Press, 1972.

Homans, George C. *Social Behavior: Its Elementary Forms.* New York: Harcourt, Brace and World, 1961, and *The Human Group.* New York: Harcourt, Brace and World, 1950.
Excellent resources for sociological theory dealing with social behavior in general and behavior in small groups respectively.

Hymes, Dell, ed. *Language in Culture and Society.* New York: Harper and Row, 1964.

Numerous points of view are presented in this symposium or collection of papers dealing with the relationship between language and culture. For the advanced student.

Lynd, Helen Merrell. *On Shame and the Search for Identity.* New York: Science Editions, Inc., 1958.

Mayer, Philip, ed. *Socialization: The Approach from Social Anthropology.* New York: Tavistock Publications, 1970.

McLuhan, Marshall. *Understanding Media: The Extension of Man.* New York: McGraw-Hill Book Co., 1964.

Merton, Robert K. *Social Theory and Social Structure.* Glencoe, Illinois: The Free Press, 1957.
The main concern is with the interplay of social theory and social research and with progressively codifying both substantive theory and the procedures of sociological analysis. Advanced.

Nierenberg, Gerard and Calero, Henry. *How to Read a Person Like a Book.* New York: Simon and Schuster, 1971.

Nisbet, Robert A. *The Social Bond.* New York: Alfred A. Knopf, 1970.
An advanced introduction to the study of society.

Parsons, Talcott. *The Social System.* Glencoe, Illinois: The Free Press, 1951.
One of the important studies based on structure-function theory in sociology.

Piaget, Jean. *Language and Thought of the Child.* New York: Harcourt, Brace and World, 1926/1932.
A classic work on adolescent psychology. A brilliant introduction to the study of child logic.

Science, Conflict and Society: Readings from *Scientific American.* San Francisco: W. H. Freeman and Co., 1969.

Skinner, Tom. *Words of Revolution.* Grand Rapids: Zondervan Publishing House, 1970.
Conflict of cultures is dealt with.

Tumin, Melvin M. *Social Stratification.* Englewood Cliffs, New Jersey: Prentice-Hall, 1967.
The forms and functions of inequality.

Turney-High, Harry Holbert. *Man and System.* New York: Appleton-Century-Crofts, Inc., 1968.
Considerations on the network of interpersonal relations and the flow of truth models. The interrelationship between man and social structure is probed.

Watson O. Michael. *Proxemic Behavior: A Cross-Cultural Study.* Paris, The Hague: Mouton, 1970.

3. Books that deal with change and the change process

Barnett, H. G. *Innovation: The Basis of Cultural Change.* New York: McGraw-Hill Book Co., 1953.
A classic work dealing with the change process.

Beals, Alan R. *Culture in Process.* New York: Holt, Rinehart and Winston, 1967.
    A general introduction to anthropology in relation to the change process with quotations from field studies.
Bennis, Warren G.; Benne, Kenneth D.; Chin, Robert. *The Planning of Change.* New York: Holt, Rinehart and Winston, 1969.
    A more recent treatment than Barnett of the change process with concepts and illustrations keyed to the average reader.
Bernard, H. Russell and Pelto, Pertti, eds. *Technology and Social Change.* New York: The Macmillan Co., 1972.
Bock, Philip K. *Culture Shock: A Reader in Modern Cultural Anthropology.* New York: Alfred A. Knopf, 1970.
    A reader in culture contact, but it does not deal with the problem of shock in the behavioral sense.
Brown, Ina Corrine. *Understanding Other Cultures.* Englewood Cliffs, New Jersey: Prentice-Hall, Inc., 1963.
    An especially interesting way of introducing the nonscholar to the field of anthropology, especially dealing with difference between societies.
Clifton, James A. *Applied Anthropology: Readings in the uses of the Science of Man.* Boston: Houghton Mifflin Co., 1970.
Cox, Harvey. *The Secular City.* New York: The Macmillan Co., 1965.
    Change and the concept of city.
Evans-Pritchard, Edward E. *The Values of Primitive Society.* Oxford: Blackwell, 1954.
    A classic work dealing with the change process from the point of view of social anthropology.
Fabun, Don. *The Children of Change.* Beverly Hills, California: Glencoe Press, 1969.
————. *Dimensions of Change.* Beverly Hills, California: Glencoe Press, 1971.
————. *The Dynamics of Change.* New York: Prentice-Hall, 1970.
    A practical, thus maximally useful, approach to the change process.
Foster, George M. *Applied Anthropology.* Boston: Little, Brown and Co., 1969.
    Presents the significant contribution of the behavioral sciences in effective communication.
————. *Traditional Cultures: and the Impact of Technological Change.* New York: Harper and Row, 1962.
    Illustration of the profound effect our involvement as a technological culture often has with examples from societies of effective and ineffective change.
Goodenough, Ward Hunt. *Cooperation in Change.* New York: Russell Sage Foundation, 1963.
    The concerns of the change agent are spelled out in some detail.
Hagen, Everett E. *On the Theory of Social Change.* Homewood, Illinois: The Dorsey Press, 1963.

An overview of the change process, especially as it relates to economic development; for the advanced student.

Herskovits, Melville. *Cultural Dynamics.* New York: Alfred A. Knopf, 1964.
A basic and thorough discussion of the change process in culture with a wealth of case study material.

Keesing, Felix M. *Culture Change.* Stanford, California: Stanford University Press, 1953.
A historical narration and a general overview of the literature of culture change.

Larson, Bruce and Osborne, Ralph. *The Emerging Church.* Waco, Texas: Word Books, 1970.

Luzbetak, Louis J. *The Church and Cultures.* Techny, Illinois: Divine Word Publishers, 1963.
Now in paperback. A general introduction to the change process with application to the Catholic Church and its mission.

Malinowski, Bronislaw. *The Dynamics of Culture Change.* New Haven, Connecticut: Yale University Press, 1945.
Various types of constructive· and destructive tension are analyzed.

Mead, Margaret, ed. *Cultural Patterns and Technical Change.* New York: A Mentor Book, New American Library, 1957.

Nida, Eugene. *Religion Across Cultures.* New York: Harper and Row, 1968.
Since biblical Christianity is a dynamic process born out of a change setting and introduces change in the life of the individuals and society, it resists being bound by the narrow ethnocentrism and restricting legalism of the church. Both the "Jesus Movement" and the small group ministry are examples of a new type of reformation.

Niebuhr, Richard. *Christ and Culture.* New York: Harper and Row, 1956.
This classic work discusses the problem, "How should the Christian involve himself in his culture?"

Price-Williams, D. R. ed. *Cross-Cultural Studies.* New York: Penguin Books, Inc., 1970.

Ray, Verne. *Social Stability and Culture Change.* Seattle, Washington: University of Washington Press, 1957.

Redfield, Robert. *The Little Community.* Chicago: The University of Chicago Press, 1955, and *The Folk Culture of Yucatan.* Chicago: The University of Chicago Press, 1941.
Discussion of the nature of society and culture using his "folk-urban" continuum, with helpful material for someone wishing to start anthropological inquiry.

————. *The Primitive World and Its Transformation.* Ithaca, New York: Cornell University Press, 1953.

Reich, Charles A. *The Greening of America.* New York: Random House, 1970.

A best-selling book dealing with the ways American society is evolving.

Rogers, Everett M. and Shoemaker, F. Floyd. *Communication of Innovations: A Cross-Cultural Approach.* New York: The Free Press, 1971.
An excellent study that could profitably follow *Christianity Confronts Culture,* since it is concerned with specific steps in the change process.

Rogers, Everett M. *Modernization among Peasants: The Impact of Communication.* New York: Holt, Rinehart and Winston, Inc., 1969.

Rugg, Harold Ordway. *American Culture: An Introduction to the Problems of.* New York: Ginn & Co., 1931.
An older analysis of American culture, yet one that provides helpful insights useful today.

Shearer, Roy. *Wildfire: Church Growth in Korea.* Grand Rapids: Wm. B. Eerdmans Publishing Co., 1966.
How God works through a culture to accomplish revival.

Spicer, Edward. *Human Problems in Technological Change.* New York: Russell Sage Foundation, 1952.
Excellent case studies in the area of change.

Toffler, Alvin. *Future Shock.* New York: Random House, 1970.
A popular book sharing the enormity of change in the world, with comments and warnings.

4. Books and sources that deal with the subject of games and simulations in approaching society

Associates of Urbanus. 3919 Willoughby Road, Holt, Michigan. Games and Materials.
Overpower. A brief version of *Star Power* of Simile II.
Strata. A simulation game teaching unknown roles for a stratificational society focusing on status-rank.
Kit for orientation of workers going overseas and returning. Tapes and exercises.

Barton, Richard F. *A Primer on Simulation and Gaming.* Englewood Cliffs, New Jersey: Prentice-Hall, 1970.

Benson, Dennis. *The Fine Art of Creating Simulation Gaming: Learning Games for Religious Education.* Nashville: Abingdon, 1971.

Berne, Eric. *Games People Play.* New York: Grove Press, 1964.

Brown, George Isaac. *Human Teaching for Human Learning.* New York: Viking, 1971. (An Esalen book.)

Buchler, Ira R. and Nutini, Hugo G. *Game Theory in the Behavioral Sciences.* Pittsburgh, Pennsylvania: University of Pittsburgh Press, 1969.
A technical introduction to the application of game theory to crosscultural data.

Davis, Morton D. *Game Theory: A Nontechnical Introduction.* New York: Basic Books, 1970.

Foster, Robert J. *An Analysis of Human Relations Training and Its Implications for Overseas Performance.* Alexandria, Virginia: Humrro Technical Report 66-15, Human Resources Research Organization, no date.

Hogan, A. J. "Simulation: An Annotated Bibliography," *Social Education,* XXXII, March 1968, 242-244.

Inbar, Michael and Stoll, Clarice S. *Simulation and Gaming in Social Science.* New York: The Free Press, 1972.

Klietsch, Ronald G. *An Introduction to Learning Games and Instructional Simulations: A Curriculum Guideline.* Newport, Minnesota: Instructional Simulations, Inc., no date.

Middleman, R. R. *The Non-Verbal Method in Working with Groups.* New York: Association Press, 1968.

Nesbitt, William A. *Simulation Games for the Social Studies Classroom.* No address: Foreign Policy Association, 1971. A practical guide with extensive bibliography.

Pfeiffer, J. William and Jones, John E. *A Handbook of Structured Experiences for Human Relations Training.* Volumes I, II, and III. Iowa City, Iowa: University Associates Press, 1971. Over seventy structured group experiences that are most worthwhile.

Simile II, LaJolla, California. Games and materials:
Crisis. Sample set $3.00. Simulation game.
Exploring Classroom Uses of Simulations. $.90.
Sitte. Simulation game.
Star Power. A simulation game. Class structure illustrated.
Using Simulations to Teach International Relations.

Stewart, Edward C.; Danielian, Jack; and Foster, Robert. *Simulating Intercultural Communication through Role Play.* Alexandria, Virginia: Humrro (Human Resources Research Office), The George Washington University, May, 1969.

Twelker, Paul A. *Instructional Simulation Systems: An Annotated Bibliography.* Corvallis, Oregon: Teaching Research, Oregon State System of Higher Education, 1969.

Werner, Roland and Werner, Joan. *Bibliography of Simulations: Social Systems and Education.* La Jolla, California: Western Behavioral Sciences Institute, 1969.

Zeiler, Richard. *Games for School Use: A Bibliography.* Yorktown Heights, New York: Center for Educational Services and Research, Board of Cooperative Educational Services, March, 1968.

5. Books that introduce one to the field of anthropology and social anthropology within the larger field of the behavioral and social sciences

Barnouw, Victor. *An Introduction to Anthropology: Ethnology.* Homewood, Illinois: The Dorsey Press, 1971.

A sociocultural treatment of anthropology oriented to schools of anthropological thought.

Beals, Ralph and Hoijer, Harry. *An Introduction to Anthropology.* New York: The Macmillan Co., 1965.

Beattie, John. *Other Cultures: Aims, Methods and Achievements in Social Anthropology.* New York: The Free Press, 1964.

Benedict, Ruth. *Patterns of Culture.* New York: Penguin Books, Inc., 1946. Republished by New American Library.
A classic discussion of distinct cultures.

Bock, Philip K. *Modern Cultural Anthropology.* New York: Alfred A. Knopf, Inc., 1969.
A significant text with a social anthropological approach.

Bouma, Donald H. *Anthropology and Missions.* Grand Rapids: International Publications, no date.
A brief pamphlet providing an introduction to the missionary's orientation in a strange culture; cultural relativism and ethnocentrism discussed.

Clifton, James A. *Introduction to Cultural Anthropology.* Boston: Houghton Mifflin Co., 1968.
An introduction to anthropology developed by having experts in their respective fields prepare the various components of the text. This is, therefore, more than a book of readings.

Cohen, Yehudi, ed. *Man in Adaptation: The Cultural Present.* Chicago: Aldine Publishing Co., 1968.
Man in the process of change, with cases discussed.

Coon, Carleton, ed. *A Reader in General Anthropology.* New York: Henry Holt and Co., 1948.
An older reader but valuable for its contributions.

Dubin, Robert. *Theory Building.* Glencoe, Illinois: The Free Press, 1969.
A working knowledge of how to construct and use conceptual models, for the serious student.

Duncan, Hugh D. *Symbols in Society.* New York: Oxford University Press, 1968.
An advanced work stressing the importance and significance of symbols for mankind. We are basically unaware of many of the symbols we use.

Durkheim, Emile. *The Elementary Forms of the Religious Life.* Glencoe, Illinois: The Free Press, 1947.
Society forms through the interaction of human beings.

Epstein, A. L. *The Craft of Social Anthropology.* London: Social Science Paperbacks in association with Tavistock Publications, 1967.
An introduction to social anthropology from the point of view of the British social anthropologists, and with emphasis on the "science" of anthropology.

Evans-Pritchard, Edward E. *The Institutions of Primitive Society.* Glencoe, Illinois: The Free Press, 1954.

An older work, but continually useful.
Firth, Raymond William. *Elements of Social Organization.* London: Watts, 1952.
Fried, Morton, ed. Readings in Anthropology (two vols.). New York, Thomas Crowell Co., 1959.
A standard reader.
Goldschmidt, Walter. *Exploring the Ways of Mankind.* New York: Holt, Rinehart and Winston, 1971.
A book of articles that contribute more as a text collection than a reader.
————. *Man's Way: A Preface to Understanding Human Society.* Henry Holt and Co., 1959.
Hammel, Eugene A. and Simmons, William S., eds. *Man Makes Sense: A Reader in Modern Cultural Anthropology.* Boston: Little, Brown and Co., 1970.
Hammond, Peter B. *An Introduction to Cultural and Social Anthropology.* New York: The Macmillan Co., 1971.
Harris, Marvin. *Culture, Man, and Nature.* New York: Thomas Y. Crowell Co., 1971.
A balanced treatment of physical and cultural concerns.
Herskovits, Melville. *Cultural Anthropology.* New York: Alfred A. Knopf, 1955.
Hoebel, E. Adamson. *Anthropology: The Study of Man.* New York: McGraw-Hill Book Co., 1972.
A popular standard text in anthropology.
Hughes, Charles C., ed. *Make Men of Them: Introductory Readings for Cultural Anthropology.* Chicago: Rand McNally & Co., 1972.
A book of readings oriented to the "science" of anthropology.
Jennings, Jesse D. and Hoebel, E. Adamson. *Readings in Anthropology.* 3rd ed. New York: McGraw-Hill Book Co., 1972.
Probably the best standard reader available today.
Keesing, Felix. *Cultural Anthropology: The Science of Custom.* New York: Rinehart and Co., 1958.
Kenyatta, Jomo. *Facing Mt. Kenya.* London: Secker and Warburg, 1938. New edition, 1962.
Kluckhohn, Clyde. *Mirror for Man.* Greenwich, Connecticut: Fawcett Publications, 1964.
An introduction to anthropology that deals with crosscultural concerns of communication.
Landar, Herbert. *Language and Culture.* New York: Oxford University Press, 1966.
Deals with many of the same problems as Hertzler and Hymes do but for more advanced students.
Levi-Strauss, Claude. *Structural Anthropology.* Garden City, New York: Doubleday and Co., 1967.
Probably the best basic work to use in understanding this structural and generative anthropologist.

Lienhardt, Godfrey. *Social Anthropology.* New York: Oxford University Press, 1966.
A statement of the interests of anthropology from the point of view of society and social structure.

Linton, Ralph, ed. *The Science of Man in World Crisis.* New York: Columbia University Press, 1945.
Valuable for insight into the kind of concerns Linton and his colleagues had.

Linton, Ralph. *The Study of Man: An Introduction.* New York: Appleton-Century Co., 1936.

Madge, John. *Tools of Social Science.* New York: Doubleday and Co., 1965.
An excellent source book for learning about the tools of research used by the behavioral scientist within the social sciences.

Maranda, Pierre. *Introduction to Anthropology: A Self Guide.* Englewood Cliffs, New Jersey: Prentice-Hall, Inc., 1972.
A practical guide to experiential learning in that which concerns the anthropologist.

Mead, Margaret. *Anthropology: A Human Science.* Princeton, New Jersey: D. Van Nostrand Co., Inc., 1964.
A valuable discussion of the perspective of anthropology with focus on the anthropologist and how he goes about his trade.

Mead, Margaret and Calas, Nicolas, eds. *Primitive Heritage: An Anthropological Anthology.* New York: Random House, 1953.
An older reader, useful for insight as to what the anthropologist thought significant in this earlier stage of study.

Minnich, R. Herbert, Jr. *A Manual of Social Science Material for Missionaries.* Elkhart, Indiana: Mennonite Board of Missions and Charities, 1958 (multilith).
A good basic survey of problems and possibilities of cross-cultural communication of new material, knowledge, attitudes and skills.

Nadel, S. F. *The Foundations of Social Anthropology.* Glencoe, Illinois: The Free Press, 1951.

Nida, Eugene. *Customs and Cultures.* New York: Harper, 1954.
Nida's earliest work and perhaps the most useful in developing awareness of cultural difference.

Oliver, Douglas L. *Invitation to Anthropology.* Garden City, New York: The Natural History Press, 1964.
A brief, concise statement of what anthropology is all about.

Pelto, Pertti J. *The Nature of Anthropology.* Columbus, Ohio: Charles E. Merrill Books, Inc., 1966.
A concise statement of the broader field of anthropology within the social sciences.

Pike, Kenneth L. *Language.* The Hague: Mouton, 1967.
For the serious and advanced student who is interested in the use and application of analytic models.

Radcliffe-Brown, Alfred R. *Structure and Function in Primitive Society*. London: Cohen and West, 1959.
The classic work in anthropology dealing with the structure-function approach to society.

Richards, Cara E. *Man in Perspective: An Introduction to Cultural Anthropology*, (with instructor's guide). New York: Random House, 1972.
A recent introduction to the broader field of anthropology with a cultural rather than social perspective.

Shapiro, Harry L., ed. *Man, Culture and Society*. New York: Oxford University Press, 1970 (first pub. 1956).
A selection of readings by some of the best-known men and women in the field.

Smalley, William. *Readings in Missionary Anthropology*. Tarrytown, New York: *Practical Anthropology*, 1967.
A collection of the most significant articles from the journal *Practical Anthropology*, extremely useful to the missionary.

Spradley, James P. and McCurdy, David W. *Conformity and Conflict*. Boston: Little, Brown and Co., 1971.
A very practical selection of readings that tunes one into behavior even more than structure.

Taylor, Robert B. *Cultural Ways: A Compact Introduction to Cultural Anthropology*. Boston: Allyn and Bacon, Inc., 1969.

*6. Books that illustrate and apply the
support model in interpersonal relations*

Abelson, Robert P. "Simulation of Social Behavior," *Handbook of Social Psychology*. 2d ed. Edited by Gardner Lindzey and Elliot Aronson. Vol. 2. Reading, Massachusetts: Addison Wesley Publishing Co., 1968.

Altman, Irwin and Taylor, Dalmas A. *Social Penetration: The Development of Interpersonal Relationships*. New York: Holt, Rinehart and Winston, Inc., 1973.
From the point of view of social psychology, the theory, supporting research and guidelines to developing interpersonal relationships are presented.

Barrett, David B. *Schism and Renewal in Africa*. Nairobi: Oxford University Press, 1968.
Sociocultural problems in communication are dealt with.

Berlo, David Kenneth. *The Process of Communication: An Introduction to Theory and Practice*. New York: Holt, Rinehart and Winston, 1960.

Bohannan, Laura. *Return to Laughter*. Garden City, New York: American Museum of Natural History with Doubleday and Co., 1964.

Boyd, Malcolm. *Crisis in Communication: A Christian Introduction to Theory and Practice*. Garden City, New York: Doubleday and Co., 1957.
Useful to those interested in evangelistic work, church public

relations and the influence of the church on media.

Byrne, Donn. *The Attraction Paradigm*. New York: Academic Press, 1971.

Cathcart, Robert S. and Samovar, Larry A. *Small Group Communication: a Reader*. Iowa: Wm. C. Brown Publishing Co., 1970.

Cherry, Colin. *On Human Communications: A Review, A Survey, and a Criticism*. Cambridge, Massachusetts: M.I.T. Press, 1957.

Dillistone, Fredrich. *Christianity and Communication*. London: Collins Press, 1956.

Doob, Leonard William. *Communication in Africa: A Search for Boundaries*. New Haven: Yale University Press, 1961.
Demonstrates effective crosscultural communication in an important area of the world.

Edel, May and Abraham. *Anthropology and Ethics*. Springfield, Illinois: Charles C. Thomas Publishing Co., 1959.

Edel, Abraham. *Method in Ethical Theory*. London: Routledge and Kegan Paul (Bobbs-Merrill Co., Inc.), 1963.

Fabun, Don. *Three Roads to Awareness*. Beverly Hills, Calif.: Glencoe Press, 1970.

Goffman, Erving. *Interaction Ritual*. Garden City, New York: Doubleday and Co., Inc., 1967.

Holmes, Monica, et al. *The Language of Trust*. New York: Science House, Inc., 1971.
Excellent case studies providing composite dialogues characterizing youth and adults of the '60s. Useful for discussion of bridging or bombing out relationships.

Jackson, B. F. Jr. *Communication — Learning for Churchmen*. Nashville: Abingdon Press, 1968.

Klapper, Joseph T. *The Effects of Mass Communication*. Glencoe, Illinois: Free Press, 1960.

Kraemer, Hendrick. *The Communication of the Christian Faith*. Philadelphia: Westminster Press, 1956.

Leonard, George B. *Education and Ecstasy*. New York: Delacorte Press, 1968.

Mayers, Marvin K. *Notes on Christian Outreach in the Philippines*. Pasadena: William Carey Library, 1970.

Mayers, Marvin K.; Richards, Lawrence; and Webber, Robert. *Reshaping Evangelical Higher Education*. Grand Rapids: Zondervan Publishing House, 1972.
Developments in education with application to a broad range of educational problems including crosscultural problems.

McGavran, Donald A., ed. *Church Growth and Christian Mission*. New York: Harper and Row, 1965.

————. *Understanding Church Growth*. Grand Rapids: Eerdmans Publishing Co., 1969.
A recent overview of this most important trend in missions.

McLaughlin, Raymond W. *Communication for the Church*. Grand Rapids: Zondervan Publishing House, 1968.

Mead, Margaret. *Culture and Commitment: A Study of the Generation Gap.* Garden City, New York: Doubleday and Co., 1970.

Nida, Eugene. *Message and Mission.* New York: Harper and Row, 1960.

Northrop, Filmer. *Cross Cultural Understanding: Epistemology in Anthropology.* New York: Harper and Row, 1964.

Nurenberg, Jesse S. *Getting Through to People.* Englewood Cliffs, New Jersey: Prentice-Hall, 1963.
A popular book on practical communications.

O'Conner, Elizabeth. *The Eighth Day of Creation — Gifts and Creativity.* Waco, Texas: Word Books, 1971.

Perception: Mechanisms and Models. Readings from *Scientific American.* San Francisco: W. H. Freeman and Co., 1972.

Peters, George. *A Biblical Theology of Missions.* Chicago: Moody Press, 1972.

————. *Saturation Evangelism.* Grand Rapids: Zondervan Publishing House, 1970.

Pike, Kenneth L. *Stir, Change, Create.* Grand Rapids: Wm. B. Eerdmans Publishing Co., 1967.
A delightful book evidencing creativity stimulated by an encounter with the behavioral sciences.

Smith, Alfred G. *Communication and Culture.* New York: Holt, Rinehart and Winston, 1966.
A good survey of the anthropological foundations for cross-cultural communication.

Tournier, Paul. *The Adventure of Living.* New York: Harper and Row, 1965.

Ward, Leo R. *Ethics and the Social Sciences.* Notre Dame: University of Notre Dame Press, 1959.

7. Books and articles referred to in Case Studies

Bowman, Norman L., ed. *Woe is Me! Case Studies in Moral Dilemmas.* Nashville: The Sunday School Board of Southern Baptist Convention, 1969.

Bredemeier, Harry C. and Stephenson, Richard M. *The Analysis of Social Systems.* New York: Holt, Rinehart, and Winston, Inc., 1962.

Buchwalter, Albert. "Victory Toba Day," *Practical Anthropology,* 2, No. 5 (Sept.-Oct. 1955), pp. 137-138, 1955.

Bynner, Witter. *The Way of Life According to Laotzu: An American Version.* New York: John Day Company, 1944.

Cairns, H. A. C. *The Clash of Cultures.* New York: Frederick A. Praeger, 1965.

Cathcart, Robert S. and Samovar, Larry A. *Small Group Communication: A Reader.* Dubuque, Iowa: Wm. C. Brown Company, 1970.

Dewey, John. *How We Think.* New York: D. C. Heath and Company, 1933.

Endo, Shusaku. *Silence.* Tokyo, Japan: The Voyagers' Press, 1969.

Ford, Leroy. *Using the Case Study in Teaching and Training.* Nashville: Broadman Press, 1969.

Gibb, Jack R. "Defensive Communication," *Journal of Communication,* 11, No..3 (Sept. 1961), pp. 141-148.

Hayakawa, S. I. "The Decision-Making Process in Japan," *The Chicago Tribune,* April 23, 1972.

Landers, Ann. *"Ann Landers Says Truth Is Stranger . . ."* Englewood Cliffs, New Jersey: Prentice-Hall, Inc., 1968, p. 198.

Lucas, W. Vincent. "The Educational Value of Initiatory Rites," *International Review of Missions,* Vol. XVI, No. 62 (April, 1972), pp. 192-198.

Phillips, J. B. *The Young Church in Action.* New York: The Macmillan Co., 1955.

Pigors, Paul, and Pigors, Faith. *Case Method in Human Relations: The Incident Process.* New York: McGraw-Hill Book Co., 1961.

Reyburn, William D. *The Toba Indians of the Argentine Chaco.* Elkhart, Indiana: Mennonite Board of Missions and Charities, 1954.

————. "The Helping Relationship in Missionary Work." Tarrytown, New York: *Practical Anthropology,* 17, No. 2 (March-April, 1970), pp. 49-59.

Rogers, Carl R. *On Becoming a Person.* Cambridge, Massachusetts: The Riverside Press, 1961.

Rubin, Irwin. "Increased Self-Acceptance: A Means of Reducing Prejudice," *Journal of Personality and Social Psychology,* 5 (1967), pp. 233-239.

Sherif, Muzafer. *The Psychology of Social Norms.* New York: Harper and Row, 1963. First published in 1936 by Harper and Brothers.

Smalley, William A. "The Cultures of Man and the Communication of the Gospel." Presented at the twelfth annual convention of the American Scientific Affiliation, August 27-29, 1957, at Gordon College, Beverly Farms, Massachusetts.

Stenzel, Anne K. and Feeney, Helen M. *Learning by the Case Method: Practical Approaches for Community Leaders.* New York: The Seabury Press, 1970.

Thomas, William I. and Znaniecki, Florian, *The Polish Peasant in Europe and America.* 5 vols. Boston: Richard G. Badger, 1918-20.

Tippet, Alan R. "Polygamy as a Missionary Problem: The Anthropological Issues," *Practical Anthropology,* 17, No. 2 (March-April 1970), pp. 75-79.

Wheeler, Ladd. *Interpersonal Influence.* Boston: Allyn and Bacon, Inc., 1970.

Zimbardo, Philip, and Ebbeson, Ebbe B. *Influencing Attitudes and Changing Behavior.* Reading, Massachusetts: Addison-Wesley Publishing Co., 1970.

index of subjects